Disturbed Consciousness

Philosophical Psychopathology

Jennifer Radden and Jeff Poland, editors

Disturbed Consciousness: New Essays on Psychopathology and Theories of Consciousness, Rocco J. Gennaro, editor (2015)

Being Amoral: Psychopathy and Moral Incapacity, Thomas Schramme, editor (2014)

A Metaphysics of Psychopathology, Peter Zachar (2014)

Classifying Psychopathology: Mental Kinds and Natural Kinds, Harold Kincaid and Jacqueline A. Sullivan, editors (2014)

The Ethical Treatment of Depression: Autonomy through Psychotherapy, Paul Biegler (2011)

Addiction and Responsibility, Jeffrey Poland and George Graham, editors (2011)

Psychiatry in the Scientific Image, Dominic Murphy (2006)

Brain Fiction: Self-Deception and the Riddle of Confabulation, William Hirstein (2004)

Imagination and Its Pathologies, James Phillips and James Morley, editors (2003)

Imagination and the Meaningful Brain, Arnold H. Modell (2003)

When Self-Consciousness Breaks: Alien Voices and Inserted Thoughts, G. Lynn Stephens and George Graham (2000)

The Myth of Pain, Valerie Gray Hardcastle (1999)

Divided Minds and Successive Selves: Ethical Issues in Disorders of Identity and Personality, Jennifer Radden (1996)

Philosophical Psychopathology, George Graham and G. Lynn Stephens, editors (1994)

Disturbed Consciousness

New Essays on Psychopathology and Theories of Consciousness

edited by Rocco J. Gennaro

The MIT Press
Cambridge, Massachusetts
London, England

MIT Press books may be purchased at special quantity discounts for business or sales promotional use. For information, please email special_sales@mitpress.mit.edu.

This book was set in Stone by the MIT Press. Printed and bound in the United States of America.

Library of Congress Cataloging-in-Publication Data

Disturbed consciousness : new essays on psychopathology and theories of consciousness / edited by Rocco J. Gennaro.
    pages   cm—(Philosophical psychopathology)
Includes bibliographical references and index.
ISBN 978-0-262-02934-6 (hardcover : alk. paper)
1. Psychology, Pathological. I. Gennaro, Rocco J.
RC454.D558   2015
616.89—dc23
2015001895

10 9 8 7 6 5 4 3 2 1

Contents

Acknowledgments   vii

1   **Psychopathologies and Theories of Consciousness: An Overview   1**
Rocco J. Gennaro

2   **Jaspers' Dilemma: The Psychopathological Challenge to Subjectivity Theories of Consciousness   29**
Alexandre Billon and Uriah Kriegel

3   **Somatoparaphrenia, Anosognosia, and Higher-Order Thoughts   55**
Rocco J. Gennaro

4   **Consciousness, Action, and Pathologies of Agency   75**
Myrto Mylopoulos

5   **Self, Belonging, and Conscious Experience: A Critique of Subjectivity Theories of Consciousness   103**
Timothy Lane

6   **From Darwin to Freud: Confabulation as an Adaptive Response to Dysfunctions of Consciousness   141**
Paula Droege

7   **Self-Deception and the Dolphin Model of Cognition   167**
Iuliia Pliushch and Thomas Metzinger

8   **Disorders of Unified Consciousness: Brain Bisection and Dissociative Identity Disorder   209**
Andrew Brook

9   **Altogether Now—Not! Integration Theories of Consciousness and Pathologies of Disunity   227**
Robert Van Gulick

10 Consciousness despite Network Underconnectivity in Autism:
    Another Case of Consciousness without Prefrontal Activity?   249
    William Hirstein

11 A Schizophrenic Defense of a Vehicle Theory of Consciousness   265
    Gerard O'Brien and Jon Opie

12 Prediction Error Minimization, Mental and Developmental Disorder,
    and Statistical Theories of Consciousness   293
    Jakob Hohwy

13 Passivity Experience in Schizophrenia   325
    Philip Gerrans

14 From a Sensorimotor Account of Perception to an Interactive
    Approach to Psychopathology   347
    Erik Myin, J. Kevin O'Regan, and Inez Myin-Germeys

Contributors   369
Index   373

Acknowledgments

I would like to thank all of the contributors to this volume. Thanks also to Phil Laughlin of the MIT Press for helping to bring this project forward, especially during the early stages. I also wish to thank the University of Southern Indiana for a 2012 Faculty Research and Creative Work Grant Award under the heading "Psychopathology and Consciousness" that enabled me to attend and present at the sixteenth annual meeting of the Association for the Scientific Study of Consciousness, the University of Sussex, Brighton, UK, in July 2012.

1 Psychopathologies and Theories of Consciousness: An Overview

Rocco J. Gennaro

The basic idea for this volume is for authors to defend, discuss, or critique at least one specific philosophical theory of consciousness with respect to one or more psychopathologies. Each essay brings together at least one theory and one psychopathology in a substantial way. Authors were asked to keep in mind such questions as: How can a (or your) theory of consciousness account for a specific psychopathological condition? How might one reply to an actual (or potential) criticism of your theory of consciousness based on a psychopathology? How might one theory of consciousness explain a psychopathology better than another theory? What difficulties arise for a specific theory of consciousness given the existence of one or more of these psychopathologies? Some work had already been done along these lines, particularly with respect to the higher-order thought (HOT) theory of consciousness on, for example, visual agnosia, autism, and somatoparaphrenia (such as Liang and Lane 2009, Rosenthal 2010, Gennaro 2012), but the time is ripe for further work with respect to various theories of consciousness (more on these theories in section 3 of this introduction). In the end, my hope is that this volume will help to spur much more interdisciplinary work along these lines.

1 A Brief Introduction to Philosophical Psychopathology

Philosophers have of course long been intrigued by disorders of the mind and consciousness. Part of the interest is presumably that if we can understand how consciousness goes wrong, then that will help us to theorize about the normal, functioning mind. Going back at least as far as John Locke (1689/1975), there has been discussion about the philosophical implications of multiple personality disorder (MPD), which is now called dissociative identity disorder (DID). Questions abound: Could there be two centers of consciousness in one body or brain? What makes a person the same person over time? What counts as a person at any given time? These questions are closely linked to the traditional philosophical problem of personal identity. Much the same can be said for memory disorders such as various forms of amnesia. Does consciousness require some kind of autobiographical memory or psychological continuity? If one loses all or most of one's episodic memory, is one literally a different person? On a related front, there has also been significant interest in experimental results from patients who have undergone a commissurotomy—a surgery performed to relieve symptoms of severe epilepsy when all else fails. During this procedure, the nerve fibers connecting the two brain hemispheres are cut, resulting in so-called split-brain patients; this calls into question the seeming "unity of consciousness" (Tye 2003, Cleeremans 2003, Dainton 2008, Bayne 2008, 2010).

Another rich source of information comes from the provocative and accessible writings of neurologists on a whole host of psychopathologies, most notably Oliver Sacks (starting with his 1987 book) and V. S. Ramachandran (2004). An additional launching point came from the discovery of the phenomenon known as "blindsight" (Weiskrantz 1986), which is frequently discussed in the philosophical literature regarding its implications for consciousness. Blindsight patients are blind (owing to cortical damage) in a well-defined part of the visual field, but yet, when forced, can guess the location or orientation of an object in the blind field with a much higher than expected degree of accuracy.

There is also philosophical interest in many other specific disorders and pathologies, such as phantom limb pain (where one feels pain in a missing or amputated limb), various agnosias (such as visual agnosia, where one is not capable of visually recognizing everyday objects), and anosognosia (which is denial of illness, such as when one claims that a paralyzed limb is still functioning or when one denies that one is blind). All of these phenomena raise a number of important philosophical questions and have forced philosophers to rethink some basic assumptions about the nature of mind and consciousness. Much has also recently been learned about autism and schizophrenia. One view is that some of these disorders involve a deficit in self-consciousness or in the ability to use certain self-concepts (Frith 1992, Stephens and Graham 2000). Others focus on the extent to which some psychopathologies should be construed as some kind of delusion (Bortolotti 2009, Radden 2010, Bayne and Fernandez 2009, Davies and Coltheart 2000). One of the exciting results in recent years is the important interdisciplinary interest that various psychopathologies have generated among philosophers, psychologists, and scientists (such as in Frith and Hill

2003, Farah 2004, Radden 2004, Feinberg and Keenan 2005, Feinberg 2011, Hirstein 2005, 2009, and Graham 2013).

Although the focus in this volume is on the above disorders and what is sometimes called "philosophical psychopathology" (Graham and Stephens 1994), it should also be noted here that some of the interdisciplinary work in what is often termed "philosophy of psychiatry" centers around the nature of mental illness and how to classify and explain it. Indeed, some even doubt the existence of mental illnesses as they are typically construed (Szasz 1974). Some argue that our current diagnostic categories, as compiled in *Diagnostic and Statistical Manual of Mental Disorders*, the DSM-5 (American Psychiatric Association, 2013), are faulty because they are derived from observable variables rather than underlying physical pathologies. Genuine mental illnesses are not just sets of symptoms but destructive pathological processes taking place in biological systems (Murphy 2009, Poland 2014).

Related to all of these areas of inquiry, one finds much interesting work on overlapping ethical issues. For example, if mental illnesses or serious abnormalities, such as psychopathy and schizophrenia, undermine rational agency, then questions arise about the degree to which the mentally ill (or those with psychopathologies) are capable of making genuinely free or voluntary decisions. This bears on central questions regarding the degree of moral and legal responsibility that those afflicted with various psychopathologies can be assigned. The topic of free will and moral responsibility is of course a major area of philosophy in its own right (e.g., Kane 2011). Further, the relevance of some neuroscientific data to ethical and legal questions has also spurred interest in recent years.[1]

2   Consciousness: Background and Terminology

The concept of consciousness is, of course, notoriously ambiguous. It is always important to make several distinctions and to define terms. The abstract noun *consciousness* is not often used in the contemporary philosophical literature, though it should be noted that it originally derives from the Latin *con* (with) and *scire* (to know). Thus, consciousness has etymological ties to one's ability to know and perceive. It should not be confused with *conscience*, which has the much more specific moral connotation of knowing when one has done or is doing something wrong. Through consciousness, one can have knowledge of the external world or one's own mental states. The primary contemporary interest, however, lies more in the use of the expressions "*x* is conscious" and "*x* is conscious of *y*." Under the former category, perhaps most important is the distinction between *state* and *creature* consciousness (Rosenthal 1993). We sometimes speak of an individual mental state, such as a pain or desire, as conscious. On the other hand, we also often speak of organisms or creatures as conscious, such as when we say "human beings are conscious" or "cats are conscious." Creature consciousness is also simply meant to refer to the fact that an organism is awake, as opposed to sleeping or in a coma. However, some kind of *state* consciousness is often implied by creature consciousness—that is, an organism that is having conscious mental states. Owing to the lack of a direct object in the expression "*x* is conscious," this is usually referred to as *intransitive* consciousness, in contrast to *transitive* consciousness, where the locution "*x* is conscious of *y*" is used (Rosenthal 1993, 1997). Most contemporary theories of consciousness are aimed at explaining state consciousness—that is, explaining what makes a mental state a conscious mental state.

It might seem that the term *conscious* is synonymous with, say, awareness or experience or attention. However, it is crucial to recognize that this is not generally accepted today. More common is the belief that we can be aware of external objects in some unconscious sense—for example, during cases of subliminal perception. The expression *conscious awareness* does not seem to be redundant. It is also not clear that consciousness ought to be restricted to attention, though some do argue that they are very closely tied (Prinz 2012). It seems plausible to suppose that one is conscious (in some sense) of objects in one's peripheral visual field even though one is only attending to some narrow (focal) set of objects within that visual field. Although perhaps somewhat atypical, one might even hold that there are unconscious experiences—depending, of course, on how the term *experience* is defined (Carruthers 2000).

Perhaps the most commonly used notion of *conscious* is captured by Thomas Nagel's famous "what it is like" sense (Nagel 1974). When I am in a conscious mental state, there is *something it is like* for me to be in that state from the subjective or first-person point of view. When I am, for example, smelling a rose or having a conscious visual experience, there is something it *seems* or *feels* like from my perspective. An organism, such as a bat, is conscious if it is able to experience the outer world through its (echo-locatory) senses. There is also something it is like to be a conscious creature, whereas there is nothing it is like to be, for example, a table or tree. This is primarily the sense of *conscious state* that authors will use throughout this book. There are still, though, a cluster of expressions and somewhat technical terms related to Nagel's sense, and some authors simply stipulate the way that they use such terms. For example, philosophers sometimes refer to conscious states as *phenomenal* or *qualitative* states. More technically, philosophers often view such states as having qualitative properties called qualia (singular, *quale*). There is significant disagreement over the nature, and even the existence, of qualia, but they are perhaps most frequently understood as the felt properties or qualities of conscious states.

Ned Block (1995) makes an often-cited distinction between *phenomenal* consciousness (or phenomenality) and *access* consciousness. The former is very much in line with the Nagelian notion described above. However, Block also defines the quite different notion of access consciousness in terms of a mental state's relationship with other mental states—for example, a mental state's "availability for use in reasoning and rationality guiding speech and action" (Block 1995, 227). This would, for example, count a visual perception as (access) conscious not because it has the *what it's likeness* of phenomenal states, but rather because it carries visual information that is generally available for use by the organism, regardless of whether or not it has any qualitative properties. Access consciousness is therefore more of a functional notion—that is, it is concerned with what such states *do*. Although this concept is useful in cognitive science and philosophy of mind generally, not everyone agrees that access consciousness deserves to be called *consciousness* in any important sense. Block himself argues that neither sense of consciousness implies the other, although others urge that there is a more intimate connection between the two.[2]

3   Some Philosophical Theories of Consciousness

Some of the theories of consciousness defended and discussed in the essays to follow include the following:

3.1   First-Order Representationalism

Many current theories attempt to reduce consciousness in mentalistic terms (as opposed to physicalistic terms). One broadly popular approach along these lines is to reduce consciousness to mental representations of some kind. The notion of a *representation* is, of course, quite general and can be applied to photographs, signs, and various natural objects, such as the rings inside a tree. Much of what goes on in the brain, however, might also be understood in a representational way—for example, as mental events representing outer objects partly because they are caused by such objects in, say, cases of veridical visual perception. Philosophers often call such representational mental states *intentional states* that have representational content, that is, mental states that are about something or directed at something, such as when one has a thought about a house or a perception of the tree. Although intentional states are sometimes contrasted with phenomenal states, such as pains and color experiences, it is clear that many conscious states have both phenomenal and intentional properties, such as a visual perception.

The general view that we can explain conscious mental states in terms of representational or intentional states is called *representationalism*. Although not automatically reductionist in spirit, most versions of representationalism do indeed attempt such a reduction. Most representationalists, then, believe that there is room for a kind of second-step reduction to be filled in later by neuroscience. The other related motivation for representational theories of consciousness is that many believe that an account of representation (or intentionality) can more easily be given in naturalistic terms, such as causal theories whereby mental states are understood as representing outer objects in virtue of some reliable causal connection. The idea, then, is that if consciousness can be explained in representational terms, and representation can be understood in purely physical terms, then there is the promise of a reductionist and naturalistic theory of consciousness. Most generally, however, we can say that a representationalist will typically hold that the phenomenal properties of experience (that is, the qualia or what-it-is-like of experience or phenomenal character) can be explained in terms of the experiences' representational properties. Alternatively, conscious mental states have no mental properties other than their representational properties. Two conscious states with all the same representational properties will not differ phenomenally. For example, when I look at the blue sky, what it is like for me to have a conscious experience of the sky is simply identical with my experience's representation of the blue sky.

First-order representational (FOR) theories of consciousness refers to theories that attempt to explain conscious experience primarily in terms of world-directed (or first-order) intentional states. Probably the two most cited FOR theories of consciousness are those of Dretske (1995) and Tye (1995, 2000), though there are many others as well (e.g., Byrne 2001, Droege 2003). Like other FOR theorists, Tye holds that the representational content of my conscious experience (that is, what my experience is about or direct at) is identical with the phenomenal properties of experience. Aside from reductionistic motivations, Tye and other representationalists often use the somewhat technical notion of the "transparency of experience" as support for their view (Harman 1990). This is an argument based on the phenomenological first-person observation, which goes back to Moore (1903), that when one turns one's attention away from, say, the blue sky and onto one's experience itself, one is still only aware of the blueness of the sky. The experience itself is not blue; rather, one *sees right through* one's experience to its representational properties, and there is nothing else to one's experience over and above such properties. Whatever the merits of the argument from transparency, it is clear that not all mental representations are conscious, and so the key question eventually becomes: What exactly distinguishes conscious from unconscious mental states (or representations)?

3.2 Higher-Order Representationalism

So one central question that should be answered by any theory of consciousness is: What makes a mental state a *conscious* mental state? There is a long tradition that has attempted to understand consciousness in terms of some kind of higher-order awareness, perhaps even going back to Locke (1689/1975), who once said that "consciousness is the perception of what passes in a man's own mind." But this intuition has been revived by a number of philosophers much more recently (Armstrong 1968, Rosenthal 1986, 1997, 2002, 2005, Gennaro 1996, 2012, and Lycan 1996, 2001). In general, the idea is that what makes a mental state conscious is that it is the object of some kind of higher-order representation (HOR). A mental state *M* becomes conscious when there is a HOR of a mental state *M*. A HOR is a metapsychological or metacognitive state—that is, a mental state directed at another mental state. So, for example, my desire to write a good introduction becomes conscious when I am (noninferentially) aware of the desire. Intuitively, it seems that conscious states, as opposed to unconscious ones, are mental states that I am "aware of" in some sense. This is sometimes referred to as the *transitivity principle*. Any theory that attempts to explain consciousness in terms of higher-order states is known as a higher-order (HO) theory of consciousness. It is best initially to use the more neutral term *representation* because there are a number of different kinds of higher-order theory, depending on how one characterizes the HOR in question. HO theories, thus, attempt to explain consciousness in mentalistic terms—that is, by reference to such notions as *thoughts* and *awareness*. Conscious mental states arise when two unconscious mental states are related in a certain specific way—namely, that one of them (the HOR) is directed at the other (*M*). HO theorists are united in the belief that their approach can better explain consciousness than any purely FOR theory that has significant difficulty in explaining the difference between unconscious and conscious mental states.

There are various kinds of HO theory, with the most common division being between higher-order thought (HOT) theories and higher-order perception (HOP) theories. HOT theorists, such as Rosenthal (2005) and

Gennaro (1996, 2012), think it is better to understand the HOR as a thought of some kind. HOTs are treated as cognitive states involving some kind of conceptual component. HOP theorists urge that the HOR is a perceptual or experiential state of some kind (Lycan 1996) that does not require the kind of conceptual content invoked by HOT theorists. Although HOT and HOP theorists agree on the need for a HOR theory of consciousness, they do sometimes argue for the superiority of their respective positions (such as in Rosenthal 2004, Lycan 2004, and Gennaro 2012).

A common initial objection to HOR theories is that they are circular and lead to an infinite regress. It might seem that the HOT theory results in circularity by defining consciousness in terms of HOTs. It also might seem that an infinite regress results because a conscious mental state must be accompanied by a HOT, which, in turn, must be accompanied by another HOT, ad infinitum. However, the standard and widely accepted reply is that when a conscious mental state is a first-order, world-directed state, the higher-order thought (HOT) is not itself conscious; otherwise, circularity and an infinite regress would follow. When the HOT is itself conscious, there is a yet higher-order (or third-order) thought directed at the second-order state. In this case, we have *introspection*, which involves a conscious HOT directed at an inner mental state. When one introspects, one's attention is directed back into one's mind. For example, what makes my desire to write a good introduction a conscious, first-order desire is that there is a (unconscious) HOT directed at the desire. In this case, my conscious focus is directed at the entry and my computer screen, so I am not consciously aware of having the HOT from the first-person point of view. When I introspect that desire, however, I then have a conscious HOT (accompanied by a yet higher, third-order, HOT) directed at the desire itself.[3]

3.3   Self-Representational Theory of Consciousness

A related version of representational theory holds that the metapsychological state in question should be understood as intrinsic to (or part of) an overall, complex, conscious state. This stands in contrast to the standard view that the HO state is extrinsic to (i.e., entirely distinct from) its target mental state. The assumption, made by Rosenthal (1986) for example, about the extrinsic nature of the metathought has increasingly come under attack, and thus various hybrid representational theories can be found in the literature. One reason is renewed interest in a view somewhat closer to the one held by Brentano (1874/1973), Sartre (1956), and others normally associated with the phenomenological tradition. To varying degrees, these views have in common the idea that conscious mental states, in some sense, represent *themselves*, which then still involves having a thought about a mental state, just not a distinct or separate state. Thus, when a one has a conscious desire for a cold glass of water, one is also aware that one is in that very state. The conscious desire represents both the glass of water and itself. It is this *self-representing* or *reflexivity* that makes the state conscious.

For example, although a HOT theorist, Gennaro (1996, 2006, 2012) has argued that, when one has a first-order conscious state, the HOT is better viewed as intrinsic to the target state so that we have a complex, conscious state with parts. Gennaro calls this the wide intrinsicality view (WIV) and argues that conscious mental states should be understood (as Kant might have understood them today) as somewhat more global brain states that are combinations of passively received perceptual input and presupposed higher-order conceptual activity directed at that input. Van Gulick (2004, 2006) has also explored the alternative that the HO state is part of an over-all, global, conscious state. He calls such states HOGS (higher-order global states), whereby a lower-order unconscious state is *recruited* into a larger state, which becomes conscious partly owing to the implicit self-awareness that one is in the lower-order state. This general approach is also forcefully advocated in a series of papers by Uriah Kriegel (e.g., Kriegel 2003, 2006), culminating in Kriegel 2009 (see also Kriegel and Williford 2006). Most recently, Kriegel (2009) calls his theory the "self-representational theory of consciousness." To be sure, the notion of a mental state representing itself, or a mental state with one part representing another part, is in need of fur-ther development and is perhaps itself somewhat mysterious. Nonetheless, these authors agree that conscious mental states are, in some important sense, reflexive or self-directed.

3.4 Multiple Drafts Theory

Daniel Dennett (1991, 2005) has put forth what he calls the multiple drafts model (MDM) of consciousness. Although similar in some ways to repre-sentationalism, Dennett is perhaps most concerned that materialists avoid falling prey to what he calls the "myth of the Cartesian theater" (Dennett 1991), the notion that there is some privileged place in the brain where everything comes together to produce conscious experience. Instead, the MDM holds that all kinds of mental activity occur in the brain by parallel processes of interpretation that are all under frequent revision (analogous to drafts of a written narrative). The MDM rejects the idea of some *self* as an inner observer; rather, the self is the product or construction of a narrative that emerges over time, which Dennett (2005) calls the "center of narrative gravity." Dennett is also well-known for rejecting the very assumption that there is a clear line to be drawn between conscious and unconscious mental states in terms of the problematic notion of qualia. He influentially rejects strong emphasis on any phenomenological or first-person approach to investigating consciousness, advocating instead what he calls *heterophenom-enology*, according to which we should follow a more neutral path "leading from objective physical science and its insistence on the third person point of view, to a method of phenomenological description that can (in principle) do justice to the most private and ineffable subjective experiences" (1991, 72). Metzinger's "self-model theory of subjectivity" (Metzinger 2003, 2011) also has some affinities to Dennett's view. There is no such ontological entity as *the* self; rather, there is a self-model and a world-model. What we folk-psychologically refer to as *the self* is not a model of a thing, but an ongoing process.

3.5 Global Workspace Theory

Bernard Baars' global workspace theory (GWT) model of consciousness is probably the most influential theory among psychologists (Baars 1988, 1997). The basic idea and metaphor is that we should think of the entire cognitive system as built on a "blackboard architecture" (Baars 1997), which is a kind of global workspace. According to GWT, unconscious processes and mental states compete for the spotlight of attention, from which information is broadcast globally throughout the system. Consciousness consists in such global broadcasting and is therefore also, according to Baars, an important functional and biological adaptation. We might say that consciousness is thus created by a kind of global access to select bits of information in the brain and nervous system. Despite Baars' frequent use of theater and spotlight metaphors, he argues that his view does not entail the presence of the material Cartesian theater that Dennett is so concerned to avoid. It is, in any case, an empirical matter just how the brain performs the functions he describes, such as detecting mechanisms of attention.

3.6 The Sensorimotor/Enactive Theory of Consciousness

In recent years, there has been increased attention to what is called an *embodied approach* to cognition that elevates the importance of bodily interactions with the world in explaining cognitive activities. With regard to consciousness, this enactive or sensorimotor theory holds that conscious experiences are inseparable from bodily activities or from sensorimotor expectations (O'Regan and Noë 2001, Noë 2004, O'Regan 2011, Hutto and Myin 2012). On this view, what we feel is determined by what we do and what we know how to do. According to the sensorimotor approach to perception, perceptual experience should be seen fundamentally as a way of interacting with the environment. What distinguishes perceptual experiences is the different ways in which a perceiver perceptually engages with the environment. What sets apart hearing from seeing, for example, are the differences between the patterns of auditory versus visual engaging with the world. Similarly, within a single (sub)modality such as color vision, what sets apart an experience of red from an experience of green are also the differences in the modes of interaction with the environment that are involved. In addition, and perhaps more radically, instead of aiming to find the neural basis for a phenomenal state, we also need to look elsewhere. In particular, if one wants to find an intelligible relation between the phenomenal and the physical, one must look at the interactions between an organism and its environment.

4 Various Psychopathologies

I mentioned at the beginning of this chapter that numerous psychopathologies are addressed in this volume, some far more than others. For those readers interested in a selected list of at least some psychopathologies, this section groups them into three categories. Many, but by no means all, of those listed below are discussed in this volume. Some readers might wish to skim this section initially, but it can also be treated as a sort of glossary to be consulted periodically while reading the essays to follow. I have organized it into three groups.

Group 1: Self-Awareness or Body-Related Psychopathologies A number of psychopathologies are commonly viewed as pathologies or delusions of self- or body-awareness in some way. For example, somatoparaphrenia is a type of body delusion where one denies ownership of a limb or an entire side of one's body. One reason that HOT theory has been critically examined in light of some psychopathologies is that, according to HOT theory, what makes a mental state conscious is a HOT of the form that "I am in mental state *M*." The requirement of an I-reference leads some to think that HOT theory cannot explain or account for some of these pathologies. Similar considerations might also apply to self-representationalism and sensorimotor theory as well as to psychopathologies such as schizophrenia/ thought insertion, dissociative identity disorder, mirror self-misidentification, and anosognosia.

Amnesia—A condition in which one's memory is lost. *Anterograde* amnesia is the loss of short-term memory, the loss or impairment of the ability to form new memories through memorization. *Retrograde* amnesia is the loss of preexisting memories to conscious recollection, beyond an ordinary degree of forgetfulness. The person may be able to memorize new things that occur after the onset of amnesia (unlike in anterograde amnesia), but be unable to recall some or all of his or her life or identity prior to the onset.

Anarchic hand syndrome—A neurological disorder caused by brain lesion in which individuals frequently perform seemingly voluntary movements that they do not consciously intend and cannot directly inhibit.

Anosognosia—A condition in which a person who suffers from a disability seems unaware of the existence of the disability. *Anton's syndrome* is a form of anosognosia in which a person with partial or total blindness denies being visually impaired, despite medical evidence to the contrary. The patient typically confabulates, that is, contrives excuses for the inability to see.

Apraxia—A form of motor (body) agnosia involving the neurological loss of ability to map out physical actions in order to repeat them in functional activities. It is a form of body-disconnectedness and takes several different forms.

Asomatognosia—A lack of awareness of the condition of all or part of one's body. A lack of awareness of paralysis because the brain is damaged.

Body swap illusion—People can be tricked into the false perception of owning another body. An illusion that can make people feel that another body, be it a mannequin or an actual person, is really theirs.

Cotard syndrome—A rare neuropsychiatric disorder in which people hold a delusional belief that they are dead (either figuratively or literally), do not exist, are putrefying, or have lost their blood or internal organs.

Dissociative identity disorder (DID)—A psychiatric diagnosis and describes a condition in which a person displays multiple distinct identities (known as alters or parts), each with its own pattern of perceiving and interacting with the environment. DID was previously called multiple personality disorder.

Mirrored-self-misidentification—The belief that one's reflection in a mirror is some other person.

Phantom limb pain/sensation—Sensations (such as cramping pain) are described as perceptions that an individual experiences relating to a limb or an organ that is no longer physically part of the body. These sensations are recorded most frequently following the amputation of an arm or a leg, but may also occur following the removal of a breast or an internal organ. Phantom limb pain is the feeling of pain in an absent limb or a portion of a limb.

Rubber hand illusion—People can be convinced that a rubber hand is their own by putting it on a table in front of them and stroking it in the same way as their real hand.

Schizophrenia—A mental disorder characterized by disintegration of thought processes and of emotional responsiveness. It most commonly manifests itself as auditory hallucinations, paranoid or bizarre delusions, or disorganized speech and thinking, and it is accompanied by significant social or occupational dysfunction. *Thought insertion* is the delusion that some thoughts are not one's own and are somehow being inserted into one's mind.

Self-deception—A process of denying or rationalizing away the relevance, significance, or importance of opposing evidence and logical argument. Self-deception involves convincing oneself of a truth (or lack of truth) so that one does not reveal any self-knowledge of the deception. A *delusion* is a false belief held with absolute conviction despite superior evidence. Unlike hallucinations, delusions are always pathological (the result of an illness or illness process). A delusion is distinct from a belief based on false or incomplete information, dogma, poor memory, illusion, or other effects of perception.

Somatoparaphrenia—A type of monothematic delusion where one denies ownership of a limb or an entire side of one's body. A body delusion.

Split-brain cases—Those patients where severing the corpus callosum blocks the interhemispheric transfer of perceptual, sensory, motor, and other forms of information in a dramatic way.

Group 2: Outer-Directed (at objects or other minds) and/or Attentional Deficits   I label as group 2 those deficits that affect mental states either directed toward other objects or minds or involving attentional deficits. For example, agnosia is a loss of ability to recognize objects, persons, sounds, shapes, or smells while the specific sense itself is not defective.

Agnosia—A loss of ability to recognize objects, persons, sounds, shapes, or smells even though the specific sense itself is not defective and there is no significant memory loss.

Akinetopsia—The loss of motion perception.

Alexithymia—A deficiency in understanding, processing, or describing emotions. It is common to around 85 percent of people on the autism spectrum and can be difficult to distinguish from, or co-occur with, social-emotional agnosia.

Autism—A disorder characterized by impaired social interaction and communication and by restricted and repetitive behavior.

Capgras syndrome—A disorder in which a person holds a delusion that a friend, spouse, parent, or other close family member has been replaced by an identical-looking impostor.

Dysexecutive Syndrome—Consists of a group of symptoms that fall into cognitive, behavioral, and emotional categories and tend to occur together. A dysfunction in executive functions such as planning, abstract thinking, flexibility, and behavioral control.

Fregoli delusion—The belief that various people who the believer meets are actually the same person in disguise.

Hemispatial neglect—Also called hemiagnosia, hemineglect, unilateral neglect, spatial neglect, unilateral visual inattention, hemi-inattention, or neglect syndrome. A neuropsychological condition in which there is a deficit in attention to and awareness of one side of space. It is defined by the inability for a person to process and perceive stimuli on one side of the body or environment and is not due to a lack of sensation.

Prosopagnosia—Also known as faceblindness and facial agnosia. Patients cannot consciously recognize familiar faces, sometimes even including their own.

Simultanagnosia—Patients can recognize objects or details in their visual field, but only one at a time. They cannot make out the scene they belong to or make out a whole image out of the details. They literally cannot see the forest for the trees. Simultanagnosia is a common symptom of Balint's syndrome.

Group 3: Other Miscellaneous Psychopathologies I place here some additional psychopathologies not easily characterized in the ways used in groups 1 and 2 (though there can be some overlap between the list in this category and the psychopathologies listed in the first two groups above).

Charles Bonnet syndrome—A condition that causes patients with visual loss to have complex and vivid visual hallucinations in which characters or objects (such as faces or cartoons) are smaller than normal.

Confabulation—The unconscious filling of gaps in one's memory with fabrications that one accepts as facts. Rationalizing what would seem to be delusional behavior.

Dependent personality disorder—A personality disorder that is characterized by a pervasive psychological dependence on other people. A long-term (chronic) condition in which people depend too much on others to meet their emotional and physical needs.

Mania—A state of abnormally elevated or irritable mood, arousal, and/or energy levels. In a sense, it is the opposite of depression.

Narcissistic personality disorder—A pervasive pattern of grandiosity, need for admiration, and a lack of empathy.

Obsessive compulsive disorder—An anxiety disorder in which people have unwanted and repeated thoughts, feelings, ideas, sensations (obsessions), or behaviors that make them feel driven to do something (compulsions).

Paranoia—A psychotic disorder characterized by delusions of persecution with or without grandeur, often strenuously defended with apparent logic and reason.

Psychopathy—A mental disorder characterized primarily by a lack of empathy and remorse, shallow emotions, egocentricity, and deceptiveness.

5   The Essays

As explained earlier, the essays included in the volume address a wide variety of psychopathologies in light of specific theories of consciousness.

Alexandre Billon and **Uriah Kriegel** (chapter 2: "Jaspers' Dilemma: The Psychopathological Challenge to Subjectivity Theories of Consciousness") hold that our conscious states often have a distinctive subjective character, or mine-ness, by virtue of which they appear to us to be ours. According to what they call "subjectivity theories," the connection between phenomenal consciousness and subjective character is necessary: all phenomenally conscious states must exhibit this mine-ness. Such theories include higher-order and self-representational theories. Billon and Kriegel consider a prima facie threat to subjectivity theories from cases of patients suffering from thought insertion, delusions of alien control, somatoparaphrenia, and depersonalization who would seem to have conscious thoughts, intentions, or bodily sensations that lack subjective character. They argue that at least some subjectivity theories can accommodate these pathologies.

Rocco J. Gennaro (chapter 3: "Somatoparaphrenia, Anosognosia, and Higher-Order Thoughts") defends the HOT theory of consciousness against the charge that it cannot account for somatoparaphrenia, a delusion where one denies ownership of a limb, and the related anosognosia, a condition in which a person who suffers from a disability seems unaware of the existence of the disability. Liang and Lane have argued that somatoparaphrenia threatens HOT theory because it contradicts the notion that, according to HOT theory, when I am in a conscious state, I have the accompanying HOT that "I am in mental state *M*." The "I" is not only importantly self-referential but essential to tying the conscious state to oneself (including one's bodily sensations) and thus to one's ownership of *M*. Indeed, it is difficult to understand how one can have a conscious state but not, at least implicitly, attribute it to oneself. Gennaro argues, for example, that understanding somatoparaphrenia as a delusion leads to a number of replies to

Lane and Liang. He also examines the central notions of "mental state own-ership" and "self-concepts" in an effort to account especially for the deper-sonalization aspect of somatoparaphrenia. Among other things, Gennaro also discusses to what extent HOT theory can make sense of Shoemaker's well-known immunity to error through misidentification (IEM) principle.

Myrto Mylopoulos (chapter 4: "Consciousness, Action, and Pathologies of Agency") discusses the traditionally neglected phenomenon of action consciousness and its breakdowns in pathological conditions. She intro-duces a novel framework for understanding action consciousness, which parallels one that is used to discuss state consciousness. In particular, she distinguishes between first-order and higher-order theories of action con-sciousness, where the former deny, but the latter affirm, the claim that an action is conscious only if one is aware of it in some suitable way. Mylo-poulos argues that higher-order theories of action consciousness enjoy sig-nificant advantages when it comes to making progress on understanding pathological cases in which action consciousness is impaired or disrupted. She focuses on anarchic hand syndrome, utilization behavior, and delu-sions of control in schizophrenia. Furthermore, although theorizing about action consciousness has typically proceeded independently from theoriz-ing about state consciousness, she highlights some ways in which theoriz-ing about consciousness as applied to these different phenomena, actions, and mental states may be fruitfully merged.

Partly in response to various aspects of the preceding three chapters, **Timothy Lane** (chapter 5: "Self, Belonging, and Conscious Experience: A Critique of Subjectivity Theories of Consciousness") offers a wide-rang-ing commentary wherein he responds to Billon and Kriegel, Mylopoulos, and Gennaro. He also clarifies and further develops some of his influen-tial previous work in this area. Subjectivity theories of consciousness take self-reference as essential to having conscious experience, but they differ with respect to how many levels they posit and to whether self-reference is conscious or not. But all treat self-referencing as a process that transpires at the personal, rather than at the subpersonal, level. Working with con-ceptual resources afforded by subjectivity theories, several attempts have been made to explain seemingly anomalous cases, especially instances of alien experience. These experiences are distinctive precisely because self-referencing is explicitly denied by the only person able to report them: those who experience them deny that certain actions, mental states, or body parts belong to self. The relevant actions, mental states, or body parts are sometimes attributed to someone or something other than self, and sometimes they are just described as not belonging to self. The cases under discussion here include somatoparaphrenia, schizophrenia, depersonalization, anarchic hand syndrome, and utilization behavior. The theories discussed include higher-order thought and self-representational. He argues that each of these attempts at explaining, or explaining away, the anomalies fails, and he calls attention to the divergent paths adopted when attempting to explain alienation experiences: some theorists choose to add a mental ingredient, and others prefer to subtract one. Lane argues that alienation from experience, action, or body parts could result from either addition or subtraction, and that the two can be incorporated within a comprehensive explanatory framework that requires self-referencing of a sort, but self-referencing that occurs solely at the level of mechanism, or at the subpersonal level.

Paula Droege (chapter 6: "From Darwin to Freud: Confabulation as an Adaptive Response to Dysfunctions of Consciousness") explains that a puzzling feature of confabulation is its selectivity: only some people confabulate in response to illness, and only some people resist correction of their inventions. So-called two-factor theories of delusion account for the latter sort of selectivity in terms of the failure of a belief evaluator. The first factor in delusion is a dysfunction in perceptual or cognitive processing and includes such cases as amnesia, feelings of unfamiliarity toward loved ones, or auditory hallucinations. Since first-factor deficits do not always cause delusions, a second factor is postulated to explain the failure of delusional patients to revise the faulty beliefs produced by first-factor deficits. For some reason—endorsement and explanationist theories differ—delusional patients maintain false beliefs in the face of counterevidence. Droege suggests that a Darwinian view of the mind can supplement two-factor theories of confabulation delusion by articulating the function of self-consciousness. If we suppose self-consciousness utilizes memories in order to maintain a sense of the self in time, then confabulation is an adaptive response to the absence of memories in order to maintain this function. Delusion differs from the everyday sort of confabulation that many of us experience in that delusions are accompanied by a second deficit in the capacity to reevaluate beliefs in light of contradictory evidence. By considering functions and failures of mental capacities, the debate between endorsement and explanationist accounts of delusion can be resolved. Droege holds a first-order representationalist theory of consciousness that also plays an important role in her chapter.

Thomas Metzinger and **Iuliia Pliushch** (chapter 7: "Self-deception and the Dolphin Model of Cognition") attempt to shed light on the phenomenon of self-deception using some of the conceptual tools offered by

Metzinger's self-model theory of subjectivity. To this end, they analyze a selected set of recent and well-documented empirical examples for human self-deception. They then offer a functionalist and representationalist analysis of how the integration of certain kinds of information into the currently active phenomenal self-model (PSM) can be blocked, thus precluding this information from becoming globally available for introspection (here, they will distinguish different kinds of introspection: for example, introspective attention as a form of subsymbolic resource allocation, and cognitive self-reference as a conceptually mediated and phenomenally opaque form of access to the currently active PSM). Owing to the transparency of the conscious model of the self, this deficit of self-knowledge mostly remains unnoticed by the self-deceived for certain periods of time, leading to sincere reports about its content of the currently active self-model that seem implausible from the third-person perspective. Interestingly, self-deception may be based on complex causal interactions between the transparent and the opaque layers of the human PSM. Their aim is to concentrate on what they take to be the most intriguing and philosophically relevant question: How is it conceivable that systematic and robust forms of misrepresentation on the level of phenomenal self-consciousness exist, and are sometimes even functionally adequate, for individual human persons as well as in an evolutionary context?

Andrew Brook (chapter 8: "Disorders of Unified Consciousness: Brain Bisection and Dissociative Identity Disorder") applies his model of unified consciousness of one's own psychological states to cases of brain bisection and dissociative identity disorder (DID). He argues that problems with Bayne's "switching model" of brain-bisected patients (wherein consciousness switches back and forth from hemisphere to hemisphere) and problems with Humphrey and Dennett's "interpretationism model" of DID are rooted in part in a common weakness: there is no reference to unified autobiographical memory of a certain special kind. Brook argues for a more commonsense picture of brain-bisection patients than Bayne's and a more realist picture of DID than Humphrey and Dennett's.

Robert Van Gulick (chapter 9: "Altogether Now—Not! Integration Theories of Consciousness and Pathologies of Disunity") explains how integration and unity play an important role in a number of current theories and models of consciousness. Normal consciousness is unified in a variety of ways, but many disorders of disunity can also occur. What can we learn from them about consciousness and unity? What theories of consciousness might help us better understand the nature and basis of such disorders? Van Gulick first surveys the diverse types of conscious unity. He then briefly describes five theories of consciousness that involve integration, that is, Baars' global workspace theory (GWT), Tononi's integrated information theory (IIT), Jesse Prinz's attended intermediate representation theory (AIR), Tim Bayne's phenomenal unity thesis, and the combination of his own HOGS (higher-order global states) model with virtual self realism (VSR). In that context, he discusses three specific pathologies of disunity—neglect and extinction, dissociative identity disorder, and split-brains—and each is considered in relation to the integration-based theories of consciousness.

William Hirstein (chapter 10: "Consciousness Despite Network Underconnectivity in Autism: Another Case of Consciousness without Prefrontal Activity?") argues that recent evidence points to widespread underconnectivity in autistic brains, which is due to deviant white-matter connections. Specifically, there is prefrontal-parietal underconnectivity and underconnectivity of the default-mode network in autistic subjects. These phenomena, along with similar data from other psychopathologies, may help shed light on the current debate in the consciousness literature about whether conscious states require prefrontal and parietal/temporal connectivity. If it can be shown that people with autism (or any other psychopathology) have conscious states despite such underconnectivity, this would constitute an argument for the claim that conscious states in the posterior cortex do not require associated prefrontal activity.

Gerard O'Brien and **Jon Opie** (chapter 11: "A Schizophrenic Defense of a Vehicle Theory of Consciousness") first present their vehicle theory of consciousness, which identifies phenomenal consciousness with the brain's vehicles of explicit representation. Given the distributed nature of neural representation, a vehicle theory is committed to the conjecture that phenomenal consciousness at each instant is a multiplicity: an aggregate of discrete phenomenal elements, each of which is the product of a distinct consciousness-making neural mechanism. This in turn implies that the single, unified, conscious subject (or "self") is a hard-won computational achievement in which myriad coconscious parts are stitched together by the brain to form an integrated and coherent whole. From the perspective of a vehicle theory of consciousness, therefore, it is not surprising that the brain sometimes fails to pull off this remarkable feat. In this chapter, they explore what light a vehicle theory sheds on familiar psychopathologies of the self, especially schizophrenia.

Jakob Hohwy (chapter 12: "Prediction Error Minimization, Mental and Developmental Disorder, and Statistical Theories of Consciousness") seeks to recover an approach to consciousness from a general theory of brain function, namely the prediction error minimization theory. The way this theory applies to mental and developmental disorder demonstrates its relevance to consciousness. The resulting view is discussed in relation to a contemporary theory of consciousness, namely, the idea that conscious perception depends on Bayesian metacognition that is also supported by considerations of psychopathology. This Bayesian theory is first disconnected from the higher-order thought theory and then, via a prediction error conception of action, connected instead to the global workspace theory. Considerations of mental and developmental disorder therefore show that a general theory of brain function is relevant to explaining the structure of conscious perception. Furthermore, Hohwy argues that this theory can unify two contemporary approaches to consciousness in a move that seeks to elucidate the fundamental mechanism for the selection of representational content into consciousness.

Philip Gerrans (chapter 13: "Passivity Experience in Schizophrenia") first explains the "predictive coding conception of cognition," which treats the mind as a hierarchy of cognitive systems devoted to the cancellation of error signals. Although the deep consequences of this theory for understanding consciousness have not been fully explored, Andy Clark has suggested that the logical consequence of the predictive coding view is that intuitive distinctions between higher- and lower-level cognitive systems need to be rethought. This suggests that conscious experience, itself produced by low-level sensory and perceptual processes, should be at the mercy of beliefs, since those beliefs can ultimately cancel the prediction errors generated by those systems. Gerrans explores this idea in the context of explanations of the sense of agency—the phenomenologically elusive experience of being the agent of an action. Much of the relevant data comes from the study of schizophrenic delusions of alien control that use predictive coding models to explain the role of correlated neural activation. Gerrans argues that the sense of agency is not as vulnerable to context effects as Clark and others have argued.

Erik Myin, **J. Kevin O'Regan**, and **Inez Myin-Germeys** (chapter 14: "From a Sensorimotor Account of Perception to an Interactive Approach to Psychopathology") explain that, according to the sensorimotor approach to perception and perceptual awareness, perceptual experience should be seen fundamentally as a way of interacting with the environment. What distinguishes different perceptual experiences is the different ways in which a perceiver perceptually engages with the environment. What differentiates hearing from seeing, for example, is the differences between the patterns of auditory versus visual engaging with the world. Similarly, within a single (sub)modality, such as color vision, what sets apart an experience of red from an experience of green is also the differences in the modes of interaction with the environment that are involved. It has been argued by sensorimotor theorists that this relocation of emphasis from the brain to the interaction with the environment dissolves many problems regarding understanding the nature of phenomenal consciousness. They argue that a similar shift of emphasis away from an internal (or brainbound) approach to an interactive one is possible in the study of psychopathology. Indeed, such a shift is implemented in approaches to psychopathology that focus on the role of person-environment interactions in the study of the positive and negative phenomena of psychosis, by means of ambulatory monitoring. Underlying this approach is a view of psychopathology as involving altered ways of interacting with one's local context. On a theoretical level, this has led to the view of schizophrenia as a "salience dysregulation syndrome." They focus on the similarities between the sensorimotor view of perception and this interactive view to psychopathology, and they discuss the gains that could be obtained by turning one's view outward.

Notes

1. For much more on mental illness and this line of research, see Radden 2004, Maibom 2005, Hirstein 2005, Fulford, Thornton, and Graham 2006, Cooper 2007, Glannon 2008, Graham 2013, Murphy 2013, Blaney, Krueger, and Millon 2014, Zachar 2014, and Kincaid and Sullivan 2014.

2. For some excellent in-depth books and anthologies on consciousness, see Block, Flanagan, and Güzeldere 1997, Chalmers 2002, Baars, Banks, and Newman 2003, Velmans and Schneider 2007, Zelazo, Moscovitch, and Thompson 2007, Revonsuo 2010, and Blackmore 2011. See also Gennaro 2014 and Van Gulick 2014 for two online encyclopedia entries on consciousness. There are major annual conferences sponsored by worldwide professional organizations, such as the Association for the Scientific Study of Consciousness, and an entire book series called "Advances in Consciousness Research" published by John Benjamins. There are also several important journals devoted entirely to the interdisciplinary study of consciousness, such as *Consciousness and Cognition* and the *Journal of Consciousness Studies*. Journals such as *Philosophy, Psychiatry, and Psychology, Cognitive Neuropsychiatry*, and *Neuro-Ethics* have also helped to foster interdisciplinary work on psychopathologies and mental illness (see also Farah 2010 and Illes and Sahakian 2011 on neuroethics). In addition to MIT Press's *Philosophical Psychopathology* book series, Oxford University Press's *International Perspectives in Philosophy and Psychiatry* series and the *Oxford Series in Neuroscience, Law, and Philosophy* are invaluable (see e.g., Malatesti and McMillan 2010, Fulford et al. 2013, and Vincent 2013).

3. Another common objection is that various animals (and even infants) are not likely to have the conceptual sophistication required for HOTs, and so that would render animal (and infant) consciousness very unlikely (Dretske 1995, Seager 2004). Are cats and dogs capable of having complex higher-order thoughts such as "I am in mental state *M*"? Although most who bring forth this objection are not HO theorists, Peter Carruthers (2000, 2005) is one HO theorist who actually embraces the conclusion that (most) animals do not have phenomenal consciousness. Gennaro (1996, 2009, 2012, chapters 7 and 8) has replied at length to this alleged inconsistency, for example, by arguing that HOTs need not be as sophisticated as it might initially appear, and there is ample comparative neurophysiological evidence supporting the conclusion that animals have conscious mental states.

References

American Psychiatric Association. 2013. *Diagnostic and Statistical Manual of Mental Disorders*, 5th ed. Washington, DC: American Psychiatric Association.

Armstrong, D. 1968. *A Materialist Theory of Mind*. London: Routledge & Kegan Paul.

Baars, B. 1988. *A Cognitive Theory of Consciousness*. Cambridge: Cambridge University Press.

Baars, B. 1997. *In the Theater of Consciousness*. New York: Oxford University Press.

Baars, B., W. Banks, and J. Newman, eds. 2003. *Essential Sources in the Scientific Study of Consciousness*. Cambridge, MA: MIT Press.

Bayne, T. 2008. The unity of consciousness and the split-brain syndrome. *Journal of Philosophy* 104: 277–300.

Bayne, T. 2010. *The Unity of Consciousness*. Oxford: Oxford University Press.

Bayne, T., and J. Fernandez, eds. 2009. *Delusion and Self-Deception*. Hove: Psychology Press.

Blackmore, S. 2011. *Consciousness: An Introduction*, 2nd ed. Oxford: Oxford University Press.

Blaney, P., R. Krueger, and T. Millon, eds. 2014. *Oxford Textbook of Psychopathology*, 3rd ed. Oxford: Oxford University Press.

Block, N. 1995. On a confusion about the function of consciousness. *Behavioral and Brain Sciences* 18:227–247.

Block, N., O. Flanagan, and G. Güzeldere, eds. 1997. *The Nature of Consciousness*. Cambridge, MA: MIT Press.

Bolton, D. 2008. *What Is Mental Disorder?* Oxford: Oxford University Press.

Bortolotti, L. 2009. *Delusions and Other Irrational Beliefs*. New York: Oxford University Press.

Bortolotti, L., and M. Broome. 2009. A role for ownership and authorship in the analysis of thought insertion. *Phenomenology and the Cognitive Sciences* 8:205–224.

Brentano, F. 1874/1973. *Psychology from an Empirical Standpoint*. New York: Humanities Press.

Broome, M., and L. Bortolotti, eds. 2009. *Psychiatry as Cognitive Neuroscience: Philosophical Perspectives*. New York: Oxford University Press.

Byrne, A. 2001. Intentionalism defended. *Philosophical Review* 110:199–240.

Carruthers, P. 2000. *Phenomenal Consciousness*. Cambridge: Cambridge University Press.

Carruthers, P. 2005. *Consciousness: Essays from a Higher-Order Perspective*. New York: Oxford University Press.

Chalmers, D., ed. 2002. *Philosophy of Mind: Classical and Contemporary Readings*. New York: Oxford University Press.

Cleeremans, A., ed. 2003. *The Unity of Consciousness: Binding, Integration, and Dissociation*. Oxford: Oxford University Press.

Cooper, R. 2007. *Psychiatry and Philosophy of Science*. London: Acumen.

Dainton, B. 2008. *The Phenomenal Self*. Oxford: Oxford University Press.

Davies, M., and M. Coltheart. 2000. Introduction: Pathologies of belief. *Mind & Language* 15:1–46.

Dennett, D. 1991. *Consciousness Explained*. Boston: Little, Brown.

Dennett, D. 2005. *Sweet Dreams*. Cambridge, MA: MIT Press.

Dretske, F. 1995. *Naturalizing the Mind*. Cambridge, MA: MIT Press.

Droege, P. 2003. *Caging the Beast*. Amsterdam: John Benjamins.

Farah, M. 2004. *Visual Agnosia*, 2nd ed. Cambridge, MA: MIT Press.

Farah, M., ed. 2010. *Neuroethics: An Introduction with Readings*. Cambridge, MA: MIT Press.

Feinberg, T. 2011. Neuropathologies of the self: Clinical and anatomical features. *Consciousness and Cognition* 20:75–81.

Feinberg, T., and J. Keenan, eds. 2005. *The Lost Self: Pathologies of the Brain and Identity*. New York: Oxford University Press.

Frith, C. 1992. *The Cognitive Neuropsychology of Schizophrenia*. Hove: Psychology Press.

Frith, C., and E. Hill, eds. 2003. *Autism: Mind and Brain*. London: Oxford University Press.

Fulford, K., M. Davies, R. Gipps, G. Graham, J. Sadler, G. Stanghellini, and T. Thornton. 2013. *The Oxford Handbook of Philosophy and Psychiatry*. Oxford: Oxford University Press.

Fulford, K., T. Thornton, and G. Graham, eds. 2006. *Oxford Textbook of Philosophy and Psychiatry*. Oxford: Oxford University Press.

Gennaro, R. 1996. *Consciousness and Self-Consciousness*. Amsterdam: John Benjamins.

Gennaro, R., ed. 2004. *Higher-Order Theories of Consciousness: An Anthology*. Amsterdam: John Benjamins.

Gennaro, R. 2006. Between pure self-referentialism and the (extrinsic) HOT theory of consciousness. In *Self-Representational Approaches to Consciousness*, ed. U. Kriegel and K. Williford. Cambridge, MA: MIT Press.

Gennaro, R. 2009. Animals, consciousness, and I-thoughts. In *Philosophy of Animal Minds*, ed. Robert Lurz. New York: Cambridge University Press.

Gennaro, R. 2012. *The Consciousness Paradox: Consciousness, Concepts, and Higher-Order Thoughts*. Cambridge, MA: MIT Press.

Gennaro, R. 2014. Consciousness [revised]. In *Internet Encyclopedia of Philosophy*. http://www.iep.utm.edu/consciou/.

Glannon, W. 2008. Moral responsibility and the psychopath. *Neuroethics* 1:158–166.

Graham, G. 2013. *The Disordered Mind: An Introduction into Philosophy of Mind and Mental Illness*, 2nd ed. London: Routledge.

Graham, G., and G. L. Stephens, eds. 1994. *Philosophical Psychopathology*. Cambridge, MA: MIT Press.

Harman, G. 1990. The intrinsic quality of experience. In *Philosophical Perspectives*, vol. 4, ed. J. Tomberlin. Atascadero, CA: Ridgeview.

Hirstein, W. 2005. *Brain Fiction: Self-Deception and the Riddle of Confabulation*. Cambridge, MA: MIT Press.

Hirstein, W., ed. 2009. *Confabulation: Views from Neuroscience, Psychiatry, Psychology, and Philosophy*. Oxford: Oxford University Press.

Hutto, D., and E. Myin. 2012. *Radicalizing Enactivism*. Cambridge, MA: MIT Press.

Illes, J., and B. Sahakian, eds. 2011. *Oxford Handbook of Neuroethics*. Oxford: Oxford University Press.

Kane, R., ed. 2011. *Oxford Handbook on Free Will*, 2nd ed. New York: Oxford University Press.

Kincaid, H., and J. Sullivan. 2014. *Classifying Psychopathology: Mental Kinds and Natural Kinds*. Cambridge, MA: MIT Press.

Kriegel, U. 2003. Consciousness as intransitive self-consciousness: Two views and an argument. *Canadian Journal of Philosophy* 33:103–132.

Kriegel, U. 2006. The same order monitoring theory of consciousness. In *Self-Representational Approaches to Consciousness*, ed. U. Kriegel and K. Williford. Cambridge, MA: MIT Press.

Kriegel, U. 2009. *Subjective Consciousness*. New York: Oxford University Press.

Kriegel, U., and K. Williford, eds. 2006. *Self-Representational Approaches to Consciousness*. Cambridge, MA: MIT Press.

Liang, L., and T. Lane. 2009. Higher-order thought and pathological self: The case of somatoparaphrenia. *Analysis* 69:661–668.

Locke, J. 1689/1975. *An Essay Concerning Human Understanding*. Ed. P. Nidditch. Oxford: Clarendon.

Lycan, W. 1996. *Consciousness and Experience*. Cambridge, MA: MIT Press.

Lycan, W. 2001. A simple argument for a higher-order representation theory of consciousness. *Analysis* 61:3–4.

Lycan, W. 2004. The superiority of HOP to HOT. In *Higher-Order Theories of Consciousness: An Anthology*, ed. R. Gennaro. Amsterdam: John Benjamins.

Maibom, H. 2005. Moral unreason: The case of psychopathy. *Mind & Language* 20:237–257.

Malatesti, L., and J. McMillan, eds. 2010. *Responsibility and Psychopathy: Interfacing Law, Psychiatry, and Philosophy*. Oxford: Oxford University Press.

Metzinger, T. 2003. *Being No One: The Self-Model Theory of Subjectivity*. Cambridge, MA: MIT Press.

Metzinger, T. 2011. The no-self alternative. In *The Oxford Handbook of the Self*, ed. S. Gallagher. Oxford: Oxford University Press.

Moore, G. E. 1903. The refutation of idealism. In *Philosophical Studies*, ed. G. E. Moore. Totowa, NJ: Littlefield, Adams.

Murphy, D. 2006. *Psychiatry in the Scientific Image*. Cambridge, MA: MIT Press.

Murphy, D. 2009. Psychiatry and the concept of disease as pathology. In *Psychiatry as Cognitive Neuroscience: Philosophical Perspectives*, ed. M. Broome and L. Bortolotti. New York: Oxford University Press.

Murphy, D. 2013. Philosophy of psychiatry. *Stanford Encyclopedia of Philosophy* (Fall 2013 Ed.), ed. Edward N. Zalta. http://plato.stanford.edu/archives/fall2013/entries/psychiatry/.

Nagel, T. 1974. What is it like to be a bat? *Philosophical Review* 83:435–456.

Noë, A. 2004. *Action in Perception*. Cambridge, MA: MIT Press.

O'Regan, K. 2011. *Why Red Doesn't Sound Like a Bell: Understanding the Feel of Consciousness*. New York: Oxford University Press.

O'Regan, K., and A. Noë. 2001. A sensorimotor account of vision and visual consciousness. *Behavioral and Brain Sciences* 24:883–917.

Poland, J. 2014. Deeply rooted sources of error and bias in psychiatric classification. In *Classifying Psychopathology: Mental Kinds and Natural Kinds*, ed. H. Kincaid and J. Sullivan. Cambridge, MA: MIT Press.

Prinz, J. 2012. *The Conscious Brain*. New York: Oxford University Press.

Radden, J., ed. 2004. *The Philosophy of Psychiatry: A Companion*. New York: Oxford University Press.

Radden, J. 2010. *On Delusion*. New York: Routledge.

Ramachandran, V. 2004. *A Brief Tour of Human Consciousness*. London: Pearson Education.

Revonsuo, A. 2010. *Consciousness: The Science of Subjectivity*. New York: Psychology Press.

Rosenthal, D. 1986. Two concepts of consciousness. *Philosophical Studies* 49: 329–359.

Rosenthal, D. 1993. State consciousness and transitive consciousness. *Consciousness and Cognition* 2:355–363.

Rosenthal, D. 1997. A theory of consciousness. In *The Nature of Consciousness*, ed. N. Block, O. Flanagan, and G. Güzeldere. Cambridge, MA: MIT Press.

Rosenthal, D. 2002. Explaining consciousness. In *Philosophy of Mind: Classical and Contemporary Readings*, ed. D. Chalmers. New York: Oxford University Press.

Rosenthal, D. 2004. Varieties of higher-order theory. In *Higher-Order Theories of Consciousness: An Anthology*, ed. R. Gennaro. Amsterdam: John Benjamins.

Rosenthal, D. 2005. *Consciousness and Mind*. New York: Oxford University Press.

Rosenthal, D. 2010. Consciousness, the self, and bodily location. *Analysis* 70: 270–276.

Sacks, O. 1987. *The Man Who Mistook His Wife for a Hat and Other Clinical Tales*. New York: Harper & Row.

Sartre, J. 1956. *Being and Nothingness*. New York: Philosophical Library.

Seager, W. 2004. A cold look at HOT theory. In *Higher-Order Theories of Consciousness: An Anthology*, ed. R. Gennaro. Amsterdam: John Benjamins.

Stephens, G. L., and G. Graham. 2000. *When Self-Consciousness Breaks: Alien Voices and Inserted Thoughts*. Cambridge, MA: MIT Press.

Szasz, T. 1974. *The Myth of Mental Illness*. New York: Harper & Row.

Tye, M. 1995. *Ten Problems of Consciousness*. Cambridge, MA: MIT Press.

Tye, M. 2000. *Consciousness, Color, and Content*. Cambridge, MA: MIT Press.

Tye, M. 2003. *Consciousness and Persons*. Cambridge, MA: MIT Press.

Van Gulick, R. 2004. Higher-order global states (HOGS): An alternative higher-order model of consciousness. In *Higher-Order Theories of Consciousness: An Anthology*, ed. R. Gennaro. Amsterdam: John Benjamins.

Van Gulick, R. 2006. Mirror mirror—is that all? In *Self-Representational Approaches to Consciousness*, ed. U. Kriegel and K. Williford. Cambridge, MA: MIT Press.

Van Gulick, Robert. 2014. Consciousness. In *The Stanford Encyclopedia of Philosophy* (Spring 2014 Ed.), ed. Edward N. Zalta. http://plato.stanford.edu/archives/spr2014/entries/consciousness/.

Velmans, M., and S. Schneider, eds. 2007. *The Blackwell Companion to Consciousness*. Malden, MA: Blackwell.

Vincent, N., ed. 2013. *Neuroscience and Legal Responsibility*. Oxford: Oxford University Press.

Weiskrantz, L. 1986. *Blindsight*. Oxford: Clarendon.

Zachar, P. 2014. *A Metaphysics of Psychopathology*. Cambridge, MA: MIT Press.

Zelazo, P., M. Moscovitch, and E. Thompson, eds. 2007. *The Cambridge Handbook of Consciousness*. Cambridge: Cambridge University Press.

2 Jaspers' Dilemma: The Psychopathological Challenge to Subjectivity Theories of Consciousness

Alexandre Billon and Uriah Kriegel

1 Introduction

According to what we will call subjectivity theories of consciousness, there is a constitutive connection between phenomenal consciousness and subjectivity: there is something it is like for a subject to have mental state M only if M is characterized by a certain mine-ness or for-me-ness. Such theories appear to face certain psychopathological counterexamples: patients appear to report conscious experiences that lack this subjective element. A subsidiary goal of this chapter is to articulate with greater precision both subjectivity theories and the psychopathological challenge they face. The chapter's central goal is to present two new approaches to defending subjectivity theories in the face of this challenge. What distinguishes these two approaches is that they go to great lengths to interpret patients' reports at face value—greater length, at any rate, than more widespread approaches in the extant literature.

2 Consciousness and Subjectivity

Compare your experiences of drinking apple juice and drinking a banana smoothie. These experiences are different in many respects: there is a gustatory apple-ish way it is like for you to have the former and a gustatory banana-ish way it is like for you to have the latter; there is a tactile juice-ish way it is like for you to have the former and a tactile smooth-ish way it is like for you to have the latter, and so on. But there is also one respect in which the two experiences are exactly the same: in both cases it is *for you* that it is like something to have them. By this we mean not only that both experiences *are* yours, but more strongly that both are *experienced* as yours. We call this the *subjectivity* of experience. Your apple-juice and banana-smoothie experiences are different in gustatory and tactile respects, but are the same in respect of subjectivity.

It is an open question what the relationship is between subjectivity and phenomenal consciousness. Call the following the *subjectivity principle*:

(SP) Necessarily, a mental state M exhibits phenomenal consciousness only if M exhibits subjectivity.

According to SP, there is a necessary, constitutive connection between phenomenal consciousness and subjectivity. Some theories of consciousness in the extant literature are committed to SP, some to ~SP, and some to neither. Call those that are committed to SP *subjectivity theories* of consciousness. According to subjectivity theories, a phenomenally conscious state that lacks this dimension of for-me-ness or subjectivity is metaphysically impossible.

There are three main kinds of subjectivity theory currently being discussed. One is higher-order representationalism. According to Rosenthal ([1990] 1997), every conscious state is a state the subject is aware of and, moreover, aware of as her own. This awareness is implemented by a higher-order representation of the subject's experience (see also Gennaro 1996, 2012). Crucially, proponents of higher-order representationalism typically hold that the phenomenal character of a conscious state is determined by the manner in which it is higher-order represented.[1] To that extent, they appear committed to SP.[2]

A second kind of subjectivity theory is self-representationalism. According to Kriegel (2009), conscious states are states the subject is aware of (as hers), not because they are targeted by higher-order representations, however, but because they are targeted *by themselves* (see also Williford 2006). Every conscious state represents itself (and, moreover, represents itself as belonging to the subject), and it is in virtue of this self-representation that the subject is aware of it (as hers). The fact that the conscious state is represented by itself means that it is represented by a conscious state, which in turn means that the subject's awareness of it (as hers) does show up in the subject's overall phenomenology. This is a clear case of a subjectivity theory, then.

A third kind of subjectivity theory is what we call acquaintance theory. According to Levine (2001), the subject's awareness of her own conscious states is not implemented in a representational state at all. Rather, it involves a sui generis awareness relation—acquaintance—that is unlike representational relations in some crucial respects, most notably by being factive (see also Billon 2005). This sui generis acquaintance relation is intended to capture the elusively immediate character of our awareness of our conscious states as it shows up in our phenomenology. It is thus intended as built into the phenomenology in the manner required by subjectivity theories.

These are the main contemporary kinds of subjectivity theory, but the latter has a long history. Already Locke wrote that "Whilst [the soul] thinks and perceives… it must necessarily be conscious of its own Perceptions" (1689/1975, 2.1.12), and of course that "It [is] impossible for any one to perceive, without perceiving, that he does perceive" (1689/1975, 2.27.9). Earlier yet, Aristotle writes in the *Metaphysics* 12.9 that "[conscious] knowing, perceiving, believing, and thinking are always of something else, but of themselves on the side (*en parergo*)" (1074b35–36).

Subjectivity theories were later pursued in the Brentano School and the phenomenological movement. Brentano himself was a self-representationalist, holding that every conscious state is intentionally directed primarily at some external object, but secondarily at itself:

[Every conscious act] includes within it a consciousness of itself. Therefore, every [conscious] act, no matter how simple, has a double object, a primary and a secondary object. The simplest act, for example the act of hearing, has as its primary object the sound, and for its secondary object, itself, the mental phenomenon in which the sound is heard. (Brentano [1874] 1973, 153–155)

Husserl, meanwhile, is an early acquaintance theorist, holding that our awareness of our own lived experience is not a standard kind of object-positing intentionality but a special, sui generis, non-object-positing intentionality:

Every act is consciousness of something, but there is also consciousness of every act. Every act is "sensed," is immanently "perceived" (internal consciousness), although naturally not posited, meant (to perceive here does not mean to grasp something and to be turned towards it in an act of meaning). (Husserl [1928] 1991, 130)

Although disagreement on the nature of subjectivity persisted among Brentano's and Husserl's students, the notion that some kind of subjectivity theory must be right became orthodox in Austro-German philosophy, including outside the Brentano School and the phenomenological movement (for example in the Heidelberg School).

An interesting case concerns the German philosopher Karl Jaspers, whose thought combines neo-Kantian, phenomenological, and existentialist elements. Jaspers started out as a psychiatrist (his doctorate was in medicine and his *Habilitation* in psychology), but converted to philosophy circa 1920. Jaspers' commitment to a subjectivity theory of consciousness is unquestionable:

Self-awareness is present in every psychic event … Every psychic manifestation, whether perception, bodily sensation, memory, idea, thought or feeling carries *this particular aspect of "being mine,"* of having an "I"-quality, of "personally belonging," of it being one's own doing. We have termed this *"personalization."* (Jaspers [1913] 1963, 121, italics original)

However, Jaspers is unique among Austro-German philosophers of the time in realizing that certain psychopathological phenomena presented a prima facie threat to subjectivity theories. This is the topic of the next section.

3 Alienation Symptoms and Jaspers' Dilemma

One of the most striking features of Jaspers' (1913) *General Psychopathology* is the treatment of certain patients, mostly schizophrenic, who expressly disown some of their mental states. One of Jaspers' patients describes some of his thoughts as follows:

I have never read nor heard them; they come unasked; I do not dare to think I am the source but I am happy to know of them without thinking them. They come at any moment like a gift and I do not dare to impart them as if they were my own. (Jaspers [1913] 1963, 123)

Such a symptom, to which Jaspers referred as "implanted thoughts," is now known as *thought insertion*. Patients suffering from thought insertion complain of having thoughts "in" them that are not theirs and seem to be merely "inserted in" them. Other patients described by Jaspers suffer from what we call today delusions of alien control. Immediately after shouting, one of them explains: "I never shouted, it was the vocal cords that shouted out of me" (Jaspers [1913] 1963, 124). Another says: "The 'shouting miracle' is an extraordinary occurrence … my muscles are subject to some influences that can only be ascribed to some external force" (ibid.).[3]

It is natural to interpret such statements as reporting conscious states lacking subjectivity: the patient does not experience the relevant conscious state *as his*. Importantly, patients suffering from thought insertion and alien control seem to mean what they say: they reject watered-down or metaphorical interpretations.[4] However, to take their reports at face value is to reject SP. Jaspers was thus confronted with the following dilemma: either (a) we can make sense of the patients' reports, but subjectivity theories should be rejected, or (b) subjectivity theories need not be rejected, but the patients' reports must be deemed unintelligible or incomprehensible. In some passages, Jaspers seems to lean toward (a): "If these psychic manifestations occur with the awareness of their not being mine … we term them depersonalization" ([1913] 1963, 121). In other places, however, he unequivocally goes for (b), claiming that the patients' reports are "in principle psychologically inaccessible to us" and incomprehensible (in the sense that we cannot understand what experience would warrant them), because "we are not able to have any clear sight of a [conscious] psychic event without our self-awareness being involved" ([1913] 1963, 578). Jaspers concluded that phenomenological psychopathology cannot make sense of thought insertion and alien control delusions; they can be addressed only neuroscientifically.

A century later, Jaspers' dilemma remains unresolved. It is fair to say, however, that intelligibility-denial is a minority position today. One reason is that there is no independent evidence for the relevant patients' irrationality. They are not generally committed to inconsistencies, at least no more than healthy controls (whose speech we would not deem unintelligible).[5] After more than sixty years, the search for abnormal patterns of deductive reasoning in deluded patients has never led to convincing results (Kemp et al. 1997, Mirian et al. 2011).[6]

Furthermore, such "alienation symptoms" (suggesting consciousness without subjectivity) can be found in patients suffering from somatoparaphrenia and depersonalization, two conditions that involve no schizophrenia or dementia. Intelligibility-denial is particularly unappealing for these patients. Patients suffering from somatoparaphrenia typically complain that one of their limbs belongs to someone else. This strange condition is often associated with hemineglect: patients neglect (are unaware of) items on one side of visual space, including the disowned limbs. Importantly for our present purposes, although most somatoparaphrenics are unable to feel sensations in the disowned limb, some (we know of four cases) do feel sensations in those limbs but feel the limbs are not theirs:

Immediately after the experiment, we asked F. B. how she could report touches on someone else's hand. Her response was initially elusive; however she eventually explained the phenomenon as follows (though adding "Yes, I know, it is strange"): her absent-minded niece would always forget her hand on the patient's bed while leaving the hospital, so that F. B. used to take care of it until the niece came back to visit her again. (Bottini et al. 2002, 251)

Specifically asked about how it was possible to perceive stimuli delivered to another's hand, another patient (A.F.) answered that "many strange things can happen in life" (Moro et al. 2004, 440). These reports suggest that patients have sensations that do not feel theirs and that, to that extent, lack subjectivity. Given the highly circumscribed character of these delusions (somatoparaphrenia is a so-called monothematic delusion), intelligibility-denial is implausible. Somatoparaphrenia thus provides another instance of Jaspers' dilemma that seems to threaten subjectivity theories.

Intelligibility-denial is even less plausible with depersonalization (Sierra 2009). Jaspers, we saw, used the term *personalization* to refer to what we call subjectivity. Even though we shall see that it is interesting and motivated, Jaspers' use of the term is somewhat idiosyncratic. The term *depersonalization* was coined by the French philosopher and psychologist Ludovic Dugas, at the turn of the century, to characterize deep and pervading modifications of the way things appeared to patients who reported a whole spectrum of abnormal experiences, ranging from the feeling of lacking bodily parts to the feeling of being unreal or of not being oneself.[7] Consider the following range of reports:

Parts of my body feel as if they didn't belong to me. (Sierra and Berrios 2000, 160)

Often I have to … enter a shop to talk, to ask for something, in order to get a new proof that I am myself. (Séglas and Meige 1895, 141)

I must be someone, I am someone, everybody else feels someone, but I am not my-self. I suddenly felt I am in half, there is two of me. (Shorvon 1946, 782)

I have stopped being. (Mayer-Gross 2011, 106)

Such patients seem to lack a sense of self, or as Simeon and Abugel (2006, 25) put it, "a clear feeling of 'I'." If they have no feeling of "I," then argu-ably their conscious states cannot be experienced as belonging to such an I. Without a felt me, there can be no felt mine-ness—no subjectivity. If so, these patients' conscious states must lack subjectivity. This includes con-scious thoughts:

I feel so detached from my thoughts that they seem to have a "life" of their own. (Sierra and Berrios 2000, 163)

As well as conscious intentions-in-action:

I would notice my hands and feet moving, but as if they did not belong to me and were moving automatically. (Sierra 2009, 29)

And even algedonic sensations of pain and pleasure:[8]

When a part of my body hurts, I feel so detached from the pain that it feels as if it were somebody else's pain. (Sierra and Berrios 2000, 163)

It was painful and my arm felt like withdrawing, but *it was not a genuine pain, it was a pain that did not reach the soul* … It is a pain, if you want, but the surface of my skin is three kilometers away from my brain, and I do not know whether I am suffering. (Janet 1928, 65, our emphasis)

When depersonalization reaches its climax, subjectivity seems to withdraw from all conscious states, leaving the subject with a bold feeling of inexistence:

Each of my senses, each part of my proper self is as if it were separated from me and can no longer afford me any sensation. ... My eyes see and my spirit perceives, but the sensation of what I see is completely absent. (Sierra 2009, 8)

There was literally no more experience of "me" at all. The experience of personal identity switched off and was never to appear again. ... The body, mind, speech, thoughts, and emotions were all empty; *they had no ownership*, no person behind them. (Simeon and Abugel 2006, 143–144, our emphasis)

What makes depersonalized patients particularly problematic for SP is that they still *believe* the states that feel alien to be theirs. Patients say that they feel *as if* those states did not belong to them. There is a feeling of alien-ness, but patients do not *endorse* the feeling. That is, they do not take the appearance of alien-ness at face value and, thus, ultimately self-attribute those states. In other words, they are not delusional.[9] Now, given that they are nondelusional, it is hard to deny that depersonalized patients' reports are sensible. Jaspers' dilemma, when extended to depersonalization, thus strongly suggests an argument against subjectivity theories of consciousness.

To summarize, Jaspers' dilemma is the forced choice between two independently unappealing options: rejecting SP, and hence subjectivity theories of consciousness, or denying the intelligibility of certain patients' reports. Although originally concerned with certain symptoms of schizophrenia, Jaspers' dilemma can be extended to somatoparaphrenia and depersonalization. In all three cases, there is an "alienation symptom," whereby patients report that some of their mental states—call them *alien states*—are not theirs (schizophrenia and most somatoparaphrenia) or at least do not *feel* theirs (depersonalization and some somatoparaphrenia). In all three cases, it seems that if we want to make sense of patients' reports, we must suppose that even though they are conscious, the alien states lack subjectivity. They thus appear to constitute counterexamples to SP.

4 Consciousness without Subjectivity?

It is generally preferable to make sense of patients' reports than to dismiss them as unintelligible. This is particularly so when the patients appear otherwise rational. Now, the most natural way of making sense of reports of the sort cited in §3 is to suppose that they involve conscious experiences that lack subjectivity. This suggests a straightforward argument from alienation against subjectivity theories. The argument proceeds in two steps.

First, if we want to make sense of patients' reports about alien states, we must suppose that these states (a) are conscious but (b) lack subjectivity. Call this the *interpretive constraint*. The rationale for this constraint is that (i) to make sense of these reports, we must treat them as the reports of someone sensible, and (ii) someone sensible would make the previously cited reports only if (a) their alien states were conscious but (b) lacked subjectivity. Plausibly, (i) is definitional. As for (ii), we must suppose (a) because the patients manage to *report* their alien states, and reportability is still our best third-person operational index of consciousness; and we must suppose (b) because the content of the reports is that the relevant states do not feel as though they belong to one, and what we call subjectivity is precisely this feeling.

With the interpretive constraint in place, it is but a short step to conclude that alien states are conscious but lack subjectivity. One only needs to assume that *we should make sense of the patients' reports*. We may call this the *rationality constraint*, since, as noted, there is good evidence that some of the relevant patients are sufficiently rational to be deemed sensible. As we have seen, the rationality constraint is particularly plausible for somatoparaphrenia, depersonalization, and other cases of nondelusional alienation symptoms (where the patients do not endorse their alienation feelings).

We may now formulate the *alienation argument* against subjectivity theories as follows:

(1) *Alienation symptom.* Some patients report that their alien states feel as though they are not theirs (that is, as though they lack subjectivity).
(2) *Interpretative constraint.* To make sense of such reports, we must suppose that alien states are (a) conscious but (b) lack subjectivity.
(3) *Rationality constraint.* We should make sense of these patients' reports.
(4) *Conclusions.* We must suppose that alien states are conscious but lack subjectivity. Accordingly, SP and the subjectivity theories are false.

As it stands, this argument applies to all subjectivity theories (higher-order, self-representational, and acquaintance theories).

A fortiori, the alienation argument applies to specific subjectivity theories. Thus, Liang and Lane (2009) have put forward a clear instance of this general schema against Rosenthal's higher-order representationalism. They argue that patient F. B. (the somatoparaphrenic who reported sensing touch in her niece's hand) represents her tactile sensations as belonging to someone other than herself (Liang and Lane 2009, 664–665). From this they conclude that F. B. has conscious sensations lacking subjectivity, and that, therefore, Rosenthal's higher-order representationalism must be rejected. They see clearly, however, that the point generalizes to other subjectivity theories of consciousness: "If the conclusions reached here are correct, Kriegel's views and the views of others who posit a necessary connection between [consciousness and subjectivity] are wrong" (Liang and Lane 2009, 667).

5   Defending Subjectivity Theories

We consider the alienation argument a genuine and important challenge to subjectivity theories of consciousness. Both of us, however, remain committed to such theories. In the remainder of this paper, we discuss the various options available to the subjectivity theorist in responding to the challenge, providing a menu of options for the proponent of SP.

The first option is to deny Premise (1) of the alienation argument, that is, deny that there really are alienation symptoms. On this view, we mischaracterize patients' reports when we say that they feel as if their alien states are not theirs. It could be argued, for example, that in truth we do not fully understand their complaints (the complaints that motivate ascribing to them experiences that are not or do not feel as their own). Alternatively, one might want to dispute the significance or the reliability of the case reports we have relied on. The standards of methodological rigor in one domain of research may be laxer than in others, after all.

Such moves have some plausibility when it comes to somatoparaphrenia (see Rosenthal 2010). For none of the patients that we know of claim feeling *sensations that are not theirs*. Rather, they say that they feel touch in someone else's limb. This does not yet imply that they feel sensations that are not their own—unless it is analytic that one cannot feel one's sensations but in one's own body, which we have phenomenological and empirical reasons to deny (de Vignemont 2007). Thus, it seems possible to experience tactile sensations at the tip of tools. When touching the ground with a cane, we can, arguably, feel the touch at the end of the cane rather than at the hand holding it (O'Shaughnessy 2003).[10] So denying Premise (1) may be plausible for somatoparaphrenics. However, it seems less so when it comes to depersonalized patients and schizophrenics suffering from thought insertion. For to have alienation symptoms *just is* to report that some mental state is not, or does not feel to be, one's own.[11] Given that the relevant patients say precisely this, and given that the huge number of converging case reports makes this claim reliable, there is no question but that they suffer from alienation symptoms (see Mullins and Spence 2003).

Thus, depersonalization and schizophrenia call for another response to the alienation argument.

One might venture to deny the rationality constraint (Premise (3) of the alienation argument). For example, Coliva (2002) argues that schizophrenics would not be classified as mentally ill if they were sensible. She asks rhetorically:

> Why should we consider her report as an expression of some kind of cognitive illusion, which we take as a symptom of mental illness, as opposed to, at most, a possible mistake in identifying the producer of the thought? And, connectedly, why should we try to cure her, rather than just, at most, correct her? (Coliva 2002, 42)

However, there are many criteria for mental illness that do not involve unintelligibility, and by which this objection is not cogent. For example, even though reports by depressed and bipolar subjects are eminently sensible, depression and bipolar disorder are usually considered mental illnesses. This classification has nothing to do with rationality or intelligibility. It stems from the distress and the disability they cause.

Still, we acknowledge that many will find attractive the claim that schizophrenics' reports do not make sense. Regardless of whether this response is plausible for schizophrenia, however, it is entirely implausible for depersonalization. Depersonalized patients, as we have seen, are not delusional. It is true that there is a syndrome that is connected to depersonalization and that involves delusions: the Cotard syndrome, often characterized as the delusional form of depersonalization (depersonalization being, conversely, the "as if" form of the Cotard syndrome).[12] There are, however, clear cases of nondelusional patients reporting alien states. Those patients, to whom we have reserved the term *depersonalization* in the first place, seem perfectly rational. Their cognitive functioning has been well studied. They were found not to differ from matched anxious or depressed patients (Sedman 1972) and to differ from normal subjects only in some specific aspects of low-level perceptual memory and attention (Guralnik et al. 2007). Their general intelligence, their executive functioning and other aspects of their memory and attention are perfectly normal. They should accordingly be no less intelligible than normal subjects.

The last option is to deny Premise (2) of the argument, the interpretative constraint. This means either denying that, to make sense of the reports, we must suppose that alien states are conscious (2a), or denying that to do so we must suppose that alien states lack subjectivity (2b). We think that these are the most plausible strategies available to the subjectivity theorist and, accordingly, discuss them more fully in the remainder of the chapter.

Indeed, the most popular subjectivist response to the alienation argument, which we may call the *agency response*, takes this form. However, we think the agency response faces tremendous difficulties, which moreover apply to other responses structurally similar to it. Instead, we offer two alternative responses to the alienation argument that we find much more plausible.

6   Subjectivity and Subjectivity*

In this section we want to discuss responses to the argument that have the following general structure. Subjectivity, it is claimed, is a slippery and potentially ambiguous notion. The fact that someone says "X is not mine" or "X does not feel mine" might therefore be interpreted in different ways, depending on the different senses of the notion. This suggests a response that claims the following:

- *Ambiguity*: that there is a sense of "subjectivity"—call it subjectivity*—different from that used in SP and subjectivity theories;
- *Rewriting*: that alien states (i) do not differ from nonalien states with respect to subjectivity, but only (ii) with respect to subjectivity*.

Call responses to the alienation argument that take this form *subjectivity* responses*. There are various subjectivity* responses, depending on the notion of subjectivity* appealed to. They all face the same twofold challenge. First of all, such responses must show that lack of subjectivity* can account for the phenomenological difference between alien states and nonalien states. They also need to show, however, that patients' behavior suggests that their alien states are indeed subjective; this task is often neglected in the literature.

When they do attend to this challenge, subjectivity* responses tend to argue as follows:

(1) The patient acknowledges, or would acknowledge, that her alien state feels *in her* or *in her mind*;
(2) Being in her (or her mind) entails being subjective in the sense relevant to SP; so,
(3) The patient effectively acknowledges, or would acknowledge, that her alien state is subjective.

Campbell (1998, 1999), Gallagher (2000), and Graham and Stephens (2000) appear to use this reasoning. Campbell writes:

The thought inserted into the subject's mind is indeed in some sense his, just because it has been successfully inserted into his mind; it has some special relation to him. He has, for example, some especially direct knowledge of it. (Campbell 1999, 610)

In the same vein, Gallagher writes:

For that reason the schizophrenic should provide a positive answer to what he might rightly regard as a nonsensical question: Are you sure that *you* are the one who is experiencing these thoughts? After all, this is precisely his complaint. *He* is experiencing thoughts that seem to be generated by others. (Gallagher 2000, 231, italics original)

In other words, the patient would not complain if it were not for the fact that some sense of mine-ness is still there.

This line of response has an obvious attraction to it. Nonetheless, we think the way it has been pursued in the extant literature faces significant difficulties and bears improvement. For starters, the argument's conclusion (that patients effectively acknowledge that their alien states are subjective) is somewhat uncharitable to the patients. It means that although patients say something like "X does not feel mine" or "X is not mine (even though it is in me/my mind)," what they really should have said is rather "X does feel mine" or "X is mine" (Billon 2013). More importantly, it is unclear how proponents of the subjectivity* response propose to account for the phenomenal difference between an alien state X and a nonalien state Y. The task is to (i) spell out what distinguishes the phenomenology of X from that of Y without appealing to a difference in subjectivity, and (ii) argue that it amounts to a difference in subjectivity*. But the standard construals of subjectivity* seem to lack the resources to manage this with plausibility.

Consider the most popular subjectivity* response in the case of thought-insertion, which identifies subjectivity* with the *sense of agency*.[13] On this view, whereas healthy subjects experience themselves as *doing the thinking*, schizophrenic patients suffering from thought insertion do not. Accordingly, inserted thoughts are not experienced by subjects as *done* or *performed* or *authored* by them. Subjects feel themselves patients rather than agents, so to speak, of the thought processes taking place in their mind. The thinking is something that happens to them, not something that they do. Nonetheless, they experience the thinking as taking place in *their* mind. The main problem with this response is that healthy subjects have many thoughts that do not seem to come with a sense of agency. Many of our daily thoughts come unbidden. Some—obsessive thoughts, for example—are even *intrusive*, occurring against our will. It is far from clear that in such cases we experience ourselves as *doing the thinking*. Yet such thoughts do not feel alien the way the schizophrenic patient's inserted thoughts do.[14] Indeed, schizophrenic patients have some intrusive thoughts as well, but they too manage to distinguish them from inserted thoughts (Eisen et al. 1997).[15]

Partly in reaction against the agency accounts of thought insertion, some have recently described the alien feeling associated with thought insertion in terms of a "sense of endorsement."[16] Inserted thoughts, on this account, are thoughts to which the patient does not feel *committed*, independently of whether she feels like the agent of those thoughts (Fernández 2010, 67, Bortolotti and Broome 2009). This lack of sense of endorsement might manifest itself in various ways: inability to provide reasons for endorsing the thought content, failure to act consistently with the thought being true, and so on (Bortolotti and Broome 2009, 210).[17] Here too, however, it is dubious that a sense-of-endorsement response can plausibly account for the phenomenal difference between alien and nonalien states. Merely intrusive thoughts often go unendorsed by their subjects, and patients suffering from obsessive thoughts typically endorse thoughts that directly contradict their intrusive thoughts (Purdon 2004). A classic example involves a caring and loving mother who is obsessed with thoughts like "I should kill my child" or "it would be better if he were dead." This mother will not only fail to behave as if she took these thoughts to be true, she will also be totally unable to find reasons for endorsing the thought. The very occurrence of the thoughts, it is true, might frighten her, with the idea that she might act upon them or have unconscious reasons for believing them. This kind of fear, however, does not amount to anything like endorsing the thought.[18] The thought remains unendorsed, yet clearly does not qualify as an inserted thought. This suggests that the phenomenal difference between inserted thoughts and intrusive thoughts is not a matter of sense of endorsement. Noninserted thoughts can lack the phenomenology of endorsement just as much as inserted thoughts.

An assumption shared by the agency and endorsement versions of the subjectivity* response is that the phenomenal difference between alien and nonalien states must amount to some feature missing from the pathological case that is present in the "normal" case. One version identifies the sense of agency as the missing feature, the other identifies it as the feeling of endorsement, but in both cases the unargued-for assumption is that patients are *missing* something. Importantly, this is a *substantive* assumption: the phenomenal difference between alien and nonalien states could just as well consist in new features being *added* to the alien states (Zahavi and Kriegel forthcoming). On this view, an inserted thought, qua inserted, instantiates all the phenomenal properties of a normal thought; but in addition, it instantiates an extra phenomenal property: *it feels inserted*. The patient complains because this extra phenomenal property is foreign, absent from normal experience.

Generalizing the strategy, one may hold that alien states exhibit a phenomenology of alienation absent from nonalien states. It may be that the phenomenology of alienation is entirely different in schizophrenia, somatoparaphrenia, and depersonalization, so that each condition involves its own distinctive extra phenomenal property, or it may be that there is an underlying phenomenal commonality among some such conditions, so it is the selfsame extra phenomenal feature exhibited in all of them. Either way, the phenomenal difference between alien and nonalien states is explained in terms of presence of an extra feature in the alien states, not in the nonalien states.

It might be objected that the *something extra* approach is methodologically problematic, compared to the *something missing* approach, insofar as it requires new posits. The "something missing" approach comports better with the so-called null hypothesis, as it posits no new features, instead explaining the data in terms of absence of already acknowledged features. The obvious response to this objection, however, is that, as we have just seen, the explanations provided by the "something missing" approach are inadequate. To be sure, some other explanation, citing a feature other than agency and endorsement, may fare better. But pending such an as yet nonexistent explanation, there is clear evidence for the existence of a phenomenology of alienation, namely, the relevant verbal reports of schizophrenia, somatoparaphrenia, and depersonalization patients. These reports constitute evidence for the existence of the phenomenology of alienation, we are suggesting, because the latter may be the best explanation of them.

Importantly, to posit a phenomenology of alienation present in alien states but absent in nonalien states is not to commit to a categorically new, sui generis type of phenomenology. For all we have said here, the phenomenology of alienation may result from an unusual combination of ordinary phenomenal elements. Compare debates on cognitive phenomenology. Some philosophers maintain that cognitive states have no phenomenology, others that they exhibit a sui generis nonsensory phenomenology. But an intermediate position is that cognitive states have a distinctive phenomenology, though one that results from a distinctive combination of sensory elements (e.g., Robinson 2006). Regardless of how plausible this is for cognitive phenomenology, we maintain that this is a highly plausible view of the phenomenology of alienation experienced by the kinds of patients discussed here.

One may speculate about a broadly "ideological" preconception of psychopathology operating in the background of the "something missing" approach. Pathology is portrayed as a kind of *imperfection*, involving a diminution of the normal state, which, in comparison, represents a kind of perfection or fullness. This "ideology" runs deep in professional psychopathology, but suffers from a distinct dearth of evidence. Intuitively, in the patients discussed in this chapter, something atypical *occurs*, takes place; it is not as though something *fails to occur* that typically does. Patients complain about something upsetting being *present* in their phenomenology; they do not bemoan the loss of something. As far as they are concerned, the problem is not that their pathological phenomenology is *impoverished* in comparison to the phenomenology they experienced prior to pathology. On the contrary, their phenomenology has been *augmented* by a new and foreign element.[19] To that extent, the "something extra" approach is much more charitable to patients, taking their reports much more at face value.

The "something extra" approach is motivated by interpretive charity toward inserted-thought subjects. However, it seems to fit less naturally depersonalization patients. The latter often explicitly report something *missing* in their phenomenology. In one of the earliest descriptions of depersonalization, Sierra mentions five patients, all of whom "complained almost in the same terms of a lack of sensations. ... To them it was a total lack of feelings, as if they were dead. ... They claimed they could think clearly and properly about everything, but the essential was lacking even in their thoughts" (Sierra 2009, 8).

If we put a premium on interpretive charity, then, we might want to seek another approach that could accommodate the relevant reports within the framework of subjectivity theories.

7 Consciousness and Consciousness*

A subjectivist tack rather neglected in the literature is what we might call the *consciousness* response*. This attempts to show the following:

- *Ambiguity*: that there is a sense of "consciousness"—call it consciousness*—that differs from the one used by SP and subjectivity theories;
- *Rewriting*: alien states resemble nonalien states (i) only with respect to consciousness* and (ii) not with respect to consciousness in the sense relevant to SP (the phenomenal sense).

It has often been noted that the notion of consciousness is multiply ambiguous. As Block (1995, 227) puts it, "There are a number of very different 'consciousnesses.' ... These concepts are often partly or totally conflated, with bad results." It may thus be that alien states are conscious in one sense of the term but not another. We might thus invoke a form of ambiguity here as well, denying that alien states are conscious in the sense relevant to subjectivity theories (*phenomenal* consciousness), even if conscious in some other (nonphenomenal) sense—the "conscious*" sense.

Consider that patients' reports indicate they are aware of their alien states in a way similar to the way we are aware of our phenomenally conscious states. In particular, they do not have to make any effort to access their alien states: the latter somehow impose themselves on them (otherwise alien states would probably not *bother* subjects). We might put this by saying that patients' access to their alien states seems "immediate." Arguably, there is a sense of "consciousness" whereby any mental state to which one has a seemingly immediate access is definitionally conscious. We might call this the *reflective* sense of "consciousness."[20] It might then be argued that reflective consciousness (= consciousness*) does not a priori entail phenomenal consciousness (= consciousness), and that even though alien states are conscious in the reflective sense, they are not conscious in the phenomenal sense.[21] The idea here is not that the subject has no phenomenology at all when in the alien state. Rather, the state itself does not *contribute* to the subject's overall phenomenology at the time. The alien state has no phenomenal character of its own, but its subject has simultaneous mental states that do. Among those is a mental state that represents her alien state as "in her." In other words, the subject has (i) a first-order state M1 that is alien but not phenomenal and (ii) a second-order state M2 that is nonalien but phenomenal and represents M1. The fact that M2 occurs and is phenomenal accounts for the subject's phenomenal awareness of M1, rendering the latter reflectively conscious; however, it does *not* render M1 *phenomenally* conscious.

To make the hypothesis more vivid, imagine the following situation. You wake up one morning and start hearing a tinnitus ringing inside your head. At first, this is just a meaningless buzz, but with time something strange happens: it begins to sound like an articulated voice. Even stranger, the voice seems to express your repressed, unconscious states. When you stand in front of someone you have reasons to detest, it says "Oh! I hate him!" It turns out, you discover, that a mad neuroscientist has implanted in your brain a small monitoring device that scans your unconscious states and expresses them through inner voices. In this case, then, you are aware of some of your phenomenally unconscious states, and moreover the awareness is phenomenally conscious (having a distinctive auditory phenomenology). Accordingly, even though the reflected-on states have no phenomenology of their own, the reflecting states do, and thus they give rise to a rich phenomenology (one you might describe as an "inner voice"). Plausibly, even if you know that the reflected-on states are *yours*, you do not *experience* them that way. On the contrary, you experience the voice as alien.

This reflective awareness response is defended by Billon (2013) for thought insertion. A partisan of this response must not only show that it is consistent with the data, but also put forward independent evidence for the claim that inserted thoughts lack phenomenality. Billon appeals to the fact that stock descriptions of thought insertions readily compare the inserted thought to representations lacking intrinsic phenomenality. Some patients talk of pictures being flashed in their mind, others of mere pieces of information, or, more frequently, of voices. All of those are representations of which we can be aware thanks to "second-order" states, but which have no phenomenality in and of themselves. Relatedly, Billon appeals to the fact that this hypothesis would neatly explain certain experimental data, such as the well-documented phenomenological and neurobiological continuity between thought insertion and alien voices (Miller 1996, Moritz and Larøi 2008, Copolov et al. 2004; see Billon 2013, 309). Admittedly, the patients we know of do not explicitly say that their inserted thoughts are unconscious in some sense. In order to say such a thing (without exposing themselves to the risk of contradiction), however, patients would need to be clear on the different senses of "consciousness." And we cannot reasonably expect them to spontaneously master some conceptual distinctions that philosophers have just started to draw rigorously.

The reflective-consciousness response can be extended to depersonalization. Indeed, it seems to work even better here, given that some depersonalized patients explicitly affirm that their alien states are unconscious even though they are conscious *of* them:

I suddenly wonder: is it really me here? Is it really me walking? Then I make enormous efforts in order to apply my consciousness to this unconsciousness ... in order to realize that I am making the walking movements. So at some point during this kind of crisis, before the absolute certainty [of being myself, before the crisis] I am conscious on one side that I am unconscious (sic) on the other side. (Séglas and Meige 1895, 147)[22]

Some suggest that there is nothing it is like for them to see anymore: "Everything in vision is dead," says a patient from Mayer-Gross (2011, 111). Or even that there is nothing it is like to *perceive*: "I can see, hear and smell but it is as if I didn't see, or hear or smell" (Dugas and Moutier 1911, 10).[23]

Even more commonly, depersonalized patients complain that their *emotional* phenomenology is blunted or absent:

The emotional part of my brain is dead. ... All my emotions are blunted. (Shorvon 1946, 784)

Kissing my husband is like kissing a table, sir. The same thing … Not the least thrill. Nothing on earth can thrill me. Neither my husband nor my child … My heart doesn't beat. I cannot feel anything. (Dugas and Moutier 1911, 109)

When depersonalization reaches its climax, subjects may describe themselves as totally unconscious, indeed as zombies:

I just sink into a kind of unconsciousness. I am just conscious enough to know that things are going on around me but nothing seems to register. (Shorvon 1946, 784)

I'm like a zombie unable to take in any information. (Sierra 2009, 51, our emphasis)

It is a state in which you feel nothing, in which you do not think, in which you do not mean what you do or think. … I am in emptiness, I am a body without a soul … I see without seeing, I am a blind man who sees. (Janet 1928, 51–52)

It's the mental sensibility that is lacking, it is not me who feels. I have no interest in what I appear to be feeling. It is someone else who feels mechanically. (Janet 1908, 515)[24]

Thus depersonalization is particularly amenable to a consciousness* response. To be sure, here as elsewhere we may choose to simply refuse to accept patients' reports, rather than try to accommodate them "as is" within a subjectivist framework. Our present point is that this is not *mandatory*: there are ways to retain SP while making sense of patients' reports more or less at face value.

The consciousness* response, in this reflective-awareness version, protects SP from its putative psychopathological counterexamples, then. Admittedly, it does so at the cost of denying that states of which we are reflectively aware must be phenomenally conscious. This is a heavy cost for most subjectivity theories, but, importantly, it is not strictly inconsistent with such theories. The response fits particularly well with *acquaintance* theories: it can be claimed that the patient is reflectively aware of her alien state but that, since reflective awareness involves a representational relation rather than the requisite acquaintance relation, the patient's alien state is not phenomenally conscious. It may also suit the self-representational approach: it might be claimed that reflective awareness involves a numerically distinct higher-order representation rather than the kind of self-representation required. As a result, the subject is reflectively aware of her alien state without the latter being phenomenally conscious. The reflective-awareness response may even be consistent with the higher-order representationalism. It may be held that not all higher-order representations yield phenomenal consciousness, only ones exhibiting certain specific features (e.g., being noninferential), and that the higher-order representation involved in a patient's reflective awareness of her alien states lacks (some of) the relevant features.[25]

8   Conclusion

Jaspers' dilemma poses a psychopathological challenge to subjectivity theories of consciousness. In the face of this challenge, it is possible, of course, to simply renounce subjectivity theories. Philosophers who have chosen to hold on to such theories have tended to respond to the challenge by dismissing patients' reports as unintelligible, or else by radically reinterpreting them. In this paper, we have attempted to articulate two new ways of defending subjectivity theories, characterized by a stronger desire to make sense of patients' reports while taking them more or less at face value. Our conviction is that it is *possible* to respect patients' rationality, sensibility, and intelligibility while holding onto subjectivity theories of consciousness in the face of what we have called the alienation argument. The "something extra" version of the subjectivity* response and the reflective-consciousness version of the consciousness* response offer, we claim, plausible ways of doing so. Importantly, the subjectivity theorist need not be wedded to a single approach for relevant psychopathological phenomena. A divide-and-conquer strategy that handles different phenomena in different ways is entirely coherent, perhaps even antecedently plausible. Our goal here has been to present a more comprehensive menu of options from which the subjectivity theorist might choose to address each challenging psychopathology.[26]

Notes

1. Thus, two subjects who differ only in that one higher-order represents his state as phenomenally F whereas the other higher-order represents his as phenomenally G will experience different overall phenomenologies.

2. Rosenthal writes: "I cannot represent my conscious pain as belonging to someone distinct from me" (Rosenthal 2005, 357); "being conscious of a mental state as belonging to someone other than oneself would plainly not make it conscious" (2005, 342).

3. Delusions of alien control and thought insertion are diagnostic symptoms of schizophrenia. Other symptoms include alien voices (patients report hearing voices), thought broadcasting (reports of thoughts being publicly accessible), thought control (reports of thoughts being controlled by an alien agency), and thought withdrawal (the patient reports that his thought suddenly vanishes, as if an external agency pulled it out of his mind).

4. See, for example, Hoffman (1986, 508).

5. Jaspers could grant the consistency of the patients. But he took it that making sense of someone required the capacity to project imaginatively being in that person's shoes and to simulate the experiences of that person. He thought that such an imaginative projection was impossible with schizophrenics suffering from the relevant symptoms. Given the independent reasons to believe that patients' reports do make sense, however, it seems that the imagination criterion might be too strong.

6. Some patients do exhibit other irrational biases, such as jumping to conclusions, but that alone does not threaten their intelligibility (see Bortolotti 2010 for a book-length defense of this claim).

7. Dugas borrowed the term "depersonalization" from the Swiss writer Amiel, who seemed to suffer from the condition and described himself in his diaries as follows: "Now I find myself regarding existence as though from beyond the tomb, from another world; all is strange to me; I am, as it were, outside my own body and individuality; I am *depersonalized*, detached, cut adrift" (Amiel [1881] 1913). He would later construe depersonalization as a withdrawal of the subjectivity from all mental states (Dugas and Moutier 1911, 13–14), which explains Jaspers' usage.

8. Indeed, the aforementioned impression of lacking bodily parts may be explained in terms of bodily sensations that lack subjectivity.

9. See Dugas and Moutier (1911, 10–11). So-called Cotard Syndrome is often said to be the delusional counterpart of depersonalization, where patients do endorse the same feelings and take the relevant appearances at face value. We follow modern classifications (ICD-10, DSN-IV) in keeping the term "depersonalization" for nondelusional patients. It should be noted, however, that some researchers, such as Janet, used the term to refer to delusional (Cotard) patients as well. There are borderline cases between delusional (Cotard) and nondelusional (depersonalized) versions, but there are also clear-cut cases of nondelusional patients.

10. Patients suffering from phantom limbs also seem to, in some sense, experience pain outside their body (Rosenthal 2010). More generally, a broad set of empirical data suggests that a region of space in which someone feels bodily sensations will not always be represented as belonging to one's body: it will only be so represented if it falls within the subject's "body schema" (de Vignemont 2007).

11. Importantly, Premise 1 of the alienation argument does not claim that the relevant patients *have* alien states, only that they *report* having them. To object to this premise is therefore to deny that they so report. But this is patently implausible.

12. It is also true that some patients, whose degree of confidence in their nonexistence often remains low, seem to be neither clearly delusional nor clearly nondelusional.

13. Sousa and Swiney (2013, 637) refer to it, justifiably we think, as "the standard approach to the core phenomenology of thought insertion."

14. Similarly, patients suffering from schizophrenia can complain of "controlled thoughts," which they take both to be their own and to be under the control of an external agency (Jaspers [1913] 1963, 122–3, Mullins and Stephens 2001). Like intrusive thoughts, controlled thoughts do not come with a sense of agency, and it is hard to see how the agency view of thought insertion could distinguish them from thought insertion (Billon 2013).

15. To distinguish the phenomenology of inserted thoughts from that of intrusive thoughts, many appeal to a form of psychological discontinuity. Intrusive thoughts, unlike inserted thoughts, feel somehow psychologically continuous with the patient's other thoughts. This psychological discontinuity can be construed as a discrepancy between the content of the thought and the subject's self-view (Graham and Stephens 2000, 173), or "the subject's long-standing beliefs and desires" (Campbell 1999, 621), or her "implicit expectancies" (Gallagher 2000). However, studies of obsessive phenomena, including intrusive thoughts, reveal that the latter's content can perfectly mirror that of inserted thoughts and feel discontinuous with the subject's self-view, long-standing beliefs and desires, and implicit expectancies (see Billon 2013, 296–298).

16. Some use the expression *sense of authorship* for *sense of endorsement*, but the former has also been used as a synonym for *sense of agency*, so we avoid it here.

17. Proponents of the endorsement approach may not have a subjectivist agenda. Bortolotti and Broome (2009) certainly claim that inserted thoughts are not experienced by the patients as their own, though Fernández (2010) seems to imply that they are subjective in our sense. In any case, our present interest is in whether the endorsement approach could be harnessed to the subjectivist agenda.

18. This kind of fear does seem to play an important role, however, in causing the recurrence of the thought (Salkovskis 1989).

19. Note, in this connection, that schizophrenics' *memoirs* of crisis and institutionalization episodes often convey a sense of new abundance and freedom in their inner life. The mid-nineteenth-century French poet Nerval declares this at the beginning of his autobiography, which focuses on his inner life during an eight-month institutionalization: "I will try … to transcribe the impressions of a long illness which took place entirely in my mind's mysteries; – and I am unsure why I use this term illness, since never, as far as I am concerned, did I feel in better health. Sometimes I felt my power and activity has doubled; it seemed to know everything, understand everything; imagination brought me infinite delights" (Nerval [1855] 1996, 3). Nerval's autobiography proceeds to describe many episodes of what we would now conceptualize as thought insertion.

20. Using Block's (1995) distinctions, we might say that a state is conscious in the reflective awareness sense when its subject is access-conscious *of* it, or when it is reflectively-conscious.

21. Notice that even higher-order representationalists can accommodate the claim that reflective awareness does not entail phenomenal consciousness. They can claim that, to make *M* phenomenally conscious, my awareness of *M* need not only to (i) seem immediate in the sense that we have specified, but also to (ii) display other specific features.

22. Notice the "sic" added by the psychiatrists, who are not sure how to understand this "consciousness of unconsciousness."

23. Interestingly, some patients say that things appear to them as through a "curtain," a "blind," a "fine wire netting," a "fine mesh," or a "glass wall" (Shorvon 1946, 784). This suggests that the phenomenality of their visual states is in some sense *attenuated*, as if only some of its standard phenomenal features are present. It is an open question how to interpret such reports of attenuated phenomenality, and how they might affect the dialectic. Here we bracket such questions.

24. Note well: by "mental sensibility" ("la sensibilité morale" in the original), people at the time meant roughly the faculty responsible for conscious thoughts in general.

25. This does require the higher-order representationalist to identify a feature that can be plausibly shown to be missing in the relevant psychopathological cases. This kind of additional burden is absent, however, in self-representational and acquaintance theories.

26. For comments on a previous draft, we would like to thank Rocco Gennaro and Tim Lane. Work for this chapter was supported by grants ANR-10-IDEX-0001–02 PSL* and ANR-10-LABX-0087 IEC.

References

Amiel, H.-F. (1881) 1913. *Amiel's Journal: The Journal Intime of Henri-Frédéric Amiel*. London: Macmillan.

Aristotle. 1908. *Metaphysics*. Trans. W. D. Ross. Oxford: Clarendon Press.

Billon, A. 2005. En Personne, la réalité subjective de la conscience phénoménale. PhD diss., École Polytechnique.

Billon, A. 2013. Does consciousness entail subjectivity? The puzzle of thought insertion. *Philosophical Psychology* 26:291–314.

Block, N. 1995. On a confusion about the function of consciousness. *Behavioral and Brain Sciences* 18:227–247.

Bortolotti, L. 2010. *Delusions and Other Irrational Beliefs*. New York: Oxford University Press.

Bortolotti, L., and M. Broome. 2009. A role for ownership and authorship in the analysis of thought insertion. *Phenomenology and the Cognitive Sciences* 8:205–224.

Bottini, G., E. Bisiach, R. Sterzi, and G. Vallar. 2002. Feeling touches in someone else's hand. *Neuroreport* 13:249–252.

Brentano, F. (1874) 1973. *Psychology from Empirical Standpoint*. Trans. A. C. Rancurello, D. B. Terrell, and L. L. McAlister. London: Routledge & Kegan Paul.

Campbell, J. 1998. Le modèle de la schizophrénie de Christopher Frith. In *Subjectivité et Conscience d'Agir: Approches Cognitive et Clinique de la Psychose*. Paris: PUF.

Campbell, J. 1999. Schizophrenia, the space of reasons and thinking as a motor process. *Monist* 82:609–625.

Campbell, J. 2004. The ownership of thoughts. *Philosophy, Psychology & Psychiatry* 9:35–39.

Coliva, A. 2002. Thought insertion and immunity to error though misidentification. *Philosophy, Psychiatry & Psychology* 9:27–34.

Copolov, D., T. Trauer, and A. Mackinnon. 2004. On the non-significance of internal versus external auditory hallucinations. *Schizophrenia Research* 69:1–6.

Dugas, L., and F. Moutier. 1911. *La dépersonnalisation*. Paris: F. Alcan. http://www.biusante.parisdescartes.fr/histmed/medica/cote?79749.

Eisen, J., D. Beer, M. Pato, T. Venditto, and S. Rasmussen. 1997. Obsessive-compulsive disorder in patients with schizophrenia or schizoaffective disorder. *American Journal of Psychiatry* 154:271–273.

Fernández, J. 2010. Thought insertion and self-knowledge. *Mind & Language* 25:66–88.

Frith, C. D. 1992. *The Cognitive Neuropsychology of Schizophrenia*. Hillsdale, NJ: Erlbaum.

Gallagher, S. 2000. Self-reference and schizophrenia: A cognitive model of immunity to error through misidentification. In *Exploring the Self: Philosophical and Psychopathological Perspectives on Self-Experience*, ed. D. Zahavi. Amsterdam: John Benjamins.

Gennaro, R. 1996. *Consciousness and Self-Consciousness*. Philadelphia: John Benjamins.

Gennaro, R. 2012. *The Consciousness Paradox: Consciousness, Concepts, and Higher-Order Thoughts*. Cambridge, MA: MIT Press.

Graham, G., and G. L. Stephens. 2000. *When Self-Consciousness Breaks: Alien Voices and Inserted Thoughts*. Cambridge, MA: MIT Press.

Guralnik, O., T. Giesbrecht, M. Knutelska, B. Sirroff, and D. Simeon. 2007. Cognitive functioning in depersonalization disorder. *Journal of Nervous and Mental Disease,* 195:983–988.

Hoffman, R. E. 1986. Verbal hallucinations and language production processes in schizophrenia. *Behavioral and Brain Sciences* 9:503–548.

Husserl, E. (1928) 1991. *On the Phenomenology of the Consciousness of Internal Time.* Trans. J. Brough. Dordrecht: Kluwer Academic.

Janet, P. 1908. Le sentiment de dèpersonnalisation. *Journal de Psychologie Normale et Pathologique* 5:514–516.

Janet, P. 1928. *De l'angoisse à l'extase (Les sentiments fondamentaux),* vol. 2. Paris: F. Alcan.   http://classiques.uqac.ca/classiques/janet_pierre/angoisse_extase_2/Janet_ angoisse_2_1.pdf.

Jaspers, K. (1913) 1963. *General Psychopathology,* 7th ed. Trans. J. Hoenig and M. W. Hamilton. Manchester: Manchester University Press.

Kemp, R., S. Chua, P. McKenna, and A. David. 1997. Reasoning and delusions. *British Journal of Psychiatry* 170:398–405.

Kriegel, U. 2009. *Subjective Consciousness: A Self-Representational Theory.* Oxford: Oxford University Press.

Krishaber, M. 1873. *De la névropathie cérébro-cardiaque.* Paris: Masson. http://gallica .bnf.fr/ark:/12148/bpt6k767014.

Levine, J. 2001. *Purple Haze.* Oxford: Oxford University Press.

Liang, C., and T. Lane. 2009. Higher-order thought and pathological self: The case of somatoparaphrenia. *Analysis* 69:661–668.

Locke, J. (1689) 1975. *An Essay Concerning Human Understanding.* Ed. P. H. Nidditch. Oxford: Oxford University Press.

Mayer-Gross, W. 2011. On depersonalization. *British Journal of Medical Psychology* 15:103–126.

Miller, L. J. 1996. Qualitative changes in hallucinations. *American Journal of Psychiatry* 153:265–267.

Mirian, D., R. Heinrichs, and S. Vaz. 2011. Exploring logical reasoning abilities in schizophrenia patients. *Schizophrenia Research* 127:178–180.

Moritz, S., and F. Larøi. 2008. Differences and similarities in the sensory and cognitive signatures of voice-hearing, intrusions, and thoughts. *Schizophrenia Research* 102:96–107.

Moro, V., M. Zampini, and S. Aglioti. 2004. Changes in spatial position of hands modify tactile extinction but not disownership of contralesional hand in two right brain-damaged patients. *Neurocase* 10:437–443.

Mullins, S., and S. Spence. 2003. Re-examining thought insertion: Semi-structured literature review and conceptual analysis. *British Journal of Psychiatry* 182:293–298.

Nerval, G. de. (1855) 1996. *Aurelia and Other Writings*. Trans. M. Lowenthal. Boston: Exact Change.

O'Shaughnessy, B. 2003. The epistemology of physical action. In *Agency and Self-Awareness*, ed. J. Roessler and N. Eilan. Oxford: Clarendon.

Purdon, C. 2004. Empirical investigations of thought suppression in OCD. *Journal of Behavior Therapy and Experimental Psychiatry* 35:121–136.

Robinson, W. 2006. Thoughts without distinctive non-imagistic phenomenology. *Philosophy and Phenomenological Research* 70:534–561.

Rosenthal, D. (1990) 1997. A theory of consciousness. ZiF Technical Report 40, Bielfield, Germany. Reprinted in *The Nature of Consciousness: Philosophical Debates*, ed. N. Block, O. Flanagan, and G. Güzeldere. Cambridge MA: MIT Press.

Rosenthal, D. 2005. *Consciousness and Mind*. New York: Oxford University Press.

Rosenthal, D. 2010. Consciousness, the self, and bodily location. *Analysis* 70: 270–276.

Salkovskis, P. 1989. Cognitive-behavioural factors and the persistence of intrusive thoughts in obsessional problems. *Behaviour Research and Therapy* 27:677–682.

Sass, L., E. Pienkos, B. Nelson, and N. Medford. 2013. Anomalous self-experience in depersonalization and schizophrenia: A comparative investigation. *Consciousness and Cognition* 22:430–441.

Sedman, G. 1972. An investigation of certain factors concerned in the aetiology of depersonalization. *Acta Psychiatrica Scandinavica* 48:191–219.

Séglas, J., and H. Meige. 1895. *Leçons cliniques sur les maladies mentales et nerveuses (Salpêtrière, 1887–1894)*. Asselin et Houzeau. http://gallica.bnf.fr/ark:/12148/bpt6k76631s.

Shorvon, H. 1946. The depersonalization syndrome. *Proceedings of the Royal Society of Medicine* 39:779–791.

Sierra, M. 2009. *Depersonalization: A New Look at a Neglected Syndrome*. Cambridge: Cambridge University Press.

Sierra, M., and G. Berrios. 1998. Depersonalization: Neurobiological perspectives. *Biological Psychiatry* 44:898–908.

Sierra, M., and G. Berrios. 2000. The Cambridge depersonalization scale: A new instrument for the measurement of depersonalization. *Psychiatry Research* 93: 153–164.

Simeon, D., and J. Abugel. 2006. *Feeling Unreal: Depersonalization Disorder and the Loss of the Self.* Oxford: Oxford University Press.

Sousa, P., and L. Swiney. 2013. Thought insertion: Abnormal sense of thought agency or thought endorsement? *Phenomenology and the Cognitive Sciences* 12: 637–654.

de Vignemont, F. 2007. Habeas corpus: The sense of ownership of one's own body. *Mind & Language* 22:427–449.

Williford, K. 2006. The self-representational structure of consciousness. In *Self-Representational Approaches to Consciousness*, ed. U. Kriegel and K. Williford. Cambridge, MA: MIT Press.

Zahavi, D., and U. Kriegel. Forthcoming. For-me-ness: What it is and what it is not. In *Philosophy of Mind and Phenomenology*, ed. D. Dahlstrom, A. Elpidorou, and W. Hopp. London: Routledge.

3 Somatoparaphrenia, Anosognosia, and Higher-Order Thoughts

Rocco J. Gennaro

Somatoparaphrenia is a pathology of self characterized by the sense of alienation from parts of one's body. It is usually construed as a kind of delusional disorder caused by extensive right-hemisphere lesions. Lesions in the temporoparietal junction are common in somatoparaphrenia, but deep cortical regions (for example, the posterior insula) and subcortical regions (for example, the basal ganglia) are also sometimes implicated (Valler and Ronchi 2009). Patients are often described as feeling that a limb belongs to another person and, thus, attribute ownership of the limb and bodily sensation to someone else. There is also some question as to whether or not the higher-order thought (HOT) theory of consciousness can plausibly account for the depersonalization psychopathology of somatoparaphrenia (Liang and Lane 2009, Rosenthal 2010, Lane and Liang 2010). Liang and Lane argue that it cannot. The HOT theory of consciousness says that what makes a mental state a conscious mental state is that it is the target of a HOT to the effect that "I am in mental state M" (Rosenthal 2005, Gennaro 2012). When the HOT is itself is unconscious, the conscious state is still outer-directed. When the HOT is conscious, we have *introspection*, and so the conscious thought is directed at the mental state. In section 1, I briefly review the previous exchange between Lane and Liang and David Rosenthal. In section 2, I further explore somatoparaphrenia and the nature of delusion while offering a number of additional replies to Lane and Liang. In section 3, I examine the central notions of *mental state ownership* and *self-concepts* in an effort to account especially for the depersonalization aspect of somatoparaphrenia against the background of HOT theory. In section 4, I argue that, to the extent that somatoparaphrenia casts doubt on the notion that some thoughts are immune to error through misidentification (IEM), the most fundamental aspect of IEM is still consistent with HOT theory. Overall, I argue that HOT theory is left unscathed by the phenomenon of somatoparaphrenia and can even help to explain what happens in these cases.

1　Lane and Liang versus Rosenthal: An Overview

Liang and Lane (2009) initially argued that somatoparaphrenia threatens HOT theory because it contradicts the notion that according to HOT theory, when I am in a conscious state, I have the accompanying HOT that "I am in mental state M." The "I" is not only importantly *self-referential* but essential in tying the conscious state to *oneself* and, thus, to one's *ownership* of M. Indeed, it is difficult to understand how one can have a conscious state but not, at least implicitly, attribute it to oneself.

Rosenthal (2010) basically responds that one can be aware of bodily sensations in two ways that, normally at least, go together: (a) aware of a bodily sensation *as one's own*, and (b) aware of a bodily sensation *as having some bodily location*, like a hand or foot. Patients with somatoparaphrenia still experience the sensation as their own but also as having a mistaken bodily location (perhaps somewhat analogous to phantom limb pain). Such patients still do have the awareness in (a), which is the main issue at hand, but they have the strange awareness in sense (b). So somatoparaphrenia leads some people to misidentify the bodily location of a sensation as someone else's, but the awareness of the sensation itself remains one's own.

Rosenthal also accepts what he calls a "more modest" version of Shoemaker's (1968) IEM principle, which says that, if the ground of my judgment is introspective, that is, "from the inside," whenever I say or think, for example, that "I feel pain," it cannot be the case that I am mistaken in thinking that the person in pain is me. The same goes for other mental states and bodily sensations. According to Rosenthal, we should at least adopt a "thin immunity principle" (TIP) such that, when I have a conscious pain (for example), I cannot be wrong about whether it's I who I think is in pain (Rosenthal 2005, 357). Elsewhere, he explains that "no error is possible about whom I am aware of as having the pain because the spontaneous awareness tacitly identifies the bearer of the pain with the bearer of the awareness" (Rosenthal 2010, 274). I will return to this theme later in section 4.

But Lane and Liang (2010) are not satisfied and, among other things, counter that Rosenthal's analogy to phantom limbs is faulty, and that he has still not explained why the identification of the *bearer* of the pain cannot also go astray, especially since Rosenthal clearly holds that misrepresentation can occur between a HOT and its object.

2 The Nature of Delusion and Further Replies to Lane and Liang

Although I largely agree with much of Rosenthal's response, I believe that there are many responses available to a HOT theorist that have thus far been neglected in this debate. I will focus on these further replies in this section, with special attention to the nature of delusion.

First, we must remember that many of these patients often deny feeling *anything* in the limb in question (Bottini et al. 2002). As Liang and Lane point out, patient FB, while blindfolded, feels "no tactile sensation" (2009, 664) when the examiner would in fact touch the dorsal surface of FB's hand. In these cases, it is therefore difficult to see what the problem is for HOT theory at all. While somatoparaphrenia is indeed a puzzling phenomenon, the HOT theorist can simply reply that there is no HOT in such cases because there is no conscious feeling (and vice versa). Since there is no conscious feeling, there is no allegedly problematic "I" in a HOT that potentially conflicts with what the patient says or feels. Moreover, HOT theory can *explain why* there is no conscious feeling, that is, because there is no HOT (with its I-concept) directed at a mental state.

Second, in those cases where FB does report feeling a tactile sensation, she is told that the examiner is about to touch her *niece's* hand. When FB is required to report touches on her niece's hand, FB's tactile perception increased dramatically, but she insisted that she was feeling touches on someone else's hand. Of course, if FB is not really feeling anything, then the reply in the previous paragraph would hold.

However, in cases where there really is a bodily sensation of some kind, a HOT theorist might plausibly argue that there are really *two* conscious states that seem to be at odds. There is a conscious feeling in a limb but also the (conscious) attribution of the limb to someone else. But it is also crucial to emphasize that somatoparaphrenia is usually characterized as a *delusion* of *belief*, often under the broader category of anosognosia, a condition in which a person who suffers from a disability seems unaware of the existence of the disability (Breen et al. 2000, de Vignemont 2010, Feinberg 2011). A delusion is often defined as a false belief that is held based on an incorrect (and probably unconscious) *inference* about external reality or oneself that is firmly sustained despite what almost everyone else believes and despite what constitutes incontrovertible and obvious proof or evidence to the contrary (Radden 2011, Bortolotti 2013). In some cases, delusions seriously inhibit normal day-to-day functioning. This doxastic conception of delusion is common among psychologists and psychiatrists (Bayne and Pacherie 2005, Bortolotti 2009). Beliefs, generally speaking, are themselves often taken to be intentional states integrated with other beliefs. They are typically understood as caused by perceptions or experiences that then lead to action or behavior. Thus, somatoparaphrenia is, in some ways, closer to self-deception and involves frequent confabulation. If this is a reasonable interpretation of the data, then a HOT theorist can argue that, in these cases, the patient has the following *two* conscious states:

(1) S1: a conscious *feeling* (i.e., a tactile sensation) in the limb in question, and
(2) S2: a conscious *belief* that the limb (and thus sensation) belongs to someone else.

Now having both S1 and S2 simultaneously might be strange and perhaps even self-contradictory in some sense, but the puzzlement has nothing to do with HOT theory. Indeed, this possibility is perfectly consistent with HOT theory. S1 would still require an unmediated HOT that "I am in M." There is no problem here for HOT theory because it is still true that one is having a conscious sensation in these cases. Note that the HOT itself is *unconscious* in these cases—the patient is not consciously entertaining the HOT or "I" in question. But what is really odd is that the person with somatoparaphrenia *also* has, as S2 indicates, a conscious belief that runs counter to, or even contradicts, S1. FB responds to questions by affirming this belief. But surely no theory of consciousness can automatically rule out such a bizarre combination of conscious states, and there is nothing in HOT theory that causes any special difficulty here. HOT theory is a theory about what makes mental states conscious and is not itself a theory of mental content, let alone a theory about the consistency of mental content. If we demand that a theory of consciousness close off the possibility of a pair of contradictory conscious states or an inconsistent pair of a feeling and verbal report, then it is unclear how any theory could pass this test. In short, HOT theory can be true even when a subject exhibits irrational thinking or behavior.

Third, it is of course normally true that when a person P feels something in his or her body, P will also believe that the limb is P's, that is, his or her own limb. Normally, there is presumably an unconscious inference or, perhaps even better, the general *presupposition* that the limb is one's own. For HOT theory, this presupposition is precisely embodied in the unmediated accompanying unconscious HOT. In cases of somatoparaphrenia, however, there might also be an erroneous or confabulated *inference* from the feeling in question to the belief that the sensation and limb are not one's own. Indeed, according to Feinberg's (2010, 2011) "ego disequilibrium theory," delusional misidentification syndromes such as somatoparaphrenia result, in part, from pathological defenses, including projection. To be sure, this is abnormal and difficult to understand to some extent, but it is not a problem specifically for HOT theory as far as I can see. These patients *do* consciously feel something that can still be explained by HOT theory in the usual way. But, in addition, there is, at least initially, an erroneous inference to the delusional belief that the sensation is not one's own. This belief is evident in FB's strange and clearly confabulatory verbal responses to questions. So what would the inference be like? Based on the above discussion, it would presumably take something like the following form:

(1)   I am having (or feel) a bodily sensation.
(2)   I do not have the limb where I feel this sensation.
(3)   *Therefore*, I feel a sensation in someone else's limb.

Further confabulation may explain who I choose as the bearer of this sensation. In the case of FB, she chooses her niece based on the examiner's questions. Yet Liang and Lane think that somatoparaphrenia presents a particular difficulty for HOT theory. But, interestingly, in Lane and Liang's counter-reply to Rosenthal, they actually say that "FB came *to believe* that her left hand belonged to her niece" (Lane and Liang's 2010, 497, added emphasis).

So I agree with Rosenthal that there are two different attributions, namely, ownership and bodily location. I agree that "FB is aware of the sensation as being her own. But she is also *aware of* the sensation as having a subjective bodily location in a hand that is not part of her own body" (Rosenthal 2010, 272, emphasis added). For the reasons given above, however, it seems better to construe the "aware of" in the previous sentence as "believes that." Lane and Liang (2010) are probably right the Rosenthal relies too heavily on the phantom limb analogy since, in phantom limb, who feels the pain is not at issue. Nonetheless, I think that Lane and Liang do not properly recognize that the tactile sensation at issue is still *felt by FB* as her own in one sense even though she *also* attributes her limb to her niece and, thus, believes that the tactile sensation is her niece's.

Liang and Lane tell us that "what seems to be happening is that these tactile sensations are *represented as belonging to someone other than self*" (2009, 664), and that is problematic for HOT theory. But this is highly ambiguous, because another way to "represent" sensations as belonging to someone else is via a propositional attitude such as a belief. And there would be no problem for HOT theory with regard to whether or not these patients can have the conscious belief in S2. That is, a patient with somatoparaphrenia would still represent that *belief* as her own. And the fact remains that no mental state of her niece's is made conscious by any HOT of FB's. It is certainly not the case that FB's niece has a conscious sensation due to one of FB's HOTs. Further, as Billon and Kriegel point out (this volume), there are no cases of patients with somatoparaphrenia claiming to *feel a sensation* that is not theirs. These last points still hold despite blindfolded FB's somewhat odd results on so-called "catch trials" in the Bottini et al. study (2002, 251). I am not quite sure that we should take all of these results at face value, especially given what I have argued above, but FB does report touches when she was cued to expect her niece's hand would be touched and when she was actually touched. However, FB reported nothing when she was cued to expect her niece's hand to be touched and her hand was not touched. Bottini et al. (2002, 251) explain that on each trial, "the examiner briefly touched the dorsal surface of FB's hand," and when she was cued to expect her niece's hand to be touched, "the examiner touched FB's left hand."

It might be objected at this point that I have ignored the endorsement and explanationist theories of delusion formation or, perhaps, have assumed the latter in laying out the inference in the previous paragraphs. The endorsement account holds that delusions are formed by endorsing as veridical the content of the unusual experience (Bayne and Pacherie 2004), whereas the explanationist account holds that delusions are formed as a way to explain an unusual experience (Maher 1999). Patients with anosognosia and somatoparaphrenia are also arguably well motivated to conjure up an explanation, for example, as a way to manage negative emotions (see McKay and Kinsbourne 2010 for much more on this line of argument). One way to frame these two theories of delusion formation is by asking the following question: Does the delusional belief occur before the person has the conscious experience or afterward? Alternatively: Are delusions bizarre convictions that alter one's way of seeing the world, or are they hypotheses formulated to account for some unusual experiences and then endorsed as beliefs?

But, as Langdon and Bayne (2010) point out, most delusions are likely hybrids of both views, especially when considered over periods of time. They instead propose a "continuum" from "received" to "reflective" delusion, whereby the former largely come to pass via the endorsement process, and the latter are formed mainly by an explanationist processes. Indeed, it seems to me that the explanationist account makes far more sense when the subject is first asked to respond to questions, such as in FB's initial examinations. Langdon and Bayne (2010) also note that we should distinguish between "spontaneous" and "provoked" confabulation, whereby the latter arises only in response to direct questioning (Kopelman 2010). After all, what makes many patient dialogues so compelling and bizarre is the clear confabulations of the patient in response to questions. For example, when FB was asked how she could report touches on someone else's hand, her "response was initially elusive; however, she eventually explained that [her] absent-minded niece would always forget her hand on [FB's] bed while leaving the hospital" (Bottini et al. 2002, 251). However, once the delusional belief has taken firm hold in the patient, it then seems more plausible from that point onward to suppose that the delusional belief (and the inference) in question is already in place prior to subsequent experiences, which is more in line with the endorsement theory. The notion that cognitive states can have an impact on one's experiences is fairly widely acknowledged.[1]

So if the argument above is plausible with regard to an initial provoked explanationist account, then the subsequent endorsement is more likely to occur unconsciously. This is because the more conceptually loaded resulting experience reflected in (3) is the *result* or *consequence* of having a delusional belief and the requisite lack of self-awareness.

It is worth mentioning that something like this analysis has been proposed as a parallel way to account for Capgras syndrome. Bortolotti (2013, 15) explains:

For some, it is correct to say that the delusional belief *explains* the experience. Others claim that the delusion is an *endorsement* of the experience. According to the *explanationist* account (Maher 1999), the content of experience is vaguer than the content of the delusion, and the delusion plays the role of one potential explanation for the experience. For instance, in the Capgras delusion, the experience would be that of someone looking very much like my sister but not being my sister. The delusion would be an explanation of the fact that the woman looks like my sister, but her face feels strange to me: the woman must be an impostor. … According to the rival account, the *endorsement* account (Bayne and Pacherie 2004), the content of the experience is already as conceptually rich as the content of the delusion. The delusion is not an explanation of the experience, but an endorsement of it: the content of the experience is taken as veridical and believed. In Capgras, the experience is that of a woman looking very much like my sister but being an impostor, and when the experience is endorsed, it becomes the delusional belief that my sister has been replaced by an impostor.[2]

Fourth, to follow up on the preceding points, it seems to me that when one has a conscious belief, such as S2, we primarily have in mind *introspecting* a belief—that is, consciously thinking about a belief. For example, FB is reporting this (false) belief in response to questions. If this is plausible, then at least some of the sting may be taken out of the idea that one can have S2 while also having S1 with its accompanying *unconscious* thought that "I am feeling a sensation." This is because S1 and S2 may not always be consciously present at the same time in these patients. That is, one may not be consciously aware of both S1 and S2 *at the same time*. Further, the HOT required for S1 is not conscious at all, but the belief in S2 is conscious. So it is unclear that whatever inconsistency might exist in FB's mind would be as obvious *to her* as we might suppose it to be.

Indeed, to the extent that somatoparaphrenia is typically thought of as a form of anosognosia, it seems plausible to suppose that it too involves a deficit of self-awareness and, thus, the unity of consciousness in some sense (including, perhaps, some memory problems as well). Recall that anosognosia involves the lack of awareness of an impairment, such as paralysis to the left side of patients' bodies. Bayne points out that anosognosic patients "are often oblivious to major changes in the contents of their own conscious states" and appear "to be impaired in tracking [their] own states of consciousness [and] a breakdown in the unity of *reflexive* consciousness" (Bayne 2011, 153; cf. Nikolinakos 2004). This bolsters the above line of argument in the sense that it can explain why FB and others with somatoparaphrenia seem to hold inconsistent beliefs or respond to questions in a way that would seem inconsistent with their beliefs (such as with S1 and S2). That is, they may not be able to hold S1 and S2 reflectively in mind at the same time owing to a deficit in self-awareness or introspection. Nikolinakos (2004, 316) explains that "Reflexive consciousness refers to the awareness of phenomenal experience [which] … is a second-order consciousness about information that appears in non-reflexive consciousness," so it is clear that by "reflexive consciousness" he is referring to what I have been calling *introspection*. This lack of monitoring or tracking of one's mental states, according to HOT theory, could be explained by an inability to form *conscious* HOTs directed at mental states—that is, as a deficit of introspective ability. What makes anosognosia so puzzling is that we would expect subjects to give up one of two inconsistent beliefs when they are clearly pointed out to that subject, but yet they do not do so. Perhaps the reason is that, from the point of view of the patient, there is an inability to hold in mind introspectively both beliefs at the same time. Much the same might be true in the case of Anton's syndrome, which is a form of anosognosia in which a person with partial or total blindness denies being visually impaired, despite clear medical evidence to the contrary. Just as one with somatoparaphrenia confabulates in response to questions about the presence of body parts, the Anton's syndrome patient typically confabulates excuses for the inability to see.

In any case, when Liang and Lane say that "patients typically *feel* that a contralesional limb belongs to someone other than self" (Liang and Lane

2009, 664, emphasis added), this, to my ear, sounds more like a belief rather than some kind of bodily sensation, especially during initial questioning and subsequent confabulation. At the very least, "feel" is ambiguous between a conscious feeling as such and the conscious belief S2. Once again, I suggest that it is the latter, partly because FB is asked to verbally respond to questions. The term *feel* in the Liang and Lane quotation seems like the generic all-encompassing *feel*, such as when one says "I feel that capital punishment is wrong" or "I feel that I can do a better job than Joe." In these cases, the term *feel* is used more like believe or think. Indeed, even just the "feel *that*" locution seems to indicate a propositional attitude rather than a bodily sensation, such as when one says "I feel pain," or "I feel cold," or "I feel tired." And when Rosenthal states that "being conscious of a state as belonging to someone other than oneself would plainly not make it a conscious state" (as quoted in Liang and Lane 2009, 662), I take it that he is again referring to a possible case where person A believes or *feels* that M is in person B. But, in such a case, M would not become conscious in person B, according to HOT theory. Even if FB does have a HOT about someone *else's* mental state M based on an inference, M would not become conscious. Thus, this line of reply, which admittedly reinterprets some of FB's reports, can be successful *contra* Liang and Lane's claim (2009, 666).

We must also remind ourselves that HOT theory comes with a well-known noninferentiality condition, such that a HOT must become aware of its target mental state noninferentially—that is, in an unmediated way. As Rosenthal repeatedly emphasizes, the point of this condition is mainly to rule out certain alleged counterexamples to HOT theory, such as cases where I become aware of my unconscious desire to kill my boss because I have consciously inferred it from a session with my psychiatrist, or where my envy becomes conscious after making inferences based on my own behavior. The characteristic feel of such a conscious desire or envy may be absent in these cases but, since awareness of them arose via conscious inference, the HOT theorist accounts for them by adding this noninferentiality condition. Thus, HOT theory requires that the HOT arises in an unmediated manner. This is also important because if there is any kind of inference to a belief, such as in S2, then the HOT would not arise in the requisite manner. So when Rosenthal says, for example, that "being aware of oneself as being in pain consists in being aware, in a spontaneous, seemingly unmediated way, of an individual's being in pain" (2010, 274), he is referring to an essential and important aspect of standard HOT theory. Lane and Liang are incorrect in treating this appeal to "spontaneous, unmediated awareness" as begging the question with regard to mental ownership

(2010, 498). It is an essential aspect of HOT theory. In a more recent paper, Rosenthal explains that "when you are aware of me as being in pain, it will not be the seemingly unmediated awareness characteristic of one's awareness of one's own pain, but we are nonetheless aware of the very same thing as being in pain" (2012, 40).

Fifth, another potential problem for Lane and Liang can also be seen by recognizing that a HOT is supposed to be a thought *about a mental state*, not about one's own (or another's) body or body part. According to HOT theory, when I am in a conscious state, I have the accompanying HOT that "I am in *mental state M*." Of course, just how bodily sensations should be categorized is a difficult issue in its own right (de Vignemont 2011, section 3), but it at least seems prima facie plausible to construe any of FB's thoughts about her limbs or her niece's limbs to be, at least in part, about a perceptual object akin to a perception. In short, we must distinguish between one's awareness of a mental state or sensation from the inside, such as a pain or other tactile sensation, and one's awareness of a body part, such as a limb. It is true that one need not visually perceive one's own limb to be aware of it in various ways, such as its spatial orientation via proprioception or where one is having pain. However, Lane and Liang do not acknowledge the fact that *if* some of FB's thoughts are not really even directed at mental states, then much of what they say is irrelevant with respect to any deep problem for HOT theory. We would no longer have an alleged problem with regard to an "I-thought" *directed at a mental state*, but instead would merely have a first-order conscious thought or belief about a body part or another's body part (more on this in section 4).

3   I-Concepts and Mental State Ownership

Recall that somatoparaphrenia is a depersonalization psychopathology, as is anosognosia (Prigatano 2010). But what exactly is meant by depersonalization? At minimum, it involves a distortion in one's self-awareness or sense of self. So there is a deficient sense of oneself and distorted self-concepts (Sierra 2009). This seems to include deficits of mental state ownership. Let us look more closely at these aspects of somatoparaphrenia.[3]

It is useful to distinguish the *feeling* of ownership from the *judgment* of ownership (de Vignemont 2007, 2011), which is neglected in Lane and Liang's arguments. As is well-known in cases of phantom pain, one may feel a pain in a limb that does not even exist. On the other hand, in cases of anesthesia or body integrity identity disorder, one might not feel any sensation in a limb that is clearly judged to be part of one's own body. So mental state ownership need not correlate with one's feeling of embodiment (de Vignemont 2007, 2011). In the now well-known rubber hand illusion, one can arguably even feel an external object (a fake rubber hand) as one's own in some sense. People can be convinced that a rubber hand is their own by putting it on a table in front of them while stroking it in the same way as their real hands.

Along similar lines, Bermúdez (2011, 161–166) distinguishes between a "sense" of ownership and a "judgment" of ownership. Recall also that a HOT theorist does not hold that HOTs are typically themselves conscious. Bermúdez argues, in the end, that the "sense" of ownership is best viewed as a "judgment" or "thought" rather than as a feeling itself. In contrast to de Vignemont (2007), Bermúdez rejects the "inflationary" conception of the sense of ownership, according to which there is a distinctive positive phenomenology of ownership, as opposed to the "deflationary" conception that consists in facts about the phenomenology of bodily sensations and in ownership judgments about the body. "There are facts about the phenomenology of bodily awareness ... and there are judgments of ownership, but there is no additional feeling of ownership" (Bermúdez 2011, 166). There are still, of course, bodily sensations and proprioceptive states. What one actually feels is the *first-order* conscious state accompanied by the unconscious judgment or thought about the mental state, as opposed to any phenomenology of "myness." Notice that this fits nicely with HOT theory, which can explain why there is a phenomenological sense of myness when one *introspects*, namely, that the HOT is itself conscious, whereas no such sense is present when one has an unconscious HOT. The concept "I" is part of a *conscious* thought in the introspective case but part of an *unconscious* thought in the first-order case. Nonetheless, it is certainly true that when there is a disturbance or abnormality in one's I-concept, such as one's bodily representation, one's consciousness will be altered and result in some odd beliefs and feelings of body *dis*ownership. But, like Bermúdez, I do not find it compelling to argue that if a deficit of bodily awareness is manifested in consciousness, then that aspect of bodily awareness is always or even normally part of our consciousness, albeit even in some peripheral way. Many abnormalities of bodily awareness can surely negatively *affect* one's consciousness but in a way where the corresponding normal functioning would not typically be part of one's consciousness. "There is no particular reason for understanding a feeling of disownership as the absence of a feeling of ownership—at least, not without prior reasons for thinking that there is such a thing as the feeling of ownership" (Bermúdez 2011, 163).

I have used something like this line of response against Ford and Smith's (2006) argument in favor of the so-called "self-representationalist" theory of consciousness, whereby first-order conscious states are always accompanied by an inner-directed peripheral conscious awareness (Kriegel 2009). Ford and Smith contend that cases of depersonalization show that something like Kriegel's view is correct based on such abnormal cases. But again, just because the removal of something—for example, normal proprioception—causes deficits in one's conscious mental states, it surely does not follow that the awareness of that thing is part of normal conscious experience. The relation could be causal instead of constitutive. That is, the typical abilities and awareness in question might merely, in the normal case, causally contribute to the phenomenology of one's conscious mental states without being part of the conscious state itself, even peripherally. There are many ways that normal consciousness can be disturbed or impaired (e.g., being unable to breathe), but surely we shouldn't conclude that every such disturbance shows that the ability in question normally shows up in our phenomenology (see Gennaro 2012, chapter 5, esp. 127–129).

Let us pursue this general theme a bit further. In previous publications, I have distinguished four degrees of I-concepts, the simplest of which is something like "I *qua* this body as opposed to other things" (Gennaro 1993, 1996). Other, more sophisticated self-concepts include "I *qua* experiencer of mental states," "I *qua* enduring thinking thing," and "I *qua* thinker among other thinkers." So bodily self-awareness is one of many ways to represent oneself. But it is clear that even this most basic I-concept is ambiguous between, for example, what has been called the body schema, which has to do with representations implicit in motor control and action, and the body image, which is one's conscious perceptions of and beliefs about one's body (Gallagher 1986). There is more than one way to represent one's body, which is presumably realized in distinct neural pathways, although the matter is not so simple (de Vignemont 2010, 2011). It is also possible, for example, to have anosognosia *without* somatoparaphrenia. These anosognosics seem to have an intact body image but a distorted body schema in the sense that their denial (or unawareness) of paralysis wrongly leads them to suppose that they are capable of normal motor action. Patients with somatoparaphrenia *also* seem to have deficit in body schema for similar reasons. They too have a severely deficient body image in that they even deny that one of their arms or legs is theirs in the first place (and thus believe that it is someone else's). For example, FB believes that she can perform certain motor tasks even though she is physically unable to do so. In other cases, a patient might insist that she can clap (or has just clapped) despite left arm paralysis and no ability to move her hand (e.g., patient CC discussed in Berti et al. 1998).[4]

Ramachandran (1996) also reports the case of a woman (FD) who suffered from a right hemisphere stroke resulting in left hemiplegia. FD could not move her left arm. But when she was asked to engage in activities that require both hands, such as clapping, she claimed that she could. Ramachandran advances the hypothesis that behaviors giving rise to confabulations and delusions are an exaggeration of normal defense mechanisms that have an adaptive and protective function (Hirstein 2005). So one reason to think that delusions and self-deception overlap is that at least some delusions, like extreme cases of self-deception, appear to have a protective and adaptive function (for much more on this theme, see the essays in Bayne and Fernández 2009). Another view about the overlap of delusions and self-deception is that the existence of delusions supports the traditional account of self-deception, such that a person has two contradictory beliefs but is only aware of one of them because she is motivated to remain unaware of the other (McKay et al. 2005, 314). This account was also suggested by some of our discussion near the end of the previous section. Levy (2009), for example, argues that the case of FD shows that a person can, at the same time, believe that her arm is paralyzed and believe that she can move her arm. But Levy rightly suggests that this awareness comes in degrees. Many people with paralysis and anosognosia simply find ways to avoid tasks that require mobility and then confabulate and make excuses for their lack of behavior in certain contexts.

4   Immunity to Error through Misidentification (IEM)

Let us return to the aforementioned and much discussed immunity to error through misidentification (IEM) principle. According to Shoemaker, a certain subset of thoughts about oneself is immune to error through misidentification (see also Evans 1982). As Shoemaker makes clear, one can think about oneself under any number of descriptions. But only some I-thoughts are immune to error through misidentification—namely, those I-thoughts that are directed at one's mind and mental life, as opposed to one's body and corporeal life. Wittgenstein ([1958] 1969) observed that I can see in the mirror a tangle of arms and mistakenly take the nicest one to be mine. I may think to myself, "I have a nice arm." In that case, I may not only be wrong about whether my arm is nice, but also about who it is that has a nice arm. Such an I-thought about my body (or body part) is not immune to error through misidentification (Kriegel 2007). In extreme abnormal cases, such as mirrored-self-misidentification, one might even believe that *one's own* reflection in a mirror is some other person.

Recall that even when Lane and Liang say that FB was feeling touches on someone else's hand, it is still the case that *she* is feeling something. So, in at least this narrow sense, there is still some level of self-awareness such that a self-referential "I" is required for the HOT that accompanies that conscious feeling. The attribution of that feeling or limb to someone else is, as I have urged, best understood as a separate false belief. But notice that there is still no possibility of error with regard to who is having the tactile sensation itself and who is aware of the feeling. Recall Rosenthal's thin immunity principle (TIP), which simply says that when I have a conscious pain (for example) I cannot be wrong about whether it's I who I think is in pain (Rosenthal 2005, 357). "No error is possible about whom I am aware of as having the pain because the spontaneous awareness tacitly identifies the bearer of the pain with the bearer of the awareness" (Rosenthal 2010, 274). TIP thus holds for FB in the sense that when FB does have a conscious feeling, FB cannot be wrong about whether it is FB who is *aware of* that feeling. The unmediated HOT in question tacitly identifies the bearer of the feeling (FB) with the bearer of the awareness of the feeling (FB). FB cannot be wrong about whether it is FB who FB thinks is having that feeling. So the identification of the bearer of the pain cannot also go astray because, whatever else FB says or does with respect to the feeling, FB still (unconsciously or implicitly) identifies herself as having that feeling. We might say that FB still owns that feeling from the inside, but she erroneously also attributes it to another person, partly due to the delusional belief that the limb is not hers. So when FB insists that she is feeling touches on someone else's hand, the fact remains that this *feeling itself* is still taken by FB to be her own. Unlike, say, mirror self-identification, which involves outward perception directed at one's body, one cannot be mistaken about the mere awareness of one's own sensation strictly from the inside. FB actually doesn't really say that the feeling is not hers, but rather that she is feeling touches in someone else's limb.

Another way to approach this matter is via the somewhat different notion of bodily immunity to error—namely, that certain judgments subjects make about their own bodies based on information gained from the first-person point of view exhibit IEM (de Vignemont 2012). The notion of bodily self-ascription is construed as ascription of bodily properties. De Vignemont (2012) favors an "inside mode account" such that bodily self-ascriptions are immune to error through misidentification if, and only if, one gains information about the body from the inside (e.g., proprioception, sense of pressure, and sense of balance). Perhaps I can be mistaken that my arms are in fact crossed, but it is difficult to see how I could be wrong that the arms that I feel are *mine*. In somatoparaphrenia, there is clearly a failure of bodily ascription, since the patient will deny ownership of the limb and attribute the limb to someone else. As we have seen, the delusional aspect of somatoparaphrenia is so strong that patients will confabulate when confronted with clear counter-evidence. However, the counter-evidence is presented via a visual modality and not from the inside, such as by pointing to the patient's arm or hand and asking whose it is. When we have some kind of feeling, sensation, or pain, we have cases of ascribing psychological properties, not bodily properties.

One might also distinguish between two ways of violating the IEM principle. Depersonalization and somatoparaphrenia do not result in *false positive errors*, that is, errors of identification in which "one self-ascribes properties that are instantiated in another individual's body" (de Vignemont, 2012, 229). Instead, they are at best *false negatives*, that is, errors of identification in which "one does not self-ascribe properties that are instantiated in one's own body" (de Vignemont, 2012, 229), though we have seen that even this type of error does not necessarily cause trouble for TIP because there is *also* an awareness of a feeling in one's own body. So although IEM is normally thought of in terms of the self-ascription of psychological properties, some have explored the possibility that some physical self-ascriptions also have IEM (Evans 1982), such as kinesthetic sensations or proprioception, and even Shoemaker (1968) discussed what he called "circumstantial" (as opposed to absolute) immunity with respect to physical self-ascriptions depending on what grounds the ascriptions are made. But there is a fine line here. On the one hand, bodily *sensations* are still mental states, such as pains and feelings in a limb, and, on the other hand, there are also judgments or feelings about the location and movement of parts of my body (Chen 2009). However, when we discover cases where a patient really *feels*, from the first-person point of view, that, say, his left arm is moving when it is not really moving, there seems to be more room to doubt that some form of IEM even applies here.[5]

Finally, let's revisit the notion of misrepresentation and HOTs. Recall that Lane and Liang protest that Rosenthal has still not explained why the identification of the bearer of the pain cannot also go astray, especially since Rosenthal clearly holds that misrepresentation can occur between a HOT and its target. But whatever one thinks of standard cases of misrepresentation between the first-order and higher-order level on HOT theory, they are not clearly relevant here because those cases involve differences in the *contents* of the two respective states.[6] Although Lane and Liang (2010, 499) claim that there should equally be the possibility of a mismatch between the "I" in the HOT and the "I" in the first-order mental state, it is unclear to me how this could be so. Wittgenstein ([1958] 1969) himself usefully distinguished between the "I-as-subject" (e.g., "I have a pain") and the "I-as-object" ("I have a broken arm"). There is never an I-as-object in the *content* of the *first-order* state, but there is an implicit (and unconscious) I-as-subject at the second-order level *as well as* an I-as-object in a typical HOT. According to HOT theory, there would only be an I-as-subject concept in a first-order state, and the content of the state refers to the outer world. This would be a kind of "raw bearer" of the state, as Rosenthal (2012) calls it. After all, if we assume that any mental state must have a bearer, then even first-order states should involve some primitive concept of I. The same is true for the unconscious HOT that accompanies a first-order conscious state, but here there is *also* an I-as-object referenced in the *content* of the HOT (i.e., "I think that *I am in M*"). Still, these I-concepts are normally parts of unconscious thoughts, and so there is little reason to suppose that there is any phenomenological sense of myness in these cases. However, when one introspects and has a conscious HOT directed at a mental state, there is not only a conscious I-as-subject concept but also a *conscious* I-as-object concept in the content of the HOT that can account for any subjective sense of myness. The fact remains, though, that there could be no mismatch between an I-as-object in the content of a mental state M and its HOT because there isn't an I-as-object concept at all in the content of M.[7]

I conclude that HOT theory can withstand the alleged threat from cases of somatoparaphrenia. Indeed, I think that HOT theory can even help to explain what happens in these cases, especially when one is clear about the nature of delusions and is careful about the concepts in question.[8]

Notes

1. For an excellent anthology on confabulation, see Hirstein 2009.

2. There is also the much-discussed, two-factor theory of confabulation, which I think I can simply take for granted in this discussion. Coltheart explains the two main factors involved in the formation of delusions as follows: "There is a first neuropsychological impairment that presents the patient with new (and false data), and the delusional belief formed is one which, if true, would explain these data. The nature of this impairment varies from patient to patient. There is a second neuropsychological impairment, of a belief evaluation system, which prevents the patient from rejecting the newly formed belief even though there is much evidence against it. This impairment is the same in all people with monothematic delusions" (Coltheart 2005, 154). I won't elaborate on this here, but see Davies et al. 2005 for some discussion of anosognosia and the two-factor theory of delusions.

3. For an excellent anthology of readings exploring numerous "self-related" pathologies, see Feinberg and Keenan 2005.

4. See also Carruthers 2009 for a nice critical discussion of de Vignemont's view and for more on the body image versus body schema distinction.

5. For much more on all things IEM, see the essays in Prosser and Recanati 2012.

6. I disagree with the way that Rosenthal handles these cases but won't pursue this here. See Gennaro 2012, especially chapter 4. Lane and Liang (2008) also take Rosenthal to task on so-called "radical confabulation" or "targetless HOT" cases. Although we may disagree about what a HOT theorist should say about possible cases of mismatches or misrepresentation between the HOT and the first-order states, we must be careful here. Although there is most certainly no infallibility in *introspection*, there is a much more intimate connection between an unconscious HOT and its first-order target state.

7. For more on IEM and somatoparaphrenia, see Lane and Liang 2011, especially 84–90, but I think the points made here apply equally to that discussion.

8. Thanks to Tim Lane for helpful comments on, and a conversation about, an earlier version of this paper.

References

Bayne, T. 2011. *The Unity of Consciousness*. New York: Oxford University Press.

Bayne, T., and J. Fernández, eds. 2009. *Delusions and Self-Deception: Affective and Motivational Influences on Belief-Formation*. Hove: Psychology Press.

Bayne, T., and E. Pacherie. 2004. Bottom up or top down? *Philosophy, Psychiatry & Psychology* 11:1–11.

Bayne, T., and E. Pacherie. 2005. In defense of the doxastic conception of delusion. *Mind & Language* 20:163–188.

Bermúdez, J. 2011. Bodily awareness and self-consciousness. In *The Oxford Handbook of the Self*, ed. S. Gallagher. New York: Oxford University Press.

Berti, A., E. Ladavas, A. Stracciari, C. Giannarelli, and A. Ossola. 1998. Anosognosia for motor impairment and dissociations with patients' evaluation of the disorder: Theoretical considerations. *Cognitive Neuropsychiatry* 3:21–44.

Bortolotti, L. 2009. *Delusions and Other Irrational Beliefs*. Oxford: Oxford University Press.

Bortolotti, Lisa. 2013. Delusion. In *The Stanford Encyclopedia of Philosophy* (Winter 2013 Ed.), ed. Edward N. Zalta. http://plato.stanford.edu/archives/win2013/entries/delusion/.

Bottini, G., E. Bisiach, R. Sterzi, and G. Vallar. 2002. Feeling touches in someone else's hand. *Neuroreport* 13:249–252.

Breen, N., D. Caine, M. Coltheart, J. Hendy, and C. Roberts. 2000. Towards an understanding of delusions of misidentification: four case studies. *Mind & Language* 15:74–110.

Carruthers, G. 2009. Is the body schema sufficient for the sense of embodiment? An alternative to de Vignemont's model. *Philosophical Psychology* 22:123–142.

Chen, C. 2009. Bodily awareness and immunity to error through misidentification. *European Journal of Philosophy* 19:21–38.

Coltheart, M. 2005. Conscious experience and delusional belief. *Philosophy, Psychiatry & Psychology* 12:153–157.

Davies, M., A. Davies, and M. Coltheart. 2005. Anosognosia and the two-factor theory of delusions. *Mind & Language* 20:209–236.

de Vignemont, F. 2007. Habeas corpus: The sense of ownership of one's own body. *Mind & Language* 22:427–449.

de Vignemont, F. 2010. Body schema and body image—pros and cons. *Neuropsychologia* 48:669–680.

de Vignemont, Frédérique. 2011. Bodily awareness. In *The Stanford Encyclopedia of Philosophy* (Fall 2011 Ed.), ed. Edward N. Zalta. http://plato.stanford.edu/archives/fall2011/entries/bodily-awareness/.

de Vignemont, F. 2012. Bodily immunity to error. In *Immunity to Error through Misidentification: New Essays*, ed. S. Prosser and F. Recanati. Cambridge: Cambridge University Press.

Evans, G. 1982. *Varieties of Reference*. Oxford: Oxford University Press.

Feinberg, T. 2010. Neuropathologies of the self: A general theory. *Neuro-psychoanalysis* 12:133–158.

Feinberg, T. 2011. Neuropathologies of the self: Clinical and anatomical features. *Consciousness and Cognition* 20:75–81.

Feinberg, T., and J. Keenan, eds. 2005. *The Lost Self: Pathologies of the Brain and Identity*. New York: Oxford University Press.

Ford, J., and D. W. Smith. 2006. Consciousness, self, and attention. In *Self-Representational Approaches to Consciousness*, ed. U. Kriegel and K. Williford. Cambridge, MA: MIT Press.

Gallagher, S. 1986. Body image and body schema: A conceptual clarification. *Journal of Mind and Behavior* 7:541–554.

Gennaro, R. 1993. Brute experience and the higher-order thought theory of consciousness. *Philosophical Papers* 22:51–69.

Gennaro, R. 1996. *Consciousness and Self-consciousness*. Amsterdam: John Benjamins.

Gennaro, R. 2006. Between pure self-referentialism and the (extrinsic) HOT theory of consciousness. In *Self-Representational Approaches to Consciousness*, ed. U. Kriegel and K. Williford. Cambridge, MA: MIT Press.

Gennaro, R. 2012. *The Consciousness Paradox: Consciousness, Concepts, and Higher-Order Thoughts*. Cambridge, MA: MIT Press.

Hirstein, W. 2005. *Brain Fiction: Self-Deception and the Riddle of Confabulation*. Cambridge, MA: MIT Press.

Hirstein, W., ed. 2009. *Confabulation: Views from Neuroscience, Psychiatry, Psychology, and Philosophy*. Oxford: Oxford University Press.

Kopelman, M. 2010. Varieties of confabulation and delusion. *Cognitive Neuropsychiatry* 15:14–37.

Kriegel, U. 2007. Self-consciousness. In *The Internet Encyclopedia of Philosophy*. http://www.iep.utm.edu/self-con/#SH5a.

Kriegel, U. 2009. *Subjective Consciousness*. New York: Oxford University Press.

Lane, T., and C. Liang. 2008. Higher-order thought and the problem of radical confabulation. *Southern Journal of Philosophy* 46:69–98.

Lane, T., and C. Liang. 2010. Mental ownership and higher-order thought. *Analysis* 70:496–501.

Lane, T., and C. Liang. 2011. Self-consciousness and immunity. *Journal of Philosophy* 108:78–99.

Langdon, R., and T. Bayne. 2010. Delusion and confabulation: Mistakes of perceiving, remembering, and believing. *Cognitive Neuropsychology* 15:319–345.

Levy, N. 2009. Self-deception without thought experiments. In *Delusions and Self-deception: Affective and Motivational Influences on Belief-Formation*, ed. T. Bayne and J. Fernández. Hove: Psychology Press.

Liang, C., and T. Lane. 2009. Higher-order thought and pathological self: The case of somatoparaphrenia. *Analysis* 69:661–668.

Maher, B. A. 1999. Anomalous experience in everyday life: Its significance for psychopathology. *Monist* 82:547–570.

McKay, R., R. Langdon, and M. Colheart. 2005. Sleights of mind: Delusions, defences, and self-deception. *Cognitive Neuropsychology* 10:305–326.

McKay, R., and M. Kinsbourne. 2010. Confabulation, delusion, and anosognosia: Motivational factors and false claims. *Cognitive Neuropsychology* 15:288–318.

Nikolinakos, D. 2004. Anosognosia and the unity of consciousness. *Philosophical Studies* 119:315–342.

Prigatano, G., ed. 2010. *The Study of Anosognosia*. New York: Oxford University Press.

Prosser, S., and F. Recanati, eds. 2012. *Immunity to Error through Misidentification: New Essays*. Cambridge: Cambridge University Press.

Radden, J. 2011. *On Delusion*. New York: Routledge.

Ramachandran, V. S. 1996. The evolutionary biology of self-deception, laughter, dreaming, and depression: Some clues from anosognosia. *Medical Hypotheses* 47: 347–362.

Rosenthal, D. 2005. *Consciousness and Mind*. New York: Oxford University Press.

Rosenthal, D. 2010. Consciousness, the self, and bodily location. *Analysis* 70: 270–276.

Rosenthal, D. 2012. Awareness and identification of self. In *Consciousness and the Self: New Essays*, ed. J. Liu and J. Perry. Cambridge, MA: Cambridge University Press.

Shoemaker, S. 1968. Self-reference and self-awareness. *Journal of Philosophy* 65: 555–567.

Sierra, M. 2009. *Depersonalization: A New Look at a Neglected Syndrome*. New York: Cambridge University Press.

Vallar, G., and R. Ronchi. 2009. Somatoparaphrenia: A body delusion: A review of the neuropsychological literature. *Experimental Brain Research* 192:533–551.

Wittgenstein, L. (1958) 1969. *The Blue and Brown Books*, 2nd ed. Oxford: Blackwell.

4 Consciousness, Action, and Pathologies of Agency

Myrto Mylopoulos

1 Introduction

We talk in a variety of ways about the property of being conscious. In some cases, we talk about a *person* being conscious ("creature consciousness"), as when we want to contrast one's current state with that of someone who is asleep, knocked out, or even in a coma. In others, we talk about mental states themselves being conscious ("state consciousness"), as when we attribute to someone a conscious belief, desire, emotion, or perception. And in yet further cases, we talk about being conscious *of* something ("transitive consciousness"), as when we want to indicate that someone is aware of or has in some way mentally registered an object or feature of their body or the environment (for the original discussion in the literature of these distinctions, see Rosenthal 1986, 2005, chap. 1).

This is all well and good. But it has been largely overlooked that we also talk of *actions* as being conscious or unconscious or as being performed consciously or unconsciously. This is an additional usage that differs from that which is present in cases of creature, state, and transitive consciousness and that merits further exploration and analysis.

When it comes to describing actions as conscious, or as consciously performed, one sometimes wants to indicate that the agent involved did something deliberately, as opposed to accidentally. For example, if someone steps in front of others in a line, we might say that they did so consciously in order to indicate that they did so on purpose and are, thus, to blame for their action. In this sense, doing something consciously is roughly synonymous with doing it intentionally.

In other cases, though—and perhaps more rarely—what one wishes to signal is that the agent involved, typically oneself, has a *subjective sense* of performing the action at the time that it is performed. The action is not something that remains outside the scope of one's awareness or attention or something that is experienced passively; rather, it is something that one experiences, and experiences *as one's own action*. In other words, one wishes to suggest that the individual has *agentive awareness* (Bayne and Pacherie 2007) or a *sense of agency* (Marcel 2003) for the action in question.

Central to this latter way of talking about actions as being performed consciously is an interest in the *phenomenology* of action or agency. The idea is that there is something it is like to perform an action—something it is like to exercise one's own bodily agency—that differs in interesting and important ways from what it is like for one's body to be moved passively.[1] As Horgan, Tienson, and Graham (2003, 323) put it: "We maintain that there is 'something it is like' to behave in a way that constitutes voluntary action, something phenomenologically distinctive that incorporates but goes beyond the phenomenology of one's own bodily motion."

This conviction has been widely echoed in cognitive psychology and neuroscience as well. For example, around the same time, Haggard and Johnson (2003, 83) remark that, "Voluntary actions, though generally neglected in psychology, have a distinctive phenomenology which can be studied both qualitatively and quantitatively." I wish to focus on action consciousness as it pertains to this subjective sense of acting.[2]

There has been much theorizing about action consciousness in this sense, focusing on the psychological mechanisms that underlie it (e.g., Wegner 2004, Pacherie 2008, Synofzik, Vosgerau, and Newen 2008, Carruthers 2012, Frith 2012), its representational content (e.g., Horgan, Tienson, and Graham 2003, Bayne and Levy 2006) and the kind of phenomenology— for example, sensory or cognitive—it involves (e.g., Bayne 2011, Horgan 2012, Mylopoulos 2015). Notably, though, such theorizing has proceeded independently of theorizing about consciousness in its other varieties. For instance, it is usually implicitly assumed that once one has a theory of action consciousness, it can be wedded comfortably with whatever theory of state consciousness one independently endorses. People working on action consciousness thus tend to stay neutral on whether higher-order theories (e.g., Rosenthal 1986, 2005, Carruthers 1996, Gennaro 1996, 2012), first-order theories (e.g., Dretske 1995, Block 2005), self-representational theories (e.g., Kriegel 2006), or attentional theories (e.g., Prinz 2012) of state consciousness—to name some of the main candidates out there—are correct. Similarly, seldom do those who theorize about state consciousness say anything explicitly about action consciousness or endorse any particular view of it.

But there is a useful way in which theorizing about state consciousness more generally can inform theorizing about action consciousness in particular: just as theories of state consciousness can be helpfully divided into higher-order and first-order theories, so too can theories of action consciousness. Higher-order theories of state consciousness accept what Rosenthal (2005, 4) calls the *transitivity principle*: mental states are conscious only if one is aware of them in some suitable way. First-order theories explicitly reject this principle (e.g., Dretske 1995). Similarly, then, I propose that *higher-order theories of action consciousness* accept an analogous transitivity principle, according to which an action is conscious only if one is aware, in some suitable way, of performing it. And I further propose that any theory that denies this may be classified as a *first-order theory of action consciousness*.[3]

In this chapter, I will work within this novel framework and make a case for higher-order theories of action consciousness. Of course, there are a number of dimensions along which a theory of action consciousness may be evaluated. The one that will take center stage in my discussion is the ability of the theory to help explain relevant pathological cases. These are cases in which action consciousness is in some way impaired, either by being absent when it would normally be present, or by being present when it would normally be absent. A complete and satisfactory theory of action consciousness ought to have something explanatory to say about why such breakdowns occur. So determining how first-order and higher-order views fare in this regard is a useful way of measuring their respective merits.

This chapter will be divided into three main parts. In the first, I describe the pathologies of action consciousness that are my main concern: (i) delusions of alien control in schizophrenia, (ii) anarchic hand syndrome, and (iii) utilization behavior. In the second part of the chapter, I argue that a first-order theory of action consciousness does not have the resources to help explain what is going on in these cases. In the third part, I show how a higher-order theory of action consciousness, by contrast, offers a more promising way forward. I will also relate such a theory to higher-order theories of state consciousness and show how core commitments of the higher-order framework can be comfortably extended to cover both mental states and actions. In doing so, I hope to begin some much-needed bridging between these two so-far independent streams of consciousness research.

2 Pathologies of Action Consciousness

Action consciousness breaks down in all sorts of surprising ways that have been well-documented in the clinical and experimental neuropsychological literature. Consider first so-called delusions of alien control in schizophrenia. These delusions are categorized as what researchers working on schizophrenia call *passivity experiences* (Frith, Blakemore, and Wolpert

2000). In general, passivity experiences involve disowning an action, mental event, or sensory experience, and, in many cases, attributing it to an external source. Perhaps one of the most well-known types of passivity experience is *thought insertion*, which involves auditory hallucinations that are experienced as coming from an outside source. For instance, one individual undergoing such hallucinations reported that "thoughts come into my mind from outer space" (Frith, Blakemore, and Wolpert 2000, 358).

In delusions of alien control, something similar happens, except that here schizophrenic individuals deny authorship of their bodily movements and report experiencing them passively, often attributing them to an outside agent. For example, one person suffering from such delusions remarked: "My grandfather hypnotized me and now he moves my foot up and down" (Frith et al. 2000, 358). Another individual insisted: "The force moved my lips. I began to speak. The words were made for me" (Mellors 1970, 18). Yet another individual, having just made an arm movement, explained: "I felt like an automaton, guided by a female spirit who had entered me during it" (Spence et al. 1997, 2001). These reports are rather striking, and especially so considering that, to the casual observer, the behavior in question seems indistinguishable from regular behavior in that it is, in many cases, complex and seemingly purposive.

Given the character of the bodily movements that schizophrenic individuals with delusions of alien control report as having an external source. One might naturally think that these individuals do not actually experience any disruptions with respect to action consciousness, but rather impairments in their belief systems, which cause them to erroneously attribute their movements to other agents despite experiencing them just as they would any of their regular actions. On this view, the impairment comes in at the level of belief rather than experience.

This picture does not fit well, however, with the two-factor model of delusion currently viewed as credible within cognitive neuropsychiatry. On this model, delusional beliefs are to be explained, in the first instance, by some antecedent impairment, most typically at the level of sensory or motor functioning (see Coltheart, Menzies, and Sutton 2010). The beliefs themselves are posited as abductive inferences on the part of the patient meant to explain the relevant impairment. It is reasonable to think that, in delusions of alien control, what needs explaining is the experience of moving passively, and that the delusional beliefs (e.g., attributing the bodily movements to an external source) are formed as a way of accounting for these experiences, albeit in ways that exhibit high degrees of irrationality. If so, then these individuals do not experience an intact sense of agency, but a marked absence of this sense.

Another pathological case that involves dramatic disruptions in action consciousness is *anarchic hand syndrome* (AHS).[4] This condition has been known to result from brain lesions in various areas of the cortex, including the supplementary motor area (SMA), the anterior corpus callosum (Della Sala 2005), and the right parietal lobe (Assal, Schwartz, and Vuilleumier 2007). These lesions cause individuals to perform sustained, goal-oriented bodily movements, all the while denying authorship or control over them. The movements of the "anarchic" hand are often triggered or driven by environmental stimuli, and in many cases, the hand plays out routine or habitual behavior. For example, in the case of one individual, JC, his affected hand "reached for light switches, repeatedly pressed buttons on the television remote control, and groped for his left hand or face during sleep" (Giovannetti, Buxbaum, Biran, and Chatterjee 2005, 77).

Sometimes an individual's affected hand will even behave at cross-purposes with the well-functioning limb and the conscious intentions of the individual. This is known as diagonistic apraxia (Biran et al. 2006). In a particularly vivid case of AHS with diagonistic apraxia, Banks et al. (1989) describe the following conflicting behaviors exhibited by one of their anarchic hand patients:

While playing checkers on one occasion, the left hand made a move he did not wish to make, and he corrected the move with the right hand; however, the left hand, to the patient's frustration, repeated the false move. On other occasions, he turned the pages of the book with one hand while the other tried to close it; he shaved with the right hand while the left one unzipped his jacket; he tried to soap a washcloth while the left hand kept putting the soap back in the dish; and he tried to open a closet with the right hand while the left one closed it. (Banks et al. 1989, 457)

People with AHS are unable to inhibit the movements of their anarchic limb except by indirect methods, such as using their other hand to stop it or sitting on top of it. Understandably, they experience great distress and frustration at their condition. Unlike schizophrenic individuals with delusions of control, however, those with AHS do not exhibit an irrational understanding of what is going on (Marcel 2003), nor do they attribute the movements of the affected limb to external agents—though they sometimes report that it is "as if" it has "a will of its own" (Marchetti and Della Sala 1998, Marcel 2003, Biran et al. 2006).

A closely related pathology, and the third one on which I will focus, is *utilization behavior* (UB). As with AHS, those with this condition—resulting from damage to the pre-SMA—exhibit repetitive, routine behavior that is strongly reactive to external stimuli. One patient, for instance, donned one pair of glasses after another as they were placed in front of him. Another drank several glasses of water consecutively, well past the point at which his thirst was quenched (Lhermitte 1983).

Though the behavior that is characteristic of UB is similar to that of AHS, the attitude that those with UB take toward their movements is notably different: they do not report distress or surprise at what they are doing, and they often confabulate if asked to explain their unusual behavior. Indeed, in the case of one individual whose *right* hand was afflicted with UB and whose *left* hand was afflicted with AHS, it was found that he was disturbed by the behavior of the latter, but not the former (Marcel 2003, see also Bayne and Pacherie 2007, for a useful discussion of the similarities and differences between AHS and UB).

What are we to make of these puzzling cases? They are all marked by an absence of action consciousness for bodily movements that seem from the third-person to be actions. Whether or not these movements truly *are* actions is not my interest here. While this is, of course, a valuable question to be pursued for its own sake, it is orthogonal to present concerns. This is because, even if the movements in question are *not* actions—according to our best theory of what actions are, whatever that may be—this would not *by itself* explain why they do not subjectively *seem* to be actions. Nor would this be explained if it turns out that they *are* actions, since we would be no clearer on what it is about engaging in action that contributes to a subjective *sense* of doing so.

A complete theory of action consciousness should have something helpful to say about these cases. I hasten to note, however, that the pathologies I have described in this section are complex, multifaceted, and far from being fully understood by theorists and clinicians alike. Quite likely, they are resistant to any general explanation of their underlying causes that is currently available to us, at least of the sort that could be laid out here. The following should be viewed, then, as an exploration of some possible *insights* or *research avenues* that we might pursue given a proper understanding of how action consciousness works in unperturbed cases. In the remainder of the chapter, then, I consider what explanatory strategies are available to first-order and higher-order theories of action consciousness, and conclude that higher-order theories offer a more promising way forward with respect to understanding pathologies of agency.

3   First-Order Theories of Action Consciousness and Pathologies of Agency

I propose that we understand first-order theories of action consciousness as being committed to both a negative and a positive thesis. The negative thesis is a denial of the transitivity principle for action consciousness: it is not the case that an action is conscious only if one is in some suitable way aware of performing it. The commitment to this negative thesis may be viewed as what separates first-order theories from higher-order theories of action consciousness.

The positive thesis, on the other hand, specifies how action consciousness *does* arise. I leave open the possibility here that action consciousness sometimes arises when no action is taking place and sometimes fails to arise when an action is taking place (*pace*, e.g., Gallagher 2007, 347). Still, it seems reasonable to work with the assumption that action consciousness *typically* accompanies actions and *typically* fails to accompany nonactions. I will stay fairly neutral on the metaphysics of action itself, but for the purposes of the present discussion, I will work within a loose causalist (e.g., Davidson [1963] 2001, Hornsby 1980, Brand 1984, Mele 1992) framework that views actions as bodily events that are suitably caused by an appropriate goal state or set of goal states (e.g., desires, reasons, intentions, or motor signals). So a natural proposal for the first-order theorist's positive thesis, and the one that will be my focus, holds that action consciousness is determined by some property that belongs to either the bodily movement itself or the relevant goal state associated with the action.

A first-order theory of action consciousness is thus committed to a conjunction of the negative thesis and the positive thesis just articulated.[5] For ease of exposition, I state this pair of theses as follows:

Negative Thesis: It is not the case that an action is conscious only if one is in some suitable way aware of performing it.

Positive Thesis: An action A is conscious in virtue of a property that belongs to either (i) the goal state that causes A, or (ii) the bodily movement associated with A.

The cases of pathology that I have discussed all involve bodily movements that seem from the outside to be actions but are not experienced as such. Presumably, the first-order theorist explains this by saying that the property responsible for action consciousness is absent in such cases. But then the first-order theorist faces the following question: What is the relevant property that the nonconscious "actions" of schizophrenic individuals with delusions of control, people with anarchic hand syndrome, and people with utilization behavior lack, but that conscious actions possess? First-order theorists must identify this property in order to make strides toward explaining the cases of pathology we have discussed. Let us dub this target property the *agentive quality*.

An inviting strategy here is to hold that the agentive quality in question is identical to some sensory quality (or qualities) of our bodily movements, as given by proprioception. Taking this route, the first-order theorist might identify the agentive quality with a type of kinesthetic sensation or with types of sensory qualities corresponding to the direction, force, or velocity of our bodily movements. Action consciousness would then amount to having a distinctive type of sensory (in this case proprioceptive) experience associated with a certain class of our bodily movements. If everything is going smoothly, presumably these sensory agentive experiences typically accompany bodily movements that are actions and typically do not accompany those that are not.

There is a simple, but I think insurmountable, challenge to this proposal. Recall that many of the disowned bodily movements in anarchic hand syndrome, utilization behavior, and delusions of control in schizophrenia are often described as being indistinguishable from the third-person from bodily movements that *are* experienced as actions. There is typically nothing in the bodily movements themselves, in isolation from the afflicted individual's reports, or their appropriateness in the present context, that indicates that something unusual is going on. Indeed, this is part of the reason why they lead to such theoretical puzzlement over the disavowals of the individuals that otherwise seem to be controlling their own behavior. But this, in turn, would seem to suggest that the disowned movements are identical—with respect to the relevant sensory qualities—to bodily movements that are subjectively experienced as actions. Thus, we cannot isolate any sensory quality of the bodily movement itself as the agentive quality that we seek, for we cannot on this basis distinguish conscious actions from nonconscious ones.

One may worry that this is too quick, at least as it applies to delusions of alien control in schizophrenia. After all, some argue that the proprioceptive experiences of schizophrenic individuals suffering from delusions lack a certain quality that typical proprioceptive experiences accompanying actions possess. More specifically, Chris Frith (1992, 2007) has proposed that proprioceptive experiences accompanying actions are sensorily *attenuated*, whereas passive movements, and those of schizophrenic individuals undergoing delusions of alien control, are not.

This attenuation may be viewed as a dampening of the subjective intensity of a sensory quality along one of its dimensions—for example, the loudness of an auditory quality. Frith offers that this attenuation is the result of *forward modeling*, which involves a predictive simulation of the bodily movements that will be generated by a given motor command in order to aid in the fine-grained, sensorimotor control of the bodily movement in question (see Wolpert, Ghahramani, and Jordan 1995, Wolpert and Miall 1996). When a forward model accurately predicts the ensuing bodily movement, the sensory properties of the bodily movement are attenuated. When the forward model prediction is absent, as in the case of passive movements, or not accurate enough, they are not.

The main line of evidence for this picture comes from a series of self-tickling studies, in which participants are asked to rate the "tickliness" and intensity of self-generated tactile stimuli compared with externally-generated tactile stimuli (Blakemore, Wolpert, and Frith 1998, 2000, Blakemore, Frith, and Wolpert 1999). It turns out that self-generated stimuli are rated on average as significantly less intense and tickly than externally-generated stimuli—in other words, people report experiencing the former as *attenuated* relative to the latter. This effect is thought to be the result of the forward model predicting the self-generated stimulus, since it is the result of the participant's motor command, but not the externally generated stimulus, since there is no motor command produced by the participant in that case, and so no forward model prediction is formed.

Importantly, such attenuation has *not* been found among schizophrenic individuals with delusions of alien control (Blakemore et al. 2000). So here we have a difference between the proprioceptive experiences of those with and without such delusions. The first-order theorist may therefore be tempted to say that the agentive quality that we are looking for is that of being a sensorily attenuated proprioceptive experience, since this property is present in typical cases of action, preceded as they are by accurate forward models, but absent for bodily movements involved in delusions of alien control, as suggested by the fact that schizophrenic individuals undergoing such delusions do not report sensory attenuation.

Along these lines, regarding the schizophrenic individual PH, Frith offers the following analysis:

I believe we can now achieve some understanding of PH's experiences because of what we have discovered about the brain. In our normal state we are hardly aware of the sensations that occur whenever we move. This is because our brain can predict these sensations and suppress our awareness of them. But what would it be like if something went wrong with the prediction and we became aware of the sensations? Normally I am only aware of the sensations when someone else moves my hand. Such a brain abnormality could explain why PH feels as if her arm is being moved by someone else. She is abnormally aware of her bodily sensations when she moves her hand. For her it really does feel as if someone else were moving her hand. (Frith 2007, 109)

I have discussed the various shortcomings of the sensory attenuation proposal in detail elsewhere (Mylopoulos 2012, Mylopoulos 2015). I briefly review these here. First, although the self-tickling studies do suggest that sensory attenuation occurs for the sensory *effects* of our bodily movements, we actually have no clear evidence that sensory attenuation occurs for proprioceptive experiences *themselves*, which is what is needed to get this type of account off the ground.

Second, many hold that the phenomenology of agency is supposed to be the basis for our agentive beliefs—that is, beliefs that we are currently doing something (e.g., Bayne and Pacherie 2007, Bermúdez 2010, Synofzik, Vosgerau, and Newen 2008). So my belief that I am typing on my computer is in some way based on my *experience* of typing on my computer, just as a belief that one is in pain is in some way based on one's *experience* of pain. There is some evidence, however, that agentive judgments drive sensory attenuation, rather than the other way around. For example, when people believe that they are causing a sensory effect to occur, they experience the effect as significantly more attenuated than when they falsely believe that it is the result of an external source (Desantis, Weiss, Schutz-Bosbach, and Waszak 2012).

A related third worry is that sensory attenuation seems to grossly underdetermine the agentive beliefs that it would be tasked with supporting. These beliefs typically describe actions at a highly conceptual level—for example, walking to the park or waving to a friend. But dampened proprioceptive experiences likely do not have sufficiently conceptually rich contents themselves in order to be the basis for beliefs with such contents.

Fourth, there may be other explanations, appealing to attentional deficits, available for why schizophrenic individuals with delusions of alien control do not experience sensory attenuation (Gold et al. 2007, Carter et al. 2010). If so, then this lack of attenuation may not be related in any way to deficits in action consciousness, though perhaps they share a common cause.

Finally, within the present context, this proposal is severely limited, as it does not help to explain the lack of action consciousness in AHS or UB. There is no empirical evidence that sensory attenuation occurs here, and no theoretical reason to think it does, given that the controlled nature of these movements at the sensorimotor level suggests that they are preceded by accurate forward-model predictions.

In light of all this, I propose that we look to the natural alternative version of the first-order account, on which the agentive quality is affixed to the goal state that causes the action, rather than the bodily movement itself. Adopting this type of view, it is open to the first-order theorist to argue that the disowned bodily movements of anarchic hand patients, schizophrenic individuals with delusions of control, and those with utilization behavior are not caused by the right kind of goal state, that is, the kind that possesses the agentive quality.

John Searle (1983) may be viewed as defending this type of first-order account in chapter 3 of his influential book *Intentionality*.[6] Searle relates action consciousness, or what he calls the *experience of acting*, to what he calls *intentions in action*. Intentions in action, according to Searle, are the causal mental antecedents of bodily movements involved in action.[7] These are propositional attitude states that are present-directed and specify action that is to be immediately performed. Searle contrasts this class of intentions with what he calls *prior intentions*, which are the more familiar intentions for future action and are expressed linguistically as "I will A" or "I am going to A." Searle posits intentions in action for the purpose of explaining, among other things, the character of spontaneous actions—for example, suddenly getting up out of one's seat while ruminating on a philosophical problem. Such actions, according to Searle, are not preceded by intentions in action—conscious or nonconscious—and yet they seem to have an intentional character to them. This is accounted for, on Searle's view, by the presence of an intention in action. He urges that "all intentional actions have intentions in action but not all intentional actions have prior intentions" (Searle 1983, 85).

An experience of acting, according to Searle, *just is* a conscious intention in action. This experience has phenomenal character and intentional content, which is simply the intentional content of the conscious intention in action that constitutes this experience. So the agentive quality that distinguishes cases of conscious action from cases of nonconscious action is, on this view, the property of being consciously intended—being caused by a conscious intention in action. This is what provides one with a subjective sense of acting.

Could such a view help to adequately account for why action consciousness breaks down in the cases I have been considering? In order to explain such cases, a proponent of this view might further appeal to a *dual control model* (cf. Norman and Shallice 1986, Humphreys and Riddoch 2003, Perner 2003, Pacherie 2008), on which there is a distinction between two levels of action control: a higher level of *intentional control* and a lower level of *sensorimotor control*.

A thumbnail sketch of these two levels of control will be useful here. At the level of sensorimotor control, action is guided primarily by way of motor commands, which specify fine-grained, detailed aspects of bodily movement, such as the precise angle of limb trajectory and the precise force with which the body will move. At the level of intentional control, bodily movements are guided primarily by way of an agent's intentions. They serve to conceptualize the bodily movement being performed—for example, getting milk from the fridge—and interact closely with an agent's practical beliefs and desires, as well as other relevant intentions, to help to ensure that the movement is going smoothly. In many, though not all, cases, these two types of control interact in rich ways. The intentions in action that guide a bodily movement at the level of intentional control will, at least typically, trigger relevant motor commands in the service of the goal that they specify.

There are several questions left open here concerning, among other things, the precise representational format and content of intentions and motor commands, how exactly they interface, and the circumstances under which they do. These questions remain largely unresolved, both from a theoretical and empirical standpoint (for some relevant work in this area, see Pacherie 2011, Butterfill and Sinigaglia 2012). But for the purposes of the view I am considering, these outstanding issues need not be settled; all that is required is that we are able to distinguish between these two types of agentive control.

Applying this distinction to the pathological cases we have been discussing, the first-order theorist may wish to say that, though the bodily movements exhibited by these individuals are initiated and guided by motor commands at the level of sensorimotor control, they are not in addition guided by intentions in action at the level of intentional control. And since, on this view, an action is conscious in virtue of being consciously intended by an intention in action, if such intentions are not involved in the sensorimotor control that governs the disowned bodily movements involved in pathological cases, this explains why these are not conscious actions.

This view does have an attractive explanation to offer when it comes to understanding what is going on in AHS and UB. It does seem more likely that the bodily movements characteristic of these conditions are *not* guided by intentions than that they *are*. The reason for this is that the bodily movements characteristic of such conditions are typically not rationally integrated into the agent's psychology at the time they are carried out. Many of the movements in question are characterized as "aimless" and "wandering," and often they involve playing out routine behaviors that are unrelated to the agent's present goals. Indeed, as mentioned, in some cases of AHS, the movements are at cross-purposes with the reported intentions of the agent.

In response, one might insist that the behavior exhibited by AHS and UB individuals is indeed guided by intentions, albeit nonconscious ones. These individuals, one may reason, are simply not aware of their intentions in the right way in order to be able to report on them. But we would be mistaken, one might urge, to conclude on this basis that the movements involved in AHS and UB are guided exclusively by motor commands rather than intentions. As evidence for this, one might cite certain cases where it is plausible that an intention is operative in guiding the relevant behavior involved in AHS or UB. Consider, in this spirit, the following description of an AHS individual, Mrs. GP:

One evening we took our patient, Mrs GP, to dinner with her family. We were discussing the implication of her medical condition for her and her relatives, when, out of the blue and much to her dismay, her left hand took some leftover fish-bones and put them into her mouth. A little later, while she was begging it not to embarrass her any more, her mischievous hand grabbed the ice-cream that her brother was licking. Her right hand immediately intervened to put things in place and as a result of the fighting the dessert dropped on the floor. She apologised profusely for this behaviour that she attributed to her hand's disobedience. Indeed she claimed that her hand had a mind of its own and often did whatever "pleased it." (Della Sala 2005, 606)

Though Mrs. GP expresses embarrassment at the behavior of her anarchic hand, perhaps it is not entirely implausible that her behavior is guided by her intentions. Perhaps she is the victim of conflicting intentions; she wants to be polite at the table, but she also has a nonconscious desire to eat the ice cream and so forms an infelicitous nonconscious intention to take it from her brother's hand.

While perhaps tempting, this does not seem to be an adequate account of the psychology underlying Mrs. GP's behavior. For one thing, Mrs. GP does not exhibit global impairments in decision-making or social interactions, and neither do individuals with AHS more generally. But it would be in violation of highly salient rational and social norms if someone were to even form the intentions that are attributed to Mrs. GP in this interpretation, let alone act on them. In addition, though it may be reasonable to suppose that Mrs. GP desires her brother's ice cream, attributing to her a desire to eat leftover fish bones is clearly more problematic. The same holds for attributing a desire to wear multiple pairs of eyeglasses, as in the case of the individual with UB described earlier.

It is much more likely that the pathological behavior in question is not guided by intentions at all, but unfolds entirely at the level of sensorimotor control via motor commands that are activated by nearby objects. Indeed, this suggestion fits well with a key marker of anarchic hand movements as being "disproportionately reactive to external environmental stimuli" (Biran, Giovannetti, Buxbaum, and Chatterjee 2006, 563). Again, such behavior is not well-integrated into the psychology of the agent, as one would expect if it were driven by intentions at the level of intentional control. And if it is not, then the first-order account we are considering may have a reasonable explanation for why action consciousness is absent.

In addition, this type of first-order account may have at least something promising to say about schizophrenic individuals with delusions of alien control. Consider the following remarks from Frith (2005), who suggests that the behavior of schizophrenic individuals during such delusions *is* intended:

This is revealed clearly in a study by Sean Spence in which such patients were asked to move a joystick in four different directions at random (Spence et al., 1997). The patients were able to perform this task normally. They made the movements at the correct time and the sequences of movements were as random as those of the controls. And yet the patients reported that their movements were being controlled by outside forces. These patients were making the movements they intended to make since they were successfully following the instructions of the experimenter. Furthermore they knew that the movements were intended since they did not try to stop the movements or correct them. Patients with delusions of control do not behave as if their actions were unintended. (Frith 2005, 756)

Suppose that we take this analysis at face value and grant that the behavior exhibited during delusions of alien control, though disowned, is nonetheless guided by intentions. On the account we are considering, the reason that the actions are disowned is that these intentions are not conscious, and so there is no experience of acting as a result.

Though all this would seem to amount to some progress in understanding pathologies of agency, there are reasons to reject the first-order account of action consciousness more generally. The problem is that consciously intending does not seem to be sufficient for action consciousness. Recall that on higher-order views of *state* consciousness, what it is for a mental state to be conscious is for one to be suitably aware of oneself as being in that state. But, just like beliefs, desires, and other propositional attitude states, intentions exhibit both mental attitude and intentional content, and when one is aware of one's intention, thereby consciously intending, one is aware of each of these components as well. If I am aware of my belief that it is sunny outside, I am aware not simply of some content, that is, that it is sunny outside, but that I *believe* this content. The same can be said of intentions, including intentions in action. I am aware not simply of *some action*, that is, the one that is specified in the content of the intention, but that I *intend* to do it.

But if so, then this account of action consciousness is problematic. It would seem to be an account of *intending* consciously, rather than *acting* consciously. There is nothing here to explain the subjective sense that one is acting rather than intending to do so. This point emerges most clearly within the framework of higher-order accounts of state consciousness, since, according to such accounts, one must be aware of a mental state, including its mental attitude, in order for it to be conscious. But it may be appreciated even if one adopts a first-order view of state consciousness. For on such views, too, if a mental state is conscious, it is so in virtue of both its mental attitude and its content, assuming it has both. And if so, then the same difficulty arises, in that consciously intending to perform an action does not seem to be sufficient for having a subjective sense of performing it—that is, for the action in question to be conscious.

There is, in addition to the above consideration, empirical evidence that strongly suggests that intentions, in particular those that are the causal mental antecedents of action—like Searle's intentions in action—become conscious earlier than actions do. And if so, then they cannot be sufficient for action consciousness, as required on the present view. In their classic study, Libet, Gleason, Wright, and Pearl (1983) set out to determine the relationship between one's intending and initiating an action and one's awareness thereof. Libet et al. asked six participants each to perform a series of simple actions—forty in total. More specifically, they were instructed in each trial to perform a "quick, abrupt flexion of the fingers and/or wrist" (625) with their right hand, at a time of their own choosing. They were encouraged not to decide in advance on a time at which to perform the act, but rather "to let the urge to act appear on its own at any time without any preplanning or concentration on when to act" (625). Participants were seated facing a specialized clock, around which a dot would revolve every 2.56 seconds. They were instructed to report the time at which they first became aware of deciding or having the "urge" to move based on the position of the dot on the clock ("W judgment"). They were also asked to report the time at which they were aware that they had "actually moved" (627) ("M judgment"). At the same time, they were hooked up to an electroencephalogram (EEG), which measured their brain activity during these tasks.

The results were that the participants reported being aware of their decision to act an average of 200 ms prior to the onset of the movement. But they were aware of *actually* moving, as indicated by their M-judgments, an average of *86 ms* prior to the movement. In other words, they had an experience of acting on average 114 ms *after* consciously deciding to act. If what it is for an action to be conscious is for it to be consciously intended, however, then one would expect that participants would, on average, report being aware of a decision to act, that is, an intention in action, and of acting, at approximately the same time. (For a more recent demonstration of the temporal gap between W-judgment and M-judgment, see Haggard & Eimer 1999.)

None of this bodes well for a first-order account of action consciousness. I therefore conclude that first-order accounts of action consciousness are inadequate for explaining what is going on in cases of anarchic hand syndrome, utilization behavior, and delusions of alien control in schizophrenia, as well as these more general problems. I now turn to showing how we can make some progress in understanding these conditions if we reflect on them from within a higher-order framework of action consciousness.

4   Higher-Order Theories of Action Consciousness and Pathologies of Agency

On a higher-order view of action consciousness, an action is conscious only if one is aware in some suitable way of performing it. This view has the benefit of preserving the commonsense intuition that drives the transitivity principle for higher-order views of state consciousness. Just as it seems correct to say that if one is in no way whatsoever aware of being in a mental state, then that mental state is not a conscious mental state, it seems correct to say that if one is in no way whatsoever aware of performing an action, then that action is not conscious.

But a higher-order view of action consciousness is faced with a prima facie difficulty: in some cases in which action consciousness is undeniably absent, the agent *does* seem to be aware of herself as performing the action. For example, individuals with AHS say things like, "of course I know it's me, it just doesn't *feel* like me" (as reported in Marcel 2003, 79). And, of course, in the anecdote previously related, Mrs. GP is highly distressed by the behavior of her "anarchic" limb at the dinner table—she is hardly unaware of it. This suggests that individuals with AHS are aware of themselves as performing these actions but nonetheless lack a subjective sense of authoring them, which is the central feature of action consciousness we are trying to understand. How can a higher-order view of action consciousness, given its central commitment to the extended transitivity principle, accommodate such cases and offer an adequate explanation of the pathologies we have been considering?

In order to deal with this challenging question, we must recognize some constraints on the type of higher-order awareness required in order for an action to be conscious. It will not do to simply be aware of an action in any way in order for that action to be conscious. Notice that the transitivity principle, both for state and action consciousness, requires that one be aware *in a suitable way* of performing an action or of being in a particular mental state. In order to flesh this out further, we can take a cue from higher-order theories of state consciousness and, in particular, Rosenthal's (2005) higher-order thought (HOT) theory. On Rosenthal's view, in order for a mental state to be conscious, one must be aware of oneself as being in that state by way of a second, higher-order state. But not just any higher-order state is suitable for playing this role. In particular, it must be the case that the higher-order state in question is *subjectively unmediated*. In other words, the individual must not have the subjective sense that she comes to be aware of the first-order state on the basis of conscious observation or on the basis of drawing some inference.

As Rosenthal (2005) notes, this helps to explain why it is that we do not view a state as conscious if we become aware of it by consciously observing what we do or say, or by relying on someone else's observation of our behavior. For example, if someone points out to us that we have been abrupt with them lately and avoided their company where possible, and reports to us their belief, on this basis, that we are angry with them, we may take their testimony at face value and also arrive at the same conclusion. But our actual emotional state of anger may nonetheless remain wholly nonconscious. It might not *seem* to us as though we are angry, despite coming to form the belief, on the basis of this third-person testimony, that we in fact are (cf. Rosenthal 2005, 310).

We can extend this important insight to apply to action consciousness as well. Doing so, the central thesis of a higher-order view of action consciousness then reads as follows: one acts consciously only if one is aware of oneself as acting in a subjectively unmediated way. It will not do to consciously observe oneself as acting and *on this basis* be aware of oneself as acting—the awareness in question must not seem to rely on conscious observation or inference.

This dovetails nicely with an independent line of thought that is popular within action theory concerning the *knowledge* we have of the intentional actions that we perform. Following Anscombe (1966), many have considered it plausible that when we act intentionally, we know what we are doing without observation—a form of what Anscombe terms *practical knowledge* (for some helpful recent discussions of practical knowledge, see also Paul 2009 and Schwenkler 2012). For instance, if I am intentionally watering the flowers in my garden, I know, according to Anscombe's thesis, that I am doing so without observation. I do not need to look and see that I am holding a garden hose over some daisies and, on the basis of this observation, infer that I am watering the flowers. This is something I know independently.[8] Anscombe's epistemic thesis is thought to capture the subjectively unmediated character that our awareness of our own actions seems to possess. On the present view, this subjective immediacy is a feature of what it is for an action to be conscious.

Relating all of this back to the pathologies of agency we have been discussing, the present proposal suggests that what is going on in AHS is that these individuals are aware that they are acting, but *only on the basis* of conscious observation of what they are doing—not in the subjectively unmediated way required for action consciousness. And the alienation they feel from their behavior is due to the necessity of conscious observation for knowing what they are doing. In an early paper, Arthur Danto and Sydney Morgenbesser (1963) articulate this idea nicely:

If one day I should notice that my arm was rising and lowering, and then realize that, if I had not noticed, I would not have known it was doing this, it would be for me a terrifying experience, a sign that I had lost contact with part of myself, that my arm had become an alien entity. (441)

This notion of "losing contact" with part of themselves is central to the phenomenology that those with AHS and other action-related pathologies experience. On the current proposal, this is neatly explained by their not having any awareness of the actions in question independently of consciously observing themselves performing them.

There is certainly some evidence that this is what is happening in AHS. Consider again the case of JC, who acquired AHS at the age of fifty-six after suffering a stroke. JC's anarchic limb executes well-coordinated movements at the level of sensorimotor control, such as reaching and grasping for objects, turning taps on and off, pressing keys, and so on. But JC is not aware of the actions as his own, reporting that the affected hand "has a mind of its own" and "wants to be the boss" (Biran, Giovannetti, Buxbaum, and Chatterjee 2006, 567).

There is good reason to think that JC may only be aware of his anarchic movements when he is consciously observing them. This seems to be what is happening in the following incident, for example, in which JC, busy with a different task and therefore not observing his "anarchic" limb, is described as being unaware of the limb's movements:

For example, in one of the testing sessions, [JC] was asked to turn pages of a magazine with his left hand. As he did this (without any difficulty), the examiner lightly touched his right fingers with a pen. The right [afflicted] hand reached towards and persisted in following the pen continuously as it was slowly moved away from the hand. ... This reaching continued until the limb was a foot above the table. JC was unaware of his arm moving on that side. (Biran, Giovannetti, Buxbaum, and Chatterjee 2006, 567)

It would seem here that unless JC *sees* what his affected hand is doing, he is not aware of its movements. More evidence is needed to fully support this hypothesis, but JC's case already lends some credence to the thought that individuals with AHS are not aware of their movements unless they consciously observe them, and that subjectively unmediated awareness is required for action consciousness to arise.

If the higher-order awareness that is central to action consciousness does not arise on the basis of conscious observation and inference, then on what basis *does* it arise? A natural response is that it arises, not on the basis of consciously observing what one's body is doing, but on the basis of the intentions that drive those bodily movements.[9] Here it will be useful to distinguish once more, along with Searle and others, between future-directed prior intentions and present-directed intentions in action.[10]

Clearly, prior intentions are not the source of action consciousness. An intention to do something this afternoon, next week, or even next year will not contribute to my being conscious of doing something *now*. Instead, we must focus on the present-directed cousins of prior intentions: intentions in action. In the course of evaluating first-order theories, I rejected the view that conscious intentions in action are solely responsible for action consciousness, as Searle maintains. But intentions in action arguably do have *some* important role to play here.

We can get a handle on what this role is by considering the kind of relationship intentions in action have with the actions that they produce. It is often said that the road to hell is paved with good intentions. It is probably also true, though less often remarked upon, that the road to heaven is paved with bad ones. This is because people often form prior intentions to perform actions sometime in the future, but then fail to act on them for a variety of reasons. Importantly, though, neither the road to heaven nor the road to hell is paved with *intentions in action*. If one forms an intention in action to do something, that action is initiated straightaway. It is only in rare cases of, for example, temporary paralysis or external interference that an intention in action will not cause the very action that it specifies. Intentions in action have a strong, reliable causal connection with the actions that they produce.

Given this strong connection, it is reasonable to suppose that when one forms an intention in action to A, not only does one A straightaway, but one is disposed to automatically infer that one is A-ing. After all, one would lose valuable time in waiting to confirm that one is A-ing by way of observation before forming the corresponding belief that one is A-ing. One can instead apply the safe default belief, acquired over the course of several successful intentions in action to A, that one's intention in action will initiate the action it specifies.

This basic supposition is also able to provide some insight as to the *type* of higher-order awareness involved in action consciousness. Higher-order views of state consciousness are divided with respect to whether the higher-order state in question is a thought (e.g., Rosenthal 2005) or a perception-like state (e.g., Lycan 2004). The most natural candidate for the type of mental state resulting from an inference on the basis of an intention in action to A is a *thought* to the effect that one is A-ing. Moreover, since I am supposing that the inference is automatic, it is also reasonable to suppose that the inference remains nonconscious, as other automatic processes do. This means that the thought that results is subjectively unmediated. So we have here the view that action consciousness is a matter of having the thought that one is A-ing on the basis of an intention in action to A. And the model on offer here is a higher-order model insofar as the thoughts that are taken to be the sources of action consciousness make one aware of oneself as performing an action, thus reflecting a commitment to the transitivity principle for action consciousness.

On such a model, there is a clear explanation, or at least the beginnings of one, for why those with AHS rely on conscious observation to be aware of their anarchic behavior. For, if the proposal I considered in the previous section is accurate, then AHS individuals do not form intentions in action for the movements of their anarchic hand—they are carried out entirely at the level of sensorimotor control. And if so, then they are unable to form the subjectively unmediated, intention-based thoughts by virtue of which an action is conscious. The same explanation could be extended to cases of UB, though a further explanation would be needed in order to understand why it is that they confabulate in the way that they do—an additional challenge that the first-order theorist faces as well.

When it comes to accounting for what is going on in the case of schizophrenic individuals with delusions of alien control, matters are a bit more complicated. For one, as mentioned, there is some evidence that the behavior from which they are alienated is, in fact, driven by intentions in action—just not conscious ones. But then it is not clear why they do not form subjectively unmediated thoughts on this basis to the effect that they are performing certain actions. One possibility is that intentions in action need to be conscious in order for one to be disposed to infer the relevant thoughts. Perhaps, if one is not aware that one intends to A now—making the relevant intention in action conscious—then one will not be disposed to infer that one is A-ing. Another possibility is that schizophrenic individuals with delusions of alien control are globally impaired in making inferences, thus blocking this particular inference—whether or not the relevant intention is conscious. Indeed, such an impairment would seem to be reflected in many of their reports attributing their actions to fantastical entities (e.g., spirits) or highly unlikely sources (e.g., their grandfather). Of course, more filling in is needed here, but at the very least, the higher-order model I have proposed offers clear pathways to explore.

Still, even if the higher-order model seems to provide a promising approach to explaining pathologies of action consciousness, one might worry that such a view is a nonstarter, since it cannot explain the *phenomenal character* that so many take to be central to action consciousness. Phenomenology is typically associated with states that possess a sensory (e.g., pains, visual sensations) or affective (e.g., emotions, urges) component and thoughts do not seem to have either of these (though see Pitt 2004).

Once again, an important parallel may be drawn here between Rosenthal's (2005) HOT theory of state consciousness and the theory of action consciousness proposed here. On HOT theory, phenomenal consciousness is a matter of mental appearances. In other words, it is a matter of how one's HOTs represent one's mental life as being. In particular, phenomenal consciousness is determined by the content of one's HOT, so what it is like for one to be in a certain mental state is determined by what mental state one's HOT represents oneself as being in. For example, if I have a HOT to the effect that I am in pain, then what it's like for me is to be in pain. This is how it *seems* to me that things currently are.

On the present proposal, the phenomenal character of action consciousness can likewise be accounted for by the content of a HOT—in this case, one that represents oneself as acting. So if I have a thought to the effect that I am walking, then it *seems* to me that I am walking, and I have a subjective sense of doing so. Moreover, the higher-order thoughts being posited here always involve first-personal reference to oneself as the agent of the action that they are about. This provides a tidy explanation of what many take to be a central aspect of the phenomenology of agency, namely the phenomenology of *self as source* (cf. Bayne 2006, Horgan, Tienson, and Graham 2003, Horgan 2012) or the explicit sense that one is, oneself, the author of the action in question.

5   Conclusion

In this chapter, I have proposed a novel framework for understanding theories of action consciousness, which parallels that within which theories of state consciousness are developed. In particular, I have drawn a distinction between first-order and higher-order theories of action consciousness, and I have argued that the latter have significant advantages over the former when it comes to offering promising ways forward with respect to explaining certain pathologies of agency. In addition, I have gestured at ways in which higher-order theories of action consciousness and higher-order theories of state consciousness can be seen as converging on some general truths about consciousness applied across a variety of phenomena.

Acknowledgments

I am very grateful to Rocco Gennaro and Timothy Lane for helpful comments on earlier drafts of this chapter and to David Rosenthal for many valuable discussions on some of the main ideas presented here.

Notes

1. I focus here on bodily actions and set aside mental actions, such as imagining a sunset on a beach or calculating gratuity on a restaurant bill. Whether or not the following treatment of bodily actions can be generalized to apply to mental actions as well is an important issue that deserves further treatment, but it is outside the scope of my present focus (for a discussion of the sense of agency for mental action, see Proust 2010).

2. I will not argue in this chapter for the claim that there *is* a phenomenology of agency in the sense described. I will take this is a starting assumption and work forward from there. So what I say here may be interpreted as conditional on accepting that there is such a phenomenology in the first place.

3. The distinction I draw here may relate in interesting ways to Gallagher's (2007) distinction between notions of action consciousness (or the sense of agency) that emphasize a "reflective" kind of awareness, involving higher-order states, versus those that emphasize a "pre-reflective" awareness, involving only first-order states. It is unclear, however, whether Gallagher allows, as I wish to do here, that "reflective" awareness may be responsible for the phenomenal character of action consciousness, rather than restricting this role to "pre-reflective" awareness.

4. Note that sometimes anarchic hand syndrome is erroneously referred to as "alien hand syndrome" (e.g., Assal, Schwartz, and Vuilleumier 2007). But the latter refers

to a disruption in the *sense of ownership* over one's limb—that is, individuals deny that the limb in question belongs to them. Those suffering from anarchic hand syndrome, by contrast, do not deny ownership of the relevant limb, but instead lack a sense of agency for its movements (cf. Marchetti and Della Sala 1998).

5. In characterizing first-order accounts in this way, I exclude so-called *matching* accounts of action consciousness, on which an action is conscious when there is a *match* in content between an appropriate goal state and an appropriate sensory experience of the action in question (e.g., Wegner 2004, Pacherie 2008, Bayne 2011). This property of registering a match does not seem to be a property of either the goal state or the bodily movement involved in the action. Indeed it is often unclear, on such accounts, to what state or event this property *does* attach and whether or not these accounts require some higher-order awareness of the successful match. For this reason, I set aside discussion of such accounts in order to focus on views that fit more clearly within the framework I wish to presently explore.

6. For other views that arguably fall in this camp, see Ginet 1990, Marcel 2003, Peacocke 2003, and Mandik 2010.

7. On Searle's view they are, in fact, part of the action itself, with an action having two components: the bodily movement and the intention in action. But this detail of his account need not concern us here.

8. Of course, Anscombe's thesis should not be taken to entail that we know *every* aspect of our intentional actions without observation, but that we at least know without observation the aspects under which they are intentional. For example, suppose that in the process of watering the flowers, I am also unintentionally drowning a family of tiny ants. The thesis does not entail that I know this unintentional aspect of my action without observation.

9. For an alternative proposal, see Stephens and Graham 2000.

10. Action theorists commonly draw a distinction between future-directed and present-directed intentions. For further examples, see Brand 1984, Bratman 1987, Mele 1992, and Pacherie 2008.

References

Anscombe, G. E. M. 1966. *Intention*, 2nd ed. Cambridge, MA: Harvard University Press.

Assal, F., S. Schwartz, and P. Vuilleumier. 2007. Moving with or without will: Functional neural correlates of alien hand syndrome. *Annals of Neurology* 62:301–306.

Banks, G., P. Short, J. Martinez, R. Latchaw, G. Ratcliff, and F. Boller. 1989. The alien hand syndrome: Clinical and postmortem findings. *Archives of Neurology* 46: 456–459.

Bayne, T. 2006. Phenomenology and the feeling of doing: Wegner on the conscious will. In *Does Consciousness Cause Behavior?* ed. W. Pockett and S. Gallagher. Cambridge, MA: MIT Press.

Bayne, T. 2011. The sense of agency. In *The Senses*, ed. F. Macpherson. Oxford: Oxford University Press.

Bayne, T., and N. Levy. 2006. The feeling of doing: Deconstructing the phenomenology of agency. In *Disorders of Volition*, ed. N. Sebanz and W. Prinz. Cambridge, MA: MIT Press.

Bayne, T., and E. Pacherie. 2007. Narrators and comparators: The architecture of agentive self-awareness. *Synthese* 159:475–491.

Bermúdez, J. 2010. Action and awareness of agency: Comments on Christopher Frith. *Pragmatics & Cognition* 18:584–596.

Biran, I., T. Giovannetti, L. Buxbaum, and A. Chatterjee. 2006. The alien hand syndrome: What makes the alien hand alien? *Cognitive Neuropsychology* 23:563–582.

Blakemore, S., C. Frith, and D. Wolpert. 1999. Spatio-temporal prediction modulates the perception of self-produced stimuli. *Journal of Cognitive Neuroscience* 11:551–559.

Blakemore, S., S. Goodbody, and D. Wolpert. 1998. Predicting the consequences of our own actions: The role of sensorimotor context estimation. *Journal of Neuroscience* 18:7511–7518.

Blakemore, S., J. Smith, R. Steel, C. Johnstone, and C. Frith. 2000. The perception of self-produced sensory stimuli in patients with auditory hallucinations and passivity experiences: Evidence for a breakdown in self-monitoring. *Psychological Medicine* 30:1131–1139.

Blakemore, S., D. Wolpert, and C. Frith. 1998. Central cancellation of self-produced tickle sensation. *Nature Neuroscience* 1:635–640.

Blakemore, S., D. Wolpert, and C. Frith. 2000. Why can't you tickle yourself? *Neuroreport* 11:R11–R16.

Block, N. 2005. Two neural correlates of consciousness. *Trends in Cognitive Sciences* 9:46–52.

Brand, M. 1984. *Intending and Acting*. Cambridge, MA: MIT Press.

Bratman, M. 1987. *Intention, Plans, and Practical Reason*. Cambridge, MA: Cambridge University Press.

Butterfill, S., and C. Sinigaglia. 2012. Intention and motor representation in purposive action. *Philosophy and Phenomenological Research* 88:119–145.

Carruthers, G. 2012. The case for the comparator model as an explanation of the sense of agency and its breakdowns. *Consciousness and Cognition* 21:30–45.

Carruthers, P. 1996. *Language, Thought, and Consciousness*. Cambridge, MA: Cambridge University Press.

Carter, J. D., J. Bizzell, C. Kim, C. Bellion, K. Carpenter, G. Dichter, and A. Belger. 2010. Attention deficits in schizophrenia—preliminary evidence of dissociable transient and sustained deficits. *Schizophrenia Research* 122:104–112.

Coltheart, M., P. Menzies, and J. Sutton. 2010. Abductive inference and delusional belief. *Cognitive Neuropsychiatry* 15:261–287.

Danto, A., and S. Morgenbesser. 1963. What we can do. *Journal of Philosophy* 60:435–445.

Daprati, E., N. Franck, N. Georgieff, J. Proust, E. Pacherie, J. Dalery, and M. Jeannerod. 1997. Looking for the agent: An investigation into consciousness of action and self-consciousness in schizophrenic patients. *Cognition* 65:71–86.

Davidson, D. (1963) 2001. Actions, reasons, and causes. In *Essays on Actions and Events*. Oxford: Oxford University Press.

Della Sala, S. 2005. The anarchic hand. *Psychologist* 18:606–609.

Desantis, A., C. Weiss, S. Schutz-Bosbach, and F. Waszak. 2012. Believing and perceiving: authorship belief modulates sensory attenuation. *PLoS ONE* 7:e37959.

Dretske, F. 1995. *Naturalizing the Mind*. Cambridge, MA: MIT Press.

Frith, C. 1992. *The Cognitive Neuropsychology of Schizophrenia*. East Sussex: Erlbaum.

Frith, C. 2005. The self in action: Lessons from delusions of control. *Consciousness and Cognition* 14:752–770.

Frith, C. 2007. *Making Up the Mind: How the Brain Creates Our Mental World*. Oxford: Blackwell.

Frith, C. 2012. Explaining delusions of control: The comparator model 20 years on. *Consciousness and Cognition* 21:52–54.

Frith, C., S. Blakemore, and D. Wolpert. 2000. Explaining the symptoms of schizophrenia: Abnormalities in the awareness of action. *Brain Research Reviews* 31: 357–363.

Gallagher, S. 2007. The natural philosophy of agency. *Philosophy Compass* 2: 347–357.

Gennaro, R. 1996. *Consciousness and Self-Consciousness*. Amsterdam: John Benjamins.

Gennaro, R. 2012. *The Consciousness Paradox: Consciousness, Concepts, and Higher-Order Thoughts*. Cambridge, MA: MIT Press.

Ginet, C. 1990. *On Action*. Cambridge, MA: Cambridge University Press.

Giovannetti, T., L. Buxbaum, I. Biran, and A. Chatterjee. 2005. Reduced endogenous control in alien hand syndrome: Evidence from naturalistic action. *Neuropsychologia* 43:75–88.

Gold, J., R. Fuller, B. Robinson, E. Braun, and S. Luck. 2007. Impaired top-down control of visual search in schizophrenia. *Schizophrenia Research* 94:148–155.

Haggard, P., and M. Eimer. 1999. On the relation between brain potentials and the awareness of voluntary movements. *Experimental Brain Research* 126 (1): 128–133.

Haggard, P., and H. Johnson. 2003. Experiences of voluntary action. *Journal of Consciousness Studies* 10 (9–10): 72–84.

Horgan, T. 2012. From agentive phenomenology to cognitive phenomenology: A guide for the perplexed. In *Cognitive Phenomenology*, ed. T. Bayne and M. Montague. New York: Oxford University Press.

Horgan, T., J. Tienson, and G. Graham. 2003. The phenomenology of first-person agency. In *Physicalism and Mental Causation*, ed. S. Walter and H. Heinz-Dieter. Imprint Academic.

Hornsby, J. 1980. *Actions*. London: Routledge & Kegan Paul.

Humphreys, G., and M. Riddoch. 2003. Fractionating the intentional control of behaviour: A neuropsychological analysis. In *Agency and Self-Awareness: Issues in Philosophy and Psychology*, ed. J. Roessler and N. Eilan. Oxford: Oxford University Press.

Kriegel, U. 2006. The same-order monitoring theory of consciousness. In *Self-Representational Approaches to Consciousness*, ed. U. Kriegel and K. Williford. Cambridge, MA: MIT Press.

Lhermitte, F. 1983. Utilization behavior and its relation to lesions of the frontal lobes. *Brain* 106:237–255.

Libet, B., C. Gleason, E. Wright, and D. Pearl. 1983. Time of conscious intention to act in relation to onset of cerebral activity (readiness-potential)—The unconscious initiation of a freely voluntary act. *Brain* 106 (Pt 3): 623–642.

Lycan, W. 2004. The superiority of HOP to HOT. In *Higher-Order Theories of Consciousness*, ed. R. Gennaro. Amsterdam: John Benjamins.

Mandik, P. 2010. Control consciousness. *Topics in Cognitive Science* 2:643–657.

Marcel, A. 2003. The sense of agency: awareness and ownership of action. In *Agency and Self-Awareness: Issues in Philosophy and Psychology*, ed. J. Roessler and N. Eilan. Oxford: Oxford University Press.

Marchetti, C., and S. Della Sala. 1998. Disentangling the alien and anarchic hand. *Cognitive Neuropsychiatry* 3:191–207.

Mele, A. 1992. *Springs of Action*. New York: Oxford University Press.

Mellors, C. 1970. First-rank symptoms of schizophrenia. *British Journal of Psychiatry* 117:15–23.

Mylopoulos, M. 2012. Evaluating the case for low-level accounts of agentive awareness. *Philosophical Topics* 40:103–127.

Mylopoulos, M. 2015. Agentive awareness is not sensory awareness. *Philosophical Studies* 172:761–780.

Norman, D., and T. Shallice. 1986. Attention to action: Willed and automatic control of behavior. In *Consciousness and Self-Regulation: Advances in Research and Theory*, ed. R. Davidson, R. Schwartz, and D. Shapiro. New York: Plenum Press.

Pacherie, E. 2008. The phenomenology of action: A conceptual framework. *Cognition* 107:179–217.

Pacherie, E. 2011. Nonconceptual representations for action and the limits of intentional control. *Social Psychology* 42:67–73.

Paul, S. 2009. How we know what we're doing. *Philosophers' Imprint* 9:1–24.

Peacocke, C. 2003. Action: Awareness, ownership, and knowledge. In *Agency and Self-Awareness: Issues in Philosophy and Psychology*, ed. J. Roessler and N. Eilan. Oxford: Oxford University Press.

Perner, J. 2003. Dual control and the causal theory of action: The case of non-intentional action. In *Agency and Self-Awareness: Issues in Philosophy and Psychology*, ed. J. Roessler and N. Eilan. Oxford: Oxford University Press.

Pitt, D. 2004. The phenomenology of cognition or what is it like to think that *p*? *Philosophy and Phenomenological Research* 69:1–36.

Prinz, J. 2012. *The Conscious Brain: How Attention Engenders Experience*. New York: Oxford University Press.

Proust, J. 2010. Is there a sense of agency for thought? In *Mental Action*, ed. L. O'Brien and M. Soteriou. Oxford: Oxford University Press.

Rosenthal, D. M. 1986. Two concepts of consciousness. *Philosophical Studies* 49: 329–359.

Rosenthal, D. M. 2005. *Consciousness and Mind*. New York: Oxford University Press.

Schwenkler, J. 2012. Non-observational knowledge of action. *Philosophy Compass* 7:731–740.

Searle, J. 1983. *Intentionality: An Essay in the Philosophy of Mind*. Cambridge, MA: Cambridge University Press.

Spence, S., D. Brooks, S. Hirsch, P. Liddle, J. Meehan, and P. Grasby. 1997. A PET study of voluntary movement in schizophrenic patients experiencing passivity phenomena (delusions of alien control). *Brain* 120:1997–2011.

Stephens, G. L., and G. Graham. 2000. *When Self-Consciousness Creaks: Alien Voices and Inserted Thoughts*. Cambridge, MA: MIT Press.

Synofzik, M., G. Vosgerau, and A. Newen. 2008. Beyond the comparator model: A multifactorial two-step account of agency. *Consciousness and Cognition* 17:219–239.

Wegner, D. 2004. Precis of *The Illusion of Conscious Will*. *Behavioral and Brain Sciences* 27:649–659, discussion 659–692.

Wolpert, D., Z. Ghahramani, and M. Jordan. 1995. An internal model for sensorimotor integration. *Science* 269:1880–1882.

Wolpert, D., and R. Miall. 1996. Forward models for physiological motor control. *Neural Networks* 9:1265–1279.

5 Self, Belonging, and Conscious Experience: A Critique of Subjectivity Theories of Consciousness

Timothy Lane

Nothing alien happens to us, but only what has long been our own.
—Rilke (1954, 50)

1 Introduction

Subjectivity theories of consciousness take self-reference, somehow construed, as essential to having conscious experience. These theories differ with respect to how many levels they posit and to whether self-reference is conscious or not. But all treat self-referencing as a process that transpires at the personal level, rather than at the subpersonal level, the level of mechanism.

Working with conceptual resources afforded by preexisting theories of consciousness that take self-reference to be essential, several attempts have been made to explain seemingly anomalous cases, especially instances of alien experience. These experiences are distinctive precisely because self-referencing is explicitly denied by the only person able to report them: those who experience them deny that certain actions, mental states, or body parts belong to self. The relevant actions, mental states, or body parts are sometimes attributed to someone or something other than self, and sometimes they are just described as not belonging to self. But all are *referred away from self.*

The cases under discussion here include somatoparaphrenia, schizophrenia, depersonalization, anarchic hand syndrome, and utilization behavior; the theories employed are higher-order thought, wide intrinsicality, and self-representational. I argue that each of these attempts at explaining or explaining away the anomalies fails. Along the way, since each of these theories seeks at least compatibility with science, I sketch experimental approaches that could be used to adduce support for my position or, indeed, for the positions of theorists with whom I disagree.

In a concluding section, I first identify two presuppositions shared by all of the theorists considered here and argue that both are either erroneous or misleading. Second, I call attention to divergent paths adopted when attempting to explain alienation experiences: some theorists choose to add a mental ingredient, and others prefer to subtract one. I argue that alienation from experience, action, or body parts could result from either addition or subtraction, and that the two can be incorporated within a comprehensive explanatory framework. Finally, I suggest that this comprehensive framework would require self-referencing of a sort, but self-referencing that occurs solely on the level of mechanism, or the subpersonal level. In adumbrating some features of this "subpersonal self," I suggest that there might be one respect in which it is prior to conscious experience.

2   Subjectivity Theories of Consciousness, Higher-Order Thought, and Belonging

Gennaro (this volume) raises a host of concerns about my interpretation of experimental data concerning some tactile experiences reported by a particular somatoparaphrenia patient.[1] Briefly, the patient (FB) reported that her left hand belonged to her niece, and that she (FB) could not feel tactile sensations in that, "her niece's" hand. In a series of controlled experiments, however, FB did report recovery of tactile sensation when the left hand was touched after FB had been told that the experimenter was about to touch her niece's hand, if in fact the left hand was touched. On catch trials, when the hand was not in fact touched, irrespective of whether the experimenter indicated intent to touch FB's left hand or "her niece's" hand, FB reported feeling nothing.

My description and interpretation of that case is part of a general critique and rejection of what Billon and Kriegel (this volume) refer to as "subjectivity theories of consciousness," or SP theories, because all are committed to a *subjectivity principle*. According to this principle, mental states can exhibit phenomenal consciousness only if they involve self-reference. Billon and Kriegel advocate a strong version of this principle, holding that it is metaphysically impossible for any phenomenally conscious state to be instantiated in the absence of subjectivity, the experience of "for-me-ness." Gennaro (2012, 299–300) advocates a weaker version, holding that it is only necessary for there to be an unconscious higher-order thought with a self-referential component.[2] But all advocates of an SP theory take self-reference to be a sine qua non.

The SP theory that concerns Gennaro is Rosenthal's (2005) higher-order thought theory of consciousness (HOT).[3] Indeed, Mylopoulos (this volume) is also principally concerned with HOT. According to HOT theory, first-order mental states are conscious only if they are targeted by HOTs with the content, "I am in a certain state." The reference to "I," understood as the owner of the state, is "unavoidable" (Rosenthal 2005, 342, 347). This necessity claim implies that "being conscious of a state as belonging to someone other than oneself would plainly not make it a conscious state" (Rosenthal 2005, 342). It is in this context that I invoked the case of FB, because it appears that she is only conscious of certain tactile states when those states are *experienced as belonging to someone other than herself,* namely, her niece.[4]

Gennaro argues that somatoparaphrenia does not constitute a challenge to HOT; Billon and Kriegel argue that it poses no challenge for SP theories in general. In crafting their arguments, they do refer to one fact that I agree to be noncontentious: thus far, published studies of somatoparaphrenia include no patient denials that reportable sensations belong to self. Emphasis is invariably placed on denial of limb ownership (e.g., Romano et al. 2014, 1216, table 2). But the point that is relevant to HOT or SP theories in general does not concern somatoparaphrenia per se; instead, it is specific to the experimental data reported by Bottini et al. (2002). In the next paragraph, I direct attention to what I take to be the critical issue, the issue that constitutes a challenge to SP theories of any stripe.[5]

Recall that, in FB's case, somatoparaphrenia was accompanied by tactile extinction, but she recovered the ability "to perceive tactile stimuli, *provided that these were referred to someone else's body*" (Bottini et al. 2002, 251).[6] During the experiment that demonstrated FB's ability to recover from tactile extinction, she was blindfolded. While blindfolded, she was advised that the examiner would touch *her* left hand. Whenever this was done, FB reported that she felt no tactile sensations. When advised that the examiner was about to touch *her niece's* hand, however, upon being touched, FB reported feeling tactile sensations. In order to ensure experiment reliability, along with the blindfold and other controls, catch trials were included, trials for which FB was led to expect touches that were not forthcoming. These trials were evenly distributed across three verbal warnings—I am going to touch your right hand, your left hand, and your niece's hand—and were administered in four sessions, two on one day, two on the next. In not even one of the thirty-six catch trials, nine each per session, did FB respond incorrectly; namely, if no touch was applied, FB reported that she felt nothing. Accordingly, we encounter an explanatory problem—why did FB report feeling the touch when primed to expect that her niece would be touched, but not when primed to expect that her left hand would be touched?

Because the causal histories of reporting and not reporting tactile sensation are nearly the same—differing only *in whom* FB expected to be touched—sensible contrastive questions that enable elicitation of causal differences can be asked (cf. Lipton 1993). In view of the controls that were in place, it seems the crucial causal difference concerned *who* was to be touched. And only when FB expected that her niece would be touched did she report tactile sensation. In other words, it seems that FB was only conscious of those sensations when she expected the touches to be applied to *someone else's* hand. It is this apparent expectation that the touch causes conscious states only when the touch is expected to be applied to someone other than self that seems to constitute a challenge for HOT and SP theories in general.

One among Gennaro's (this vol.) explicit concerns is that FB might be reporting a belief or a judgment rather than an experience. Since HOT theory allows for the possibility that HOTs can misrepresent first-order sensory states that they are about,[7] a HOT theorist could argue that FB is reporting a belief or judgment that misrepresents what FB experiences. In this context, since somatoparaphrenia is classified as a delusion, Gennaro raises two concerns about how to interpret delusional reports: one pertains to the endorsement/explanationist distinction. On the endorsement account of delusion, patients are endorsing as veridical the content of unusual experiences; on the explanationist, they are attempting to explain unusual experiences. Gennaro's second concern relates to the distinction between "spontaneous" and "provoked" confabulations, the latter only occurring when patients are questioned directly. Regarding provoked confabulations, Gennaro then proceeds to emphasize FB's initial elusiveness when asked how she could report touches on someone else's hand. Gennaro argues that the endorsement interpretation of FB's reports is more likely appropriate only after the delusional belief has taken firm hold. Before the delusion has taken firm hold, a "provoked explanationist" account should be favored. The implication of Gennaro's interpretation seems to be that at least at first, when FB is responding to touches, it is more likely the case that she is explaining something odd, rather than endorsing as veridical the content of her experiences. If this is the case, then it would weaken the force of my criticism of HOT.

Gennaro's explication of FB's case, however, appears not to address the explanatory problem posed by the experimental results. Among other things, "provoked" is ambiguous: it is the case that in the experimental context, FB was asked to report touches. So, one could say that she was provoked. But Gennaro's emphasis is not here; instead, he is concerned with the provoking that occurred later, when FB was queried as to how she was able to report touches on someone else's hand. Her simple responses were not problematic; one might even say they were spontaneous. It was only when she was asked to *explain* those spontaneous responses that FB seemed elusive.

Consider as well that Gennaro—along with Rosenthal, Mylopoulos, Billon, and Kriegel—all emphasize the importance of spontaneous, unmediated awareness. Gennaro accurately reports that this is essential to Rosenthal's construal of HOT theory.[8] Indeed, FB's reports of tactile sensation when her niece's hand was actually touched appear to be instances of spontaneous, unmediated awareness.

In short, it seems that Gennaro's argument turns on an ambiguity and a red herring: a simple response concerning whether a hand was touched is not the type of provoking that Gennaro needs, and emphasizing FB's elusiveness when she was asked to explain how such touches could be reported distracts us from the explanatory contrast problem I've articulated. FB appears to have done nothing more than affirm the occurrence of tactile sensations in some instances while denying their occurrence in others. The only difference between the two cases was in how she was primed: your left hand or your niece's hand. In view of the controls that were in place, as well as the apparent absence of mediation, FB seems to merely be endorsing that a tactile experience was instantiated. That such an instantiation might be unusual and in need of explanation results from the prompting to explain how such a thing could occur. In other words, FB is reporting a sensation, not a belief. If FB was reporting a belief, she should also have done that during the "your niece" catch trials, because she would have been unable to distinguish touch from its absence. But recovery from tactile extinction only occurred (i) when she was primed in the right way and (ii) when she was actually touched.

There is, however, a glaring gap in the data, one that Gennaro, as well as Billon and Kriegel, correctly point out. Bottini et al. did not explicitly inquire as to whether the tactile sensations belonged to FB or to her niece (cf. Feinberg and Venneri 2014). My interpretation of the data is an inference to the best explanation: I am making the case for a conditional claim— if FB feels those sensations belong to her niece, that experience would best explain her ability to recover from tactile extinction only when primed in the right way and only when actually touched. But reasoning in this way obviously does not establish that FB has alienation experiences of the type described by Billon, Kriegel, and Gennaro.

Although I believe this issue might be resolvable on conceptual grounds, it should be emphasized that Rosenthal regards the HOT theory as an empirical theory that is testable (e.g., Lau and Rosenthal 2011). Likewise, Gennaro (2012, 269–302) argues that his "wide intrinsicality view" (WIV) of HOT can inform a neurophysiological research program; Kriegel (2009, 233–265) argues that his self-representational theory can answer some of the principal scientific questions of consciousness. Indeed, when first responding to Rosenthal (Lane and Liang 2010, 500), I acknowledged the desirability of beginning to monitor somatoparaphrenia patients and conducting a refined set of probes in order to more adequately address worries of the type expressed by Gennaro, Billon, and Kriegel. Here I propose a more formal attempt to operationalize HOT and treat somatoparaphrenia as a test case for SP Theories.

The relevant issue concerns what to make of FB's differential responses to passive touch.[9] Because I endorse Billon and Kriegel's view that depersonalization is also a potential counterexample to SP theories, a natural place to look for refined probes of FB-like patients is *The Cambridge Depersonalization Scale* (Sierra 2009, 161–168). Question 22 on that scale typifies the type of item that could easily be adapted to serve as a suitable probe: "When a part of my body hurts, I feel so detached from the pain that it feels as if it was 'somebody else's pain.'" But I believe we can do much more than systematize probes of subjective report. A pincers maneuver, whereby data on subjective report and data from objective measures converge, is called for. As for the latter, the means for differentiating self from nonself are already available.

For two decades, evidence for the existence of a mirror neuron system in the motor domain has been accumulating (Kilner and Lemon 2013). Whereas some neurons modulate their activity only when a person observes the actions of others, but not when self performs those same actions, a special class of neurons modulate their activity both when executing an action and when observing that action performed by someone else. In effect, what we see mirrors what we feel. Of more direct relevance to the case of FB, mirroring has recently been identified for the experience of, and the observation of, touch: observation of someone else being touched induces activation of neural circuitry in both the primary (SI) and secondary (SII) somatosensory cortices (Schaefer et al. 2009).

The sensory overlap between what is seen happening to others and what is experienced in self presents an experimental opportunity. It is not the overlap per se that matters, it is the opportunity afforded by mirroring experiments to distinguish between self and nonself. Consider, for example, the findings of Keysers et al. (2004): in an fMRI study of the relationship between the observation of touch in others and the experience of touch in self, they discovered that the SII was activated both when participants were touched and when they observed someone else being touched. SI, on the other hand, was just weakly activated when observing touch. The authors interpret their findings thus (2004, 342): "It might be that SII activation in the context of weak SI activation only evokes a concept of touch that is relatively detached from our own immediate bodily experience."

If we were to apply findings of this type to an investigation of subsequent FB-like recoveries of tactile sensation in alien limbs, in order to seek confirmation of my hypothesis that patients only became conscious of certain tactile states when those states are experienced as belonging to someone other than themselves, we would need to proceed in two stages: first, we would attempt to replicate the Bottini et al. experiment, including the blindfold, the catch trials, and other controls. If we were to succeed at that, including successful recovery of tactile sensation on being primed to expect that *someone other than oneself* was to be touched, we should proceed to stage two. Here we could dispense with the blindfold and the catch trials. Instead, having in stage one already confirmed that actual contact and the right prime are necessary for recovery of sensation, we would use fMRI to compare patient (a) reactions when primed to expect that oneself would be touched with (b) reactions when primed to expect that someone other than oneself would be touched.[10] Since we would now allow the patient to observe what was being done, based upon the mirroring effects described above, we would expect overlap between experiencing touch in self and seeing touch applied to someone else. If my working hypothesis is correct, I would expect that when priming to expect someone else will be touched enables recovery of tactile sensation, we will observe SII activation in the context of weak SI activation. In other words, the patient's experience is that of observing someone else being touched, not of experiencing touch for him- or herself.

My claim is not that this would settle the issue. Rather, my intent—both here and in the remainder of this chapter—is to reorient the debate concerning HOT and all other SP theories, situating them squarely in an experimental context, since I believe we have already entered an era when significant aspects of SP theories are empirically tractable. We have amassed sufficient evidence concerning many types of alien experience, have developed novel experimental methods that enable teasing apart *self* and *nonself* experiences, and have developed technologies that enable application of those methods to both healthy and patient populations. Progress toward settling disagreements regarding how best to explain what I have elsewhere referred to as problems of belonging (Lane 2014, 54–56) can be made in the laboratory.

As regards FB-like cases, the hypothesis and approach indicated here are not sufficient, but vicarious somatosensory activation has been explored using other technologies as well, such as EEG (Bufalari et al. 2007), magnetoencephalography (Avikainen et al. 2002), and transcranial magnetic stimulation (Bolognini et al. 2011). Moreover, subregions within SI and SII that differentially contribute to distinguishing self from nonself experiences (Keysers et al. 2010) and trait differences that affect responsiveness to observed touch (Schaefer et al. 2012) have already been identified. In sum, an experimental platform from which sophisticated probes of FB-like cases can be launched already exists.

3 A "Something Extra" Self-Representational Hypothesis of Alienation

In their survey of a select set of alienation experiences—schizophrenia, somatoparaphrenia, and depersonalization—when reflecting on the challenge that these pose for SP theories, Billon and Kriegel (this vol.) consider the possibility that the phenomenal difference between alien and nonalien states could either involve the *addition* or the *subtraction* of a phenomenal feature. In building a defense of SP, they aspire to show that alienation experiences are compatible with their preferred theory of phenomenal consciousness, a theory that is distinctive in at least two ways: first, unlike the HOT theory, here conscious states are taken to be conscious because these mental states target themselves. In a word, this is a self-representational position. Second, they emphasize that subjects *experience* these states as belonging to self: that is, awareness of a state as belonging to self "does show up in the subject's overall phenomenology."

They observe that the most widely favored subtraction, or "something missing," position, is that patients possess thoughts (in the case of thought-insertion) that they did not *author*. On this view then, *belonging* and *agency* dissociate: subjects may have thoughts despite lacking a sense of agency for them (Gallagher 2000). But Billon and Kriegel proceed to object that, even for healthy subjects, many thoughts running through our minds come unbidden or feel intrusive, without causing us to experience those thoughts as distinctively alien (cf. Bayne 2010, 156–162, Billon 2013, 296–302, Lane 2012, 279–280). Therefore, it seems that the "something missing" view is explanatorily inadequate.

Motivated by this worry about the "something missing" view, they propose a "something extra" hypothesis of alienation experiences. For example, in the case of schizophrenic thought insertions, an inserted thought instantiates many properties of a normal thought[11] *plus* it instantiates an extra phenomenal property—it *feels* inserted. They begin defense of their position by distinguishing phenomenal consciousness—the object of their concern—from "reflective" consciousness, a distinction that they acknowledge to be similar to Block's distinction between phenomenal and "access" consciousness (Block 2007, 166–178, cf. Billon 2013, 305–306). In effect, what Billon and Kriegel suggest is that their version of SP theory concerns phenomenal consciousness, and alienation worries can be explained as relevant only to reflective, or access, consciousness. Billon (2013, 307) has written of such patients that they have reflective awareness of "their inserted thoughts, but … lack phenomenality and subjectivity altogether."

On the assumption that Billon and Kriegel's distinction is in most important respects similar to Block's, it is worthwhile to consider the latter's original example of access dissociated from phenomenal consciousness, blindsight (Block 2007, 172–173). Blindsight patients, despite suffering from cortical blindness, are able to make accurate forced choices about things presented to those visual fields for which they claim to have no visual experiences. Although blindsight patients apparently have the relevant unconscious "perceptual or quasi-perceptual states," they seem to lack both phenomenal and access consciousness. Block claims, however, that perhaps there could be "super-blindsighters" who learn to prompt themselves, such that they would guess without being told to do so. Super-blindsighters then would have access (or reflective) consciousness without having phenomenal consciousness. In other words, they would "just know," despite not having visual experiences, rather in the way that people can just know time or direction without having any relevant conscious experiences.

Let us return to consideration of Billon and Kriegel: they argue that alienation experiences occur when a first-order, nonphenomenal, alien mental state occurs in simultaneity with a second-order, nonalien, phenomenal state that represents the first-order state. The second-order state is claimed to represent the first-order state as belonging to self, albeit without rendering the latter phenomenally conscious.[12] In this way, SP might be saved because the mental state that exhibits phenomenal consciousness also exhibits belonging, while the state that does not exhibit belonging is assigned to a distinct category of consciousness, one that is accessed but nonphenomenal.[13]

In order to cast this in less abstract terms, they propose a thought experiment: imagine that, on awakening one morning, you experience tinnitus. Over time, what was once a meaningless ringing in the ears begins to sound like a voice, a voice that expresses repressed, unconscious states. Within the plotline of this thought experiment, it develops that you eventually realize a neuroscientist has implanted a device in your brain that monitors repressed states and translates them into phenomenally conscious states; the auditory hallucinations symptomatic of schizophrenia are taken to be one example of translated results. Accordingly, if you are in the presence of someone you have reason to dislike, albeit without being consciously aware of the dislike, the monitor might detect a first-order repressed state that it expresses with the rich auditory phenomenology of an inner voice, such as "Oh, I hate him." Billon and Kriegel further claim that although the reflected-on states belong to you, you experience them as alien.[14]

The first concern about this explanatory framework is that it is ad hoc for advocates of a self-representative view to invoke second-order thoughts that somehow translate first-order thoughts into phenomenally conscious states, without making those first-order states phenomenally conscious. Second, one of Billon and Kriegel's goals is to explain the phenomena while taking patient reports more or less at face value, but it is not clear that the reflective-consciousness argument achieves this goal. If the nonphenomenal first-order state is represented by the second-order phenomenal state as belonging to self, then wherefrom comes the experience that the voices one hears are alien?[15] Perhaps the idea is that the alien experience is explainable as owing to the repressed nature of the unconscious state. But if that is the idea, the conjectured relationship between repression and alienation must be explicated, and that would not be easy, because although repressed thoughts or the processes of repression can become conscious, there is no evidence to suggest that such thoughts or processes are thereby experienced as alien (cf. Boag 2010).

Since on this view the first-order state is nonphenomenal (intrinsically), and since it is represented as belonging to the person who experiences the auditory hallucinations, the alien dimension seems to be lost from the subjective experience. SP's metaphysical commitment to "for-me-ness" as appearing in a subject's overall phenomenology can perhaps be defended in this way, but then it is not clear that patient reports of their phenomenology are being taken at face value. In other words, the reflective-consciousness view might help explain how the auditory hallucination "Oh, I hate him" can be experienced as being for-me; it is not clear, however, in what respect this framework helps to explain how a nonphenomenal state represented by the auditory hallucination can be explained, if we are committed to taking seriously patient reports that these voices seem alien.[16] One way of expressing this worry is that it seems a something extra has been added to the explanans; meanwhile, something has been subtracted from the explanandum.

Nevertheless, since Billon and Kriegel acknowledge that their reflective/phenomenal distinction is similar to Block's access/phenomenal distinction, and since efforts have been made to identify the neural correlates of these two types of consciousness (Block 2005), it should be possible to adduce empirical evidence to assess the neural plausibility of their hypothesis. In particular, some progress has been made with respect to the neural correlates of visual consciousness (Block 2005, 47–48); evidence suggests that the neural basis of *access* involves activation of the superior parietal and the dorsolateral prefrontal cortices. For example, binocular rivalry occurs when two distinct patterns are shown, one to each eye of a participant, in these bi-stable perception experiments. Because the two patterns are so different, the brain does not fuse them; instead, a rivalry ensues. Subjects see one pattern for a few seconds; then the other, for a few seconds; after that, the visual experience shifts back again. Subject reports of conscious contents correlate with activation in these frontal and parietal areas.

The details of bi-stable perception need not detain us here, and it must be admitted that much work remains to be done before one can assert with confidence that the neural correlates of any given instantiation of access consciousness have been identified. But experimental work carried out to date suggests a critical role for the frontoparietal network. A starting point then in the search to seek empirical confirmation of the Billon-Kriegel framework would be evidence of fronto-parietal activity in the absence of phenomenal consciousness. This seems to be a reasonable expectation, at least on the assumption that not all first-order mental states instantiated within schizophrenics are represented by second-order states. And, because the Billon and Kriegel thought experiment concerns first-order states that are repressed, if we take repression as paradigmatic, it is necessarily the case that most first-order states are never expressed on a phenomenal level (cf. Boag 2010, 174), irrespective of whether the relevant phenomenology is extrinsic or intrinsic.

The problem is that not only is there no evidence of fronto-parietal activity in the absence of phenomenal consciousness, but most neuroscientific studies show conscious awareness of an event requires recruitment of widespread brain activation. Frontal and parietal areas, in particular, are implicated (e.g., Baars 2007). In other words, even though it may be conceptually possible for access to occur without phenomenal consciousness, there is nothing to suggest that it is empirically possible.[17] On the contrary, it seems unlikely, at least, that is, if the nonexistence of super-blindsight can be regarded as instructive. If, on the other hand, the suggestion is that the relevant second-order states are intrinsically wedded to the first-order states represented, then we would need some account of why and how these second-order states sometimes occur.

Taking the repression thought experiment as a literal expression of the main idea, the crux of the issue is that reflective- or access- consciousness seems to implicate fronto-parietal activity, but this pattern of activity seems to play no distinctive role in repression. What evidence there is concerning repressed impulses, thoughts, or desires does not implicate fronto-parietal activity (Berlin 2011). We can, however, infer that the amygdala plays an important role in repression (Berlin 2011, 15), and separate evidence suggests that hyperactivation of receptive language areas in the left temporal lobe mediates auditory verbal hallucinations (Hugdahl et al. 2012).[18] If we consider the Billon-Kriegel hypothesis against this backdrop, it would seem that the repressed first-order state must somehow involve the amygdala, and the translation of that state must somehow involve the left temporal lobe. But if these regions are the ones that we can, with some measure of confidence, claim to mediate repression and hallucination, it remains unclear how the seemingly essential fronto-parietal activity could be assimilated to explanation of alien experience.

In sum, three principal worries append to the reflective-consciousness hypothesis as it applies to first-rank schizophrenic symptoms. First, it is ad hoc. In Ptolemaic fashion it adds an ingredient—one that carries a not inconsiderable amount of conceptual baggage—to the self-representational theory of consciousness solely in order to account for a phenomenon that self-representational theory itself is unable to explain. Unfortunately, unlike Ptolemy's epicycles, the something extra here seems not to increase our explanatory leverage. Second, by failing to specify how repression is related to alienation, it seems to have omitted the phenomenon that is in need of explanation. Although the conceptual footwork might save the theory, the cost seems to have been a sacrifice of the phenomenon that stands in need of explanation. And, third, the hypothesis seems to lack neural plausibility. Just as there is no empirical evidence to suggest that Block's super-blindsight is ever instantiated, so too there is no empirical evidence to suggest that the neural substrates of reflective and phenomenal consciousness ever dissociate or interact in the requisite way.

So this strategy seems not to ease the explanatory burden of accounting for schizophrenia's first-rank symptoms. But might it help with other types of alienation? Billon and Kriegel suggest that the reflective-consciousness hypothesis can be extended to depersonalization. Indeed, they argue that it might work even better here, because "some depersonalized patients explicitly affirm that their alien states are unconscious even though they are conscious *of* them." And it is in fact the case that some patients describe their experiences in such terms.

But as Billon and Kriegel observe, the feeling that one's "emotional phenomenology is blunted or absent" is a *far more common* symptom of depersonalization. It seems these symptoms of depersonalization are mediated by "fronto-limbic suppression" (Sierra 2009, 146): that is, the amygdala, the anterior insula, and perhaps other limbic areas are suppressed due to abnormal prefrontal regulatory activity. Not only is this suppression hypothesis supported by abundant experimental evidence, it would also help explain most of depersonalization's symptoms.

Nevertheless, the symptom that is of most concern to Billon and Kriegel, however, does seem to be consistent with their reflective-consciousness hypothesis, so it warrants close examination. Recall that, according to their hypothesis, it can be the case that "alien states are unconscious even though (patients) are conscious *of* them" (this vol.). Bearing this in mind, take note of the patient's descriptions—"I suddenly wonder: is it really me here? Is it really me walking?" This is followed by what they regard as a highly significant passage: "Then I make enormous efforts in order to apply my consciousness to this unconsciousness ... in order to realize that I am making the walking movements." Is this truly a case wherein the patient has access to a nonconscious state, somewhat like a super-blindsighter, perhaps the equivalent of forcing oneself to guess?

First, take note that the patient's description concerns the act of walking. Second, further note that currently the most influential theory of depersonalization is the "two-neural-network" model (Sierra 2009, 146). The first network is the fronto-limbic suppression network described above. The second network involves parietal regions that seem to mediate the experience of embodiment and agency. For example, elevated activation in the angular gyrus and decreased activity in the posterior insula have been observed in patients who report the absence of agentive feelings. Those patients who exhibit decreased activity in the posterior insula report so striking an absence of agentive feeling that when they move it seems "they are watching the movements of another person."

Now once again consider (i) the hypothesis that "alien states are unconscious even though (patients) are conscious *of* them" along with (ii) the patient who, while walking, wonders whether it is really self who is walking, and who must exert strenuous effort in order to be certain that it is in fact self. It appears to be the case that what troubles this patient is the *loss* of agency. My suggestion here is that this case is adequately explained by the second component of the two-neural-network model. Naturally, were we to encounter a patient who described symptoms in these terms, in order to confirm my hypothesis, we would want to check angular gyrus and posterior insula activity. But if the *absence* of agency is the critical factor here, then the Billon and Kriegel attempt at developing a "something extra" explanation fails.

It might appear to be the case that now I am omitting something important from the explanandum, to wit—the patient's effort "to apply my consciousness to this unconsciousness." But this omission is only apparent. For quotidian instances of action, I see no reason to presuppose that a conscious agentive state is instantiated (Lane 2014, 64–69).[19] On this characterization then, one could still say that the patient is conscious of something unconscious, at least in the sense that the patient is aware that something is amiss, an awareness that precipitates inferring the absence of a typically unconscious ingredient. Therefore, we can still take the patient's description at face value, but the hypothesis is markedly different than that of Billon and Kriegel. Here I am not positing a reflective- or access- state that is somehow independent of a phenomenal state. Instead, I am suggesting that there are agentive mental states (whether conscious or not), and that these can go missing when the angular gyrus exhibits elevated activity and the posterior insula, decreased activity. This interpretation might even be a bit closer to Block's example of access- without phenomenal- consciousness: there do seem to be times when we "just know" that something is missing or that something has changed.[20]

Regarding the explanandum, one final point remains to be made. Billon and Kriegel have also assembled a selection of depersonalization self-descriptions that suggest the patients are "totally unconscious" in a way that is "particularly amenable" to their hypothesis. It is the case that one patient records "I'm like a zombie"; another, "I am in emptiness." Indeed these descriptions might be amenable to the "totally unconscious" characterization. But it is obvious that these are tropes, attempts at applying natural language to experiences for which it was not designed. My claim is that not all tropes are alike: some characterize the phenomenon in question with greater accuracy than do others. Of the examples cited by Billon and Kriegel, I submit that a more accurate trope is "it is not me who feels." This seems not to be a denial that conscious feelings are instantiated; rather, it seems to be an assertion that there are conscious feelings of which I am directly aware that do not belong to self.[21]

I believe this is not just a matter of cherry-picking. The principal reason is that converging lines of evidence suggest that being uniquely situated to report instantiation of a conscious experience dissociates from belonging or personal ownership (Lane 2012, Klein 2014). Unlike the tropes cited by Billon and Kriegel, these descriptions appear to have identified a distinctive conscious experience that has previously gone underreported. Neither "I'm like a zombie" nor "I am in emptiness" can be said to enjoy such a felicitous fit with an emerging body of scientific description.

Regarding the explanans, likewise, one final point remains to be made. Sierra (2009, 143) opines, regarding the first component of the two-neural-network model of depersonalization, that "an 'emotion coloring' mechanism is likely to be a major contributor to feelings usually described in terms of 'immediacy.'" Billon and Kriegel, along with most others who weigh in on consciousness, take "seemingly immediate access" be part of the explanans of "consciousness," part of what makes a state conscious. I believe this view to be mistaken. Sierra here suggests one component of felt immediacy; I believe there are others (e.g., Lane 2012, 258–259). Felt immediacy, I submit, does not so much inform as regards what makes an experience conscious, as it does regarding to whom that conscious experience belongs.

4   A "Something Missing" HOT Hypothesis of Alienation

Mylopoulos's concern (this volume) is to explain alien action, in particular schizophrenic passivity experiences, anarchic hand syndrome (AHS), and utilization behavior.[22] As her point of departure, she presupposes that in nonpathological or nonaberrant cases there is a "subjective sense of performing the action at the time"—what is variously referred to as "phenomenology of agency," "agentive awareness," or "action consciousness"—something that she takes to be missing when alien actions occur.[23] Action here is taken to be a bodily event that is "suitably caused by an appropriate goal state or set of goal states (e.g., intentions, desires, reasons, motor commands)." Action consciousness, then, is determined by some property—an "agentive quality"—that "belongs to" the bodily movement or the goal state associated with the action. She considers various candidates for the missing "agentive quality"—for example, proprioception or sensory attenuation—but dismisses both. Instead, she derives a proposal for understanding agentive quality from a version of the HOT theory according to which action consciousness results from "thinking that one is A-ing on the basis of an intention in action to A." One supposed virtue of HOT theory in this context is that it can explain the phenomenal character that she presupposes to be "central to action consciousness," because all that matters is whether the relevant HOT "represents oneself as acting." In sum, if a HOT of this kind is missing, then action consciousness is missing, and the attribution of agency can go awry.[24]

In developing her hypothesis, Mylopoulos draws a distinction between two types of action control, intentional and sensorimotor. For the latter, action is guided primarily by motor commands that specify fine-grained features of movement—for example, angle of trajectory and grip aperture. For intentional, movements are "guided by way of intentions that relate to any agent's practical beliefs and desires." She also emphasizes that the relevant sense of "intentional" here is "intention in action," a concept borrowed from Searle that underscores *present*-directedness; in other words, intentions so understood are "the direct mental antecedents of bodily movements involved in action." As this distinction applies to the pathologies considered here, the claim is that alien movements are guided by motor commands, but not by "intentions in action at the level of intentional control."

Although acknowledging that in most cases the sensorimotor and the intentional interact, Mylopoulos argues the two can dissociate and that AHS and utilization behavior are examples of such dissociation. AHS and utilization behaviors, on this view, seem not to be preceded by intentions in action. In a word, *something is missing*. It is for this reason—the absence of intentions in action—that these behaviors are felt to be alien. And, the absence of intention in action is due to the absence of a higher order thought "that one is A-ing on the basis of an intention in action to A."[25]

One among the reasons that Mylopoulos recruits HOT theory for her attempt to explain these aberrant behaviors is that—like Gennaro, Billon, and Kriegel—she accurately notes that, on Rosenthal's theory, thoughts of the right sort must be direct or noninferential (e.g., Rosenthal 2002, 408–411). Applying this hypothesis then to AHS, she says that subjects feel the behaviors to be alien because they lack the feeling of immediacy, the sense that awareness of these behaviors is "subjectively unmediated." And this absence of immediacy is due to the absence of a HOT "that one is A-ing on the basis of an intention in action to A." For patients with AHS, the anarchic behaviors are just what they observe, from the outside; hence, awareness of these behaviors is indirect or mediated.

Why should this matter? Mylopoulos emphasizes that speed counts. If formulation of a belief about action were dependent upon *observing* self in action, such mediation, or the inferences that need to be made, would cause us to "lose valuable time." But here is where the difficulties begin.

First, Mylopoulos emphasizes "the *subjectively* unmediated, intention-based higher-order thoughts."[26] But the *subjective sense* that something is unmediated does not imply that it is unmediated. More importantly, since on Rosenthal's theory HOTs can radically misrepresent (Lane and Liang 2008), there is no necessary connection between how things seem and the objective passage of time. What Mylopoulos needs—something HOT theory does not provide—is objective rather than subjective speed and efficiency. Note too that Rosenthal (e.g., Lau and Rosenthal 2011, 366) takes pains to emphasize that HOT theory is neutral as regards whether conscious awareness "adds significant utility or immediate impact on behavior and task performance." He proceeds to emphasize that for most cognitive and perceptual tasks, performance does not depend upon higher-order representations; in fact, "because conscious awareness can differ even if all first-order representations remain completely unchanged, such awareness itself might serve little function." If speed is a critical issue, and if HOT theory cannot help with explaining speedy action responses in ecological contexts, then one wonders why insist upon a "subjective sense of performing the action at the time," especially given that consciousness is notoriously slow (Dehaene 2014, 115–160).

Second, to support her view that AHS results from sensorimotor rather than intentional action control, which the agent can know of only on the basis of "conscious observation," she cites the case of JC, who appears only to be aware of anarchic movements when he sees them. Of course this concerns a straightforward empirical issue, but at the current stage of knowledge there is no consensus regarding the facts of the matter. Indeed, Marcel (2003, 81–82) describes a patient who "was aware of the anarchic actions performed by his left hand even when out of his sight." So even though conscious observation was not involved, the patient reported feeling "as if someone else was doing the actions."

Third, the degree of efficiency that can be achieved when depending on observation of one's own body, while acting, has yet to be fully explored. But the case of IW's neuropathy is instructive in this regard (McNeill et al. 2010). When he was nineteen years old, as the apparent result of an auto-immune reaction triggered by a severe fever, IW suffered a deafferentation of his body from the neck down: that is, he underwent a nearly complete loss of peripheral sensory feedback, including tactile and proprioceptive sensations. Although neither was he paralyzed nor was his motor system affected, unless he could look to see what his body was doing, he had no control over what his body did. In a word, visual observation of his body became essential to the exercise of control over his body—everything from simple sitting up or walking, to the complex actions required for his vocation.

Although the initial prognosis was that IW would be confined permanently to a wheelchair, he designed a program aimed at relearning how to move. Using vision to guide him, while carefully thinking about each motion, he practiced moving his body, repetitively and in various combinations—different trajectories, distances, and velocities. Despite this constant need to maintain visual contact with his body and the environment, especially with objects that he must manipulate, IW has learned how to perform at levels all but indistinguishable from healthy persons.

The point of citing IW's case is not to deny the distinction that Mylopoulos draws between intentional and sensorimotor control. Indeed, Mylopoulos agrees that in many cases "these two types of control interact in rich ways." But I believe she overstates the role that dissociation between these two, or the idea of "losing contact" with self, might play in explaining phenomena like AHS. No doubt IW's effective training incurs a cognitive and perceptual cost in the distribution of mental resources—he must devote resources to motor activity that most of us can reserve for other purposes. Nevertheless, he is capable of maintaining contact with and control over his body, visually. The degree to which IW recovered suggests that intentional and sensorimotor control might be so seamlessly connected to one another that Mylopoulos's explanatory strategy is blocked.

Fourth, Wegner's (2002) Ouija-like experiments that suggest we can quite easily be fooled into thinking that we are acting when that could not possibly be the case are also relevant here. What most concerns with regard to Mylopoulos's "intention in action" hypothesis is Wegner's (2002, 179) suggestion that much of human behavior "seems to occur without much influence by intentions, especially when the behavior is not particularly discrepant from prior beliefs." Wegner's (2002, 180) experiments seem to show that many of our reported intentions are "post hoc inventions" or "fabrications" that depend more upon an idealized image of self as agents than upon actual choice of actions "with foreknowledge and in accord with our conscious intentions." As for the case of IW, it seems that vision plays *more* of a role than Mylopoulos's hypothesis implies; Wegner's experiments, on the other hand, seem to show that intention in action plays *less* of a role than Mylopoulos's hypothesis suggests.

Finally, perhaps we are at a moment in time when the hypothesis can be operationalized and tested. First, although strictly speaking, HOT theory does not specify neuroanatomical detail (Lau and Rosenthal 2011, 366), the relevant higher-order representations might be mediated in virtue of dorsolateral prefrontal (DLPFC) activity (Lau and Rosenthal 2011, 367–370).[27] Second, since fMRI studies have shown that intentions in action can be analyzed to a sufficiently fine-grained level of detail such that brain activity can distinguish among distinct grasping actions prior to the initiation of those actions (Gallivan et al. 2011), it should be possible to devise a suitable action-involving paradigm. Third, neurodisruption techniques (e.g., transcranial magnetic stimulation [TMS]) could be applied in order to determine whether or not targeting a specific area (e.g., the DLPFC) interferes with the hypothesized HOT in such a way as to induce an experience of alien action. And, fourth, TMS has already been successfully applied to the DLPFC, effectively creating patterns of neurodisruption (Bilek et al. 2013).

Briefly, TMS makes it possible to assess the role of brain regions in cognitive activity, by creating virtual lesions: that is, it can be targeted to specific brain areas, causing temporary disruptions of activity, thereby providing information about the functional relevance of a brain region (e.g., the DLPFC).[28] Sidestepping many technical details for the nonce, what I am suggesting is that repetitive TMS be applied within an action paradigm, to the DLPFC, and at different parameters, in order to both enhance and inhibit cognitive processes. The hypothesis to be tested is Mylopoulos's application of HOT theory to action: if that hypothesis is correct, parameters that enhance relevant cognitive processes should enhance the feeling of control, and those that inhibit should diminish the feeling of control or engender a sense of alien action.

In fact, recently, Dienes and Hutton (2013) have taken the first steps in this direction. Their concern was not with action per se; instead, they were testing a HOT interpretation of the cold control theory (CCT) of hypnotic suggestion. The specific hypnotic suggestion in this instance was magnetic hands; experimenters suggest to subjects that their hands are like magnets, and are thereby able to attract or repel one another. According to the HOT interpretation of CCT, hypnotic responses are constituted by (i) intentions to perform actions, even though (ii) hypnotized subjects think they do not intend those actions. The phenomenology of hypnosis, the feeling that the arms move by themselves, results then from intentions of which one is not aware. To express this idea in terms of HOT theory: "hypnotic response is all due to the formation of inaccurate ... HOTs" (Dienes and Hutton 2013, 387). On the assumption that the left DLPFC mediates the formation of *accurate* HOTS, Dienes and Hutton applied low-frequency repetitive TMS to the left DLPFC, predicting that the resulting disruption of activity would enhance the hypnotic effect, because by hypothesis disruption would increase the likelihood of inaccurate HOTs being formed (cf. Rounis et al. 2010). Indeed, the authors did find some evidence to indicate that TMS-induced neural disruption of left DLPFC activity enhanced hypnotic response, thereby suggesting inaccurate HOTs might be playing a role in the alien experiences associated with hypnotic experiences.[29]

The intent in citing this experiment is not to imply that Mylopoulos's hypothesis has already been tested. The intent is only to add substance to the claim that the hypothesis is already empirically tractable. Doubtless though, a suitable test would need to consider the relationship between the formation of inaccurate HOTs along with the formation of actual intentions,[30] and both of these in the context of a paradigm devoted not to suggestion as such, but to action.

It goes without saying that many additional details would need to be taken into consideration. What is more, as is true for all empirical hypotheses, the results of one set of experiments could be used to adduce support for or against a hypothesis, but such results could not be claimed to settle the matter once and for all. Nonetheless, I think the time has arrived that we should begin adding a set of constraints to the many conjectures on offer in this vicinity. The constraints I have in mind are those that are commonplace when one seeks to operationalize and test in experimental settings.

5 Concluding Remarks and the Subpersonal Self

My first major concern is that each of the theories discussed above presupposes that consciousness includes an element of self-reference. I have argued that this presupposition is erroneous whether that self-referential element is conscious or not, but my focus here is on the gratuitous explanatory burden created by theories that attempt to explain both (i) the experience of alienation and (ii) the experience of belonging. If it were the case that strong evidence existed for the simultaneous occurrence of (i) and (ii), this would then be a necessary explanatory challenge. We should not subtract from the explanandum for the sake of convenience. But although it is clear that (i) occurs in certain pathological, illusory or otherwise atypical conditions, it is not obvious that (ii) is a necessary component of all conscious experiences. In fact, there are reasons to be wary of presupposing the latter (e.g., Prinz 2012, 213–240).

Kriegel (2009, 121, n. 32) acknowledges that he is aware of no experimental evidence showing that "phenomenal consciousness involves for-me-ness." But he (2009, 175) "cannot envisage what it would be like to have a phenomenology lacking the kind of inner awareness that constitutes for-me-ness." Although I do not share his intuitions, I do share his concern that when considering the phenomenology of consciousness theorists should avoid glib rejection of one another's phenomenological pronouncements, if these are based solely upon dissonance between what different persons envisage. After all, as Kriegel rightly avers, "there are certainly facts of the matter pertaining to phenomenology," and these are critical to getting clear about the explanandum.[31]

Where we disagree is on how to regard these issues from the perspective of scientific explanation. Although there is much that distinguishes early views of explanation from more recent views, the two converge on a willingness to allow for the addition of entities or processes whose existence is uncertain, just so long as they enhance explanatory adequacy; such liberality though is usually not extended to the phenomena under scrutiny (e.g., Hempel 1965, Craver 2007). As this relates to alien experiences, I submit that many of the difficulties we encounter when trying to achieve adequate explanation derive from having inflated the explanandum.[32]

Concerning the explanandum, Kriegel pitches his view as a conditional (2009, 67): "*if* the phenomenology has the features I say it does, *then* self-representationalism is true." As to whether the antecedent of this conditional is true, two empirical points can be made. First, there appear to be an ever-increasing number of counterexamples to the for-me-ness feature of the phenomenology. The seeming counterexamples I have in mind are not restricted to somatoparaphrenia, passivity experiences, or depersonalization: they include visual experiences (Zahn 2008), nonpathological "switching" away from self and back in a way that corresponds to changes in hemispheric dominance (Gott et al. 1984), episodic memory (Klein 2014, 103–109), fibromyalgia pain (Valenzuela-Moguillansky 2013), pain asymbolia (Klein forthcoming) and so forth (cf. Lane 2012). But we can do more than cherry pick examples from the scientific literature; we can design experiments. Recall that Kriegel "cannot envisage what it would be like to have a phenomenology lacking the kind of *inner awareness* that constitutes *for-me-ness*."[33] Now consider the possibility that (i) the neural substrate of "inner awareness" supervenes on our primary interoceptive system (Craig 2003), and (ii) it is in virtue of a representation of the primary system realized in that anterior insula that we have "the feeling that 'I am'" (Craig 2009, 65). If Kriegel's "inner awareness" approximates the neural substrate that Craig identifies as mediating interoception, and if "the feeling that 'I am'" approximates "for-me-ness," then it should be possible to begin testing whether, for example, anterior insula activation that is hypothesized to be essential for (2) ever fails to occur when we have conscious experiences. Once again, the claim is not that this would settle the issue, but it would enable us to begin moving beyond comparison of what one another envisage as possible.[34]

My second major concern is that each theory of consciousness considered in this chapter—HOT, wide intrinsicality, self-representational, or HOT as applied to agency—emphatically takes *seeming* directness, immediacy, or noninferential access to be an integral component of conscious experience.[35] Moreover, they link experienced immediacy to the position that phenomenally conscious states all "contain a crucial self-referential element" (Gennaro 2006, 221). Although it may be the case that, somehow understood, *experienced immediacy* plays a role along the lines suggested by these theories, experienced immediacy does not entail self-reference or belonging.

For those whose intuitions incline them to endorse the presupposed link between immediacy and self-reference, consider the example of craniopagus twins who are connected at the thalamus (cf. Lane 2014, 55). Although these sisters have not been tested under controlled conditions, they seem to share interoceptive or introspective access to conscious experiences such as thirst. But shared access does not imply inability to distinguish between sensations "that belong to self and those that belong to her sister" (Bor 2012, 29).[36] Whereas typically when reflecting on whether two persons could share conscious experiences philosophers have had to resort to thought experiments (e.g., O'Brien 2007, 206), craniopagus twins appear to show that not only what Hirstein (2012) refers to as "mindmelding" can occur, but also that it can dissociate from belonging. It seems to be the case that one sister can be aware of thirst without referring that sensation to self.[37]

Felt immediacy, however, does not only dissociate from belonging during interoception or introspection; it can be experienced even when we are observing the external world and exhibit no confusion as regards belonging attributions. We are extremely sensitive to certain signals in the external world, such as changes in the scleral field size (eye white area) of conspecifics: that is, we quickly and efficiently detect fear and certain other emotions in others (Tsuchiya et al. 2009, Hardee et al. 2008, Yang et al. 2007). But we do not misattribute the conscious experience of fear to self. Naturally, the neural substrates of personal and observed fear overlap in important respects, but in quotidian circumstances we can easily distinguish between the two. The essential point is that it is not obviously the case that self-reference is intrinsically bound to *seeming* immediacy, directness, or noninferential access.

I suspect that the ill-advised emphasis placed on felt immediacy arises because SP theories, albeit in distinct ways, link consciousness to self-reference, somehow understood, which in turn suggests a link to self-knowledge. And knowledge of self's mental states is commonly claimed to be epistemically direct, immediate, or noninferential (e.g., Macdonald 2009, 741). But some cases suggest that conscious states can occur when felt immediacy is absent (e.g., Zahn et al. 2008, Sass and Parnas 2003, 438). In sum, my concern is not only that felt immediacy does not entail belonging; I also suspect that the presupposition of a link between self-reference and consciousness misleads us in our efforts to characterize that which we hope to explain.

My third major concern is that amid the debate over whether it is preferable to add or subtract ingredients from the explanans, perhaps we are overlooking an alternative, ecumenical option. Elsewhere I have argued that distinct "molecular" or "isomeric" arrangements play a role in causing alienation experiences (Lane 2012, 2014). What happens in quotidian cases is that mental states cluster in specific ways—for example, pain's sensory-discriminative component seems intrinsically bound to its affective-motivational component. In a word, when we feel pains we don't like them. But sometimes the affective-motivational component is *subtracted* from the overall experience (e.g., pain asymbolia) such that we no longer care. The pains don't bother us; they might even feel alien. Alternatively, in the quotidian case, actions exhibit intentional binding and sensory attenuation. In a word, when we act, sensory experiences are either altogether absent or vanishingly thin. But sometimes something is *added* to actions: that is, sensory experiences are accentuated. When these sensory experiences are added, actions can be felt to be alien (e.g., passivity experiences). In short, the addition and subtraction hypotheses do not conflict with one another; instead, they can be combined in a comprehensive model of alienation experiences.

What I am suggesting is that when standard expectations concerning how mental states should cluster are confounded, the likelihood of alienation experiences is high. I say the likelihood is high, because alienation is not guaranteed by the mere awareness that mental states are clustering in unexpected ways. For example, we can be aware that mental states are clustering in atypical ways when we observe people with whom we are intimately familiar, as in Capgras syndrome. Capgras syndrome appears to be importantly analogous to pain asymbolia, in that sensory-discriminative components are intact, but the affective-motivational components are missing. Unlike pain asymbolia, however, here the problem seems to be that a person with whom we are deeply familiar seems alien. It is not an instance wherein conscious experiences that we host seem not to belong to self. Therefore, I previously recommended that when seeking to explain alienation experiences, not only do we require awareness that mental states are clustering in unexpected ways, we also need to distinguish among stimuli (either extero- or interoceptive) that are related to self, to persons with whom we are familiar, and to persons or things that are related neither to self nor to an intimate. Only when an awareness of confounded expectations is accompanied by self-referencing stimuli do alienation experiences occur.

It may appear that I am now preparing to recant on my rejection of the role that self-reference is proclaimed to play in SP theories, but that is not the case. First, I am only claiming that self-reference, paradoxically, plays an important role in alienation experiences. Second, Kriegel's (2009) self-reference is part of the conscious experience and, though Gennaro's (2012) is not part of the conscious experience, it is characterized as an unconscious psychological phenomenon. But the type of self-reference that matters to explaining alienation experiences is neither conscious nor psychological; instead, it is a neuronal or subpersonal process. Baldly, this is a subpersonal self.

Northoff and Bermpohl (2004) and Northoff et al. (2006) have previously argued that stimuli, irrespective of sensory modality, if related to self, are processed in virtue of neural activity in the brain's cortical midline structures (CMS). Many additional findings have followed in the wake of this discovery: First, Northoff et al. (2010) have adduced evidence to suggest that high resting state activity (RSA)—activity that occurs in the absence of external stimuli—is prevalent throughout the brain and that it can both shape and be shaped by stimulus-induced activity. Second, Qin and Northoff (2011) have shown that the perigenual anterior cingulate cortex (PACC) is specifically involved in the processing of self-referential stimuli, in a way that clearly distinguishes self from that which is familiar or that which concerns stimuli of other types. Third, Schneider et al. (2008) discovered "overlap" between RSA and self-referential activity in anterior CMS, such as the PACC; in these regions, high self-referential activity correlates with less deviation from RSA, relative to low self-referential activity.

Building upon these and related findings, Huang et al. (2014) have investigated vegetative state (VS) patients. Although VS patients exhibit no indication of purposeful behavior, language comprehension, awareness of sensations, or of self, an *active* paradigm was used. The questionnaire comprised both self-referential (e.g., "Have you been to Taiwan?") and nonself-referential (e.g., "Are there sixty minutes in one hour?"). The "task" itself consisted of four fMRI scanning runs, and each run comprised twenty self-referential and twenty nonself-referential questions. Findings were striking: first, the greater the PACC signal change during self-referential, compared to nonself-referential questions, the higher the degree of consciousness.[38] Second, RSA was lower for the patients than for the control subjects. And, third, two of the patients who exhibited the highest signal changes in the PACC recovered two months after the fMRI scanning.

Obviously, much more would need to be said about this experiment and its findings, and experimental probes of this kind are in need of refinement. But the principal implications of relevance here are these: because of the RSA's unique relationship with the self, if self-referential questions are to elicit distinctive neural activity, RSA must have achieved a minimum threshold. If that threshold has been achieved, even for patients with serious disorders of consciousness, PACC signal changes evoked in response to self-referential questions can be used to predict the degree of consciousness. And, strikingly, these PACC signal changes—these distinctive reactions to self-referencing stimuli—might serve as predictive markers of future capacities for consciousness.

Above I argued that theories of consciousness that presuppose conscious or psychological self-reference all fail to adequately explain alienation experiences. But studies of VS patients suggest that self might be related to consciousness in a manner previously unrecognized. It seems that self is *prior to* our experience of the world: recall, self overlaps with the resting state, the state in which subjects are not being exposed to external stimuli.[39] What is more, self, understood in this neuronal sense, seems to be essential to conscious experience: the *subpersonal self* exhibited in VS patients—PACC activation in response to self-referential questions when subjects appear to be wholly unconscious—is, potentially, an indicator of whether the capacity for consciousness is recoverable. Simplifying, self is intrinsically related to RSA; RSA is a precondition for self-reference; self-referencing precedes recovery of consciousness. In this respect, the subpersonal self is essential to conscious experience. If a slogan is called for, self is prior to consciousness.

I opened this essay with an epigraph from Rilke: "nothing alien happens to us, but only what has long been our own." There is, I believe, a sense in which this is true. Alienation experiences are robust conscious experiences. But if the model I propose is true, they only occur when stimuli interact with the brain in a way that implicates self. On a neuronal level this self-referencing occurs when stimuli interact with the brain in such a way as to evoke just minimal deviation from RSA; it is in virtue of this close matching of external stimuli to the RSA (the brain's intrinsic activity) that stimuli are perceived as and judged to be self-referencing. Because neuronal self-referencing is essential to the having of alien experiences, it can truly be said that what seems alien has long been our own. Indeed this is why alienation experiences are robust: expectations concerning what to expect from self-referential stimuli are confounded, and the confounding of expectations occasions a thickening of conscious experience.

Acknowledgments

I express my heartfelt gratitude to Rocco Gennaro, Alexandre Billon, Uriah Kriegel, and Myrto Mylopoulos for their generosity in allowing me to read early and penultimate versions of their manuscripts. I am also grateful to David Rosenthal for many helpful discussions concerning his higher-order thought theory of consciousness, as well as to Georg Northoff and Pengmin Qin for discussions regarding technical aspects of experimental research on what I refer to as the subpersonal self. Funding for this research was, in part, provided by National Science Council of Taiwan research grants, 100-2410-H-038-009-MY3, 102-2420-H-038-001-MY3, and 104-2420-H-038-001-MY3.

Notes

1. Previously, I discussed this case in Lane and Liang 2010, 2011 and Liang and Lane 2009. Rosenthal (2010) responded to those interpretations, concerning their possible implications for his higher-order thought theory of consciousness, and developed a response that is partially endorsed by Gennaro (this volume). I later argued that this case can be understood within a comprehensive explanatory framework for *belonging* or *mental ownership*, a relationship between selves and conscious experiences, whether those experiences pertain to mental states, actions, or bodies (Lane 2012, 2014).

2. For more detail concerning Gennaro's views on the kind of self-reference essential to conscious experience, see 2012, 103–134, 220–221. I return to this issue in the manuscript's concluding section.

3. It should be noted that Gennaro's version of HOT theory differs from Rosenthal's in certain important respects; for a summary of the former's "wide intrinsically view" (WIV) see Gennaro 2012, 55–59. What matters for our purposes here is that Gennaro is committed to a self-referential condition: for example, "what makes mental states conscious is *intrinsic* to conscious states ... a kind of *inner* self-referential and relational element is ... present *within* the structure of such states" (2012, 55).

4. See Liang and Lane 2009 and Lane and Liang 2010.

5. Billon and Kriegel also suggest that degree of methodological rigor might be a concern here. With this too, I am in agreement, and that is why I take the Bottini et

al. (2002) case to be just a starting point or motivation for further inquiry (Lane and Liang 2010, 500). I expand on this point below.

6. Italics added.

7. HOT theory even allows for the possibility of what I have elsewhere dubbed "radical confabulation" (Lane and Liang 2008)—representation of first-order states that do not even exist. See Gennaro 2012, 59–70, for some of his views on misrepresentation and "targetless" HOTs.

8. As for the passage from Lane and Liang (2010, 498) that concerns Gennaro, the point I intended there was not to deny that this is an essential component of Rosenthal's theory. Instead, my point was that even if spontaneity and the absence of mediation are critical to understanding consciousness, this alone does not imply that FB's HOT represents recovered tactile sensations as belonging to her.

9. For the distinction, as revealed by functional magnetic resonance imaging (fMRI), between active and passive touch, see Gardner and Johnson 2013, 522.

10. Applying touches to a patient's hand such that the patient can see what is being done, while undergoing fMRI, does pose many technical difficulties. But that these can be overcome is suggested by the methodology adopted by Ehrsson et al. (2004) in their fMRI study of the rubber hand illusion.

11. Billon (2013, 307) describes inserted thoughts thus: They differ "from the patient's ordinary thoughts by being phenomenally unconscious for him ... [they are] akin to sentences, images, unconscious computational processes, and other people's conscious thoughts." He adds, however, that they differ from sentences, images, and so forth, in that they are "apparently in the patient."

12. According to Billon (2013, 307), "this does not mean that there is no phenomenology associated with thought insertion, only that it is, so to speak, an extrinsic, or a 'second-order phenomenology.'"

13. When arguing that there can be more than one type of consciousness, one phenomenal and the other not, Billon and Kriegel emphasize that what the two share is immediacy, or "immediate access." Elsewhere I have argued that although "immediate access" is relevant to these discussions, the lack of immediacy is one factor that can contribute to the experience of alien mental states (Lane 2012, 257–267; cf. Klein 2014, 101–103). Below I expand on this concern about the presumed significance of immediacy.

14. Billon (2013, 304) cites an actual instance of thought insertion that might be adduced to support the distinction they adopt here: according to one frequently cited description of thought insertion, it is like having "a screen" in the middle of one's skull on which pictures can be flashed, conveying thoughts that seem not to belong to self.

15. Elsewhere Billon (2013) emphasizes that, in order to develop an adequate explanation, we must allow for the possibility that two sets of features—the "phenomenal" and the "spatial"—are dissociable. There are many problems with this approach,
not the least of which is the requirement that we accept the explanatory utility of
distinguishing between intrinsic and extrinsic phenomenology. But setting these
thorny conceptual issues aside, consider only the weight assigned by Billon to the
spatial dimension and how this relates to the first-rank symptoms of schizophrenia.
He says that "in me" is plausibly understood as "always where I am, that follows me
around" (Billon 2013, 303–304). Arguably, giving emphasis to spatial phenomenology helps, in a rather straightforward way, to make sense of thought insertion. But
ego-boundaries are permeable in two directions: some thoughts are inserted, while
others "fly" to others, who can "catch" them (Mullins and Spence 2003, 294). In the
latter case it is less clear how we should understand the spatial phenomenology,
especially given Billon's (2013, 296) expressed intent "to save the meaningfulness
and the intelligibility of the patients."

16. I should add that although I am in sympathy with interpretations of patient
reports as reflecting actual patient phenomenology, there is need for caution when
interpreting schizophrenic speech. Language disturbance—in particular incoherent
or desultory content—is one of the primary behaviors by which diagnosis is made
(Hyman and Cohen 2013, 1391). An example of this "loosening of associations"
characteristic of much schizophrenic speech is: "I don't think they care for me
because two million camels … 10 million taxis … Father Christmas on the rebound."

17. Here Billon (see 2013, 306, fn. 4) might insist that what is accessible or "reportable" bears no necessary connection to phenomenal consciousness.

18. Note that this role identified for receptive language areas in the left temporal
lobe fits well with subjective reports, since the "near-universal experience" is of
these voices "as being like an auditory percept" (Garrett and Silva 2003, 454). But it
should also be noted that my claim in the text concerns empirical evidence about
receptive areas, and that Billon (2013, 311) claims (a) the same does not hold for *productive* areas and (b) auditory cortex activation has only been observed "in a subgroup of patients." Of course, getting straight about the facts of the matter in this
vicinity will require much more work but, as regards (a), the subjective reality of
auditory hallucinations correlates with activity in Broca's area (Raij et al. 2009) and,
even when subjective reality is not controlled for, activity in the right hemisphere
homolog of Broca's area correlates with auditory hallucinations (Sommer et al.
2008). As regards (b), one reason why auditory cortex activation might have been
observed only in a subgroup of patients is a failure to adequately distinguish between
the relative significance of resting state vis-à-vis stimulus-related activity (cf. Northoff 2013, 351; Kompus et al. 2011).

19. I expand on this point below.

20. As an analogy, consider commonplace awareness of change in a person or place, but change in features that typically go unnoticed. Such aspects of a person or place can be noticed when absent, even if we are unable to articulate or identify what is missing. Applying this idea to action, note that subliminally-processed stimuli can induce motor cortex activations enabling accurate responses to a target (Dehaene 2014, 129). Now consider the patient who wonders, "Is it really me walking?" My suggestion is that a degree of incompatibility between anticipation mechanisms and motor responses might be sufficient to cause patients to become aware of a disturbance to agency. What Poincaré dubbed the "subliminal self" can fail, thereby drawing attention to its absence, and causing mobilization of "enormous efforts in order to apply … consciousness" toward rectifying motor responses that ordinarily do not require intervention by a conscious, agentive self (cf. Dehaene 2014, 86).

21. I expand upon this point in the concluding section.

22. All three are alien in the sense of seeming not to be controlled by self, but only for the passivity experiences of schizophrenics is it commonplace to attribute agency to some external source. For AHS this is less common. Utilization behavior refers to the compulsive grabbing and use of objects without regard to need or social situation, for example, reaching for and eating food even when not hungry or when the food belongs to someone else (Rizzolatti and Kalaska 2013, 883).

23. Mylopoulos is here endorsing a distinction between the phenomenology of bodily motion and of agency. As Horgan (2011, 64) characterizes the difference, the former involves a visual, kinesthetic, and so forth what-it's-like; agency, however, places emphasis upon the "what-it's-like of *self as source.*"

24. I do not agree with Mylopoulos that action consciousness occurs in ordinary cases; at best we *just know* that self performs a given action (Lane 2014, 64–65), and this seems to be what Block intends by suggesting the conceptual possibility of access- without phenomenal- consciousness. If this distinction does apply here, there is no agentive quality or phenomenal character that need concern us. In other words, what Mylopoulos suggests has gone missing, was not there in the first place. Neither do I endorse her dismissal of sensory attenuation as relevant to these discussions; there seems to be abundant experimental data to show that, pace Mylopoulos, sensory attenuation does occur in persons who have passivity experiences (e.g., Shergill et al. 2005 and Teufel et al. 2010), who have just been awakened from REM sleep (Blagrove et al. 2006), and so forth.

25. I here devote most of my attention to AHS because Mylopoulos takes that to be the example that most clearly supports her hypothesis. Concerning utilization behaviors, however, it is worth noting that recent experimental results show, at least for some of its manifestations, movements are more "rationally integrated into the agent's psychology at the time" than Mylopoulos suggests. For example, Besnard et al. (2010) have adduced evidence to suggest that the frequency of utilization behaviors depends upon their relationship with the content of a task (involving a verbal-

ized script). If the task counts as an important part of the agent's psychology at the time, then many utilization behaviors are "rationally integrated."

26. Italics added.

27. Note that the conjectured association between HOTs and PFC activity is not universally endorsed (Gennaro 2012, 279–280).

28. For a succinct review of some relevant technical matters, see Rossi et al. 2009.

29. Because my concern here is only to argue that the Mylopoulos hypothesis is empirically tractable, I will not discuss methodological worries or the degree to which the data can plausibly be claimed to support the hypothesis that HOTs are misrepresenting actual intentions.

30. A possible neural substrate for intention-to-act has been suggested by Andersen and Cui 2009.

31. That the issues here are difficult is undeniable, and it may surprise some to know that it is not only philosophers who worry about for-me-ness. The cognitive neuroscientist, Revonsuo (2006, 32), for example, observes that "The study of consciousness is, first and foremost, the study of the world-for-me. … That is the principal explanandum for the science of consciousness. Accordingly, the most fundamental concept in the study of consciousness should capture the essence of the world-for-me." By way of contrast, some philosophers whose main concern is the "phenomenal self" allow that "there are occasions—when we drift into reverie, or similar conditions—when we are not particularly aware of ourselves *as* selves at all" (Dainton 2008, 147).

32. Among my reasons for being disinclined to endorse Kriegel's view of subjective character is that he consigns it to "fringe" or "peripheral" consciousness (2009, 47–52). The result seems to be a compounding of our explanatory burden, adding not one but two contentious posits to the explanandum.

33. Italics added.

34. I am aware of the pitfalls of trying to operationalize before we have achieved sufficiently mature levels of conceptual sophistication (on the philosophical side) and methodological as well as technological sophistication (on the scientific side). And it is unlikely that anyone will soon pass a Turing test of consciousness science (cf., Revonsuo 2006, 300–303). But every intellectual choice involves a degree of risk: I am betting that we have already achieved levels of sophistication—on both sides—such that we are poised to eclipse "sketches of, or promises for, arguments" (Kriegel 2009, 312).

35. Kriegel's (2006, 156) view is distinctive in that he holds "the awareness we have of our conscious states is immediate simply because it *really is* unmediated."

36. I regard this as an instance wherein a person can "host" a conscious experience without that experience belonging to the person who is introspectively aware of it (cf. Lane 2012, 260). This is a somewhat different sense of "host" than that employed by Kriegel (2009, 8) when he asserts that "conscious experiences are not states that we may *host...*"

37. For a detailed analysis of this case and its possible relevance to "immunity to error through misidentification," see Langland-Hassan (forthcoming).

38. To distinguish among various degrees of consciousness, minimally conscious patients were included in the sample. Assessment included use of the Coma Recovery Scale (Revised).

39. If "self" so used still seems to intimate the mental, then substitute, "this organism, here, now."

References

Andersen, R., and H. Cui. 2009. Intention, action planning, and decision-making in parietal-frontal circuits. *Neuron* 63:568–583.

Avikainen, S., N. Forss, and R. Hari. 2002. Modulated activation of the human SI and SII cortices during observation of hand actions. *NeuroImage* 15:640–646.

Baars, B. 2007. Attention and consciousness. In *Cognition, Brain, and Consciousness: Introduction to Cognitive Neuroscience*, ed. B. Baars and N. Gage. New York: Academic Press.

Bayne, T. 2010. *The Unity of Consciousness*. New York: Oxford University Press.

Berlin, H. 2011. The neural basis of the dynamic unconscious. *Neuro-psychoanalysis* 13:5–31.

Besnard, J., P. Allain, G. Aubin, F. Osiurak, V. Chauvire, F. Etcharry-Bouyx, and D. Le Gall. 2010. Utilization behavior: Clinical and theoretical approaches. *Journal of the International Neuropsychological Society* 16:453–462.

Bilek, E., A. Schafer, E. Ochs, C. Esslinger, M. Zangl, M. Plichta, U. Braun, et al. 2013. Application of high-frequency repetitive transcranial magnetic stimulation to the DLPFC alters human prefrontal-hippocampal functional interaction. *Journal of Neuroscience* 33:7050–7056.

Billon, A. 2013. Does consciousness entail subjectivity? The puzzle of thought insertion. *Philosophical Psychology* 26:291–314.

Blagrove, M., S.-J. Blakemore, and B. Thayer. 2006. The ability to self-tickle following rapid eye movement sleep. *Consciousness and Cognition* 16:285–294.

Block, N. 2005. Two neural correlates of consciousness. *Trends in Cognitive Sciences* 9:46–52.

Block, N. 2007. On a confusion about a function of consciousness. In *Consciousness, Function, and Representation: Collected Papers*, vol. 1. Cambridge, MA: MIT Press.

Boag, S. 2010. Repression, suppression, and conscious awareness. *Psychoanalytic Psychology* 27:164–182.

Bolognini, N., A. Rossetti, A. Maravita, and C. Miniussi. 2011. Seeing touch in the somatosensory cortex: A TMS study of the visual perception of touch. *Human Brain Mapping* 32:2104–2114.

Bor, D. 2012. *The Ravenous Brain: How the New Science of Consciousness Explains Our Insatiable Search for Meaning*. New York: Basic Books.

Bottini, G., E. Bisiach, R. Sterzi, and G. Vallar. 2002. Feeling touches in someone else's hand. *Neuroreport* 13:437–443.

Bufalari, I., T. Aprile, A. Avenanti, F. Di Russso, and S. Aglioti. 2007. Empathy for pain and touch in the human somatosensory cortex. *Cerebral Cortex* 17:2553–2561.

Craig, A. D. 2003. Interoception: The sense of the physiological condition of the body. *Current Opinion in Neurobiology* 13:500–505.

Craig, A. D. 2009. How do you feel—now? The anterior insula and human awareness. *Nature Reviews: Neuroscience* 10:59–70.

Craver, C. 2007. *Explaining the Brain: Mechanisms and the Mosaic Unity of Neuroscience*. New York: Oxford University Press.

Dainton, B. 2008. *The Phenomenal Self*. New York: Oxford University Press.

Dehaene, S. 2014. *Consciousness and the Brain: Deciphering How the Brain Codes Our Thoughts*. New York: Viking.

Dienes, Z., and S. Hutton. 2013. Understanding hypnosis metacognitively: rTMS applied to left DLPFC increases hypnotic suggestibility. *Cortex* 49:386–392.

Ehrsson, H., C. Spence, and R. Passingham. 2004. That's my hand! Activity in premotor cortex reflects feeling of ownership of a limb. *Science* 305:875–877.

Feinberg, T., and A. Venneri. 2014. Somatoparaphrenia: Evolving theories and concepts. *Cortex*. doi:10.1016/j.cortex.2014.07.004.

Gallagher, S. 2000. Self-reference and schizophrenia: A cognitive model of immunity to error through misidentification. In *Exploring the Self: Philosophical and Psychological Perspectives on Self-Experience*, ed. D. Zahavi. Philadelphia: John Benjamins.

Gallivan, J. P., D. A. McLean, K. F. Valvear, C. E. Pettypiece, and J. C. Culham. 2011. Decoding action intentions from preparatory brain activity in human parieto-frontal networks. *Journal of Neuroscience* 31:9599–9610.

Gardner, E. P., and K. Johnson. 2013. Touch. In *Principles of Neural Science*, 5th ed., ed. E. Kandel, J. Schwartz, T. Jessel, S. Siegelbaum, and A. Hudspeth. New York: McGraw Hill.

Garrett, M., and R. Silva. 2003. Auditory hallucinations, source monitoring, and the belief that "voices" are real. *Schizophrenia Bulletin* 29:445–457.

Gennaro, R. 2006. Between pure self-referentialism and the extrinsic HOT theory of consciousness. In *Self-Representational Approaches to Consciousness*, ed. U. Kriegel and K. Williford. Cambridge, MA: MIT Press.

Gennaro, R. 2012. *The Consciousness Paradox: Consciousness, Concepts, and Higher-Order Thoughts*. Cambridge, MA: MIT Press.

Gott, P., E. Hughes, and K. Whipple. 1984. Voluntary control of two lateralized conscious states: Validation by electrical and behavioral studies. *Neuropsychologia* 22: 65–72.

Gullivan, J., D. McLean, K. Valyear, C. Pettypiece, and J. Culham. 2011. Decoding action intentions from preparatory brain activity in human parieto-frontal networks. *Journal of Neuroscience* 31:9599–9610.

Hardee, J., J. Thompson, and A. Puce. 2008. The left amygdala knows fear: Laterality in the amygdala response to fearful eyes. *Social Cognitive and Affective Neuroscience* 3:47–54.

Hempel, C. 1965. *Aspects of Scientific Explanation*. New York: Free Press.

Hirstein, W. 2012. *Mindmelding: Consciousness, Neuroscience, and the Mind's Privacy*. New York: Oxford University Press.

Horgan, T. 2011. From agentive phenomenology to cognitive phenomenology: A guide for the perplexed. In *Cognitive Phenomenology*, ed. T. Bayne and M. Montague. New York: Oxford University Press.

Huang, Z., R. Dai, Z. Yang, D. Liu, J. Hu, L. Gao, W. Tang, et al. 2014. The self and its resting state in consciousness: An investigation of the vegetative state. *Human Brain Mapping* 35:1997–2008.

Hugdahl, K., E.-M. Loberg, L. Falkenberg, E. Johnsen, K. Kompus, R. Kroken, M. Nygard, R. Westerhausen, K. Alptekin, and M. Ozgoren. 2012. Auditory verbal hallucinations as aberrant lateralized speech perception: Evidence from dichotic listening. *Schizophrenia Research* 140:59–64.

Hyman, S., and J. Cohen. 2013. Disorders of thought and volition: Schizophrenia. In *Principles of Neural Science*, 5th ed., ed. E. Kandel, J. Schwartz, T. Jessel, S. Siegelbaum, and A. Hudspeth. New York: McGraw Hill.

Keysers, C., J. Kaas, and V. Gazzola. 2010. Somatosensation in social perception. *Nature Reviews: Neuroscience* 11:417–428.

Keysers, C., B. Wicker, V. Gazzola, J.-L. Anton, L. Fogassi, and V. Gallese. 2004. A touching sight: SII/PV activation during the observation and experience of touch. *Neuron* 42:335–346.

Kilner, J., and R. Lemon. 2013. What we currently know about mirror neurons. *Current Biology* 23:R1057–R1062.

Klein, C. Forthcoming. What pain asymbolia really shows. *Mind.*

Klein, S. 2014. *The Two Selves: Their Metaphysical Commitments and Functional Independence.* New York: Oxford University Press.

Kompus, K., R. Westerhausen, and K. Hugdahl. 2011. The "paradoxical" engagement of the primary auditory cortex in patients with auditory verbal hallucinations: A meta-analysis of functional neuroimaging studies. *Neuropsychologia* 49: 3361–3369.

Kriegel, U. 2006. The same-order monitoring theory of consciousness. In *Self-Representational Approaches to Consciousness*, ed. U. Kriegel and K. Williford. Cambridge, MA: MIT Press.

Kriegel, U. 2009. *Subjective Consciousness: A Self-Representational Theory.* New York: Oxford University Press.

Lane, T. 2012. Toward an explanatory framework for mental ownership. *Phenomenology and the Cognitive Sciences* 11:251–286.

Lane, T. 2014. When actions feel alien—an explanatory model. In *Communicative Action*, ed. T. W. Hung. Singapore: Springer Science+Business Media.

Lane, T., and C. Liang. 2008. Higher-order thought and the problem of radical confabulation. *Southern Journal of Philosophy* 46:69–98.

Lane, T., and C. Liang. 2010. Mental ownership and higher-order thought. *Analysis* 70:496–501.

Lane, T., and C. Liang. 2011. Self-consciousness and immunity. *Journal of Philosophy* 108:78–99.

Langland-Hassan, P. Forthcoming. Introspective misidentification. *Philosophical Studies.*

Lau, H., and D. Rosenthal. 2011. Empirical support for higher-order theories of conscious awareness. *Trends in Cognitive Sciences* 15:365–373.

Liang, C., and T. Lane. 2009. Higher-order thought and pathological self: The case of somatoparaphrenia. *Analysis* 69:661–668.

Lipton, P. 1993. Constrastive explanation. In *Explanation,* ed. D. H. Ruben. New York: Oxford University Press.

Macdonald, C. 2009. Introspection. In *The Oxford Handbook of Philosophy of Mind,* ed. S. Walter, A. Bechermann, and B. McLaughlin, 741–766. Oxford: Oxford University Press.

Marcel, A. 2003. The sense of agency. In *Agency and Self-Awareness: Issues in Philosophy and Psychology,* ed. J. Roessler and N. Eilan. New York: Clarendon Press.

McNeill, D., L. Quaeghebeur, and S. Duncan. 2010. The man who lost his body. In *Handbook of Phenomenology and Cognitive Sciences,* ed. S. Gallagher and D. Schmickin. New York: Springer.

Mullins, S., and S. Spence. 2003. Re-examining thought insertion: Semi-structured literature review and conceptual analysis. *British Journal of Psychiatry* 182:293–298.

Northoff, G. 2013. *Unlocking the Brain,* vol. 2: *Consciousness.* New York: Oxford University Press.

Northoff, G., and F. Bermpohl. 2004. Cortical midline structures and the self. *Trends in Cognitive Sciences* 8:102–107.

Northoff, G., A. Heinzel, F. Bermpohl, H. Dobrowolny, and J. Panksepp. 2006. Self-referential processing in our brain: A meta-analysis of imaging studies on the self. *NeuroImage* 28:440–457.

Northoff, G., P. Qin, and T. Nakao. 2010. Rest-stimulus interaction in the brain: A review. *Trends in Neurosciences* 33:277–284.

O'Brien, L. 2007. *Self-Knowing Agents.* New York: Oxford University Press.

Prinz, J. 2012. *The Conscious Brain: How Attention Engenders Experience.* New York: Oxford University Press.

Qin, P., and G. Northoff. 2011. How is our self related to midline regions and the default mode network? *NeuroImage* 57:1221–1233.

Raij, T., M. Valkonen-Korhonen, M. Holi, S. Therman, J. Lehtonen, and R. Hari. 2009. Reality of auditory hallucinations. *Brain* 132 (Pt. 11): 2994–3001.

Revonsuo, A. 2006. *Inner Presence: Consciousness as a Biological Phenomenon.* Cambridge, MA: MIT Press.

Rilke, R. M. 1954. *Letters to a Young Poet,* rev. ed. New York: W. W. Norton.

Rizzolatti, G., and J. Kalaska. 2013. Voluntary movement: The parietal and premotor cortex. In *Principles of Neural Science,* 5th ed., ed. E. Kandel, J. Schwartz, T. Jessel, S. Siegelbaum, and A. Hudspeth. New York: McGraw Hill.

Romano, D., M. Gandola, G. Bottini, and A. Maravitaa. 2014. Arousal responses to noxious stimuli in somatoparaphrenia and anosognosia: Clues to body awareness. *Brain* 137:1213–1223.

Rosenthal, D. M. 2002. Explaining consciousness. In *Philosophy of Mind: Classical and Contemporary Readings*, ed. D. Chalmers. New York: Oxford University Press.

Rosenthal, D. M. 2005. *Consciousness and Mind*. New York: Oxford University Press.

Rosenthal, D. M. 2010. Consciousness, the self, and bodily location. *Analysis* 70: 270–276.

Rossi, S., M. Hallett, P. Rossini, and A. Pascual-Leone. 2009. Safety, ethical considerations, and application guidelines for the use of transcranial magnetic stimulation in clinical practice and research. *Clinical Neurophysiology* 120:2008–2039.

Rounis, E., B. Maniscalo, J. Rothwell, R. Passingham, and H. Lau. 2010. Theta-burst transcranial magnetic stimulation to the prefrontal cortex impairs metacognitive visual awareness. *Cognitive Neuroscience* 1:165–175.

Sass, L., and J. Parnas. 2003. Schizophrenia, consciousness, and the self. *Schizophrenia Bulletin* 29 (3): 427–444.

Schaefer, M., B. Xu, H. Flor, and L. Cohen. 2009. Effects of different viewing perspectives on somatosensory activations during observation of touch. *Human Brain Mapping* 30:2722–2730.

Schaefer, M., H.-J. Heinze, and M. Rotte. 2012. Embodied empathy for tactile events: Interindividual differences and vicarious somatosensory responses during touch observation. *NeuroImage* 60:952–957.

Schneider, F., F. Bermpohl, A. Heinzel, M. Rotte, W. Tempelmann, C. Wiebking, H. Dobrowolny, H. Heinze, and G. Northoff. 2008. The resting state and our self: Self-relatedness modulates resting state neural activity in cortical midline regions. *Neuroscience* 157:120–131.

Shergill, S., G. Samson, P. Bays, C. Frith, and D. Wolpert. 2005. Evidence for sensory prediction deficits in schizophrenia. *American Journal of Psychiatry* 162:2384–2386.

Sierra, M. 2009. *Depersonalization: A New Look at a Neglected Syndrome*. New York: Cambridge University Press.

Sommer, I., K. Dierderen, J. Blom, A. Willems, L. Kushen, K. Slotema, M. Boks, et al. 2008. Auditory verbal hallucinations predominantly activate the right inferior frontal area. *Brain* 131 (Pt. 12): 3169–3177.

Teufel, C., A. Kingdon, J. Ingram, D. Wolpert, and P. Fletcher. 2010. Deficits in sensory prediction are related to delusional ideation in healthy individuals. *Neuropsychologia* 48:4169–4172.

Tsuchiya, N., F. Moradi, C. Felsen, M. Yamazaki, and R. Adolphs. 2009. Intact rapid detection of fearful faces in the absence of the amygdala. *Nature Neuroscience* 12:1224–1225.

Valenzuela-Moguillansky, C. 2013. Pain and body awareness: An exploration of the bodily experience of persons suffering from fibromyalgia. *Constructivist Foundations* 8:339–350.

Wegner, D. 2002. *The Illusion of Conscious Will*. Cambridge, MA: MIT Press.

Yang, E., D. Zald, and R. Blake. 2007. Fearful expressions gain preferential access to awareness during continuous flash suppression. *Emotion* 7:882–886.

Zahn, R., J. Talazko, and D. Ebert. 2008. Loss of the sense of self-ownership for perceptions of objects in a case of right inferior temporal, parieto-occipital, and precentral hypometabolism. *Psychopathology* 41:397–402.

6 From Darwin to Freud: Confabulation as an Adaptive Response to Dysfunctions of Consciousness

Paula Droege

Cognitive psychology is a biological science, which means that its job is to study how the cognitive systems *work*. ... The job of core psychology is not to predict behavior but to explain the mechanisms, including contributions of supporting environmental structures, that together account for cases of *proper* cognitive functioning.

—Ruth Millikan, *White Queen Psychology* (1993)[1]

I began this project by reading the excellent anthology *Delusion and Self-Deception* (Bayne and Fernández 2009), and before long I was wondering if I had been deceiving myself into thinking I had anything original to add to the reams of recent publication on confabulation. My error does not count as delusional, thank goodness, because I am reconsidering the mistake. My ability to reevaluate my beliefs in light of counterevidence is a good way to distinguish nonpathological forms of error such as self-deception from pathological delusions.

A puzzling feature of confabulation is its selectivity: only some people confabulate in response to illness, and only some people resist correction of their inventions. So-called *two-factor theories of delusion* explain the difference by the failure of a belief monitor or evaluator. The first factor in delusion is a dysfunction in perceptual or cognitive processing and includes such cases as amnesia, feelings of unfamiliarity toward loved ones, or auditory hallucinations. In themselves, first-factor deficits do not always cause delusions, so a second factor is postulated to explain the failure of delusional patients to revise the faulty beliefs produced by first-factor deficits. For some reason—endorsement and explanationist theories differ—delusional patients maintain false beliefs in the face of counterevidence. This two-factor account seems right to me, so my remarks will focus on what first- and second-factor deficits reveal about the functions of consciousness and self-consciousness. In particular, I suggest that the function of self-consciousness is to utilize memories in order to maintain a sense of the self in time, and confabulation is an adaptive response to the absence of memories in order to serve this function. Delusional confabulation is maladaptive, however, because it undermines the social value of the self.

1 The Function of Consciousness and Self-Consciousness

This is the age of biological and neural materialism. Mapping and manipulation of genetic sequences has led to speculations about the biological basis of everything from personality to language (Gjerde et al. 2012, Powers et al. 2013). Simultaneously, advances in neural imaging technology have given researchers new insight into the brain structures underlying memory, emotion, and other mental processes (Addis et al. 2012, Panksepp 2011). Scientific research on consciousness has been an important part of the movement to identify the physical basis of psychological phenomena, but consciousness research faces a difficulty that other research does not. The function of consciousness is not obvious; indeed, some argue there is not or cannot be a function of consciousness (Rosenthal 2008, Chalmers 1997). As long as we accept this assumption, solutions to the hard problem of consciousness will be limited to correlations between neural and phenomenal processes. We will never be able to say with assurance that *this* neural process is a conscious process, because any correlate neural process might be functioning in the absence of consciousness.

These concerns do not apply to theories about the physical realization of other psychological processes such as language production. Though it is an enormously complicated business to explain how humans comprehend and produce language, no one is inclined to say that researchers may have accounted for the *functions* related to language but have left out *language itself*. The functions of parsing, grammatical sentence production, semantic association, and so forth just are language. With regard to consciousness, on the other hand, no proposed function seems adequate to determine when creatures are conscious and when they are not.

There are (at least) two reasons for the difference in treatment between language and consciousness:

(1) A legacy of the computational theory of mind is a tendency to break down mental processes into abstract, interchangeable components that can be effectively modeled by algorithmic equations. Where input and output can be described in terms of data structures, and processing involves operations over those structures, a computational analysis neatly matches mental functions with the physical systems that perform those functions.

Language, sensation, and many other mental processes fit this model well. Consciousness does not.[2]

(2) A related reason that consciousness does not seem to have a function is a reluctance to think of the mind as a biologically evolved feature of the body. To think of the mind as a computer is, perhaps counterintuitively, more in keeping with dualist tradition than it is to the Darwinian view of the mind as an adaptation to environmental conditions. The computational model allows us to think of ourselves as *software* running on hardware, performing *calculations* according to *rules* and processing *information*. This picture is not so far from René Descartes's ideal rational agent, contemplating the essences of things without that messy body muddying up the clarity and distinctness of pure intellection. A Darwinian model gives us nothing but that messy body with all its rigged-up contraptions and flaws. Natural selection only promises a system that is good enough to promote survival and reproduction enough of the time to be worth the cost of maintenance. When we're lucky, a series of mutations produces an organ that is remarkably sophisticated and effective, such as the eye. When we're not so lucky, vestigial structures such as the appendix may cause illness or death because they are not sufficiently problematic to get culled from the genetic code.

None of this random contingency fits well with the feeling we have of ourselves from the inside as essentially separate from the world, secure in our own minds so long as we restrict ourselves to logical inference patterns. Descartes's picture is tempting, especially for philosophers who yearn for the Ideal, but it is a mistaken picture. Our minds, like our bodies, are subject to the forces of evolution. Minds are designed by natural selection to fulfill various functions and so can fail to fulfill those functions. Contradictory beliefs, equivocal concepts, inference failures, and all the other manifest failures of human thought are the natural consequence of a system that functions *just well enough* to help the organism survive and reproduce. In contrast, a faculty of reason dedicated exclusively to truth and knowledge cannot account for its own deep and abiding errors.[3]

Returning now to consciousness theory, a Darwinian view of the mind begins with the assumption that consciousness has a function. Though some features of organic life are spandrels, piggy-backing on the evolutionary value of coincident properties, somewhere in the story a function figures in the explanation of every attribute. Either consciousness itself serves some purpose, or it is paired with something else that serves a purpose. In any case, the first question is: What might consciousness *do*?

This question can be profitably approached from several different directions. I'll discuss two approaches and then consider how to combine them into a plausible theory.[4] One of the earliest and most useful neuropsychological approaches is a contrastive analysis of the sort proposed by Bernard Baars (1988, 1997, Baars and Newnan 1994). A comparison of the processes that occur consciously and those that occur unconsciously can provide a sense of what consciousness adds to otherwise unconscious sensory and cognitive events. Some illuminating contrasts are the following: unconscious processes tend to be quick and accurate, involve habituated, routine responses, can be done in parallel with other processes, are initiated and conducted involuntarily, and are limited to a narrow range of contents; conscious processes tend to be slow and error-prone, involve novel responses, occur serially, are initiated voluntarily, and integrate a wide range of contents. Baars concludes from this comparison that consciousness prioritizes sensory input, thought, and action in accordance with goals. So long as the situation is familiar and predictable, no conscious adjustments are necessary. But in the face of a new opportunity or obstacle, plans may need to be altered or abandoned. According to Baars, the single most important function of consciousness is to provide access to a variety of sources of information in order to select and combine the bits relevant to the situation at hand. Consciousness is a *global workspace*—it serves as a hub for collecting and relaying information (Baars 1997).

A second approach to determining the function of consciousness adopts the diametrically opposite perspective of Cartesian self-reflection. Though we are clearly not ideal rational agents, Descartes was not wrong to look inside the mind for insights into the nature of consciousness. His error (or one of them) was to take consciousness to be an absolute foundation for knowledge. So long as we keep in mind the Darwinian project of functional explanation, introspection can reveal features that uniquely characterize conscious experience.

Phenomenologist Edmund Husserl set himself the task of identifying the essential structural features of consciousness by means of self-reflection. In Husserl's view, Descartes's error was his metaphysical dualism of mind and world, so Husserl proposed we eliminate, or *bracket*, metaphysics entirely and limit ourselves to an investigation of the world from inside the mind. I won't pause to say why I think this, too, is a mistake; I'd rather focus on the virtue of Husserl's approach in revealing the way the world appears to reflective consciousness. First and foremost, a world *appears*. Consciousness represents there to be objects, colors, sounds, a body uniquely and intimately connected to thought and feeling amid bodies that act similarly to mine. In the words of Husserl's teacher, Franz Brentano, "consciousness is always consciousness *of*" (Husserl [1913] 1970): consciousness represents a world. Second, the world appears from a *point of view*: consciousness is perspectival. As I sit here in my study, the desk extends in a trapezoid before me and to each side. If I get up and move around, the appearances of the desk's shape shift even while I represent the desk as retaining its size and place. Indeed, the form of conscious perception must change with each change in perspective in order to represent the world as stable (Husserl [1905] 1990).

A third feature of conscious experience is an essential counterpart to its perspectival structure: consciousness is temporal. The world appears before me *now* (Husserl [1905] 1990). Time is so important to consciousness that its role is rarely noticed. In the same way that earth and air form the environment necessary for human action, space and time form the structure of conscious perception. But time, like air, is difficult to grasp. Invisible and ubiquitous, time has the additional quality of flux. There is no way to stop time to examine its features in the way one can reflect on spatial relations. Of course, as Einstein has shown, we cannot stop space either—space and time shift in synch. *Consciously*, however, we represent space as static positions in an external world and time as dynamic changes in position. We do this in order to orient ourselves in a stable environment and attend to only those changes that affect our needs and goals. Here we come to the function of consciousness, as I interpret the insights from Husserl's phenomenological analysis for a Darwinian theory of the mind.[5] Consciousness represents the world at the present moment so that creatures can assess current conditions in light of their goals (Droege 2003, 2009). Changes in the appearance of the desk as I occlude one or another segment with books and papers do not change its effectiveness as the support of my computer and research material. Leaves swaying in the wind outside do not change the effectiveness of the tree to maintain its shape and shade. The sudden sound of a ball against window, on the other hand, consumes my consciousness until I am sure that nothing is broken, and the source of the sound takes his ball elsewhere. What changes over time and what remains the same, as represented in consciousness, depends on the situation of the creature in its environment. Waterfalls, traffic noise, and the motion of waves while riding in a boat are examples of environmental change that can be represented as stable after a period of adjustment.

Notice that the contrastive and phenomenological approaches to the function of consciousness have produced compatible results. In both cases, consciousness integrates information to present the world to a creature in a way uniquely relevant to that creature at that moment. In global workspace theory, the importance of accessing information and relaying it to the rest of the system takes precedence. In phenomenology, the spatiotemporal relation of the contents of consciousness to the subject is most important. But the information accessed by the workspace would be of no value unless it were coded relative to the subject, and the spatiotemporal array of experience would be no more than a solipsistic cinema unless it is integrated into a sensorimotor system capable of perceiving and acting in the world.

So, my suggestion is that the function of consciousness is to represent the world at the present moment. This might seem trivial: Don't all sensations and actions represent the world as present? The critical distinction to make is between representations that *occur* in the present and representations *of* the present. Although all representations occur at the moment that they are causally effective (the trivial bit), a representation *of* the present requires that time be part of the *content* of the representation. On a Darwinian view of the mind, an item has the function of representing something (an apple, geomagnetic north, time) just in case it has the function of varying isomorphically with that thing. This representational function is secured when it has been used often enough by consumer devices to fulfill their proper functions.[6] To be a representation *of* presence, on this theory, is to vary in accord with the present moment so that other devices can use this representation to help the organism survive and reproduce. A way to see the difference is to notice that a representation that occurs in the present cannot fail to occur when it occurs. However, a representation *of* the present *can* fail. Events can be represented as present when they are merely anticipated or have already ceased. The flash-lag illusion is a good example of anticipation.[7] If a light is flashed directly above a bar moving right to left, subjects will report seeing the bar as located left of the flash. The location of the moving bar is projected forward in space to anticipate where it is *now* rather than where it was at the moment the stimulus signal was received (Eagleman and Sejnowski 2000, Nijhawan 1994). Though bar and light *occur* simultaneously, they are not *represented as* simultaneously occurring.

If the function of consciousness is to represent the present moment, what is the value of this representation? Creatures that inflexibly respond to stimuli in fixed patterns have no need of temporal representation. Their responses must occur at the appropriate times, and so their representational systems may incorporate timing mechanisms to track the time of day or cycles of the moon. Such creatures use time but do not represent time. Temporal representation becomes valuable, indeed necessary, when a creature is able to respond to a situation in more than one way. Where different responses are possible, a creature must be able to assess the situation *now* in order to determine the best action in light of its goals. In sum, consciousness has the function of integrating information about the world as it is now presented to the subject to aid the pursuit of goals.

It is worth noting how this temporal representation theory of consciousness differs from other philosophical theories. In contrast with other first-order theories, such as Fred Dretske's representational naturalism (1995), the function of consciousness is distinct from other functions such as sensation, thought, or integration. The representational content of consciousness is the present moment, and its function is to facilitate flexible response.[8] In contrast with higher-order theories, such as higher-order thought (Rosenthal 2005, Gennaro 2012) and higher-order perception (Carruthers 2004, Lycan 2004) theory, conscious representation is a direct relation. I am conscious of the world by having a representation of the world as it is now. On a higher-order theory, I represent my sensations of the world in order to be conscious of it. A full argument against higher-order theory would require another chapter to consider the deep and subtle differences among these theories, but let me give just one general objection: higher-order representations are unnecessary.[9] Unless the quite sophisticated apparatus of higher-order representation is required to explain the difference between conscious and unconscious representation, a simpler form of representation is preferable. As we will soon see, the capacity for higher-order representation usefully marks a different distinction crucial to understanding confabulation: the distinction between consciousness and self-consciousness.

Careful consideration of representational function illuminates this distinction. To the extent that the *self* refers to the sensations of one's own body, self-consciousness is an aspect of consciousness. The representation of pain in my arm is particularly salient to me but is not a different kind of representation than the representation of green on the leaves of the tree.[10] Representations of one's own bodily states are part of the world that one represents as present in consciousness. Or, as is often the case, bodily states are *not* conscious because they are not the most relevant information to goal-directed behavior.

Self-consciousness serves a distinct representational function when it involves consciousness of one's *representational* states. This sense of self-consciousness will be the primary topic in this chapter. *Higher-order representation* is a representation about another representation, and so self-consciousness is a form of higher-order representation that constitutes an extended sense of self. Creatures develop the capacity for representing their own representations when they need to be able to keep track of their past and plan for their future.

Again, it might seem that all creatures must be able to represent them-selves in time in order to flexibly pursue their goals. Although a creature must be able to distinguish the present from past and future, it does not need to represent its own experiences of past events, nor does it need to rep-resent its expectations about its own future experiences, where *experience* is a conscious representation as described above.[11] Arguably, the ability to keep track of *one's own* past and future arises with the development of com-plex social systems and goes beyond simple goal-directed behavior. Having a theory of mind—the representation of representations—facilitates inter-actions with others by anticipating their desires, understanding their fears, and thwarting their deceptions (Perner 1991, Humphrey 1987). Applying these skills to one's self allows for the collection of information about one's own thoughts and feelings over time to form an autobiographical narrative about the sort of person one is and the sorts of things one does.

2   Varieties of Misrepresentation

Thus far I have proposed a functional theory of consciousness and self-consciousness in terms of temporal representation. Consciousness is a representation of the present moment in order to determine appropriate goal-directed action. Self-consciousness is a representation of one's past and future representations in order to form a sense of one's self as extended in time. In addition, a functional theory can help diagnose *dysfunctions* of vari-ous kinds. When something goes wrong, we want to know why. Sometimes the machinery is functioning perfectly, but the environment fails to coop-erate: even a new car will not run underwater. Sometimes the machinery itself is at fault, and it would be useful to know exactly where the malfunc-tion has occurred in order to affect repair. In this section, I'll look at two ways these representations might fail: consumer error and producer error.

According to Ruth Millikan's teleosemantic theory of mental represen-tation, two types of function operate in coordination to secure represen-tational success. A representation *producer* has the function of getting the representation to vary according to a rule with the item it represents. To represent the location of the moving bar described in the flash-lag illusion in the previous section, the visual system produces a representation that continually updates the representation of the bar position as it moves from right to left. A representation *consumer* has the function of utilizing the rep-resentation relation to aid survival and reproduction. If the representation fails to accord with the item it represents, then the consumer will not be able to fulfill its function, except by chance (Millikan 1993, 287).

(1) *Consumer error.* Illusions such as flash-lag can be explained by looking at how consumers may fail even when producers are functioning properly. In order to capture moving prey or escape an oncoming predator, a creature needs to anticipate the location of the target based on its trajectory. The creature needs to know where the target is *now*, not where the light-reflectance signal began its journey several hundred milliseconds ago. In contrast, stationary targets such as the flash should be represented at the time and place where they occurred. The difference in function translates into a representation of the moving bar to the left of the flash, even though the bar and flash were presented simultaneously at the same location.

Many perceptual illusions exploit just this sort of gap between functional design and unusual situation to produce an inaccurate representation. In the Müller-Lyer illusion, the lines are actually the same length, but one line looks longer than the other (see fig. 6.1).

How can a teleofunctional theory of representation account for this failure when the system is fully functional? Remember that the producer function is to get representations to vary according to a rule with the item they represent, so that consumers can aid the creature in survival and reproduction. Because it has been adaptively successful to represent lines with tips extending outward as concave shapes and lines with tips extending inward as convex shapes, consumers read concave lines as further away and, therefore, longer than convex lines. The job of consumers is to interpret representational content in a way that has been successful enough of the time to warrant continued production. But there is no guarantee that every situation will conform to the felicitous conditions that occurred in the past. Indeed, there are many reasons that the consumers of perceptual representations fail to fulfill their functions. A common reason for failure is simply the inability to capture prey, avoid a predator, or accomplish whatever goal was intended. In the case of the Müller-Lyer illusion, the failure is due to deliberate manipulation that thwarts normal functioning.[12] These failures accentuate function rather than undermine it. We learn how

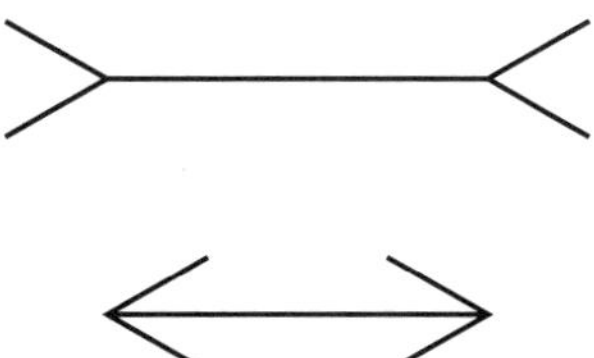

Figure 6.1
The Müller-Lyer illusion.

limited perceptual input is interpreted as shaped, located far or near, moving or still. An understanding of perceptual illusions should not incline us to try to fix the visual system so that it does not produce these errors. Enough of the time, the system functions to tell us what we need to know about our environment.

(2) *Producer error*. Another sort of representational error occurs when a system represents one thing as another, takes two things to be one and the same, or produces a representation in the absence of any referent at all. This sort of error may be considered (oxymoronically) true misrepresentation since it involves a failure of the representation to accord by a rule with the item it represents. Someone might mistake a bush for a person when walking home on a dark night or be unable to distinguish between beech and elm trees. Misrepresentations occur when consumers of a representation p have successfully utilized a relation to one thing, such as a person, to fulfill their function, and representation p is caused by another thing, such as a bush. Equivocal representations occur when misrepresentations are not corrected, and two things, such as beech and elm trees, come to be represented as the same.

Empty representations have caused a great deal of trouble in philosophy of mind because representation is a relation, and relations traditionally require two existent relata. If a representation is empty, there would seem to be only one item, the representation, without anything to serve as the item represented. Say that I come to think that today I will finally see the King of France. This thought has come about through a poor understanding of European history and government as well as the announcement of a parade through Paris of all French dignitaries and officials. There is no King of France to stand in relation to my representation, so no consumers could have utilized this relation to successfully fulfill their functions. But notice that concepts about kings as heads of state and kings of France during various periods of history do have referents that test-taking consumers may have utilized to good effect. Empty representations indicate that the system is malfunctioning in some way, as in this case, where I have confused historical and contemporary facts to produce a nonreferring representation. In general, a teleofunctional solution to the problem of the missing relatum is to admit there is no representational relation when there is no referent. The system is mistaken in taking there to be a relation where one does not exist.[13]

3   Confabulation as Misrepresentation

Given that the function of consciousness and self-consciousness is temporal representation—of the world now and of oneself over time, respectively—we are in a position to consider the specific dysfunction of confabulation. In keeping with my focus on self-consciousness as the representation of one's self in time, I will restrict my discussion to classic cases of confabulation involving the production of false memories. Other forms of confabulation, such as occur in conjunction with hemiplegia or Anton's syndrome, are beyond the scope of this chapter.[14]

The clearest cases of confabulation occur in Korsakoff patients who suffer from severe amnesia. Oliver Sacks offers a vivid description of the situation for one of his patients:

Abysses of amnesia continually opened beneath him, but he would bridge them, nimbly, by fluent confabulations and fictions of all kinds. For him they were not fictions, but how he suddenly saw, or interpreted, the world. Its radical flux and incoherence could not be tolerated, acknowledged, for an instant—there was, instead, this strange, delirious, quasi-coherence, as Mr. Thompson, with his ceaseless, unconscious, quick-fire inventions, continually improvised a world around him—an Arabian Nights world, a phantasmagoria, a dream, of ever-changing people, figures, situations—continual, kaleidoscopic mutations and transformations. (Sacks 1970)

According to Gianfranco Dalla Barba and Marie-Francoise Boissé (2010), *temporal consciousness* is the ability to keep track of the self in time, and so its function is similar to the function of self-consciousness described above. When temporal consciousness malfunctions, as in Korsakoff syndrome, a person has difficulty organizing memories and tends to conflate and reorder events. Unlike cases of amnesia without confabulation, the confabulating person retains a sense of herself in time but constructs an alternate timeline out of misremembered and invented fragments (Dalla Barba 2009).

Despite the similarities between temporal consciousness and self-consciousness, there are instructive differences in how these notions figure in a theory of consciousness. Most significantly, temporal consciousness is not dependent in any way on unconscious representations. Whereas, in my view, consciousness and self-consciousness are particular sorts of representation that serve particular functions not performed by, but dependent on, unconscious representations. Consciousness selects and combines otherwise unconscious representations into a representation of the present moment in order to facilitate flexible, goal-directed action, and self-consciousness emerges as a representation of one's own past, present, and future representations in order to keep track of oneself in relation to others belonging to complex social networks.

Dalla Barba would object that this theory suffers from the *fallacy of the homunculus* (Dalla Barba 2002, 2009, Dalla Barba and Boisse 2010). Because consciousness is necessary for meaning, he argues, unconsciousness can be nothing more than a physical, causal process. This objection, as well as phenomenology in general, rests on a Cartesian rather than a Darwinian view of the mind. Consciousness and meaning (and usually self-consciousness too) appear fully formed in the mature, intact, reflective mind, and the mystery is how they could possibly be produced by brain processes. Descartes, of course, concluded that they couldn't possibly and so were nonphysical. Neurophenomenologists, such as Dalla Barba, reject dualism but not the Cartesian commitment to consciousness as the mark of the mental. The problem with this commitment from a Darwinian point of view is the difficulty in explaining how consciousness and meaning suddenly appear out of nowhere. Evolutionary explanation depends on a series of small mutations over the course of generations, where each mutation confers some selective advantage that accounts for its reproduction. To claim that consciousness and meaning are not rooted in unconscious processes is to sever the mind from its evolutionary ancestry.[15]

The rejection of unconscious representation also raises the question of how past experiences influence present consciousness. Dalla Barba and Boissé (2010) suggest that "modifications" in the brain cause temporal consciousness, even though these causes have no representational content. Magically, these contentless bits are combined more or less accurately into narratives of a personal past and future, depending on the integrity of the brain. Neuropsychological structures, from Hebbian synaptic connections to dynamic systems of neural networks, may be causal precursors to consciousness, but, since they have no content, they cannot be used to explain why some of a person's representations of her past are correct and others are confabulated. Conscious content is created sui generis—how it succeeds or fails to represent anything is a mystery.

An adequate theory of conscious memory must explain how a person is plausibly connected to her past experiences in ways that justify the accuracy of her memories. On a Darwinian account, representations of the past are produced in a similar way to other sorts of representations: they are designed to vary isomorphically with the item represented so as to aid survival and reproduction. The survival value of episodic memories is social, given the function of self-consciousness developed above. Memories endow a person with the sense of who she has been and how she has interacted with others over the course of her life. Perhaps more important, episodic memories help a person imagine how her future might take shape in satisfying ways based on how things have gone well or badly in the past (Schacter and Addis 2007). In light of these functions, the partial, errorprone, constructive character of memory can be seen as an effective way to balance the dual desiderata of accuracy and action-orientation. A tape-recorder memory would be perfectly accurate but would lack the ability for quick generalization and recombination necessary for situation-specific application. On the other extreme, a self tailored precisely to meet current demands would fail to have the continuity and stability that others expect. Though I might perform better on many tasks without the baggage of my personal past, it is just that baggage that anchors me in a particular community and defines me for family, friends, and acquaintances. In other words, the Darwinian view explains why memory is both accurate and inaccurate in predictable ways.

All of which brings us back to confabulation. How might a Darwinian theory of self-consciousness explain confabulation? If the function of conscious memory is to produce a temporally extended self, confabulation performs this function by adding false content to remembered experiences in order to produce a plausible narrative of a self over time. Representation producers generate false memories that conflate or invent past events and confuse historical with personal events. Confabulations feel like real memories because they are produced by the same system, designed to serve the same function. The memory production system lacks the proper input—missing, partial, or contradictory information—so it constructs a story on the basis of whatever bits are available. Confabulation is an adaptive response to memory dysfunction; it preserves a sense of self in time despite the loss of reliable information about past experiences.

4 Rational Confabulation

If we take confabulation to be adaptive—as what the system is supposed to do, in some sense—does that also mean it is rational? The answer, of course, depends on what we count as rationality. On a Darwinian view, rationality must be tied to fitness: it is rational to desire things that aid survival and reproduction and to believe things that help satisfy those desires. Beliefs and desires are reproduced because they have been useful in some way, by leading to appropriate responses or participating in valid inferences. Note that in a social and linguistic world the survival value of beliefs and desires may be quite indirectly tied to biological need. Learning to appropriately apply the word *Monet* will not, in itself, do much to help me or my genes proliferate. A single representation, such as *Monet*, or a belief, such as "Monet is an artist," is derived from a system of representation producers and consumers operating in tandem to design a mind that fits its environment. The sorts of representations that aid in flourishing in rural

Pennsylvania will differ from those useful to residents of Cairo. What all representations have in common is that their value is tied to their success in guiding action in the world.

In considering whether confabulation is rational on this account, it will be useful to discuss two other delusions that have been described as rational: Capgras syndrome and schizophrenic thought insertion. Patients manifesting Capgras syndrome claim that imposters have been substituted for loved ones. They recognize that the person looks identical to their spouse, sibling, or parent but claim it is nonetheless not that person. On a two-factor account, neurological damage to the right hemisphere accounts for the first factor of this delusion. A lesion that severs connectivity between face identification systems and affective responses leads to the sense that the person looks just like a loved one but is unfamiliar (Ellis and Young 1990, Ellis et al. 1997, Stone and Young 1997, Coltheart, Menzies, and Sutton 2010). Brian McLaughlin (2009) describes the situation as an *affective illusion*: the lack of input from the affective system leads to misrepresentation despite functional face identification systems. Because the person has a genuine feeling of unfamiliarity along with the identification of a familiar person, Brendan Maher (1974) has suggested that the "imposter hypothesis" is a rational solution to the problem posed by the patient's aberrant experience. But as McLaughlin counters, this solution cannot be rational because it conflicts with evidence accepted as true by the patient (2009).

Here is where the consideration of function can be illuminating. If the function of consciousness is to produce a representation of the present moment, then the representation *imposter* does indeed conform to function. The Capgras patient consciously represents the person as both familiar and unfamiliar at the same time, and imposters are the only sort of people who fit this description. Nonetheless, the falsity of the imposter hypothesis is revealed by its inconsistency with additional evidence, and so it should not be accepted. In the frame of a two-factor account, we can say that imposter hypothesis that results from the first-factor deficit is rational, but the persistence in believing this hypothesis in the face of counterevidence is irrational to the point of delusional.

Thought insertion in schizophrenia admits to a similar sort of explanation. One prominent neuropsychological account proposes a mismatch between predicted action and actual action owing to the malfunction of a module called a *comparator* (Frith, Blakemore, and Wolpert 2000, Carruthers 2012). Predicted action is the source of the feeling of agency that normally is confirmed by perceptual feedback indicating the action was performed. On the comparator model, thought insertion is the result of conscious thoughts in the absence of the signal that normally produces the feeling of agency accompanying conscious thoughts. The result is that the schizophrenic person has conscious thoughts that feel to her as if they were produced by someone other than herself. As with Capgras syndrome, the hypothesis that someone is inserting thoughts into her mind is a rational response to her aberrant experiences.[16] But in maintaining this hypothesis in the face of counterevidence and manufacturing elaborate scenarios to reinforce it, schizophrenic thought insertion is delusional.

With these two cases in mind, the question about whether confabulation is rational has a clear answer. As with Capgras syndrome and thought insertion, the absence of essential input produces faulty but reasonable results. Confabulators invent and recombine memories to produce an extended sense of self as a way to rationally compensate for memories lost to amnesia. Those of us who confabulate regularly and are willing to revise our memories in light of evidence illustrate how memory errors can be produced in minds that are not damaged in any way. Confabulation is delusional when a second deficit in monitoring or evaluating these memories endorses them despite their implausibility or conflict with other evidence. Neurological evidence for damage to executive processes in confabulation supports this account (Nahum et al. 2012, Dalla Barba and La Corte 2013, Gilboa 2010).

5 Content and Consciousness

Participants in recent debates about delusion may wonder whether the account just described is an *endorsement* or *explanationist* account. In an endorsement account, strange experiences produced by first-factor deficits are simply taken to be veridical. There is a general tendency to endorse the deliverances of perception and memory. Seeing is believing, after all. Even so, two-factor theorists recognize that strange experiences alone do not explain why the delusional person continues to maintain faulty beliefs. So some endorsement theorists have suggested that emotions and motivations are the second factor. These privilege the faulty experiences in a way that overrides normal forms of belief evaluation such as tests for consistency, plausibility, or available confirming and disconfirming evidence (McLaughlin 2009, McKay and Kinsbourne 2010, Davies 2009, Fotopoulou 2010).

An objection to the endorsement view is the *experiential encoding problem* (Langdon and Bayne 2010). Perceptual experience may seem too cognitively thin to carry sophisticated conceptual content, such as *imposter*. On this view, perceptual experience is like a canvas of colors and shapes awaiting the thoughtful interpretation of the viewer,[17] who applies the content *imposter* to explain the anomalous experience.

In contrast to endorsement, the advocate of an explanationist account emphasizes the inference processes that follow strange experiences. Here is how Robyn Langdon and Tim Bayne describe the two accounts:

> The explanationist and the endorsement accounts are alike with regard to the role of inferential transitions in the formation of delusions, the two accounts differ only in where they locate such transitions in relation to experience. The explanationist account of the route from experience to a reflective delusion locates most of the inferential processing downstream of experience, in the processes of hypothesis generation and evaluation, whereas the endorsement account locates it upstream of experience, before the received delusion is endorsed. (Langdon and Bayne 2010)

This description of the difference between explanationist and endorsement accounts highlights a serious problem. The difference is cast in terms of the content of consciousness, whether inferences occur prior to consciousness, giving the person cognitively thick experiences, or whether inferences occur after relatively thin experiences.

This difference is reminiscent of Daniel Dennett's distinction between Stalinesque and Orwellian revision (1991, Dennett and Kinsbourne 1992). Does delusional belief occur before the person has a conscious experience or afterward? Dennett argued that this question could not be answered in principle, and so there could be no fact of the matter about the contents of consciousness. I disagree and have argued that there is indeed a fact of the matter about the contents of consciousness: consciousness represents the present moment (Droege 2003). To the extent it is possible to determine how the system is functioning, it is possible to determine what it represents.

So the problem with the endorsement/explanationist distinction is not that there is no way to determine the content of consciousness. The problem is that the distinction assumes that the delusional content is fixed in place either prior to or after consciousness. Either inferences happen prior to experience and the Capgras patient has a feeling that the person is an imposter, *or* she simply has a feeling of unfamiliarity and then infers that the person must be an imposter. You have to pick one account or the other.

I have described the experiences of Capgras patients as including the feeling that a person is an imposter and the experiences of schizophrenics as conscious thoughts inserted into the mind by someone else. These experiences are endorsed by a faulty monitoring or evaluative system that maintains the delusional beliefs in the face of counterevidence. Am I therefore offering an endorsement account of delusion? No. The inferential processes that sustain delusional beliefs do not end with their acquisition. The explanation of strange experiences is ongoing, especially when the delusional belief is challenged as implausible or inconsistent with other beliefs or evidence. Delusions involve endorsing aberrant experiences *and* explaining them despite assaults on their plausibility.

With regard to confabulation, it is even more apparent that delusional inferences are not exclusively prior to or following confabulated self-conscious content. Conscious memory functions to represent a past experience as part of a present experience in order to connect experiences of the past and present (and future) into a temporally extended self (Droege 2013). The self is continually fabricated in response to cues that trigger the retrieval of relevant past experiences. When confabulators produce irrelevant or false memories, there is no reason to doubt that they experience these memories in the same way they experience true memories. Even so, memories are constructed, not recorded and replayed, which means that cognitive processes of interpretation and conjecture operate to produce and justify memories. In other words, confabulators consciously experience false memories that are the result of an attempt to explain the gaps in memory over time.

Langdon and Bayne recognize the problem in trying to draw a line between explanation and endorsement, noting that most delusions seem to be a hybrid of both accounts. Their solution is a continuum from received to reflective delusion: received delusions are formed largely by endorsement processes, and reflective delusions are formed largely by explanationist processes (Langdon and Bayne 2010, 330). Langdon and Bayne put confabulation toward the received end, although they suggest that purely reflective confabulations may occur.

I would go further and argue that the endorsement and explanationist accounts be eliminated in favor of an account that acknowledges the dependence of conscious content on both perceptual and cognitive processes. Furthermore, remembered content is subject to ongoing revision. On a Darwinian view, representations earn their keep by helping their bearer to navigate in a changing environment. Though they may fail to fulfill this function, and in the case of delusion they fail systematically, conscious representations had best be designed to incorporate both perceptual and conceptual information in order to provide a useful approximation of how things are now and have been.

6 At Last to Freud

The main argument in this chapter has been that a functional account of consciousness and self-consciousness is a useful tool for understanding confabulation and other delusions such as Capgras syndrome and schizo-phrenic thought insertion. In closing, let me say a word about how all this connects to psychodynamic approaches to delusion pioneered by Sigmund Freud (1923).

Though all but the most committed analysts doubt the validity of Freud's singular psychosexual explanation of the origin of neuroses and psychoses (as well as civilization and its discontents), Freudian notions like repres-sion, projection, and sublimation continue to be productive in explaining human motivation and action. A Darwinian account of the mind as com-posed of representations designed to aid survival and reproduction need not reject the view of a self struggling to maintain itself in a world of com-plex and competing demands. Freud imagined a battle between an instinc-tive drive toward the satisfaction of bodily pleasures and the constraints on that satisfaction imposed by a social order. Enculturation is a process of inculcating that order within the psyche of the individual, so the battle becomes an internal war of the id (pleasure) against the superego (culture). The ideal result is a stalemate that allows a stable and functional ego to walk precariously and obliviously between these two factions as she goes about her daily life. According to Freud, this pitched internal battle rages entirely outside consciousness, the only signs of its progression appearing in the form of inexplicable actions such as parapraxis (Freudian slips) and other manifestations of the subconscious such as dreams.

Freud was the first theorist to propose an active and symbolic uncon-scious, an astute innovation that is only beginning to gain widespread acceptance as we continue to discover how much mental processing occurs outside the light of consciousness. The dramatic description of the subcon-scious—as I will call the specifically Freudian unconscious—certainly has had its adherents. But it suffers from Dalla Barba's *fallacy of the homunculus*. Freud offered no explanation of where instinctual drives originate, how social order is internalized, or, most critically, how id and superego compete with one another for control of the ego. By contrast, a Darwinian theory of the unconscious draws on evolutionary history to show how representa-tions develop from simple sensory-response couplings to complex concep-tual structures (Millikan 2004, Dennett 1995). Unconscious representations need not be the uncontrollable or oppressive forces posited by Freud; they include mundane capacities such as walking on an uneven path or parsing speech in a familiar language.

This is not to say that unconscious representations are always so benign. The human social and cultural environment forms one important set of parameters within which our representational system operates. An argument could be made that social/cultural regulations are an even more important factor in determining the survival of representations for a contemporary human than physical or biological constraints. Consequently, a full understanding of delusions like confabulation requires an examination of the social and cultural forces that shape the formation and maintenance of mental illness.[18]

In my view, consciousness is a representation of the present moment, developed in order to assess the progress of goal-directed behavior. Self-consciousness includes a representation of past experience as part of a conscious state in order to keep track of the self in time. Self-consciousness emerges from consciousness in response to social demands to maintain a consistent identity. Failure to fulfill this identity-maintenance function is often caused by neurological damage, but it may also be caused by radical disruptions in the social environment in relation to which the self was constructed. In other words, brain damage is not the only source of delusions, and brain interventions—such as drug therapy or neurosurgery—are not the only cure. A Darwinian view of the mind is inclusive in its consideration of possible explanations and pragmatist in its evaluation of them. When self-consciousness breaks, the best approach effects repair.

Notes

1. The bit omitted from the quote makes the point that psychology should not study systems that fail, since successful function must be determined first. I agree that a basic understanding of function should precede a discussion of malfunction but will argue here that malfunction can also help clarify proper function.

2. John Searle (1980) famously pointed this out in the heyday of computational theory. Despite the many responses by computational theorists since the article first appeared, conscious robots figure more prominently in science fiction than in artificial intelligence research programs.

3. See Ruth Millikan's sustained argument for this point in the title article from *White Queen Psychology and Other Essays for Alice* (1993). See also Daniel Dennett's *Darwin's Dangerous Idea* (1995) for a general argument in favor of Darwinian thinking.

4. A third approach, comparative ethology, looks at behavioral and physical features that characterize conscious creatures as distinct from unconscious creatures. The difficulty in this approach, of course, is to determine which creatures are which without begging the question about the function of consciousness to be answered. Even so, as a supplement to cognitive and phenomenological considerations, comparative ethology can add an important dimension to discussions about the evolutionary value of consciousness (see, for example, Droege and Braithwaite 2014).

5. Husserl himself offered no functional analysis of consciousness because he took consciousness to be the ground of existence. Consciousness is simply given in the "natural attitude," it requires no explanation (Husserl 1905). A similar mistake is shared by current advocates of neurophenomenology. Consciousness is simply described phenomenologically and then correlated with neural structures. Even Evan Thompson, who develops an intricate biological base for the phenomenological mind, gives consciousness a wholly mysterious ground in the "absolute flow" of time consciousness (Thompson 2010, 323–328).

6. This broad gloss on Millikan's teleosemantics (2004, 1993, 1989, 1984) is meant to point toward a Darwinian theory of representation, not to wage a full defense. I will explain a bit more about the relation between producer and consumer function in the next section, but more curious or skeptical readers should consult Millikan's own careful and comprehensive arguments in support of the theory.

7. In the next section I will argue that this illusion is not a case of representation failure after all, or at least it is not a simple case. By anticipating the trajectory of the bar, the representation producing system is functioning properly. The error is that the location of the bar is represented as *to the left of* the flash when they were actually located at the same place.

8. Ned Block (1997) and Michael Tye (1995, 2000) both suggest that consciousness makes content "poised." The integration of information into a representation of the present moment may be a way to make this rather vague term concrete.

9. For more argument, see Droege 2003, chapter 2. See also Rosenthal (2005) and Gennaro (2012) for further defense of higher-order theory. Readers are encouraged to draw their own opinions on higher-order theory by considering the other worthy contributions to this volume.

10. Technically, there are no representations *of* pain and green; they are qualities of the sensory system that represent properties such as bodily tissue damage and light reflectance (Clark 2000, Tye 2000, Rosenthal 2005).

11. For a full explanation of how a representation of the present moment can also represent a past or a future moment, see Droege (2013).

12. In Millikan terms, the situation is not Normal; the conditions do not conform to those that have accounted for the historical success of the consumer in performing its function.

13. As far as I can tell, this solution eludes the problems with representational theories of consciousness raised by Pete Mandik's Unicorn Argument (2009).

14. It is worth noting that these sorts of *perceptual* or *intentional* confabulations involve memory retrieval processes in producing the false report about what was seen or intended. A patient without control of her arm must use her memory of reasons she might not have wanted to move it in order to manufacture her response.

These need not be, and probably are not, episodic memories, and so are not the sort of self-conscious representations under consideration here. But they may involve the same or similar deficits as false episodic memories.

15. John Searle's "connection principle" (1992) rests on a similar Cartesian assumption, despite Searle's avowed commitment to biological naturalism. According to the connection principle, unconscious representations must be accessible to consciousness, because only consciousness can fix aspectual shape. The Cartesian assumption is that consciousness is necessary for determining representational content as, for example, water rather than H_2O (163–164). A teleofunctional theory explains exactly how to individuate representational content as a precursor to consciousness and so offers a step-wise account of their evolution. In our commitment to a biological and teleological account of consciousness, Searle and I are in agreement. See *Consciousness and Language* (Searle 2002, chapter 5) for a straightforward argument that representation is simply part of nature.

16. On this point, I side with John Campbell in his debate with Annalisa Coliva (Campbell 2001, 2002, Coliva 2002a, 2002b). Thought insertion indicates that introspection is not immune to error through misidentification. People with schizophrenic auditory hallucinations maintain a sense of ownership (these thoughts are in my head), but they have lost a sense of agency (these thoughts were not produced by me).

17. Note that this description is precisely the opposite of Dalla Barba's, where consciousness alone produces meaning. Oppositions such as this hint that the correct view must be somewhere in between.

18. Thanks to Jesse Ballenger, Greg Eghigian, and Sandy Lindenbaum for reminding me of the essential role social factors play in the manifestation of mental illness and especially in theory and treatment.

References

Addis, D., K. Knapp, R. P. Roberts, and D. L. Schacter. 2012. Routes to the past: Neural substrates of direct and generative autobiographical memory retrieval. *NeuroImage* 59:2908–2922.

Baars, B. 1988. *A Cognitive Theory of Consciousness*. Cambridge: Cambridge University Press.

Baars, B. 1997. *In the Theater of Consciousness: The Workspace of the Mind*. Oxford: Oxford University Press.

Baars, B., and J. Newnan. 1994. A neurobiological interpretation of global workspace theory. In *Consciousness in Philosophy and Cognitive Neuroscience*, ed. A. Revonsuo and M. Kamppinen. Hillsdale, NJ: Erlbaum.

Bayne, T., and J. Fernández, eds. 2009. *Delusion and Self-Deception: Affective and Motivational Influences on Belief Formation*. Hove: Psychology Press.

Block, N. 1997. Biology versus computation in the study of consciousness. *Behavioral and Brain Sciences* 20:159–166.

Campbell, J. 2001. Memory demonstratives. In *Time and Memory: Issues in Philosophy and Psychology*, ed. Christoph Hoerl and Teresa McCormack, 169–186. Oxford: Oxford University Press.

Campbell, J. 2002. The ownership of thoughts. *Philosophy, Psychiatry & Psychology* 9:35–39.

Carruthers, G. 2012. The case for the comparator model as an explanation of the sense of agency and its breakdowns. *Consciousness and Cognition* 21:30–45.

Carruthers, P. 2004. HOP over FOR, HOT Theory. In *Higher-Order Theories of Consciousness*, ed. R. Gennaro. Amsterdam: John Benjamins.

Chalmers, D. 1997. Facing up to the problem of consciousness. In *Explaining Consciousness: The "Hard Problem,"* ed. J. Shear. Cambridge, MA: MIT Press.

Clark, A. 2000. *A Theory of Sentience*. Oxford: Oxford University Press.

Coliva, A. 2002a. Thought insertion and immunity to error through misidentification. *Philosophy, Psychiatry & Psychology* 9:27–34.

Coliva, A. 2002b. On what there really is to our notion of ownership of a thought. *Philosophy, Psychiatry & Psychology* 9:41–46.

Coltheart, M., P. Menzies, and J. Sutton. 2010. Abductive inference and delusional belief. *Cognitive Neuropsychiatry* 15:261–287.

Dalla Barba, G. 2002. *Memory, Consciousness, and Temporality*. Norwell: Kluwer Academic Publishers.

Dalla Barba, G. 2009. Temporal consciousness and confabulation: Escape from unconscious explanatory idols. In *Confabulation: Views from Neuroscience, Psychiatry, Psychology, and Philosophy*, ed. W. Hirstein. Oxford: Oxford University Press.

Dalla Barba, G., and M. Boissé. 2010. Temporal consciousness and confabulation: Is the medial temporal lobe "temporal"? *Cognitive Neuropsychiatry* 15:95–117.

Dalla Barba, G., and V. La Corte. 2013. The hippocampus: A time machine that makes errors. *Trends in Cognitive Sciences* 17:102–104.

Davies, Martin. 2009. Delusion and motivationally biased belief: Self-deception in the Two-factor Framework. In *Delusion and Self-Deception: Affective and Motivational Influences on Belief Formation*, ed. T. Bayne and J. Fernández. Hove: Psychology Press.

Dennett, D. C. 1991. *Consciousness Explained*. Boston: Little, Brown.

Dennett, D. C. 1995. *Darwin's Dangerous Idea: Evolution and the Meanings of Life*. New York: Simon & Schuster.

Dennett, D., and M. Kinsbourne. 1992. Time and the observer: The where and when of consciousness in the brain. *Behavioral and Brain Sciences* 15:183–247.

Dretske, F. 1995. *Naturalizing the Mind*. Cambridge, MA: MIT Press.

Droege, P. 2003. *Caging the Beast: A Theory of Sensory Consciousness*. Amsterdam: John Benjamins.

Droege, P. 2009. Now or never: How consciousness represents time. *Consciousness and Cognition* 18:78–90.

Droege, P. 2013. Memory and consciousness. *Philosophia Scientiae* 17:171–193.

Droege, P., and V. Braithwaite. 2014. Framework for investigating animal consciousness. In *Ethics in Behavioural Neuroscience*, ed. F. Ohl, G. Lee, and J. Illes. New York: Springer.

Eagleman, D., and T. Sejnowski. 2000. Motion integration and postdiction in visual awareness. *Science* 287:2036.

Ellis, H., and A. Young. 1990. Accounting for delusional misidentifications. *British Journal of Psychiatry* 157:239–248.

Ellis, H., A. Young, A. Quayle, and K. De Pauw. 1997. Reduced autonomic responses to faces in Capgras delusion. *Proceedings of the Royal Society of London, Series B: Biological Sciences* 264:1085–1092.

Fotopoulou, A. 2010. The affective neuropsychology of confabulation and delusion. *Cognitive Neuropsychiatry* 15:38–63.

Freud, S. (1923) 1989. *The Ego and the Id*. New York: W. W. Norton.

Frith, C., B. Blakemore, and D. Wolpert. 2000. Abnormalities in the awareness and control of action. *Philosophical Transactions of the Royal Society of London, Series B: Biological Sciences* 355:1771–1788.

Gennaro, R. 2012. *Consciousness Paradox: Consciousness, Concepts, and Higher-Order Thoughts*. Cambridge, MA: MIT Press.

Gilboa, A. 2010. Strategic retrieval, confabulations, and delusions: Theory and data. *Cognitive Neuropsychiatry* 15:145–180.

Gjerde, L., N. Czajkowski, E. Røysamb, R. Orstavik, G. Knudsen, K. Ostby, S. Torgersen, J. Myers, K. S. Kendler, and T. Reichborn-Kjennerud. 2012. The heritability of avoidant and dependent personality disorder assessed by personal interview and questionnaire. *Acta Psychiatrica Scandinavica* 126:448–457.

Humphrey, N. 1987. The inner eye of consciousness. In *Mindwaves: Thoughts on Intelligence, Identity, and Consciousness*, ed. C. Blakemore and S. Greenfield. Oxford: Blackwell.

Husserl, E. (1905) 1990. *On the Phenomenology of the Consciousness of Internal Time (1893–1917)*. Trans. John Barnett Brough. *Husserliana: Collected Works*, Book 4. Dordrecht: Kluwer Academic.

Husserl, E. (1913) 1970. *Logical Investigations*. Trans. J. N. Findlay. New York: Humanities Press.

Kriegel, U. 2009. *Subjective Consciousness: A Self-Representational Theory*. Oxford: Oxford University Press.

Langdon, R., and T. Bayne. 2010. Delusion and confabulation: Mistakes of perceiving, remembering, and believing. *Cognitive Neuropsychiatry* 15:319–345.

Lycan, W. 2004. The superiority of HOP to HOT. In *Higher-Order Theories of Consciousness*, ed. R. Gennaro. Amsterdam: John Benjamins.

Maher, B. 1974. Delusional thinking and perceptual disorder. *Journal of Individual Psychology* 30:98.

Mandik, P. 2009. Beware of the unicorn: Consciousness as being represented and other things that don't exist. *Journal of Consciousness Studies* 16 (1): 5–36.

McKay, R., and M. Kinsbourne. 2010. Confabulation, delusion, and anosognosia: Motivational factors and false claims. *Cognitive Neuropsychiatry* 15:288–318.

McLaughlin, B. 2009. Monothematic delusions and existential feelings. In *Delusion and Self-Deception: Affective and Motivational Influences on Belief Formation*, ed. T. Bayne and J. Fernández. Hove: Psychology Press.

Millikan, R. 1984. *Language, Thought, and Other Biological Categories*. Cambridge, MA: MIT Press.

Millikan, R. 1989. Biosemantics. *Journal of Philosophy* 86:281–297.

Millikan, R. 1993. *White Queen Psychology and Other Essays for Alice*. Cambridge, MA: MIT Press.

Millikan, R. 2004. *Varieties of Meaning*. Cambridge, MA: MIT Press.

Nahum, L., A. Bouzerda-Wahlen, A. Guggisberg, R. Ptak, and A. Schnider. 2012. Forms of confabulation: Dissociations and associations. *Neuropsychologia* 50: 2524–2534.

Nijhawan, R. 1994. Motion extrapolation in catching. *Nature* 370:256–257.

Panksepp, J. 2011. The basic emotional circuits of mammalian brains: Do animals have affective lives? *Pioneering Research in Affective Neuroscience: Celebrating the Work of Dr. Jaak Panksepp* 35:1791–1804.

Perner, J. 1991. *Understanding the Representational Mind*. Cambridge, MA: MIT Press.

Powers, N., J. Eicher, F. Butter, Y. Kong, L. Miller, S. Ring, M. Mann, and J. Gruen. 2013. Alleles of a polymorphic ETV6 binding site in DCDC2 confer risk of reading and language impairment. *American Journal of Human Genetics* 93:19–28.

Rosenthal, D. 2005. *Consciousness and Mind*. Oxford: Oxford University Press.

Rosenthal, D. 2008. Consciousness and its function. *Neuropsychologia* (special issue): *Consciousness and Perception: Insights and Hindsights: A Festschrift in Honour of Larry Weiskrantz* 46: 829–840.

Sacks, O. 1970. *The Man Who Mistook His Wife for a Hat and Other Clinical Tales*. New York: Harper Perennial.

Schacter, D., and D. Addis. 2007. The ghosts of past and future. *Nature* 445:27.

Searle, J. 1980. Minds, brains, and programs. *Behavioral and Brain Sciences* 3: 417–424.

Searle, J. 1992. *The Rediscovery of the Mind*. Cambridge, MA: MIT Press.

Searle, J. 2002. *Consciousness and Language*. Cambridge: Cambridge University Press.

Stone, T., and A. Young. 1997. Delusions and brain injury: The philosophy and psychology of belief. *Mind & Language* 12:327–364.

Thompson, E. 2010. *Mind in Life: Biology, Phenomenology, and the Sciences of the Mind*. Cambridge, MA: Harvard University Press.

Tye, M. 1995. *Ten Problems of Consciousness*. Cambridge, MA: MIT Press.

Tye, M. 2000. *Consciousness, Color, and Content*. Cambridge, MA: MIT Press.

7 Self-Deception and the Dolphin Model of Cognition

Iuliia Pliushch and Thomas Metzinger

They call him Flipper, Flipper, faster than lightning,
No-one you see, is smarter than he,
And we know Flipper lives in a world full of wonder,
Lying there under, under the sea!
—William B. Dunham, lyrics for the theme song for the 1964 *Flipper* television
series and for the film *The New Adventures of Flipper*

We may not be fully aware of all the aspects and implications of our experiences,
but we do seem to keep track of them. Tibetan scholars express this idea by saying
that there is no person whose mental states are completely hidden to him- or
herself.
—G. Dreyfus and E. Thompson

1 Introduction

Our aim in this chapter is to develop a number of fresh perspectives on the
problem of self-deception. We will focus on its phenomenological profile
and on the empirical plausibility of new conceptual tools. Our aim is to
concentrate on what we take to be the most intriguing and philosophically
relevant question: How is it conceivable that systematic and robust forms of
misrepresentation on the level of phenomenal self-consciousness exist, and
are sometimes even *functionally adequate*, for individual human persons as
well as in an evolutionary context?

To answer this question, we will analyze a selected set of recent and
well-documented empirical examples of human self-deception from the
perspective of the self-model theory of subjectivity (SMT, Metzinger 2003a,
2003b, 2006, 2007). We will then sketch a functionalist and representationalist analysis of how the integration of certain kinds of information into
the currently active phenomenal self-model (PSM, see section 3) can be

blocked, thus precluding this information from becoming globally available for introspection. A PSM is an integrated, conscious model of the person as a whole, including psychological and social properties. In the first section, we will briefly explain what self-deception is and highlight some of the standard issues in classical philosophical debates. In the second and third sections, we will select three conceptual tools from an empirically grounded philosophical theory of self-consciousness and apply them to our current understanding of this specific target phenomenon. Owing to the transparency of the conscious model of the self, the deficit of self-knowledge that characterizes self-deception mostly remains unnoticed by the self-deceived subject, leading to sincere reports about its content that seem implausible from the third-person perspective. Interestingly, self-deception shows causal interactions between the unconscious and consciousness as well as between transparent and opaque layers of the human PSM. Transparent layers (e.g., in conscious body representation) are experientially real; opaque layers (such as conscious thoughts or occurrent beliefs) are subjectively experienced *as* representations. One of our more general goals is to isolate a set of particularly promising contact points connecting philosophy of mind, psychiatry, and cognitive neuroscience, thus laying the groundwork for more fruitful forms of interdisciplinary cooperation in the future.

The tentative answer to the question is as follows: transparency of the PSM is the centrally relevant, causally enabling condition for the existence of robust forms of misrepresentation. The functional adequacy is to be looked for at the subpersonal, computational level, for which the currently best available framework is that of predictive coding (see section 3.3); the dolphin model of cognition (section 4.2) accounts for the phenomenal adequacy. An evolutionary explanation should encompass the interaction of competing distal goals, such as the goal to deceive others (e.g., Trivers's offensive function of self-deception [SD]) or the avoidance of existential anxiety and terror of death (as in terror management theory (TMT) see Solomon, Greenberg, and Pyszczynski 1991, 2004, Greenberg, Solomon, and Pyszczynski 1992).

2   The Phenomenon of Self-Deception

What exactly is the *explanandum* for a theory of self-deception—the scientific target phenomenon in need of explanation? What is a conceptually adequate way to *frame* it? Let us begin by looking at some traditional philosophical and psychological ways of approaching these two questions. Typically, these approaches still make use of the folk-psychological distinction

between desires and beliefs, and they rarely take data from cognitive neuropsychiatry or empirically grounded theories of mental representation
such as connectionism[1] (Churchland 1989, Clark 1993, Ramsey, Stich, and
Garon 1991) or predictive coding (Friston 2010, Hohwy 2013, Clark 2013)
into account. This is not to say that folk psychological distinctions cannot
be useful, but that an explanation of the phenomenon on a folk-psychological level alone is obviously insufficient and incomplete.

Before offering a short overview of some classical positions, we want to
lay our cards on the table and briefly state our own working definition of
self-deception, which will be elucidated at the end of this section.

SD_{Def}: Self-deception (SD) is

(1) a motivated kind of
(2) hypothesis-testing, that
(3) results in an evidence-incompatible mental representation of reality,
which
(4) fulfills a belief-like role.

Motivated means causally driven by goal-representations, which may be
conscious or unconscious. *Hypothesis-testing* is here (in part, metaphori-
cally) understood as a process that is mostly unconscious and typically
involves nonpropositional representational formats, as in predictive coding approaches to cognition (Friston 2010, Hohwy 2013). The relationship
to the evidence points to the fact that self-deceivers are perceived as possessing an inconsistent system of beliefs from a third-person perspective,
leaving open the possibility that there is no such perceived inconsistency
from a first-person perspective. The fourth point characterizes the role of
self-deceptive representations in folk-psychological terms.

Our short review of the literature is structured according to three building blocks that are typically emphasized in the literature and also reflected
in our definition: the nature of the motivation (1), the process (2), and
the final effect or "product"[2] (3 and 4) (Van Leeuwen 2007, Nelkin 2012,
Funkhouser 2009). It is guided by three main questions: What is the driving
force behind SD? Which *kind* of reasoning process led to its occurrence, and
how was it influenced by the initial motivation? What exactly marks out
the resulting cognitive attitude?

We want to begin by drawing the reader's attention to a first general
feature shared by all accounts presented here: they all regard SD as a personal-level phenomenon (for discussion of the personal-level distinction,
see Bermúdez 2000a, Colombo 2013, Drayson 2012). Can personal-level
accounts using "the folk-psychological notions of 'belief,' 'deception,' and

'self,'" to use Borge's words (2003, 4), be successful in explaining self-deception? Donald Davidson (1985, 79) warned that personal-level explanations of irrationality might explain it away by inventing some form of rationalization.[3] A brief look at the literature on self-deception shows that although there is no consensus on the definition of self-deception, some authors have clearly recognized the limits of folk-psychological explanations of the phenomenon, a fact that is, to some degree, reflected in the accounts they propose (e.g., Borge 2003, Funkhouser 2009, Porcher 2012; for a teleofunctionalist account, see Smith 2014).

2.1 Motivation

Let us now begin our brief look at the literature with those accounts that specify the motivation of the self-deceiver. There is widespread disagreement both about which kind of *attitude* the motivation is (intention, desire, goal) and what *content* it has (desire that p, desire to believe that p, disagreement about what p is). To give an example, Sayers and Perera (2002) confronted doctors with vignettes describing terminally ill patients to see whether they would refrain from life-prolonging treatment ("passive euthanasia") and which reasons they would give for their decision. The result was that doctors typically did take medical, but rarely ethical, reasons into account. Accepting Barnes's (1997) theory of self-deception, Sayers and Perera hypothesized that this may be the case because doctors had an *anxious desire* not to intend death (but not an *intention* to relieve their anxiety), so focusing on medical reasons precluded them from making the inference from denying nonbeneficial treatment to the fact that nontreatment accelerated patients' death. It is clear, however, that the motivation for self-deception has to be broad enough to include cases of self-deception, yet narrow enough to exclude cases that are not those of self-deception ("content dilemma," Nelkin 2002, 393). *Content dilemma* is to be applied independently of the basis on which the motivation is established (intuitions, folk-psychology, commonly accepted cases of SD etc.). We will briefly mention the different alternatives and argue that the motivation for self-deception is best understood in terms of subpersonal goal representations. To begin with, we consider the debate between intentionalists, or those claiming SD to be a result of intentional action, and proponents of a deflationist approach, or those claiming it to have another "motivational or affective basis" (Scott-Kakures 2012, 18). In the last decade, the scale between intentionalist (e.g., Davidson 1985, 1998, Pears 1991, Rorty 2009, Fingarette 2000, Bermúdez 2000b, Talbott 1995) and deflationary approaches (e.g., Bach 1981, Barnes 1997, Johnston 1988, Mele 2001, 2012) has tipped in favor of the latter.[4] For reasons of completeness, we will nevertheless mention the two possible intentionalist positions (Mele 2001, 18):

(1) Intentional activities "engaged in as part of an *attempt* to deceive oneself" (e.g., Pears 1991, Davidson 1985; for critique see, e.g., Lazar 1999, Mele 2001),

(2) Intentional activities otherwise directed—for example, to reduce anxiety (e.g., Johnston 1988, Barnes 1997, Galeotti 2012).

What unifies intentionalist approaches is that an explanation of self-deception is couched in personal level terms. That is why Mele (2001) calls intentionalist positions the "agency view." An important point against intentionalist approaches recently made by Scott-Kakures (2012) is that there cannot be two diametrically opposed conscious intentions at the same time—that is, the intention of deceiving oneself and the other aimed at discovering the truth. To further elaborate on this point, we might have an objective, third-person theory about the causal relationship between intention and self-deception, but this theory could only explain the functional structure of self-deception and not the first-person phenomenology of the self-deceived individual in question. The latter is the case simply because the intention to deceive oneself, per definition, cannot become conscious as such. The subjective phenomenology might systematically, and perhaps necessarily, misrepresent the actual causal relation between explicit goal-representation and one's own behavior. In other words, what is a *logical* possibility (i.e., self-deception as an explicit goal-representation occurring in a given cognitive system) might not be a *phenomenological* possibility (because it threatens the integrity of the conscious self-model, Metzinger 2003a, 2007). Hence, given that intentionalist theories must exclude the scope of phenomenology, let us now look at deflationary alternatives.

Though Van Leeuwen (2007) mentions desires as well as goal-directed practical attitudes as alternatives to intention, desire is, probably, the most popular deflationary alternative:

• a desire to obtain a *first-order* belief (e.g., Mele 2001, Barnes 1997), henceforth called a *desire-that-p* account, and

• a desire to obtain a *second-order* belief (Funkhouser 2005, Nelkin 2002, 2012), henceforth called a *desire-to-believe* account.

To briefly distinguish between the two by giving an example: if one's self-deceptive belief in the faithfulness of one's spouse is the result of one's desire that the spouse be faithful, then it is one's desire for a *first-order* belief that motivated this instance of self-deception. If the given belief is the result of the desire *to believe* that one's spouse is faithful, then it is the desire for a *second-order* belief. Nelkin's (2002, 2012) main reason for a desire-to-believe account is the emphasis on the need to explain how self-deceivers can be held responsible for their self-deception. Her explanation is that the self-deceptive desire has to fulfill the condition that if self-deceivers were to become aware of their desire and the product, they would recognize the causal connection between the two (Nelkin 2002, 404, n. 36). Nelkin (2002) argues that her account fits the experimental data discussed by Mele, a proponent of a desire-that-*p* view (398). For reasons of space, we skip any discussion of the question, which account explains the subject's responsibility in a better way.

The appeal by both to the same empirical data poses the question whether one can empirically distinguish between the two. Funkhouser's (2005) reason for a desire-to-believe account is that it better explains the avoidance behavior of the self-deceiver (e.g., if I believe that my spouse is cheating on me, I do not drive by the house where the suspected lover lives, although it is the shortest path home). Thus, it is the interpretation of the behavior of self-deceivers that tips the scale in favor of the desire-to-believe account: if self-deceivers exhibit avoidance behavior, then the desire that motivates them to engage in self-deception is the desire to change their own mental state, but not the world. Consequently, self-deceivers are taken to be driven by a desire-to-believe and not a first-order desire.

Pedrini (2012) argues on the basis of the behavior of self-deceivers (more precisely, the fact that their defense of the self-deceptive belief is often effortful and quite sophisticated, p. 149) for a view opposed to Funkhouser's. She interprets Funkhouser (2005) as claiming that the self-focused desire to believe that *p* is primary in self-deceivers, but the world-focused desire that *p* is contingent. She disagrees with this claim, calling Funkhouser's explanation of self-deceptive behavior being driven by a self-focused desire to be a "(largely undeclared) inference to the best explanation about the motivation for avoidance behavior" (146).

This selective review of the literature on the motivation of self-deception shows that, though there are a wide variety of positions on the motivation of self-deception, different conceptual constraints are formed, largely, in the philosophical armchair, on the motivation behind self-deception. The existing empirical evidence does not, however, permit any definitive choice among the proposed kinds of motivation. The fact that behavior is brought in as an argument in favor of a certain kind of motivation also makes it clear that a good theory of self-deception could be adequate in at least two different ways: in explaining the overt behavior of self-deceived individuals and in achieving *phenomenological* adequacy—helping us to understand what is so hard to understand, namely, *what it is like* to be self-deceived[5] from the inside. The description of the fine-grained causal mechanisms internally leading to overt SD is a way often pursued to achieve both. It is important not to confuse these different sets of adequacy conditions.

2.2 Hypothesis Testing

In the last subsection, we highlighted some aspects from the literature concerning the motivation for self-deception. This subsection offers another selective mini-review of recent empirically tested psychological theories that specify the second building block, or the process by which self-deception is accomplished.

Traditionally, the self-deceptive process is one of belief acquisition and maintenance. On the personal level of description, the term *reasoning* is used to denote belief-forming processes. In case of self-deception, it may mostly be *subpersonal* belief-forming processes that stand in the foreground. Yet, because no sharp distinction has been drawn between the two in the self-deception literature, and because at least some of the resulting mental representations of subpersonal, self-deceptive, belief-forming processes are conscious, we use the term *reasoning* to denote both personal and subpersonal belief-forming processes in this review section. The main question, here, concerns the role of motivation in influencing self-deceptive, belief-forming processes. This is evident in Helzer and Dunning's (2012) claim that "motivated reasoning" is a "paradigmatic case of self-deception" (380), where the motivation is to arrive at a certain conclusion instead of establishing the truth.[6]

Given that, in the next section, we will argue that the self-deceptive process is a kind of *subpersonal* hypothesis-testing, we review in this subsection two self-deception theories that argue that it is a *personal* kind of hypothesis testing: Mele's (2001, 2012) and Scott-Kakures's (2009). Mele's popular deflationary theory of self-deception is based on Friedrich's (1993) and Trope and Liberman's (1996) error minimization accounts. The core idea behind error minimization is that there are false negative and false positive errors.[7] The desire to avoid these errors influences the setting of thresholds for accepting and rejecting hypotheses.

Thresholds are important insofar as they determine the duration of the process (how quickly do we stop?) and the process itself (what evidence do we consider?). The aim of an error-minimization account is, in Trope and Liberman's (1996) words, that the error-minimization model explains how any motivation "can be translated into *common* epistemic terms of error minimization and guide the hypothesis testing process" (254). Namely, it does so, first, by influencing the decision threshold, and/or second, by biasing the generation and evaluation of the hypothesis (Trope and Liberman 1996, 258–260). Mele (2001, 2012) takes the decision threshold and, thus, the gathering of evidence as differing in self-deceivers compared to nonmotivated subjects. For example, individual thresholds for accepting the claim that a corrupted CIA agent is innocent may diverge in his colleagues and in his parents (Mele 2001, 64).

Scott-Kakures (2009) bases his personal hypothesis testing account on Festinger's (1957) cognitive dissonance paradigm and Kruglanski and Webster's (1996) research on the need for "cognitive closure."[8] The idea is that self-deception is motivated by the desire to find out the truth, yet that certain sources of cognitive dissonance lead to a biased treatment of the evidence:

(1) desire for "cognitive closure" on the one hand and the uncertainty whether p or not-p (openness of the question) on the other, and
(2) desire-driven *expectations* of the self-deceiver on the one hand and the openness of the question on the other.[9]

The comparison of these two theories shows that if attention is paid to the formulations used, both are personal-level hypothesis testing accounts. The question is whether the underlying empirical theories are intended to encompass the phenomenology and the ease with which they can do so. Theories formulated in personal-level terms whose scope excludes phenomenology are theories operating with hypothetical constructs. Kruglanski and Webster (1996, 279) argue, in the case of cognitive closure, that it may be a hypothetical construct, but that hypothetical constructs are nonetheless useful if they can account for experimental data. We argue that the same might be the case with respect to error minimization. The cognitive dissonance paradigm, on the other hand, does include the measurement of tension[10] by asking participants whether they were "uneasy," "uncomfortable," and "bothered" by cognitive dissonance[11] (Cooper 2007). Affirmative responses to these questions indicate that the phenomenological level has been encompassed, yet pose the question about the distinction between the concepts of tension in self-deception and in other psychological models. Is it the same kind of tension by which self-deception, cognitive dissonance, and (if ever) cognitive closure are characterized? A more finegrained description of the phenomenological component is clearly needed. For example, Slotter et al. (2010) found that after romantic breakup, the clarity of the self-concept (or the degree of conviction and certainty with which beliefs referring to specific aspects of the self-model are held) is not only diminished, but that the transition also leads to emotional distress. Granted that self-deception influences the self-concept, does it always evoke the same kind of discomfort as romantic breakup, or is there a phenomenological spectrum of *types* of subjective discomfort that could be interestingly explored in a more detailed manner?

This brief review has highlighted the difficulty of construing a personal-level model of the process of self-deception that takes empirical data into account. To give one last example, we will consider Michel and Newen's (2010) attempt to construe a personal level explanation of self-deception by using Greve and Wentura's (2010) empirical account of self-immunization. Self-immunization is the phenomenon that consists in participants changing the description of a certain psychological trait that is important to them, in order to be able to further ascribe this desirable trait to themselves in cases in which their prior description of the trait does not fit anymore.[12] For example, which knowledge domains one actually rates to be diagnostic of general knowledge (e.g., history, natural sciences, politics, fine arts) changes, depending on in which of those domains "participants were made to believe that they were worse" (Greve and Wentura 2003, 45). Given that the self-immunization process analyzed by Greve and Wentura (2010) is subpersonal and Michel and Newen's (2010) theory of self-deception is a personal-level one, this leads to an inconsistency in the explanation: on the one hand, Michel and Newen (2010) claim that it is the personal-level interpretation of data that account for self-deception. On the other hand, the consideration of empirical data leads to the claim that "dual rationality will typically be observable in *'automatic' or unreflected adaptation* and this is one reason for criticizing S's activity from a rational point of view" (741, italics are our own emphasis). This suggests that a subpersonal interpretation is doing the explanatory work (for further details and references regarding the personal-subpersonal distinction, see Metzinger 2013a, 7–8).

2.3 The "Product": Global Effects

In the last subsection, we pointed out some of the difficulties that folk-psychological explanations encounter when considering the motivation and reasoning process. In this subsection, we will briefly summarize recent accounts (Funkhouser's, Lynch's, and Porcher's) that show similar difficulties for the question of the *product* of self-deception.

Funkhouser (2009) raises doubts that the folk-psychological concept of belief can explain the self-deceptive representation, given the indeterminacy of belief ascription to the self-deceiver (11). He relinquishes the assumption that nonlinguistic behavior is to be preferred when determining what someone believes and opts for a lower-level explanation—regarding-as-true stances (13). The latter reflect the domains in which a proposition might be regarded as true or false—theoretical or practical reasoning, behavior, and so forth. Notice there might be opposition regarding the truth-value of a proposition across domains, which is particularly true for self-deception (9). Funkhouser (2009) claims that "belief reduces to, or is nothing over and above, these regarding-as-true stances" (9); regarding-as-true stances serve as belief-indicators, depend on the context, and are not to be privileged one over the other in establishing the beliefs of the self-deceived (10–12).

Other authors defend similar accounts insofar as they agree with Funkhouser (2009) that the concept of belief is not fine-grained enough. For example, Lynch (2012) argues that the product of self-deception can be characterized by degrees of conviction. His solution[13] is to speak of degrees of conviction, instead of beliefs, as "in a state where one's confidence level ranges between wholehearted belief and disbelief, it would be natural to expect the aforementioned tensions to appear" (440). In this context, having a belief that p means having a high degree of confidence in p (Lynch 2012, 439). Self-deceivers, according to Lynch (2012), have unwarranted degrees of conviction in a proposition insofar as this degree deviates from the degree of confidence their impartial cognitive peers would have if they considered the evidence[14] (439). He criticizes Mele for not explaining how nagging doubts and the personal stakes in the matter (e.g., caffeine-lovers being less convinced by arguments emphasizing the risk of caffeine consumption, Lynch 2012, 437) influence the mental state of the self-deceiver, arguing that the combination of both leads to attempts to justify the unwarranted position that do not succeed completely (Lynch 2012).

The third view to be mentioned is that of Porcher (2012) who argues that the indeterminacy of belief ascription to self-deceivers indicates the limits of our practices of belief attribution, conceptualizes self-deceptive belief as an *in-between belief* in Schwitzgebel's sense (78), and emphasizes that the degree of confidence is not fixed, but oscillates with time:

This *shifting back and forth* [of the degree of confidence in the belief that p] could easily be explained as the product of the subject's relationship with the threatening data (e.g., through the activation of certain memories, through the admonishing of relatives and friends, through direct contact with the evidence, etc.). One's confidence in the self-deceptive belief would fluctuate and thus manifest itself in behavior that at one time would point toward a higher, and at other times toward a lower, confidence in p. (Porcher 2012, 77, our emphasis)

All accounts presented in this section emphasize the limits of folk-psychological belief-ascription in case of self-deceivers, yet do not abandon it. Though self-deception is mostly characterized as belief that is unwarranted by the evidence available to the self-deceiver and motivated by a desire, this characterization of self-deception has not led to a satisfactory explanation of self-deception. Moreover, these accounts view beliefs as *dispositional* attitudes (for an opposing view that self-deceptive attitudes might be constructed each time on the spot given the available context see Michel 2014). Most recently, Baghramian and Nicholson (2013) have voiced the concern about the lack of consistency in philosophical explanations of self-deception and suggested that they should take empirical data into account. Yet explanations of self-deception in folk-psychological terms have so far been unsuccessful to fulfill the given demand.

2.4   The Explanandum for a Theory of SD

After we have considered the self-deception literature, let us ask about the explanandum and the way of framing self-deception. The explananda for a theory of self-deception are the behavior and the phenomenology of the self-deceiver (for a dispositional, phenomenological account of belief, see Schwitzgebel 2002). By contrast, the acceptance of a certain framework in which the explanation for self-deception is given (e.g., a folk-psychological one) is not part of the explanandum, but a *means* of explanation. Moreover, behavior and phenomenology are used in the self-deception literature as arguments for preferring one kind of folk-psychological description to another.

The behavior of the self-deceiver includes at least two components:

(1) The behavior of the self-deceiver is *inconsistent* and precludes an unequivocal belief ascription. Typical examples are either behaving in a specific way while asserting the possession of an inconsistent or contradictory belief, or behaving in a contradictory way at different points in time while claiming an invariance of one's belief.

(2) The self-deceiver is prone to justify her self-deceptive behavior—for example, to provide reasons for it.

The phenomenology that characterizes the self-deceiver also involves at least two components:

(1) The self-deceiver experiences *tension*—for example, feelings of uneasiness and distress (see Proust 2013 for an extended discussion of metacognitive feelings in reasoning and Pliushch 2015 for the claim that self-deceptive tension is a kind of a metacognitive feeling).

(2) The *retrospective recognition* of one's own self-deception leads to a certain phenomenology, coupled with reports typically described as "How could I have been so blind, when it was so obvious?"

This is not to say that this first- and third-person description is complete, or that it states the *necessary and sufficient* conditions for SD to arise, because the latter has been impossible to achieve so far, as can be seen in the fact that Mele (2001, 2012) proposes only *jointly sufficient* conditions for acquiring self-deception. Thus, it is unclear whether necessary and sufficient conditions for self-deception can be formulated or even whether one should aim at formulating them. Instead, we provide a first- and third-person redescription that can be enriched in the face of new empirical findings. Further, the framing of self-deception should be different on the personal and subpersonal levels. The motivation for self-deception is best described as emerging from multiple, continuously competing subpersonal goal-representations, whose counterpart on the personal level, if it is present, can be described by the folk-psychological notion of desire or *goal* that is now experienced as *my own* goal.[15] Employing this description of the motivation for self-deception opens up a new perspective and poses new questions neglected so far. If we have to consider multiple goal-representations, then it does not make sense to ask which single goal-representation led to self-deception. Rather, we should ask about the *relationship* among the multiple goal representations and which *circumstances* trigger which goal representations to influence self-deception.

To give an example, von Hippel and Trivers (2011) recently argued that self-deception serves the offensive function of deceiving others, and they suggested that self-enhancement is a kind of self-deception. By contrast, proponents of terror-management theory (TMT) argue that self-esteem serves as a means to reduce the anxiety of death and that mortality salience (MS) induction leads to certain self-serving biases (Pyszczynski, Greenberg, Solomon et al. 2004). Granting that self-enhancement is a kind of self-deception and that it is achieved by enhancing self-esteem, what exactly is the relationship between the goal of deceiving others and the goal of reducing the anxiety of death? An intriguing possibility worth empirical examination is that TMT serves the ultimate goal of deceiving others by convincing them of one's own worth, because it is not possible to withstand the anxiety of death on one's own.

The description of the *process* of self-deception should also acknowledge the distinction between levels of description. Explicit reference to an inference to the best explanation in the self-deception literature—for example, by Mele (2001) and the sheer abundance of different (mostly personal-level) explanations of the process of self-deception—point to the fact that there is little consensus on how higher-order cognition in general and its conscious counterpart, guided by an explicit representation of "reasons," actually takes place. The construction of psychological models of cognition serves the primary aim of explaining empirical data—behavior and assertions of participants in studies. The employment of personal-level concepts in the construction of these models, such as Mele's reducing false positive or false negative error, should be distinguished from the claim that such psychological models provide a description of the reasoning process on the conscious, personal level.

3   Conceptual Tools for SD: A Look at SMT

Let us now look at three ideas offered by the self-model theory that may be helpful in gaining a fresh perspective and laying the conceptual foundations for a more data-driven, scientific explanation of self-deception. One important metaphysical background assumption of this theory is that there is no such ontological entity as "the" self (Metzinger 2011; for the theory itself see Metzinger 2003a; shorter summaries can be found in Metzinger 2006, 2007, 2008; a popular account is Metzinger 2010). There is a self-*model* and a world-*model*, and what we folk-psychologically refer to as *the self* in sincere autophenomenological reports is the content of a self-model, which is mostly transparent. The phenomenal self-model (PSM) is characterized by transparency (see section 3.1), introduces boundaries on the possible kinds of knowledge (see section 3.2) and, at the microfunctional level, can be fruitfully described as a generative model (see section 3.3).

Importantly, a self-model is not a model of a thing, but an ongoing process. This process can vary along a large number of functional and phenomenological dimensions. For example, a human being's self-model is very different in the dream state (Windt and Metzinger 2007, Metzinger 2013a, Windt 2015), or during an episode of schizophrenia, naturally occurring out-of-body experiences, or neurological conditions like anosognosia (Metzinger 2003a, 2010). Although we tend to linguistically reify the introspectively accessible representational content of this ongoing, dynamic process by speaking about *a* self-model or *a* conscious self, what we are referring to never is a static representation of some static intentional object, but a time-slice of an inner process evolving over time. In self-deception, there never is "a" self that is being deceived—all that exists is a self-model with highly specific and slightly deviant functional properties. Self-modeling is a continuous, context-sensitive tracking of global properties of the organism, including personal-level and social properties. *Tracking* means reducing uncertainty by *predicting* global system properties, using a single, integrated data-format, using a single self-model: self-consciousness just *is* this data-format as it appears to the person as whole, and all of its content is *counterfactual* content, a probability density distribution, the best hypothesis the system currently has about its own global state (Friston 2010, Hohwy 2013, Clark 2013).

3.1 Phenomenal Transparency

Transparency (as the term is used in this contribution) is a property of conscious representations, namely, that they are not experienced *as* representations. This means that the system has no introspective access to nonintentional properties of its own representations, that it is necessarily unaware of the construction process (see Metzinger 2003a: 3.2.7 and Metzinger 2003b, 354 for details). Therefore, the subject of experience feels as if being in direct and immediate contact with their content. An opaque phenomenal representation is one that is experienced *as* a representation—for example, in pseudohallucinations or lucid dreams (in which the dreamer has become aware of the fact that he or she is dreaming, see Windt and Metzinger 2007, Metzinger 2013a, Metzinger 2003a, 169–173). Unconscious representations are neither transparent nor opaque. First, transparent conscious representations create the phenomenology of naïve realism. Second, there exists a graded spectrum between transparency and opacity, determining the variable phenomenology of *mind-independence* or *realness*. Third, if we move from the representationalist to the functionalist level of analysis, we may interpret experiential realness as the Bayes-optimality[16] or dynamical stability of the generative models employed (see section 3.3). If, on the microfunctionalist level, phenomenal realness is Bayes-optimality, then given the second point, there exists a gradient of realness with maximal realness corresponding to phenomenal transparency.

If we return to the representationalist level, we can understand the key step in SMT, namely, applying these considerations to the special case of conscious self-representation—a *phenomenal self* that is the content of a *transparent* self-model. Consequently, the origin of the consciously experienced first-person perspective is not tied to a specific form of *content*, but always to the region of maximal invariance, that is, to the most robust, dynamically stable, and Bayes-optimal region in the overall model of reality (Blanke and Metzinger 2009, Metzinger 2013a, 2013b, Limanowski 2014, Limanowski and Blankenburg 2013). Because the phenomenal self is transparent, we necessarily *identify* with its content. It is important to note that while the PSM, viewed in isolation, is itself a subpersonal entity, the fact that the organism as a whole *identifies* with its content causally enables the emergence of personal-level properties, given an appropriate social context.

3.2 Phenomenal Self-Reference and Autoepistemic Closure

The content of the *phenomenal* self-model (PSM) consists of bodily sensations, emotions, and the contents of phenomenally experienced cognitive processing (Metzinger 2003a, 299). The knowledge we can gain by introspecting the contents of our phenomenal world- and self-model is bound by the principle of autoepistemic closure, as well as by the principle of phenomenal self-reference. The *principle of phenomenal self-reference* constrains the *amount* of subjective knowledge we can get: nothing over and above the contents of our currently active self-model is introspectively available to us (Metzinger 2003a, 236). The *principle of autoepistemic closure* bounds the *kind* of knowledge we can get: our attentional processing is closed or bounded with respect to certain aspects of our own internal representational dynamics, for example, because we cannot phenomenally represent the fact that most phenomenal representations are counterfactual simulations, that they are probability distributions and not external reality (Metzinger 2003a, 57, Madary 2012). Thus, we experience the phenomenally transparent parts of our world- and self-model as real and as immediately given and are able to use them as a background for those cognitive simulations that we actually phenomenally represent *as* simulations—for example, as conscious thought, future planning, episodic memories, and so forth.

Furthermore, certain aspects of the contents of our phenomenal models that are available for attention, cognition, and control of behavior may be functionally dissociated. Thus, while the *global availability*[17] *constraint* states that it is the contents of our phenomenal mental models "which are, functionally speaking, globally available for cognition, attention, and the

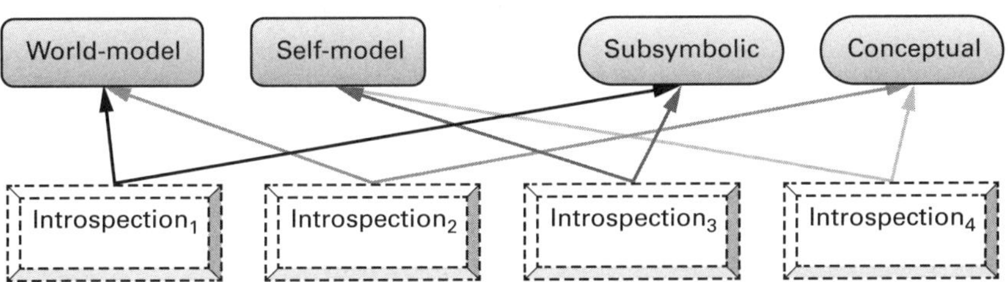

Introspection₁—Resulting phenomenology: "External attention"
Introspection₂—Resulting phenomenology: "Consciously experienced cognitive reference"
Introspection₃—Resulting phenomenology: "Inward attention"
Introspection₄—Resulting phenomenology: "Consciously experienced cognitive self-reference"

Figure 7.1

Kinds of introspection, differentiated by intentional object and representational format (adapted from Metzinger 2003a, 36).

immediate control of behavior" (Metzinger 2003a, 210), the global availability for one component of the three does not necessarily imply its availability for the other two. There may be *degrees* of awareness and availability. For example, an internal model could control external behavior via the motor system, but not be available for introspective attention or an updating of the cognitive self-model.

3.3   The Self-Model as a Generative Model

Above, we stated that, on the informational-computational level of description, a conscious model makes specific information available for introspection, rational thought, and flexible behavioral control. On the microfunctional level, the model can be interpreted as a Bayes-optimal region in state space (see section 3.1). To speak of *a* self-model, strictly speaking, is a conceptual reification that results from only looking at a temporal segment of the continuous neural dynamics in our heads—in reality, self-consciousness never is a thing, but always a process.

Predictive coding is the implementation of empirical Bayes where the latter is a procedure for representational learning and inference that is assumed to occur in the human brain (Friston 2003, 2005). Bayesian models have as their core the premise that representational learning and inference abide by the Bayes theorem, according to which the posteriori probability of a representation's being true is equal to its prior probability times the likelihood. Predictive coding has at its core the idea that representational learning and inference in the brain occur as a result of the propagation of precision-weighted prediction errors along the hierarchy of levels at each of which they are compared with the corresponding predictions, so that the latter can be updated according to the Bayesian principle. The merit of predictive coding is that it provides a unifying framework for perception, action, and cognition (Clark 2013, Hohwy 2013).

Hence, conscious models of the self and of reality can be described as internal instruments generating *predictions* for an organism, aspects of a causally fine-grained functional anatomy that continuously minimizes prediction errors (Friston 2010, Hohwy 2013, Clark 2013). The content of phenomenal self-consciousness is simply the best global hypothesis the organism has about its own current state. Mathematically, what we consciously experience as *ourselves* is a complex probability distribution, yielding a global model of the system in which this very process is unfolding.

To give a preview of what is to come in section 4 and to sum up the conceptual tools introduced so far: because of the *transparency* of our PSM, we subjectively experience most of its content as real, as immediately and noninferentially given, and as a form of self-knowledge endowed with the phenomenal signature of certainty. Because all nonlinguistic, pretheoretic self-knowledge we may have—or which we may *not* have—is mediated through this model (the *principle of phenomenal self-reference*), we cannot know anything else beyond the content of this model from a purely first-person perspective (*the principle of autoepistemic closure*). Of course, there are many ways to transcend this situation via high-level, symbolic cognition, intersubjective communication, and scientific theory formation. Yet the phenomenology itself is robust, and (not only) in the case of self-deception it is generated not by conflicting homunculi in our heads or by a hierarchy of beliefs and desires, but by dynamical self-organization of subsymbolic structures in the brain. The phenomenology is determined by a process that is aimed at minimizing prediction error and at any given instant generates a global, Bayes-optimal system model. This globally available system model is what drives the behavior of normal people as well as that of self-deceived subjects, and it is the *introspectively available* partition of this model that we describe in sincere, truthful reports about ourselves—whether we are self-deceived or not.

4   Applying SMT to SD

Before applying the conceptual tools introduced in section 3 to self-deception, let us note that the core hypothesis of the SMT about the inexistence of the ontological entity of the self does not preclude the applicability of SMT to self-deception. The "self" in self-deception should not be taken literally: a self-model is not a thing but a process, namely, the process of continuously tracking global properties of the organism and representing them in a unified and dynamical data-format. What is deceived is not a mysterious self, but the organism/cognitive system/person as a whole. And, of course, there is also no internal agent *doing* the deceiving.

4.1   Motivation

In section 2.4 we stated that the motivation for self-deception is best described as emerging from multiple, continuously competing, subpersonal goal-representations. The distinction between the phenomenal self-model as "the decisive tool for transforming subpersonal properties of a conscious system into personal-level features" (Metzinger 2003a, 424) and an unconscious self-model allows us to understand the conceptual transition from a subpersonal goal-directed framework to a traditional belief-desire framework operating on the personal level of introspectively available goal-states, subjectively experienced as *one's own* goals. If subpersonal goal-representations win the dynamic competition, then they may either directly influence behavior (causing goal-directed behavior without a corresponding "phenomenal model of the intentionality relation" (PMIR), see Metzinger 2003a, 424, 2007), or, by becoming integrated into the PSM, they may become available for more flexible, context-sensitive, and selective forms of action control. What has been frequently overlooked in the past is that the classical intentionality-relation (Brentano [1874] 1973) can *itself* form the content of a conscious mental representation. In beings like us, there exists a phenomenal model *of* the intentionality relation. We have, as it were, the capacity to catch ourselves in the act: at times we have higher-order conscious representations of ourselves *as* representing. On the other hand, from a purely empirical point of view, it is highly plausible to assume that many nonhuman animals are intentional systems, but that their nervous systems do not allow them to ever become aware of this fact. In self-deception, we may therefore have configurations where human beings do *mis*represent, but have locally lost the ability to become aware of the fact *that they are representing*, in a specific domain. The central idea is that the intentionality-relation can itself be a form of phenomenal content, and that this will typically be a form of dynamical, subsymbolic content (as, for example, in the subjective experience of attending to a visual object or of being currently directed at an action goal). The core idea behind the theoretical notion of a PMIR is that human beings do not only represent individual objects or goal states, but that in many representational acts we also corepresent the *representational relation* itself—and that this fact is relevant for understanding what it means that the contents of consciousness are experienced as involving a first-person perspective. Using this new conceptual instrument, one might say that self-deception is a domain-specific loss of the first-person perspective.

One constraint on those goal representations is that they have to be evaluated as desirable for the system. Yoshie and Haggard (2013) manipulated the emotional valence of action outcomes by following participants' key-press actions with negative or positive emotional vocalizations. They demonstrated that the sense of agency can be modulated by the emotional effects of an action. The results of their study suggest that the sense of agency is attenuated for negatively valenced events, and that this effect may possess a low-level sensorimotor basis,[18] indicating that the process of desirability evaluation is a subpersonal one. The further value of Yoshie and Haggard's study is that the desirability has been dissociated from context, because the negatively valenced event is a negatively perceived sound stripped of any informational context. This indicates that, in the case of self-deception, the mechanism described in the study may be responsible for changes in the desirability of goal-representations that lead to changes in the belief-forming processes and their outcomes. If this is the case, then self-deception might often be much less of a higher-order cognitive phenomenon than has been assumed so far. This conclusion is further supported by McKay et al.'s (2013) study in which optimism has been tested to be susceptible to caloric vestibular stimulation (cold water is applied to the left or right ear canal to elicit rapid eye movements), as anosognosia is. Both have been argued to be cases of self-deception (for anosognosia see, e.g., Ramachandran 1996; for unrealistic optimism, see Taylor 1989). The results of McKay et al.'s (2013) study indicate that left caloric vestimular stimulation reduces unrealistic optimism which leads them to conclude that anosognosia and optimism might share the same mechanism. Preuss et al. (2014, 137) have further tested that for emotionally positive stimuli affective control increased during right ear CVS and decreased during left ear CVS. The results of the aforementioned studies suggest that the interaction between subpersonal goal representations and interoceptive signals might be worth exploring in the case of self-deception.

4.2   The Dolphin Model of Cognition

What could be an intuitive image that captures as many aspects of our preceding discussion as possible? We argue that the self-deceptive reasoning process can be described by what we call the dolphin model of cognition. Dolphins frequently leap above the water's surface. One reason for this behavior could be that, when traveling longer distances, jumping can save the dolphins energy, as there is less friction while in the air. Typically, the animals will display long, ballistic jumps, alternated with periods of swimming below, but close to the surface. Porpoising is one name for this high-speed surface-piercing motion of dolphins and other species, in which leaps are interspersed with relatively long swimming bouts, often about twice the length of the leap. Porpoising may also be the energetically cheapest way to swim rapidly and continuously and to breathe at the same time.

We think that, just as dolphins cross the surface, thought processes often cross the border between conscious and unconscious processing as well, and in both directions. For example, chains of cognitive states may have their origin in unconscious goal-commitments triggered by external stimuli, then transiently become integrated into the conscious self-model for introspective availability and selective control, only to disappear into another unconscious "swimming bout" below the surface. Conversely, information available in the conscious self-model may become repressed into an unconscious, modularized form of self-representation where it does not endanger self-esteem or overall integrity. However, in the human mind, the time windows in which leaps into consciousness and subsequent "underwater" processing unfold may be of a variable size—and there may actually be more than one dolphin. In fact, there may be a whole race going on.

The dolphin model of cognition has the advantage that it can be gradually enriched by additional assumptions. For example, we can imagine a situation where only one dolphin at a time can actually jump out of the water, briefly leaping out of a larger, continuously competing group. In real-world dolphins, synchronous surfacing also may serve to enhance bonding and appears to have a distinctly social component—here, we can imagine the process of becoming conscious as a process of transient, dynamic integration of lower-level cognitive contents into extended chains, as a process of cognitive binding with the new and integrated contents becoming available for introspection$_3$ or introspection$_4$ (see figure 7.1 and Metzinger 2003a). We can also point out that dolphins are often so close to the surface that they are actually half in the water and half in the air. Another possibility to envision could be that the tourist in the boat sometimes doesn't notice how one dolphin has taken over the position of another one. This could take place during a short moment when they were both invisible, perhaps because the tourist was briefly distracted (the *tourist* is the model of an epistemic agent, the *seeing self* that is also part of our intuitive image). But it is also possible that one and the same dolphin might suddenly reappear in the distance, on the other side of the boat as it were, changing its position from the self-model to the external reality-model, now perhaps not even being recognized as the same dolphin anymore (and thus selectively becoming available for introspection$_1$ and introspection$_2$ only, instead of introspection$_3$ and introspection$_4$). This intuitive and oversimplified model of cognitive processing may, as we believe, turn out to be heuristically fruitful in understanding the transitions and interactions between personal and subpersonal level in phenomena such as self-deception or mind-wandering. Importantly, and given new empirical data, the spatial metaphor present in the dolphin model is open to continuous modification in order to further enhance its heuristic fecundity.

Before proceeding with the characterization of the belief-forming process of the self-deceiver, let us introduce two more conceptual tools: mental autonomy (M-autonomy) and the notion of an epistemic agent model (EAM; Metzinger 2013a, 2013b). M-autonomy is the ability to control the conscious contents of one's mind in a goal-directed manner and functionally presupposes the ability to suspend or terminate cognitive processes at will, by means of attentional or cognitive agency. Cognitive processing *becomes* a personal-level phenomenon by being functionally integrated into an EAM, which is a transparent conscious self-representation of possessing the capacity for epistemic agency and/or actually executing epistemic actions, where epistemic agency involves attentional agency (the ability to selectively focus one's attention) and cognitive agency (the ability to control goal-directed thought). Metzinger (2013a, 2013b) applies these conceptual tools to the phenomena of dreaming and of mind wandering, and we will here apply them to self-deception. The involvement of belief-forming processes is a characteristic of self-deception that differentiates it from cases in which goal representations influence the behavior directly. As Donald Davidson (1985) puts it, self-deception is a "weakness of the warrant," to be differentiated from the weakness of the will.

Mind wandering is a phenomenally represented, but subpersonal, form of cognitive processing (Metzinger 2013b). The self-deceptive, belief-forming process is subpersonal cognitive processing as well, yet it is an open question whether it is always phenomenally represented. Moreover, this question is independent of the one of whether tension is a necessary phenomenological component in self-deception: "I feel discomfort and identify its origin in my possessing certain representations" does not imply "I am an epistemic agent engaged in cognitive processing and I feel tension *because* something is wrong with the latter."

Taking for granted that at least some self-deceptive, subpersonal belief-forming processes are phenomenally represented, let us draw the analogy between these instances and mind wandering. If subpersonal cognitive processing is like a group of dolphins traveling below the surface, then mind wandering is like an absent-minded tourist passively monitoring a single dolphin's path. This happens in the absence of an EAM, whereas normal as well as self-deceived reasoning is like tracking an individual animal's leaps plus an experience of being able to control its trajectory, perhaps even involving the phenomenology of identification. What this analogy does not capture, however, is that we do not experience reasoning as singled out splashes, but as a connected whole. Just as real-life dolphins are often still visible below the surface or even partly in the water and partly above it, and therefore effortlessly perceived as one and the same dolphin over time, cognitive processing on the level of the EAM is experienced as stringent and internally connected. What conscious reasoning shares with the blind spot in vision and inattentional blindness in perception is the common characteristic that, though only parts come to consciousness, we experience the overall process as complete and without gaps. Let us call this *cognitive binding*. The continuous process of integrating cognitive processing into an EAM may result in a glossing over of temporal discontinuities.

Let us make this claim more precise. Keeping in mind the three levels of the reasoning process (unconscious, conscious and uncontrolled, conscious and controlled), the mind-wandering process is an uncontrolled one that is at certain points coupled with the phenomenology of control owing to a transient integration into the EAM. The general point about conscious cognition, which, however, has to be accounted for in explanations of self-deception, is that, even when we have the phenomenology of a controlled reasoning process, it can arise from the conscious experience of only some *parts* of the subpersonal reasoning process being currently integrated into an EAM, which themselves may be nonveridical or appear outright hallucinatory when detected from a third-person stance. We may experience ourselves as epistemic agents while we are not. In philosophical and psychological models of reasoning, introspectively accessible parts that are specified as conscious, and those containing biases that might or might not be conscious, are often combined without specifying how exactly conscious and unconscious parts are dynamically integrated into a holistic PSM. This problem is different from Bermúdez's (2000) interface problem, insofar as this is not the problem of how to describe the *transition* from subpersonal to personal-level states, but how to explain their interaction in creating a unified experience of the EAM in general and a unified experience of a continuous reasoning process in particular.

Cognitive binding is a different possibility from those so far considered in the literature about the relationship between conscious and unconscious belief-forming processes. For instance, Evans (2009), a proponent of dual-system theories of reasoning, considers the two possibilities to be either that an unconscious reasoning process is tracked, monitored, and corrected by the conscious one, or that both independently run in parallel. Yet both models leave unaccounted the possibility we introduce, namely, that the reasoning process as consciously experienced and controlled is the result of parts of the unconscious reasoning process being sporadically integrated into the unified EAM. Cognitive binding should also be differentiated from the "illusion of objectivity" or the control exercised by the agent over the reasoning process to appear unbiased (e.g., Pyszczynski, Greenberg, and Solomon 1999, 839).

There are two inferences to be drawn from cognitive binding. First, verbal reports about participant's reasoning processes generated in the context of empirical studies may actually refer to the introspectively available results of cognitive binding. Second, the need to justify the mental representations derived from reasoning processes that involve cognitive binding will lead to attempts of justification that, by necessity, can at best be only partially correct, because they must rely on what is introspectively available. In principle, it would be possible that one dolphin changes positions with another without you, the tourist, noticing this fact. The tourist is the EAM, and like any model, it can always be false or incomplete.

Let us conclude this section with a few more comments about the functional level. First, explanations of higher-order cognition using predictive coding should avoid the equivocation of the concepts of reasoning and inference. The hierarchical inference of causes using prediction errors is not to be confused with the personal-level notion of inference. To illustrate this point, Blokpoel, Kwisthout, and van Rooij (2012) argue that it may be difficult to explain higher-order cognition with predictive coding, because of the complexity of causal models at higher levels required for Bayesian inference to take place. They make clear their point by citing the Dr. Jekyll and Mr. Hyde thought experiment discussed by Kilner, Friston and Frith (2007) from Jacob and Jeannerod (2005): imagine that you are observing the identical movements of a person that, in one case, is Dr. Jekyll having an intention to cure and, in another case, is Mr. Hyde having an intention to hurt. The difficulty is to distinguish whether this person performing the same movements has the intention to cure or to hurt. Kilner, Friston, and Frith (2007) argue that it is possible to distinguish these two intentions owing to the dependency of prediction error on context. Yet it is not the case that a personal-level inference is responsible for the given discrimination. Thus, it does not follow from predictive coding that the conscious reasoning process, as well as the EAM, involves Bayesian reasoning on the level of its content, even if both arise out of a subpersonal process approximating Bayes-optimality. Second, although a thorough account of higher-order cognition in terms of predictive coding, in particular that of self-deceptive, belief-forming processes, is still to come, we want to point out that it is not only external evidence that has to be considered, but also itinerant fluctuations of ongoing brain activity that provide the "brain's internal context for processing external information and generating behavior"[19] (Sadaghiani et al. 2010, 12). Self-deceptive, belief-forming processes are highly dynamic and context-sensitive, so there will never be a static resulting mental representation with a fixed and determinate content. In the next section, we will consider those properties of SD that change over time.

4.3   Resulting Mental Representations

In this section, we will first argue that the majority of the empirical literature suggests that inconsistency is not part of the self-deceiver's PSM. Second, we will attempt to show how our conceptual tools offer a better description of the phenomenology of self-deceivers.

The kind of self-deception elaborated in the philosophical literature typically is one in which there is an inconsistency in the PSM that is globally accessible for attention, cognition, and action. Take, for example, Amelie Rorty's (1988) hypothetically constructed example of self-deception: a cancer specialist denies that she has cancer, yet exhibits behavior consistent with the proposition that she has cancer—for example, writing farewell letters to friends. In this case, the self-deceiver can plausibly be asked to explain the reasons for her behavior, and the inconsistency can be made available for conscious cognition. Take another often-constructed example of a wife who denies that her husband cheats on her, yet avoids visiting locations that would confirm this being the case (see section 2.1). It seems that in this case, too, the aim was to construct a hypothetical example of self-deception in which the inconsistency can be made introspectively available for attention and cognition, which can only be the case if it can become part of the phenomenal self-model.

If one looks at the empirical psychological literature on self-deception, however, it will often suffice to assume that there is an inconsistency between the phenomenal and the unconscious self-model. To demonstrate this point, let us consider some of the examples interpreted[20] as cases of self-deception by von Hippel and Trivers (2011). As one example, they describe a study by Ditto and colleagues that shows that "when people are led to believe that color change is a good thing, they wait more than 60% longer for the test strip to change color than when they believe color change is a bad thing" (von Hippel and Trivers 2011, 8). Another example they describe is a study by Epley and Whitchurch who found that, if asked to identify their own photo, "participants were more likely to choose their photo morphed 10% with the more attractive image than either their actual photo or their photo morphed with the unattractive image" (von Hippel and Trivers 2011, 5). A third example we want to mention is a study conducted by Snyder and colleagues. They found that if participants are given the choice of sitting either next to or away from a disabled person, and if the television in front of the two open seats shows the same program, they sit next to the person, presumably to demonstrate to self and other that they are not prejudiced against disabled people. However, if there are two different television programs, participants choose the seat further away (von Hippel and Trivers

2011, 10). What these studies clearly show is that not every self-related bit of information and not every self-related preference represented in the system becomes part of the PSM, and that overt action may often be guided by goal-representations that are not part of the phenomenal self-model.

Yet, what such studies do *not* show is that there actually is some phenomenally represented inconsistency in the self-deceiver. To give one more example, Greve and Wentura (2010, 728) describe self-immunization (see section 2.2) as "personal/consciously experienced stability versus sub-personal/cognitively adaptive dynamics" (where stability refers to trait *ascription* and the dynamics is related to trait *description*) and note that self-deception is not resolvable purely on the personal level. This is not only the case for self-immunization, but for many other cases described in the psychological literature as well. Thus, although in philosophical thought experiments self-deceivers can often plausibly be asked to justify their inconsistent behavior, because the inconsistency is in principle globally available for attention and cognition, in empirically plausible psychological cases the inconsistency is often accessible to the third-person observer only, but not to the self-deceivers themselves, because it is not a part of the PSM. We find a corresponding disagreement in the self-deception literature about the definition of self-deception (Baghramian and Nicholson 2013, 1025). Along similar lines, Van Leeuwen (2013) criticizes Trivers (2011) for making the categorization of self-deception so broad and diffuse that it precludes a scientific investigation (Van Leeuwen 2013, 148). Is every bias self-deceptive? Is every misrepresentation self-deceptive? Is every goal-directed misrepresentation self-deceptive, the one whose content can be manipulated by triggering different goals (compare the color change example mentioned in the previous paragraph)? Does self-deception involve a certain phenomenology—for example, an unspecific, vague feeling of uneasiness? Why does this feeling not lead to the revision of the misrepresentation? Perhaps because of a systematic causal misattribution of the feeling to some other source?[21] Still, do self-deceivers *permanently* experience this feeling of uneasiness? Here, the central point is that the phenomenological level is not to be taken lightly in the discussion of self-deception, and that it is difficult to prove that self-deception involves an inconsistency in the PSM.

Another example for the latter claim are Paulhus and Buckels's experiments that attempt to show that self-deception "requires not only motivated cognition but also the additional feature of discrepant representations" (Paulhus and Buckels 2012, 367). Paulhus and Buckels (2012) summarize two experiments conducted following the Quattrone-Tversky paradigm (370): participants had to take an achievement test and were given the freedom to terminate the test even after the fixed amount of time that was given. The context the experimenters provided about getting high scores on the test (being successful or being prone to schizophrenia) affected the amount of time participants worked on the task, leading the authors to conclude that "subjects can be motivated to excel or fail on a test that is supposed to inform them about their current ability level" (371). The authors present this as a case of self-deception, because the manipulation of the time spent working on the test should have precluded participants from concluding that the results of the test indicated their performance level (372). Participants, however, justified the accuracy of the scores achieved by such cheating (371). They seem not to *experience* the contradiction between the time they took to accomplish the tasks and the conclusions they drew about their performance (and there is no information about physiological or some other measurements of tension).

Further, it is possible that the inconsistency in self-deception between the contents of the unconscious self-model and the PSM is not an inconsistency between two representations resulting from the belief-forming process, but between one representation resulting from such a process and a goal-representation influencing behavior directly. Another interesting point is that it is not only the case that changes in the unconscious self-model may lead to unnoticed changes in the PSM, as the literature mentioned so far already suggests, but also vice versa. Khemlani and Johnson-Laird (2012) conducted experiments in which participants had to detect logical inconsistencies. Their results suggest that the additional fact that participants actively construct explanations of the inconsistencies makes it harder for participants to detect those afterward. Khemlani and Johnson-Laird (2013) further constrained the interpretation of their previous study as far as inconsistencies were harder to detect only if participants had to explain both consistent and inconsistent sets of assertions. With respect to self-deception, and given that the behavior of the self-deceiver indicates the possession of inconsistent representations and that justification of self-deceptively acquired mental representations is often part of this behavior, a number of new targets and avenues for empirical research suggest themselves. For example, it would be interesting to experimentally test how the *type* of personal-level justification that self-deceivers have to construct actually changes their unconscious self-model in order to stabilize and strengthen their self-deception.

Let us now come to the phenomenology of the self-deceiver. We argue that the following properties of self-deceptive phenomenal representations can vary:

(1) The degree to which they are conscious (e.g., Demos 1960, Billon 2011, von Hippel and Trivers 2011),

(2) The phenomenology of certainty—that is, the phenomenal experience of their subjective epistemic status (see section 2.3), and

(3) Phenomenal transparency (realness and mind-independence).

In the remaining section we will focus on the third point, because it has not yet been considered in the literature. Recently, the term *transparency* has been used in explanations of self-deception (Galeotti 2012, Bagnoli 2012, Marraffa 2012). Its meaning, however, is different from the notion of phenomenal transparency introduced by us in the previous section. These authors use term *transparency* either in the sense of cognitive lucidity[22] or in the sense of inaccessibility of whole processes or mental operations.[23] We understand transparency as *inaccessibility of earlier processing stages* that leads to a specific kind of phenomenology—the one of perceptual presence, realness, and mind-independence. Thus, our use of the transparent—opaque distinction is not a substitute for the conscious/unconscious distinction. On the representational level, the transparency constraint allows for the possibility of unnoticeable self-misrepresentations (Metzinger 2003a, 431–432). If a certain conscious content is transparent, then it is experienced as real, and the subject is certain of its existence. In the human PSM, one disadvantage of transparency of is that the resulting introspective$_{3/4}$ unavailability of the content's causal history severely restricts introspective self-knowledge (435).

So, how far does the notion of phenomenal transparency help clarify the phenomenon of self-deception? First, let us draw attention to the difference between (a) transparent mental representations and (b) mental representations that have transparent mental representations as their content. This distinction is important to differentiate our analysis of the formation and the functional role of self-deceptive phenomenal representations from the process of their justification.

(a) Transparent representations, owing to their being perceived as real, form a background model that serves as a basis for building simulation models (cf. Metzinger 2003a). Those transparent representations contain transparent parts of the phenomenal world- and self-model, the epistemic status of which we never question, owing to their not being experienced *as* representations, but as the real world and the real me (e.g., we simply see the book in our hands and perceive both the book and our hands as real, cf. Metzinger 2003a, 165–166).

(b) We can form thoughts *about* the content of such transparent representations—for example, *de re* beliefs about this book in our hands. Conscious thoughts, however, are (mostly) *opaque*, experienced as simulations—mental representations that might be true or false. One argument of the self-model theory is that this causally enables modal competence—the ability to distinguish between what is real and what is only possible and to compare self-generated models of reality with a preexisting default model, continuously marked out as real.

Armed with this distinction, let us tackle self-deceptive phenomenal representations. Typically, they are taken to be beliefs that we take to be true. Thus, the most straightforward suggestion would be that they are opaque. Yet we will argue that, like thoughts in mind wandering and dreaming episodes (Metzinger 2003a, 172), self-deceptive thoughts are often exceptions to the rule—they may be transparent, which is the case when they have been integrated into the *reality model*. Our point is that there may actually be mind-independent thoughts, thoughts that cannot be experienced *as* thoughts anymore, because self-deception often occurs exactly when cognitive contents have acquired the experiential status of mind-independence. Their content is then only accessible to introspection$_{1/2}$, but not to introspection$_{3/4}$ anymore. Phenomenal transparency leads to a different kind of subjective feeling of epistemic reliability, which is not to be equated with the epistemic status of beliefs on the one hand and the feeling of epistemic reliability accompanying opaque mental representations on the other. Further, the transparency of self-deceptive representations is compatible with them having to be justified by the self-deceiver, in which case a self-deceiver forms an opaque thought *about* a now-transparent, self-deceptive representation.

At least four points speak in favor of phenomenal transparency as a frequent property of self-deceptive representations. First, it is an established fact that emotions, which may oscillate between transparency and opacity, play a role in self-deception (Mele 2000, 2001, Damm 2011). This directs attention to the necessity to carefully consider transitions between transparency and opacity of self-deceptive representations. Second, Gendler (2007) also points in the same direction, as far as she conceives of the self-deceiver as somebody who make-believes/imagines/fantasizes that something is the case. We argue that it is the transition from imagination to *being-the-case* that is relevant. Third, anosognosia is often mentioned in the literature as a case of self-deception (e.g., selected chapters of Bayne and Fernández 2009, Ramachandran 1996). However, the semantic overlap of our concepts of delusion and self-deception (their motivated nature and resistance against available evidence) does not imply an overlap of *phenomena*, or that all motivated delusions are instances of self-deception. Thus, remaining neutral to the question of whether anosognosia is an instance of self-deception, we want to argue that another reason, apart from motivation and resistance against counterevidence (which makes the ascription of self-deception to anosognostics so popular in the literature), is that in anosognosia, or denial of illness, the misrepresentation that one is healthy or that one's arm is not paralyzed has become a transparent part of their PSM. It is now a robust part of one's phenomenal body-model, experientially mind-independent, and thus makes it resistant to counterevidence. Fourth, transparency provides a better explanation for real-world cases of self-deception, for example, the air crash example described in Trivers (2010), in which a pilot and a copilot argue about the appropriateness of weather conditions for takeoff. The copilot's behavior changes from, first, pointing out the danger of the weather conditions to, eventually, agreeing with the pilot, boarding the plane, and taking off. How can the copilot agree to board the plane, given his knowledge of ice on the wings, his warnings to the pilot, and so on, if it means gambling his life? The self-deceptive representation is now not part of the opaque, doubtful cognitive self-model anymore, because it has become a part of the transparent, external situation model, and therefore is experientially mind-independent. Our speculative hypothesis is that the transition from the opaque self-model into the transparent model of external reality sometimes takes a detour through the transparent layers of the somatic and emotional self-model—that is, first establishing mind-independence and realness and then gaining the status of externality (see, e.g., Thagard 2006 for self-deception as a result of an emotional skewer). It would then be the *emotional* state of the self-deceived person that is responsible for the phenomenological projection of a cognitive misrepresentation into the outside world. Thus, as such it is not questioned (it *cannot* be questioned), and there are no simulations performed according to which it is false. Accordingly, the question is not one of entertaining a certain belief *as a belief* (being aware that it can be false), but rather one of being gradually drawn into a certain *model of reality*. The new model of reality may include a new and transparent self-model (e.g., of a nonparalyzed body, available for introspection$_{3/4}$) or, in the second case, adopting not only a view that it *is* secure to fly (while emotionally oscillating between certainty and uncertainty), but a full-blown and transparent situation model (available for introspection$_{1/2}$). Thus, the point is that after a belief is adopted and owned as part of the cognitive self-model, its truth-value is (usually) not questioned, because it has subsequently "escaped" to become part of the transparent PSM, or the external situation model, in this way guiding behavior *and* shaping our external phenomenal reality as well.

5   Conclusion

At the beginning, we asked three questions. First, how is it conceivable that systematic and robust form of misrepresentation on the level of phenomenal self-consciousness exist? We argued that transparency of the PSM is a sufficient condition for not noticing the fluctuations in content properties of our self-deceptive phenomenal representations, as well as for our blindness to the fact of our reasoning process having been influenced by unconscious goal-representations and resulting from cognitive binding.

Second, how can systematic misrepresentations be *functionally adequate* for individual human persons? Here, we argued that much of the evidence cited in this chapter suggests that self-deceptive misrepresentations arise out of Bayes-optimal neural processes that are internally characterized by itinerant fluctuations and depend on external information received over time. Self-deceptive processes are part of the self-model that, of course, is itself a dynamic, generative model that is continuously optimized (Limanowski and Blankenburg 2013). Given Friston et al.'s (2013) claim that high precision biases perception in the direction of one's goals (as an explanation of optimism bias), and our own description of self-deception as a goal-directed misrepresentation with a specific phenomenological profile, preservation of the overall *integrity of the self-model*[24]—which reflects *organismic* integrity—is an unconscious, high-level goal that is deeply grounded in any biological system's continuous battle to sustain its own existence. Sometimes this process will therefore have to sacrifice epistemic reliability in order to preserve the overall integrity of the self-model *and* the body. Clearly, the integrity of the self-model is a deep normative constraint for unconscious processing, but many open questions remain and, in itself, this often-neglected fact will not suffice for a convincing explanation of SD.

Third, why could such SD processes have evolved? We argued that self-deception emerges from multiple competing goal representations. We further emphasized the importance of the new hypothesis, offered by Robert Trivers, stating that the goal to deceive *others* may well be the overarching evolutionary goal in self-deception, the decisive new capacity. Combining these two points, it is the exploration of the *connection* of this goal with other relevant constraints (e.g., to continuously avoid anxiety of death and achieve a stable form of mortality denial, which, for TMT, is another maximally important goal, or the successful maintenance of an autobiographical self-model, see Metzinger 2013b) that may prove fruitful in unriddling self-deception. If a generative model accurately extracts those aspects of the causal structure of the world that are responsible for reproductive fitness of an organism, its epistemic status will not matter. In a purely evolutionary context, self-deception may therefore be functionally adequate, leading to new mental properties that propagate through populations and across generations. The dolphin model of cognition will pave the way toward understanding the proximal and "porpoising" belief-forming processes that, in the individual organism, are influenced by specific, self-deceptive goal-representations. The dolphin model is not meant as an intuition pump, but as a flexible heuristic tool that can be adapted to generate more specific questions—and hopefully answers.[25]

Notes

1. Notable exceptions are Sahdra and Thagard (2003), who offer a connectionist account of SD. There is also Bayne and Fernández's (2009) collected volume on the relationship between delusion and self-deception that takes data from cognitive neuropsychiatry into account, yet remains in the boundaries of the folk-psychological description.

2. Van Leeuwen (2007) proposes calling "the attitude that results from self-deception the *product of self-deception*" (421). In this article, he also gives a brief overview of what he calls the "strategies" for solving the paradox of self-deception (i.e., believing in obviously contradictory propositions).

3. Paradox of irrationality: "On the one hand, it is not clear that there is a genuine case of irrationality unless an inconsistency in the thought of the agent can be identified, something that is inconsistent by the standards of the agent himself. On the other hand, when we try to explain in any detail how the agent can have come to be in this state, we find ourselves inventing some form of rationalization that we can attribute to the self-deceiver, thus diluting the imputed inconsistency" (Davidson 1985, 79).

4. For comparison purposes, Demos (1960), who is said to have set the stage for the debate about self-deception (Clegg and Moissinac 2005), has claimed that self-deception can be explained by the distinction between two kinds of awareness: "simple awareness" and awareness that is coupled with attention. Awareness presupposes consciousness. Yet the assumption that consciousness and attention can be dissociated is debatable (Bor and Seth 2012).

5. In this chapter, we do not make a sharp distinction between self-deceiver (active) and the self-deceived (passive), because it would communicate a wrong picture of homunculi in our heads that try to deceive each other.

6. Kunda's (1990) distinction between two kinds of motivation—accuracy and directional goals—underlies this claim. Kunda (1990) defined motivation as "any wish, desire, or preference that concerns the outcome of a given reasoning task" (480). It is interesting to note that this distinction is neither exhaustive, nor exclusive: there might be other types of goals, and one might at the same time want to arrive at the truth and at a specific (namely, a true) conclusion.

7. "The *acceptance threshold* is the minimum confidence in the truth of a hypothesis that the perceiver requires before accepting it, rather than continuing to test it, and the *rejection threshold* is the minimum confidence in the untruth of a hypothesis that the perceiver requires before rejecting it, and discontinuing the test" (Trope and Liberman 1996, 253, our emphasis).

8. Cognitive dissonance theory was originally developed by Festinger (1957, further developments are discussed in Cooper 2007). Festinger (1957) claimed that inconsistency among cognitions is followed by a feeling of discomfort and leads to strategies of dissonance reduction. According to Cooper (2007), cognitions are any "pieces of knowledge," which also include actions and attitudes, because the latter have a "psychological representation" (6).

Kruglanski and Webster (1996) define the need for cognitive closure as an "individual's desire for a firm answer to a question and an aversion toward ambiguity," noting that this need is "akin to a person's goal" (264). The need for closure affects, according to them, the knowledge-construction process in a biasing way. The underlying assumption is that "people under a heightened need for closure experience its absence as *aversive*. They may, therefore, wish to terminate this unpleasant state quickly (the urgency tendency) and keep it from recurring (the permanence tendency)" (265, our emphasis).

9. To exemplify the second *source:* "If, by her current lights, the question 'Do I or do I not have a typically lethal cancer?' is open, it can hardly be the case that 'It is far more likely that I will send my daughter to college than that I will not send my daughter to college,' and so on" (Scott-Kakures 2009, 100).

10. Lynch (2012) gives a nice summary of how different authors define tension in self-deception.

11. There is an interesting inference one can draw from cognitive dissonance theory concerning the theory of von Hippel and Trivers (2011), who advocate that self-deception has an offensive evolutionary function to deceive others. Von Hippel and Trivers (2011) claim that self-enhancement is a kind of self-deception, as well as that self-deception can be tested by the self-affirmation paradigm. Steele (1988), who developed the self-affirmation theory as a further elaboration of the cognitive dissonance theory, claims that cognitive dissonance can be explained in terms of self-affirmation. Yet, von Hippel and Trivers (2011) argue that tension is not a necessary requirement for self-deception, although the paradigm they use builds on this assumption.

12. In Slotter et al.'s (2010) terms: self-immunization is about self-concept content change, in comparison to self-concept size or clarity.

13. Lynch (2012) argues that his solution explains the tension (feeling of uneasiness and discomfort) inherent in self-deception, because humans are generally responsive to evidence and "this is not a contingent truth about self-deceivers" (2012, 442).

14. Mele (2001) proposed the impartial-observer test as the one that differentiates cases of self-deception, which Lynch (2012) embraces here: "S's degree of conviction in the proposition that p will be unwarranted if it deviates to a noteworthy degree from that which her ICPs [impartial cognitive peers] would form on the basis of considering the same information that S was acquainted with, and deviates in the direction of what S wants to be true" (2012, 441).

15. For a recent theory arguing that human behavior is influenced by competing goals, see Huang and Bargh (2014).

16. Bayes-optimality is the property of processing available information according to the Bayes's law, which is an appropriate (optimal) way to handle uncertainty inherent in that information (Clark 2013, 9).

17. The notion of global availability has been developed by Bernard Baars (1988, 1997) and David Chalmers (1997).

18. Noteworthy is that exaggerated belief in one's personal control has been suggested by Taylor (1989) to be one of the three self-deceptive illusions, along with self-enhancement and unrealistic optimism.

19. Sadaghiani et al. (2010) argue that the itinerant fluctuations provide a link to mind wandering: "Itinerant fluctuations of this [ongoing brain] activity reflect the dynamic nature of the underlying internal model that does not remain locked in a stationary mode but remains malleable by continuously exploring hypotheses regarding future experience and action" (10).

20. An empirical example of self-deception that satisfies all four of the constraints mentioned in section 2.4 is hard to find, not least due to the impossibility of controlling the termination of self-deception under experimental conditions. Religion and global warming as examples (or at least consequences of our ability) of self-deception can be found in Varki and Brower (2013), who propose that full-blown theory of mind capacities could only evolve in humans owing to the existence of self-deception as a mechanism by which anxiety about one's death could be managed.

21. See Cooper 2007 for a short elaboration on Schachter and Singer's (1962) misattribution of arousal paradigm that would suggest an affirmative response to the latter question.

22. Galeotti (2012, 55) uses the term *transparency* in the sense of cognitive lucidity: "The second difference is that the non-transparency of the SD process is a specifi-

cally thematic one. It is not simply that we do not master our cognitive processes and that cold biases are pervasive and beyond our control, that, again, is common to any cognitive enterprise and in no way can single out, let alone explain, SD. The *non-transparency* of SD is a special kind of overall *opacity* possibly caused by the strong emotional state of the subject, which somehow *impairs her cognitive lucidity about the whole process and its outcome"* (italics are our own emphasis).

23. Bagnoli (2012, 100–101) uses transparency as accessibility of mental processes and operations: "We ordinarily assume self-transparency, even though we know that there are large areas of our mental processes and operations that remain *inaccessible*. One solution is to treat self-deception as a case where our mind is *opaque*, as it happens for many mental sub-personal processes and operations. But the interesting aspect of self-deception is that it concerns beliefs and mental states that are normally accessible. Hence, the selective character posits an obstacle to reducing self-deception to a general case of the opacity of the mind because it appears to exhibit some sort of finality. That is, it concerns a selected cluster of *beliefs that whose knowledge the agent has an interest in blocking*, even though she may not intend to block it" (italics are our own emphasis).

24. See, e.g., Metcalfe 1998 for the stress-reducing function of SD, or Barnes 1997 for its anxiety-reducing function.

25. We are very grateful to Jennifer Windt and Michael Madary for valuable comments and help with the English version. Iuliia Pliushch's PhD project is funded by the Barbara Wengeler foundation.

References

Baars, B. J. 1988. *A Cognitive Theory of Consciousness*. Cambridge: Cambridge University Press.

Baars, B. J. 1997. *In the Theater of Consciousness: The Workspace of the Mind*. Oxford: Oxford University Press.

Bach, K. 1981. An analysis of self-deception. *Philosophy and Phenomenological Research* 41:351–370.

Baghramian, M., and A. Nicholson. 2013. The puzzle of self-deception. *Philosophy Compass* 8:1018–1029.

Bagnoli, C. 2012. Self-deception and agential authority: A constitutivist account. *Humana.Mente: Journal of Philosophical Studies* 20:99–116.

Barnes, A. 1997. *Seeing through Self-Deception*. Cambridge Studies in Philosophy. Cambridge: Cambridge University Press.

Bayne, T., and J. Fernández, eds. 2009. *Delusion and Self-Deception: Affective and Motivational Influences on Belief Formation*. New York: Psychology Press.

Bermúdez, J. L. 2000a. Personal and sub-personal: A difference without a distinction. *Philosophical Explorations* 3:63–82.

Bermúdez, J. L. 2000b. Self-deception, intentions, and contradictory beliefs. *Analysis* 60:309–319.

Billon, A. 2011. Have we vindicated the motivational unconscious yet? A conceptual review. *Frontiers in Psychology* 2:224.

Blanke, O., and T. Metzinger. 2009. Full-body illusions and minimal phenomenal selfhood. *Trends in Cognitive Sciences* 13:7–13.

Blokpoel, M., J. Kwisthout, and I. van Rooij. 2012. When can predictive brains be truly Bayesian? *Frontiers in Psychology* 3:406.

Bor, D., and A. Seth. 2012. Consciousness and the prefrontal parietal network: Insights from attention, working memory, and chunking. *Frontiers in Psychology* 3:63.

Borge, S. 2003. The myth of self-deception. *Southern Journal of Philosophy* 41:1–28.

Brentano, F. (1911) 1971. *Psychologie vom empirischen Standpunkt, Zweiter Band: Von der Klassifikation der psychischen Phänomene*. Hamburg: Meiner.

Brentano, F. (1874) 1973. *Psychology from an Empirical Standpoint*. Ed. O. Kraus. English edition ed. L. McAlister. Trans. C. Antos, R., D. B. Terrell, and L. McAlister. London: Routledge & Kegan Paul; New York: Humanities Press.

Chalmers, D. 1997. Availability: The cognitive basis of experience? In *The Nature of Consciousness: Philosophical Debates*, ed. N. Block, O. Flanagan, and G. Güzeldere, 421–424. Cambridge, MA: MIT Press.

Churchland, P. M. 1989. *A Neurocomputational Perspective: The Nature of Mind and the Structure of Science*. Cambridge, MA: MIT Press.

Clark, A. 1993. *Microcognition: Philosophy, Cognitive Science, and Parallel Distributed Processing*, 4th ed., vol. 6. Cambridge, MA: MIT Press.

Clark, A. 2013. Whatever next? Predictive brains, situated agents, and the future of cognitive science. *Behavioral and Brain Sciences* 36:181–204.

Clegg, J., and L. Moissinac. 2005. A relational theory of self-deception. *New Ideas in Psychology* 23:96–110.

Colombo, M. 2013. Constitutive relevance and the personal/subpersonal distinction. *Philosophical Psychology* 26:547–570.

Cooper, J. 2007. *Cognitive Dissonance: Fifty Years of a Classic Theory*. Los Angeles: Sage.

Damm, L. 2011. Self-deception about emotion. *Southern Journal of Philosophy* 49:254–270.

Davidson, D. 1985. Deception and division. In *The Multiple Self*, ed. J. Elster, 79–92. Studies in Rationality and Social Change. Cambridge: Cambridge University Press. Reprint, 1989.

Davidson, D. 1998. Who is fooled? In *CSLI Publications*, vol. 69: *Self-Deception and Paradoxes of Rationality*, ed. J.-P. Dupuy, 1–18. Stanford, CA: Center for the Study of Language and Information.

Demos, R. 1960. Lying to oneself. *Journal of Philosophy* 57:588–595.

Drayson, Z. 2012. The uses and abuses of the personal/subpersonal distinction. *Philosophical Perspectives* 26:1–18.

Evans, J. S. 2009. How many dual-process theories do we need? One, two, or many? In *In Two Minds: Dual Processes and Beyond.*, ed. J. S. Evans and K. Frankish, 33–54. Oxford: Oxford University Press.

Festinger, L. 1957. *A Theory of Cognitive Dissonance*. Stanford, CA: Stanford University Press. Reprint, 1968.

Fingarette, H. 2000. *Self-Deception*. Berkeley: University of California Press.

Friedrich, J. 1993. Primary error detection and minimization (PEDMIN) strategies in social cognition: A reinterpretation of confirmation bias phenomena. *Psychological Review* 100:298–319.

Friston, K. 2003. Learning and inference in the brain. *Neural Networks* 16:1325–1352.

Friston, K. 2005. A theory of cortical responses. *Philosophical Transactions of the Royal Society of London, Series B: Biological Sciences* 360:815–836.

Friston, K. 2010. The free-energy principle: A unified brain theory? *Nature Reviews Neuroscience* 11:127–138.

Friston, K., P. Schwartenbeck, T. FitzGerald, M. Moutoussis, T. Behrens, and R. J. Dolan. 2013. The anatomy of choice: Active inference and agency. *Frontiers in Human Neuroscience* 7:598.

Funkhouser, E. 2005. Do the self-deceived get what they want? *Pacific Philosophical Quarterly* 86:295–312.

Funkhouser, E. 2009. Self-deception and limits of folk psychology. *Social Theory and Praxis* 35:1–16.

Galeotti, A. 2012. Self-deception: Intentional plan or mental event? *Humana.Mente: Journal of Philosophical Studies* 20:41–66.

Gendler, T. 2007. Self-deception as pretense. *Philosophical Perspectives* 21:231–258.

Greenberg, J., S. Solomon, and T. Pyszczynski. 1992. Why do people need self-esteem? Converging evidence that self-esteem serves an anxiety-buffering function. *Journal of Personality and Social Psychology* 63:913–922.

Greve, W., and D. Wentura. 2003. Immunizing the self: Self-concept stabilization through reality-adaptive self-definitions. *Personality and Social Psychology Bulletin* 29:39–50.

Greve, W., and D. Wentura. 2010. True lies: Self-stabilization without self-deception. *Consciousness and Cognition* 19:721–730.

Helzer, E., and D. Dunning. 2012. On motivated reasoning and self-belief. In *Handbook of Self-Knowledge*, ed. S. Vazire and T. Wilson, 379–396. New York: Guilford Publications.

Hohwy, J. 2013. *Predictive Mind.* Oxford: Oxford University Press.

Huang, J., and J. Bargh. 2014. The selfish goal: Autonomously operating motivational structures as the proximate cause of human judgment and behavior. *Behavioral and Brain Sciences* 37:121–135.

Jacob, P., and M. Jeannerod. 2005. The motor theory of social cognition: A critique. *Trends in Cognitive Sciences* 9:21–25.

Johnston, M. 1988. Self-deception and the nature of the mind. In *Topics in Philosophy*, vol. 6: *Perspectives on Self-Deception*, ed. B. McLaughlin and A. Rorty, 63–91. Berkeley: University of California Press.

Khemlani, S., and P. Johnson-Laird. 2013. Cognitive changes from explanations. *Journal of Cognitive Psychology* 25:139–146.

Khemlani, S., and P. Johnson-Laird. 2012. Hidden conflict: Explanations make inconsistencies harder to detect. *Acta Psychologica* 139:486–491.

Kilner, J., K. Friston, and C. Frith. 2007. Predictive coding: an account of the mirror neuron system. *Cognitive Processing* 8:159–166.

Kruglanski, A., and D. Webster. 1996. Motivated closing of the mind: "Seizing" and "freezing." *Psychological Review* 103:263–283.

Kunda, Z. 1990. The case for motivated reasoning. *Psychological Bulletin* 108: 480–498.

Lazar, A. 1999. Deceiving oneself or self-deceived? On the formation of beliefs "under the influence." *Mind* 108:265–290.

Limanowski, J. 2014. What can body ownership illusions tell us about minimal phenomenal selfhood? *Frontiers in Human Neuroscience* 8:946.

Limanowski, J., and F. Blankenburg. 2013. Minimal self-models and the free energy principle. *Frontiers in Human Neuroscience* 7:547.

Lynch, K. 2012. On the "tension" inherent in self-deception. *Philosophical Psychology* 25:433–450.

Madary, M. 2012. How would the world look if it looked as if it were encoded as an intertwined set of probability density distributions? *Frontiers in Psychology* 3:419.

Marraffa, M. 2012. Remnants of psychoanalysis: Rethinking the psychodynamic approach to self-deception. *Humana.Mente: Journal of Philosophical Studies* 20: 223–243.

McKay, R., C. Tamagni, A. Palla, P. Krummenacher, S. Hegemann, D. Straumann, and P. Brugger. 2013. Vestibular stimulation attenuates unrealistic optimism. *Cortex* 49:2272–2275.

Mele, A. 2000. Self-deception and emotion. *Consciousness and Emotion* 1:115–137.

Mele, A. 2001. *Self-Deception Unmasked*. Princeton Monographs in Philosophy. Princeton, NJ: Princeton University Press.

Mele, A. 2012. When are we self-deceived? *Humana.Mente: Journal of Philosophical Studies* 20:1–15.

Metcalfe, J. 1998. Cognitive optimism: Self-deception or memory-based processing heuristics? *Personality and Social Psychology Review* 2:100–110.

Metzinger, T. 2003a. *Being No One: The Self-Model Theory of Subjectivity*. Cambridge, MA: MIT Press.

Metzinger, T. 2003b. Phenomenal transparency and cognitive self-reference. *Phenomenology and the Cognitive Sciences* 2:353–393.

Metzinger, T. 2006. Précis: *Being No One. Psyche* 11:1–35.

Metzinger, T. 2007. Self models. *Scholarpedia* 2:4174.

Metzinger, T. 2008. Empirical perspectives from the self-model theory of subjectivity: A brief summary with examples. *Progress in Brain Research* 168:215–278.

Metzinger, T. 2010. *The Ego Tunnel: The Science of the Mind and the Myth of the Self*. New York: Basic Books.

Metzinger, T. 2011. The no-self alternative. In *The Oxford Handbook of the Self*, ed. S. Gallagher, 279–296. Oxford: Oxford University Press.

Metzinger, T. 2013a. Why are dreams interesting for philosophers? The example of minimal phenomenal selfhood, plus an agenda for future research. *Frontiers in Psychology* 4:746.

Metzinger, T. 2013b. The myth of cognitive agency: Subpersonal thinking as a cyclically recurring loss of mental autonomy. *Frontiers in Psychology* 4:931.

Michel, C. 2014. *Self-Knowledge and Self-Deception: The Role of Transparency in First Personal Knowledge*. Münster: mentis.

Michel, C., and A. Newen. 2010. Self-deception as pseudo-rational regulation of belief. *Consciousness and Cognition* 19:731–744.

Nelkin, D. 2002. Self-deception, motivation, and the desire to believe. *Pacific Philosophical Quarterly* 83:384–406.

Nelkin, D. 2012. Responsibility and self-deception: A framework. *Humana.Mente: Journal of Philosophical Studies* 20:117–139.

Paulhus, D., and E. Buckels. 2012. Classic self-deception revisited. In *Handbook of Self-Knowledge*, ed. S. Vazire and T. Wilson, 363–378. New York: Guilford Publications.

Pears, D. 1991. Self-deceptive belief formation. *Synthese* 89:393–405.

Pedrini, P. 2012. What does the self-deceiver want? *Humana.Mente: Journal of Philosophical Studies* 20:141–157.

Pliushch, I. 2015. The extension of the indicator-function of feelings: A commentary on Joëlle Proust. In *Open MIND*, ed. T. Metzinger and J. M. Windt, 31C. Frankfurt am Main: MIND Group.

Porcher, J. 2012. Against the deflationary account of self-deception. *Humana.Mente: Journal of Philosophical Studies* 20:67–84.

Preuss, N., G. Hasler, and F. W. Mast. 2014. Caloric vestibular stimulation modulates affective control and mood. *Brain Stimulation* 7:133–140.

Proust, J. 2013. *Philosophy of Metacognition: Mental Agency and Self-Awareness*. Oxford: Oxford University Press.

Pyszczynski, T., J. Greenberg, and S. Solomon. 1999. A dual-process model of defense against conscious and unconscious death-related thoughts: An extension of terror management theory. *Psychological Review* 106:835–845.

Pyszczynski, T., J. Greenberg, S. Solomon, J. Arndt, and J. Schimel. 2004. Why do people need self-esteem? A theoretical and empirical review. *Psychological Bulletin* 130:435–468.

Ramachandran, V. 1996. The evolutionary biology of self-deception, laughter, dreaming, and depression: Some clues from anosognosia. *Medical Hypotheses* 47: 347–362.

Ramsey, W., S. Stich, and J. Garon. 1991. Connectionism, eliminativism, and the future of folk psychology. In *Philosophy and Connectionist Theory*, ed. W. Ramsey, S. Stich, and D. Rumelhart, 199–228. Hillsdale, NJ: Erlbaum.

Rorty, A. 1988. The deceptive self: Liars, layers, and lairs. In *Topics in Philosophy*, vol. 6: *Perspectives on Self-Deception*, ed. B. McLaughlin and A. Rorty, 11–28. Berkeley: University of California Press.

Rorty, A. 2009. User-friendly self-deception. A traveler's manual. In *The Philosophy of Deception*, ed. C. W. Martin, 244–259. Oxford: Oxford University Press.

Sadaghiani, S., G. Hesselmann, K. Friston, and A. Kleinschmidt. 2010. The relation of ongoing brain activity, evoked neural responses, and cognition. *Frontiers in Systems Neuroscience* 4:20.

Sahdra, B., and P. Thagard. 2003. Self-deception and emotional coherence. *Minds and Machines* 13:213–231.

Sayers, G., and S. Perera. 2002. Withholding life prolonging treatment, and self-deception. *Journal of Medical Ethics* 28:347–352.

Schachter, S., and J. Singer. 1962. Cognitive, social, and physiological determinants of emotional state. *Psychological Review* 69:379–399.

Schwitzgebel, E. 2002. A phenomenal, dispositional account of belief. *Noûs* 36: 249–275.

Scott-Kakures, D. 2009. Unsettling questions: Cognitive dissonance in self-deception. *Social Theory and Practice* 35:73–106.

Scott-Kakures, D. 2012. Can you succeed in intentionally deceiving yourself? *Humana.Mente: Journal of Philosophical Studies* 20:17–39.

Slotter, E., W. Gardner, and E. Finkel. 2010. Who am I without you? The influence of romantic breakup on the self-concept. *Personality and Social Psychology Bulletin* 36:147–160.

Smith, D. L. 2014. Self-deception: A teleofunctional approach. *Philosophia* 42: 181–199.

Solomon, S., J. Greenberg, and T. Pyszczynski. 1991. A terror management theory of social behavior: The psychological functions of self-esteem and cultural worldviews. *Advances in Experimental Social Psychology* 24:93–159.

Solomon, S., J. Greenberg, and T. Pyszczynski. 2004. The cultural animal: Twenty years of terror management theory and research. In *Handbook of Experimental Existential Psychology*, ed. J. Greenberg, S. Koole, and T. Pyszczynski, 13–34. New York: Guilford Press.

Steele, C. 1988. The psychology of self-affirmation: Sustaining the integrity of the self. In *Advances in Experimental Social Psychology*, ed. L. Berkowitz, vol. 21, 261–302. San Diego, CA: Academic Press.

Talbott, W. 1995. Intentional self-deception in a single coherent self. *Philosophy and Phenomenological Research* 55:27–74.

Taylor, S. 1989. *Positive Illusions: Creative Self-Deception and the Healthy Mind*. New York: Basic Books.

Thagard, P. 2006. *Hot Thought: Mechanisms and Applications of Emotional Cognition*. Cambridge, MA: MIT Press.

Trivers, R. 2010. Deceit and self-deception. In *Mind the Gap: Tracing the Origins of Human Universals*, ed. P. Kappeler and J. Silk, 373–393. Berlin: Springer.

Trivers, R. 2011. *Deceit and Self-Deception: Fooling Yourself the Better to Fool Others*. London: Allen Lane.

Trope, Y., and A. Liberman. 1996. Social hypothesis testing: Cognitive and motivational mechanisms. In *Social Psychology: Handbook of Basic Principles*, ed. E. Higgins and A. Kruglanski, 239–270. New York: Guilford Press.

Van Leeuwen, N. 2007. The product of self-deception. *Erkenntnis* 67:419–437.

Van Leeuwen, N. 2013. The folly of fools: The logic of deceit and self-deception in human life. *Cognitive Neuropsychiatry* 18:146–151.

Varki, A., and D. Brower. 2013. *Denial: Self-Deception, False Beliefs, and the Origins of the Human Mind*. New York: Twelve.

von Hippel, W., and R. Trivers. 2011. The evolution and psychology of self-deception. *Behavioral and Brain Sciences* 34:1–16.

Windt, J. M. 2015. *Dreaming: A Conceptual Framework for Philosophy of Mind and Empirical Research*. Cambridge, MA: MIT Press.

Windt, J., and T. Metzinger. 2007. The philosophy of dreaming and self-consciousness: What happens to the experiential subject during the dream state? In *The New Science of Dreaming*, vol. 3: *Cultural and Theoretical Perspectives*, ed. D. Barrett and P. McNamara, 193–247. Westport, CT: Praeger Publishers/Greenwood Publishing Group.

Yoshie, M., and P. Haggard. 2013. Negative emotional outcomes attenuate sense of agency over voluntary actions. *Current Biology* 23 (20): 2028–2032.

8 Disorders of Unified Consciousness: Brain Bisection and Dissociative Identity Disorder

Andrew Brook

1 Disorders of Unified Consciousness: Two Kinds

One of the most interesting ways to study consciousness is to see what happens when it takes an abnormal form or breaks down. A phenomenon that looks simple and seamless when functioning smoothly reveals all sorts of structure when it functions abnormally. Abnormal forms (it would beg questions to say malfunctions) of unified consciousness are particularly interesting in this regard.

Abnormalities of unified consciousness take two broad forms. In the form that we will discuss in this paper, one finds, rather than a single instance of unified consciousness in a single human body, what appears to be two or more instances of it. The two cases we will examine are people whose brains have been bisected (usually by cutting the corpus callosum; these operations are more properly called "commissurotomies") and people who have what is now known as dissociative identity disorder (hereafter DID) (previously known as multiple personality disorder, a name that made all kinds of assumptions about the nature and reality of the condition). In these two cases, it is natural to think that (under special laboratory conditions in the case of brain bisections) unified consciousness has split: one has become two, or, in the case of DID, often more than two.

Another form of abnormality of unified consciousness is, or certainly appears to be, more radical, in which it is more natural to think that unified consciousness has shattered rather than split. In these conditions, even if there was unified consciousness once, now there is little or none.

Here is the plan. Abnormalities of the first kind will be the main topic of the chapter. However, we will begin with some examples of the second kind of abnormality. They provide a useful contrast. Then we will characterize the abnormalities of the first kind in somewhat greater detail than is often the case. Next, we will look at where two influential accounts go wrong: one is an account of what might be going on in brain bisection cases (Bayne 2010), and the other is an account of cases of DID (Humphrey and Dennett 1989). The problems with both have at least one common root: insufficient attention to the role of autobiographical memory. Out of these two critiques, what I hope is a more adequate account will grow.

2   Disorders in Which Unified Consciousness Appears to Have Shattered

Schizophrenia

In some particularly severe forms of schizophrenia, a person seems to lose the ability to have an integrated, interrelated experience of his or her world and self altogether. The person speaks in "word salads" that never get anywhere, indeed often never even become complete sentences. The person is unable to put together perceptions, beliefs, and motives into simple plans of action or to act on such plans if formed, even plans to obtain sustenance, tend to bodily needs, escape painful irritants, and so on. The behavior of these people seems to express what we might call mere experience-fragments, the contents of which are so narrow and unintegrated that the subject is unable to cope with their life and interact with others in the ways that, for example, split-brain subjects easily do.

Dysexecutive Syndrome

In schizophrenia of the severe sort just described, the shattering of consciousness is part of a general breakdown or deformation of mental functioning: affect, desire, belief, even memory all suffer massive distortions. In another condition, normal unity of consciousness seems to be just as absent, but there does not seem to be the same sort of general cognitive or affective disturbance. This is true of what some researchers call dysexecutive syndrome (Dawson, 1998, 215, for example). What indicates breakdown in the unity of consciousness is that these subjects are unable to consider two things together, even things directly related to one another. For example, such people cannot figure out whether a piece of a puzzle fits into a certain place even when the piece and the puzzle are both clearly visible and the piece obviously fits, they cannot crack an egg into a pan, and so on.

Trevarthen (1984) reports a similar syndrome even in a few brain bisection patients. In the cases he reports, patients are conscious of some object seen in the right side of the visual field by the left hemisphere (controlled so that the information is received by only that hemisphere) until an intention is formed to reach for it with the left hand, controlled by the right hemisphere. Somehow the intention to reach for it seems to obliterate consciousness of it in the hemisphere that controls speech, presumably the left hemisphere. However, if the object is slid over to the left visual field, then the speech-controlling hemisphere reports that it can see the object again— even though the object can now be seen only by the right hemisphere and the left still controls speech!

Simultagnosia

A disorder presenting symptoms similar to those of dysexecutive syndrome is simultagnosia or Balint's syndrome (Balint was an early twentieth-century German neurologist). In this disorder, patients see only one object located at one "place" in the visual field at a time. Outside of a few degrees of arc in the visual field, these patients say they see nothing but an "undifferentiated mess" and seem to be receiving no information about objects (Hardcastle 1997, 62).

What is common to dysexecutive disorder, Trevarthen's cases, and simultagnosia is that subjects seem not to be conscious of even two objects at the same time in a single conscious state. They cannot, for example, compare the objects (in Trevarthen's cases, the object of a perception with the object of an intention). Nor are they like commissurotomy cases. In commissurotomy cases, there is evidence (discussed in the section introducing these cases) that a conscious experience of the second item exists within another unified consciousness. Whatever may be true of those cases, there is no like evidence here. If there is any experience of a second or third item at all, it would appear that it is not conscious. Instead of consciousness being split into two discrete parcels, there is just one radically diminished parcel. The rest of the conscious experiencing that is typical of normal consciousness has disappeared.

In all these cases, it is plausible to suggest that the unity of consciousness has shattered rather than split. There are, of course, many different theories about what is going on in severe schizophrenia, dysexecutive syndrome, and simultagnosia/Balint's syndrome. Some hold that the deficits are not deficits of unified consciousness at all; they are deficits in the capacity to process perceptual information. Consciousness remains unified, but patients can no longer take in what is happening. Whatever exactly we want to say about these cases, they all display two features. First, unified consciousness is greatly diminished, in ways that limit patients' abilities dramatically, and second, whatever unified consciousness there is, there are not two or more apparent instances of it. In both respects, brain bisection and DID are utterly different.

3   Disorders in which Unified Consciousness Appears to Have Split

Brain Bisection Operations

No medical procedure having to do with consciousness has received as much philosophical attention in recent times as brain bisection operations (commissurotomies). Nagel (1971) was perhaps the first philosopher to write about them; his paper continues to be influential. Since then, Puccetti (1973, 1981), Marks (1981), Hirsch (1991), Lockwood (1989), Hurley (1998), Bayne (2008, 2010), Schechter (2010) and many, many other philosophers have written on these operations. Indeed, the strange behavior that can be generated in these patients in controlled conditions was one of the things that brought the unity of consciousness back into prominence.

Brain bisection operations are done to prevent the spread of severe epileptic seizures from one cerebral hemisphere to the other, a spread that can be lethal. In the procedure, the corpus callosum is partially or entirely severed. The corpus callosum is a large strand of about 200 million neurons running from one hemisphere to the other. When present, it is the chief channel of communication between the hemispheres. These operations were done mainly in the 1960s but have been reintroduced recently in a somewhat modified form. (For more details, see Sperry 1984, Bogen 1993, or Gazzaniga 2000.)

In everyday life, these patients show little effect of the operation. In particular, their consciousness of their world and themselves appears to remain as unified as it was prior to the operation. How this can be has puzzled a lot of people (Hurley 1998). Even more interesting for our purposes, however, is that, under certain laboratory conditions, these patients behave as though two "centres of consciousness" (Sperry 1984) have been created in them. The original single instance of unified consciousness seems to have been replaced, for a short time, by two instances of unified consciousness, each associated with one cerebral hemisphere.

Here are a couple of examples of the kinds of behavior that prompt that assessment. The human retina is split vertically in such a way that the left half of each retina is primarily hooked up to the left hemisphere of the brain, and the right half of each retina is primarily hooked up to the right hemisphere of the brain. Now suppose that we flash the word TAXABLE on a screen in front of a brain-bisected patient in such a way that the letters TAX hit the left side of the retina and the letters ABLE the right side, and we put measures in place to ensure that the information received by each half of the retina goes only to one lobe and does not get to the other. If such a patient is asked what word is being shown, the mouth, controlled usually by the left hemisphere, will say TAX, while the hand controlled by the hemisphere that does not control the mouth (usually the left hand and the right hemisphere) will write ABLE. Or, if the hemisphere that controls a hand (usually the left hand) but not speech is asked to do arithmetic in a way that does not penetrate to the hemisphere that controls speech, and the hands are shielded from the eyes, the mouth will insist that it is not doing arithmetic, has not even thought of arithmetic today, and so on—while the appropriate hand is busily doing arithmetic!

Dissociative Identity Disorder

Another candidate phenomenon for splitting without shattering is dissociative identity disorder (DID). Everything about this phenomenon is controversial, including whether there is any real multiplicity of consciousness at all (Hacking 1995, Humphrey and Dennett 1989). DID can take two forms. The more common form is often described as the dissociated units (persons, personalities, sides of a single personality, or whatever they are) taking turns, usually with pronounced changes in personality. When one is active, the other(s) usually is (are) not. Here the most prominent symptom is usually strange memory gaps (amnesias) in each unit for periods when the body in question was clearly conscious and active but apparently in the control of another unit. These amnesias will play a prominent role in my own account of the condition.

In the other, less common form, two or more units are present at the same time. The unit in control of speech, for example, will report that another "person" inside her is talking to her or giving her orders, these orders being experienced not from the standpoint of giving them but from an external standpoint, as coming from another person. This form of DID is called the coconscious form in the literature. Note that this term names something very different from what, for example, James or Parfit had in mind when they said that (what they call) coconsciousness is central to unified consciousness. Among other things, the unit in control of speech and the "little person inside me talking to me," as she might put it (DID occurs about 80 percent of the time in women), are not experienced as parts of one integrated field of experience and agency. Though the "little person" is experienced as part of unified consciousness, she is experienced as a separate entity in it and a separate center of intentions and actions.

In what follows, we will focus on the serial form of DID in which different units take turns, though near the end we will make one suggestion about the coconscious variety. In the coconscious form, rotating amnesias usually play little or no role; they are central in the serial form. Indeed, the coconscious form resembles thought insertion (Billon and Kriegel, this volume), and even anarchic hands (Mylopoulos, this volume), more closely than it does serial DID.

4 Other Disorders of Unified Consciousness

We have examined abnormalities of unified consciousness in which unified consciousness appears to have either split or shattered. There are also abnormalities of unified consciousness in which neither appears to be happening. For the sake of completeness, we should say a word about them before we move on (see also Gennaro, this volume).

From Somatoparaphrenia to Hemineglect

In one set of conditions, subjects cease to be aware of or deny ownership of a body part, half the body, or even the whole body. The deficit takes many different forms. There is somatoparaphrenia, in which, for example, patients deny that one of their own limbs is part of them, or asomatognosia, which is a lack of awareness of one's body or parts of it. A third condition is anosognosia. In this condition, a person who has suffered a loss of function is unaware of the deficit. Thus, a person now blind will insist that she can see—and will stumble about in a room bumping into things. A person whose limbs are now paralyzed will insist that his limbs are moving—and will become furious when family and caregivers say that they are not. A fourth condition is hemineglect. Here, one loses all feeling, all proprioceptive awareness, of one side of one's body and even all perception of it. Sometimes the condition can extend to losing experience of one half (divided vertically) of everything spatial in one's experience. And so on.

What distinguishes these cases from cases in which unified consciousness appears to have shattered is that unified consciousness is (largely) intact. What distinguishes them from cases in which unified consciousness has split is that, in each of the various conditions, there remains but one instance of it. What seems to have happened in every case is that the range of things that get integrated into unified consciousness has become bizarrely circumscribed. The various conditions encompass a denial that limbs are felt proprioceptively (i.e., are within unified consciousness) or a claim that one can experience only half of one's body or of all objects seen. Or that the range of things within unified consciousness no longer includes how certain bodily parts (eyes, limbs) are, or are not, functioning. Where, in those with "normal" consciousness, there would be perception and proprioception of the whole body and whole objects, these patients perceive and propriocept much less of body and objects.

Since in none of these cases is there even apparent splitting of a single instance of unified consciousness into two or more instances of it within a single body, we will say no more about them.

Finally for this section, a quick look at mirror twins. In brain bisection cases and DID, it appears that one body has two centers of unified consciousness, either at a time or over time. In a condition that is broadly the reverse of brain bisection cases, some theorists believe that, in certain mirror twins, one center of unified consciousness spans two bodies. There are problems with these cases, the most important of which is that no professional studies of them have been reported, but the idea is so interesting that it is worth saying a few words about one such case. Mirror twins are identical twins who insist on mirroring one another to the greatest extent possible. They dress alike, spend hours side-by-side or facing one another, often cannot stand to be separated, finish each other's sentences, and the like.

Our example is the case of Greta and Freda Chaplin. The person/s in these two bodies drew herself/themselves to the attention of authorities in Yorkshire beginning in the 1970s because they had developed a strong erotomania for a postman. Two bodies were involved, and they were mirror twins. On this, all agreed. However, the bodies acted in some respects as though a single instance of unified consciousness spanned them. Each body could finish sentences started by the other. There is some suggestion that, say, the left body could report on scenes that only the right body could see. The two bodies could speak spontaneously constructed sentences in perfect unison. The two did everything they could together, even wanting to have both right hands on a frying pan. When separated by more than a few meters, they complained bitterly, each body reporting that it felt like a part of itself was being ripped out. And so on. As I said, there are no professional studies of the case (it was widely reported in the press at the time, for example, in *Time*, Apr. 6, 1981) but some of the treating health professionals came to the view that what was presented to them was a her, not a them.

5   Brain Bisection Patients in the Lab and the Switch Hypothesis

Most theorists view the archetypical brain bisection behavior, behavior in which there is good evidence (reports, for example) of unified consciousness of representations A, B, C, but not of D, E, F in the same brain (and expressed by the same body), and good evidence (the subject's deliberate, integrated actions, for example) of consciousness of D, E, F, but not of A, B, C, as evidence of two simultaneous, internally integrated streams of consciousness that are not integrated with each other. (Producing such behavior requires careful manipulation of flows of information in a lab. Dissociated behavior appears neither in brain bisection patients outside the lab nor in the acallosal, those born without a corpus callosum. There is now a literature on why there is not more disunity in these cases, but I have to set that issue aside.) In his interesting 2010 book, Tim Bayne assays another option: That consciousness switches back and forth between the two streams.[1]

The advantage to this "switch model," as Bayne calls it (2010, 210), is that it allows him to continue to maintain, against the prima facie evidence, that there is but one stream of unified consciousness in brain bisection cases. This, in turn, removes the danger that brain bisection cases pose for his unity thesis, the thesis that

Necessarily, for any conscious subject of experience (S) and any time (t), the simultaneous conscious states that S has at t will be subsumed by [roughly, will be parts of] a single conscious state. (16)

Since the two streams are both states of a single human subject, the unity thesis holds that they must be subsumed by a single conscious state.

Interesting as it is, the onus is on the switch model. It makes a strong claim, much stronger, for example, than a weaker claim (with which it could be confused) that also preserves the unity thesis by claiming that consciousness is necessarily unified within each stream, but that, sometimes, there are two such streams within one brain. The issue between switchers and dual streamers is this:

Can all the conscious states in both hemispheres at a given time and over time be tied together in one unified stream of consciousness?

Switchers say that there are conscious states in only one hemisphere at a time, so the answer is yes. Dual streamers say that there are simultaneous conscious states in both hemispheres, so that answer is no.

Problems Facing the Switch Hypothesis

As Schechter has pointed out (2011, 7), a single example of two conscious states in one subject (say, one per hemisphere) that are simultaneous and yet not "subsumed by a single conscious state" would be enough to sink the switch hypothesis—as, for that matter, would two conscious states in a single subject at different times that are not thus subsumed. We will return to this issue.

A second, even more pressing issue is whether the switch hypothesis can accommodate brain bisection patients' sense (which is as robust as it is in those with normal states of consciousness) of having a single unified stream of consciousness over time without any breaks. A brain-bisected person continues to believe not just that something persists across time in both everyday life and the apparent duality created in the lab, but that s/he does. If the claim is to fly, it has to be able to account for this strong sense. One would expect that a switch from one hemisphere to the other would produce a break in this sense of continuity.

Autobiographical Memory

To see how we should think about the second issue, we need to link unified consciousness to memory of a certain kind, something not often done in the literature. Let me start by isolating a specific kind of memory. When taxonomizing memories, it is common to view episodic memory as a subclass of declarative memory and autobiographical memory (most of it anyway) as a subclass of episodic. So we get a nesting:

Declarative (episodic [autobiographical])

I want to go further and break autobiographical memories into two groups. In the first group, we remember *experiencing* the recalled experience, *feeling* the feeling, *doing* the action, and so forth. The second group consists of all the rest: autobiographical memories that we have because someone told us something about ourselves and the like. So we have one more nesting. For the former group, it goes like this:

Declarative (episodic [autobiographical (recalled as experienced, had, or done)])

Call these autobiographical memories as experienced (AME). And my proposal is simple: if consciousness can access a rich store of common AMEs whichever hemisphere it is seated in at any given moment—if in either place, it recalls having had much the same earlier experiences, and so forth—then consciousness can switch without any breaks in the single unified stream of consciousness over time. Is this possible?

Notice, first, that if unified consciousness retains access to the same AMEs whichever hemisphere it has switched to, switching will make remarkably little difference. Unified centers of consciousness have no information about where they are located in the brain, so the center in question will not only retain the same sense of who it was, but it will not even have any direct sense that it has switched, though it may be able to infer that it has from the fact that it has (mostly) lost control of one arm and leg and gained control over the others and, if the switch was to the subdominant lobe, has lost a raft of important cognitive facilities, including language and the ability to engage is most linear thinking.

Next, ask this question: Is there a common store of AMEs, the requisite, I suggested, of maintaining a sense of single unified stream of consciousness? For if there is not, then a switch to the other hemisphere will be accompanied by a switch to an alternative set of AMEs, which would utterly transform the center of consciousness's sense of who it was earlier.

Whether there is no split in the pool of AMEs in the special laboratory settings in which two centers of consciousness appear to emerge is not easy to determine. Subjects clearly retain a store of earlier AMEs and create new ones—they are not amnesic in any significant way. However, I could not find any direct evidence touching on the question of whether the subdominant hemisphere (SDH) in particular creates new AMEs while dissociated from the dominant hemisphere or whether consciousness seated in that hemisphere can access existing AMEs.

That said, there is indirect evidence. When the SDH through the left hand is doing tasks that the dominant hemisphere denies (through the mouth) that it is doing—adding up numbers shielded from the eyes, for example, while the mouth denies that it is doing arithmetic—the SDH keeps track of where it is in, for example, the activity of adding, thus where it has been, and doing this would seem to require new, at least short-term, AMEs or something very much like them. Since the dominant hemisphere clearly has no access to these memories (or it would not deny that it is doing arithmetic), it would follow that AMEs to which one hemisphere has no access are being created. And from this it should follow that when unified consciousness switches back to that lobe, its sense of its earlier self will change. Since such breaks do not seem to exist in actual brain bisection patients, all this counts against the switch hypothesis. (It is easy to think of further relevant tests. For example, we could ask the SDH to draw what it had for breakfast, where it was a week ago, how it feels about answering all these silly questions, and the like, and see what the left hand does.)

Then there is the problem that Schechter raised—conscious states existing simultaneously in each hemisphere. This would seem to be both the most obvious and the most serious problem facing the switch hypothesis, yet, strangely, when Bayne considers objections to the switch hypothesis (2010, chapter 9.6, 214–221), it is not among the five objections that he considers. Yet it arises in the very way the disunity in brain bisection patients is usually described. The usual description, which we have already seen, goes as follows. There is evidence of unified consciousness of A, B, C— on the basis of being conscious of A, B, C by having them—but not of D, E, F in a single body and brain, evidenced by avowal of A, B, C, for example, and disavowal of D, E, F, and there is evidence of unified consciousness of

D, E, F—on the basis of being conscious of D, E, F by having them—but not of A, B, C, evidenced by expressing D, E, F on demand, for example, while responding not at all to requests concerning A, B, C. (The information has to reach just one hemisphere without reaching the other in each case; think again of the example of doing and disavowing doing arithmetic.)

The only natural way to make sense of the description just given of the situation of brain bisection patients, or, for that matter, of the dissociation of AMEs discussed two paragraphs ago, is to ascribe simultaneous conscious states to the two hemispheres. There is a problem with doing so because the evidence for consciousness in the SDH is much weaker than the evidence in the dominant hemisphere. This makes it possible to suggest that, when consciousness is seated in the dominant hemisphere, the representational states in the SDH are not conscious states (Bayne 2010, 210). And a case can be made for the suggestion. First, we distinguish between being conscious of the world (and one's own body) and being conscious of one's experiences. (Put in the language of phenomenality, this would be the distinction between the world being like something for me and my experiences being like something for me.) Then we suggest that when consciousness is not seated in the SDH hemisphere, maybe there will be consciousness of the world in the SDH but there is no consciousness of those experiences of the world. To get that, that is, for those experience to become like anything to the SD hemisphere, consciousness must switch to that hemisphere.

I have two comments on this suggestion: (1) it works much better for the SDH than for the dominant hemisphere, and (2) if the cognitive and representational activities of the SDH are sometimes not conscious, or not fully conscious, then one would think that there would be some big change when consciousness switches to that hemisphere. There is no evidence of any such change.

In short, though thinking through the implications of AMEs lent some initial support to the switch hypothesis, following those implications further and adding evidence of how much goes on simultaneously in the two hemispheres ultimately undermines the hypothesis. The natural way of thinking of these cases—one stream of consciousness temporarily becoming two in the laboratory, then remerging into one—remains the way of thinking that best fits the evidence.

6   Dissociative Identity Disorder

Like brain bisection operations, dissociative identity disorder (DID) has also received significant attention from philosophers. An early study, and still one of the best because it was rooted in extensive hands-on experience, was Humphrey and Dennett (1989). Not long after, Hacking wrote a large book on the subject (1995). And the interest continues. For example, Bayne (2010) devotes part of a chapter to the topic (chapter 7.3, 162–71). I have written on Hacking and Bayne elsewhere (Brook 1997, 2014), so here I will focus on Humphrey and Dennett. Their study has both strengths and weaknesses that have not often been appreciated. The main strength is that the two of them spent a year interviewing "multiples" and their therapists and attending both patient and professional conferences and meetings. As was partly true with respect to Bayne on brain bisection cases, the main weaknesses in Humphrey and Dennett's treatment flow from their neglect of autobiographical memory and closely related aspects of unified consciousness.

DID has been greeted with every possible reaction on the credibility scale—from extreme credulity to outright incredulity. Part of what makes it controversial is that it has appeared in only a few regions (Austria/Germany/the Netherlands and the United States/Canada) and in only a few periods in history (late nineteenth century and the past forty or fifty years for the former, mostly the past fifty years for the latter), and it favors women at least four to one.

As we sketched earlier, DID has four main characteristics:

(1) More than one personality, each with unified consciousness and unified focus on self and world, appears, or appears to appear, in a single body. The number of personalities can vary from two to hundreds. At least three is typical.
(2) The personalities appear either *seriatim* or simultaneously. The latter is called coconsciousness; the former is more common.
(3) The multiple personalities lack either (a) memory "from the inside" of one another *(seriatim)* or (b) introspective access to one another (coconsciousness).
(4) The personalities have different identities (in the psychological, not the philosophical, sense of "identity"), dress very differently, and even vary in such things as handwriting. Often the personalities are very one-sided and specialized for a particular role or emotion.

As I also said, here we will focus mainly on *seriatim* DID, with a suggestion about the coconscious variety near the end. The first question that arises with respect to DID is whether it is real. That is the question that Humphrey and Dennett address. In a moment, we will see what the question meant to them, but what it means to me is this: in cases of DID (or at least many cases diagnosed as DID), is the structure of unified consciousness different in relevant, significant respects from what it is in people who do not have DID, or is DID just a form of self-interpretation, a story self-constructed, probably, for self-protective reasons but reflecting no differences from non-DID people deeper than that? And our conclusion will be that, in the same way that unified consciousness really splits into two "streams" in brain bisection patients under certain laboratory conditions, unified consciousness really is different in (at least many) DID patients from what it is in people who do not have DID. There are facts of the matter, not just differing narratives.

What do Humphrey and Dennett think? They draw five conclusions about DID (1989, 94). The relevant two are these:

1. While the unitary solution to the problem of human selfhood is for most people socially and psychologically desirable, it may not always be attainable. ...

5. The end result [in DID] would appear to be in many cases a person who is genuinely split. That is, the grounds for assigning several selves to such a human being can be as good as—indeed the same as—those for assigning a single self to a normal human being. (Humphrey and Dennett 1989, 94)

These conclusions might appear to have a realist cast—until we ask what they take the grounds "for assigning a single self to a normal human being" to be. How real are normal single selves for them? Here it is helpful to look back on what it would it mean for them for DID to be "real."

We suggest that, if the model we have outlined is anything like right, it would mean at least the following:

1. The subject will have, at different times, different "spokesmen," corresponding to separate Heads of Mind. Both objectively and subjectively, this will be tantamount to having different "selves" because *the access each such spokesman will have to the memories, attitudes and thoughts of other spokesmen will be, in general, as indirect and intermittent as the access one human being can have to the mind of another.* (Humphrey and Dennett 1989, 81, my italics)

The part that I have italicized sounds pretty good to anyone with realist inclinations. However, they immediately go on to say:

2. Each self, when present, will claim to have conscious control over the subject's behavior. That is, this self will consider the subject's current actions to be her actions, experiences to be her experiences, memories to be her memories, and so on. (At times the self out front may be conscious of the existence of other selves—she may even hear them talking in the background—but she will not be conscious *with* them). (Humphrey and Dennett 1989, 81)

By contrast with (1), this sounds like pure interpretationism. The background is Dennett's view that a self, a unit of unified consciousness, is merely a story that a person has constructed about him- or herself, what Dennett once (1992) called a center of narrative gravity. And, of course, the multiple selves in cases of DID will be as real as *that!*

In my view, Dennett's account works quite well as an account of the *content* of the self, as a story about how one views oneself, what kind of person one takes oneself to be. However, concerning the *structure* of the self, what a self is, there is more than interpretation. There are some facts of the matter, facts about how selves are built—facts that Humphrey and Dennett overlook.

Recall AMEs, autobiographical memories of earlier experiences and other earlier events recalled from the same point of view as that from which the events were originally experienced ("from the inside" in S. Shoemaker's useful metaphor [1968 and later works]). Thus, one remembers not just an experience, a thought, or whatever; one remembers having the experience, thinking the thought, or whatever. One remembers not just an action; one remembers doing the action. One remembers not just a feeling; one remembers having the feeling, And so on.

If I remember having had an experience and the like, it will appear to me that I had that experience, and so forth. I will appear to myself to be that person. (And this appearance will generally be correct. When I remember the experiences of some person from the standpoint of having had the experiences and absent a countervailing factor, such as, for example, memory leading back to one person, everything else leading back to another, or—maybe—radical transformation of character, if I have autobiographical memory "from the inside" of having, doing, feeling an earlier person's thoughts, experiences, actions and feelings, that is near-conclusive reason to take myself to be that person.) In short, AMEs are central to our experience of ourselves as beings persisting over time.

That said, there is a certain artificiality in what we have said about memory up to now. Contrary to what has been said so far, we seldom remember having or doing or feeling individual experiences or actions. Usually, what we remember about ourselves is far "bigger" than that. Memories "from the inside" are usually a kind of global representation:

Global representation: Representing many objects as a single complex object.

What characterizes a global representation is that the representation of the elements of its object is united: One is aware of all the elements together, in a single conscious act, and one is aware of them not just as individual items but as a group.

To see how this works, consider representation of items that could be expressed by these sentences:

(1) I am reading the words on the screen in front of me.
(2) I am puzzled by your comments.
(3) I am enjoying the music I hear outside.
(4) I believe our agreement was to meet at 6:00.
(5) I thought I understood Kant's notion of the object.
(6) I wish the world were a fairer place.

Here there are three different elements that could be united in a single global representation, (a) what I am representing, (b) the acts (act when unified) of representing them, and (c) myself as the subject doing the representing, as follows:

c.	b.	a.
1. I	am reading	the words on the screen in front of me
2. I	am puzzled	by your comments
3. I	am enjoying	the music I hear outside
4. I	believe	our agreement was to meet at 6:00
5. I	thought	I understood Kant's notion of the object
6. I	wish	the world were a fairer place

Similarly for memory—when I remember, for example, doing something, I usually remember not just what I did but also how I felt at the time, what I experienced at the time, the outcome of the action and how I felt about that, and so on (all probably with some measure of inaccuracy). If memories are about many things at once, not just one, memories are *global representations* that represent a *unified group* of earlier experiences and actions.

Now we can see what is missing from the Humphrey and Dennett account of *seriatim* DID. When the rotating amnesias so characteristic of the disorder are present, there are earlier global memories that the unit of unified consciousness currently in charge of the body *cannot* access "from the inside." And this is a fact about them, not just a self-interpretation—a fact of the matter.

Indeed, something similar can be said about the so-called coconscious variety of DID. When alternative personalities appear to the unit of unified consciousness in charge, even though the alter(s) appear(s) to be part of oneself, one will experience what the alter(s) say(s) and do (does) from the standpoint of observing the sayings and doings (even though one recognizes them to be a part of oneself), not from the standpoint of doing them. Thus, these sayings and doings will not be part of the current global representation of what the unit in charge is currently experiencing, saying, and doing.

7   Conclusion

Our conclusions, then, are that in brain bisection patients, unified consciousness really splits into two "streams" under appropriate laboratory conditions, and that unified consciousness really is different over time in *seriatim* DID patients and may well be different at a time in coconscious DID patients from what it is in the relevantly similar situations in people who do not have DID. These are hard facts, as hard as any facts about human cognition and consciousness, not just matters of self-interpretation.

Note

1. There are actually two different versions of the switch hypothesis. One holds that the seat of consciousness is in some brain area common to both hemispheres, and what switches is the focus, the content of conscious experience. The other holds that the seat of consciousness itself, consciousness, not just what one is conscious of, hops from one hemisphere to the other. Bayne does not distinguish them but seems to have had the latter, stronger version in mind.

References

Bayne, T. 2008. The unity of consciousness and the split brain syndrome. *Journal of Philosophy* 105:277–300.

Bayne, T. 2010. *The Unity of Consciousness*. Oxford: Oxford University Press.

Bogen, J. 1993. The callosal syndromes. In *Clinical Neuropsychology*, ed. K. Heilman and E. Valenstein. Oxford: Oxford University Press.

Brook, A. 1997. Review of Ian Hacking, *Rewriting the Soul* (Princeton, 1995). *Canadian Philosophical Reviews* 16:402–406.

Brook, A. 2014. Review of Tim Bayne, *Unity of Consciousness* (Oxford, 2010). *Australasian Journal of Philosophy* 90 (3): 599–602.

Brook, A., and P. Raymont. 2001/2010. Unity of consciousness. *Stanford Encyclopedia of Philosophy* (plato.stanford.edu), on which parts of this chapter draw.

Dawson, M. 1998. *Understanding Cognitive Science*. Oxford: Blackwell.

Dennett, D. 1992. The self as center of narrative gravity. In *Self and Consciousness: Multiple Perspectives*, ed. F. Kessel, P. Cole, and D. Johnson. Hillsdale, NJ: Erlbaum.

Gazzaniga, M. 2000. Cerebral specialization and interhemispheric communication: Does the corpus callosum enable the human condition? *Brain* 123:1293–1336.

Hacking, I. 1995. *Rewriting the Soul: Multiple Personality and the Sciences of Memory*. Princeton, NJ: Princeton University Press.

Hardcastle, V. 1997. Attention versus consciousness: A distinction with a difference. *Cognitive Studies: Bulletin of the Japanese Cognitive Science Society* 4:56–66. Reprinted in *Neural Basis of Consciousness*, ed. N. Osaka (Amsterdam: John Benjamins, 2003).

Hirsch, E. 1991. Divided minds. *Philosophical Review* 100:3–30.

Humphrey, N., and D. Dennett. 1989. Speaking for our selves: An assessment of multiple personality disorder. *Raritan* 9:68–98.

Hurley, S. 1998. *Consciousness in Action*. Cambridge, MA: Harvard University Press.

Lockwood, M. 1989. *Mind, Brain, and the Quantum*. Oxford: Blackwell.

Marks, C. 1981. *Commissurotomy, Consciousness, and Unity of Mind*. Cambridge, MA: MIT Press.

Nagel, T. 1971. Brain bisection and the unity of consciousness. *Synthese* 22: 396–413.

Parfit, D. 1984. *Reasons and Persons*. Oxford: Oxford University Press.

Puccetti, R. 1973. Brain bisection and personal identity. *British Journal for the Philosophy of Science* 24:339–355.

Puccetti, R. 1981. The case for mental duality: Evidence from split-brain data and other considerations. *Behavioral and Brain Sciences* 4:93–123.

Schechter, E. 2010. Individuating mental tokens: The split-brain case. *Philosophia* 38:195–216.

Schechter, E. 2011. Comments on Tim Bayne's *Unity of Consciousness*. American Philosophical Association, December 2011.

Shoemaker, S. 1968. Self-reference and self-awareness. *Journal of Philosophy* 65: 555–567.

Sperry, R. 1984. Consciousness, personal identity, and the divided brain. *Neuropsychologia* 22:661–673.

Trevarthen, C. 1984. Biodynamic structures: Cognitive correlates of motive sets and the development of motives in infants. In *Cognition and Motor Processes*, ed. W. Prinz and A. F. Sanders. Berlin: Springer.

9 Altogether Now—Not! Integration Theories of Consciousness and Pathologies of Disunity

Robert Van Gulick

In the *Meditations on First Philosophy* (1642), René Descartes famously wrote of mental unity,

For in truth, when I consider the mind, that is, when I consider myself in so far only as I am a thinking thing, I can distinguish in myself no parts, but I very clearly discern that I am somewhat absolutely one and entire; and although the whole mind seems to be united to the whole body, yet, when a foot, an arm, or any other part is cut off, I am conscious that nothing has been taken from my mind; nor can the faculties of willing, perceiving, conceiving, etc., properly be called its parts, for it is the same mind that is exercised [all entire] in willing, in perceiving, and in conceiving, etc. (Descartes [1642] 1935, Meditation VI, section 19)

However, contemporary psychology and neuroscience recognize a great diversity of modules and mechanisms within the mind and many dimensions in which minds are organized and structured, some of which involve conscious mentality and others of which concern unconscious aspects of mind. Various types of unity or integration can apply or not apply both within and between those modules and along those multiple conscious and nonconscious dimensions. As with other aspects of mind, valuable evidence about those various unities can be gained by considering pathological cases in which normal forms of unity are absent or altered and significantly diminished. However, before considering any clinical cases, it will be useful to get a general overview of the various types of unity and how they figure in current integrative theories of consciousness. Given that context, we can then consider several pathologies of disunity and their implications.

Notions of unity play a central role in many theories and models of consciousness. Some treat unity of one type or another as either a necessary or sufficient condition for consciousness. And even those that regard it as neither may nonetheless count it as an important property or dimension that we need to include in our theory to fully understand the nature and function of consciousness. In some cases the relevant sort of unity is a type of conscious unity, but in other cases it may concern types of nonconscious unity that underlie consciousness at the functional or neural level. Understanding the relation between consciousness and unity is thus not a single question but a large family of interrelated questions, and getting a clear overview of the relevant distinctions is essential at the outset. Only after the various questions have been clearly distinguished can one turn to their likely answers and to the evidence to be gained from pathological cases.

In distinguishing among the many respects in which consciousness or conscious mental states can be unified, perhaps the largest division is that between forms of *synchronic* unity and those of *diachronic* unity. That temporal division crosscuts all the other categories; each of the many types of conscious unity exist in both a synchronic and diachronic form. Pathologies of conscious unity can affect a patient in one temporal form but not another. Amnesic patients with severe anterograde amnesia, like the famous HM, may lack diachronic unity of personal memory, though they possess such unity for short temporal intervals. Cases of the converse sort are less common, but they are possible. Simultagnosia might be one such case. Patients suffering from simultagnosia can consciously perceive only one object at a time and cannot visually perceive multiple objects as unified in a scene (Kinsbourne and Warrington 1962). Thus, simultagnosia presents a case in which there is no conscious synchronic scene-unity, but the patient might build up a unified scene representation of some sort diachronically through memory from a succession of isolated object representations. He can consciously perceive only one item on the table at a time—the fork, the spoon, the knife, the plate—but using memory he builds a representation of the unified scene—of the place setting and the larger table. That resulting state might not be a unified *visual experience* of the scene nor in the format of visual experience, but it would nonetheless still be a conscious representation and awareness of the unified scene, one constructed diachronically.

Unities of both temporal sorts can occur in diverse forms and along multiple mental dimensions. Many of them might count as forms of *representational unity.* Such unities may apply either to the integration (unity) of the *contents* of those states, that is, to *what they represent,* or to the *vehicles* or *structures* that *do the representing* by carrying or encoding the relevant contents. Representational unity admits of many degrees, and information or content can be partially or fully integrated along multiple dimensions, that is, integrated with respect to some functions such as motor control while being less integrated in other respects such as explicit inference. The integration of disparate information is a key feature of many models of consciousness, but none of those theories assume that conscious information is always (or ever) *fully integrated* to the *highest degree* in *all respects*. Even attentive conscious contents are less than fully integrated in some respects. In our most attentive moments, we still fail to grasp some of the joint implications of the contents of which we are conscious. Nonetheless, conscious contents do in general involve a high degree of integration along multiple dimensions, and evidence from pathological cases in which such integration fails to occur may provide important insights into the nature and basis of consciousness.

A great many forms of mental unity might be considered subtypes of representational unity. In particular, object-unity, scene-unity and world-unity can be viewed as progressively more encompassing forms of representational unity—as the representation of individual features integrated into the representation of a unified object, the representation of such objects integrated into the representation of overall scene, and the representation of many such locations and objects integrated into the representation of a larger environment or world, including many local scenes. Again, pathologies can occur at any of these stages, and the effect of such deficits on consciousness can be an important source of evidence. In addition to that continuum of unity along increasing spatial scope, there is also a progression along the dimension of *integrating information from multiple sources*, including *multisensory* integrations of many types: visual-auditory, visual-tactile, visual-proprioceptive, and others. Such multisensory integration can be compromised both in cases of pathology and in normal subjects under restricted conditions of exposure studied in the laboratory. The multisource integration of information can also include information from *nonsensory* sources such as memory and belief, all of which can again be compromised in some cases of pathology.

Other forms of conscious unity are less clearly representational, especially those associated with the *unity of the self*, whether as a subject of *experience* or of *action*. Traditionally, the experiences associated with a given person or organism are regarded as all being *experienced* by a single, unified subject or self. The conscious subject that visually perceives is the same subject that consciously hears, feels, thinks, and desires. There is one single, unified self who has all these experiences, one subject by whom they are all experienced, or so, at least, it has been traditionally held. Moreover, as Bayne (2010) has argued, not only is the subject unified but the *totality of experiences* had by a conscious subject at a time are also *phenomenally unified* in a "what-it-is-like" sense that goes beyond representational unity. According to Bayne's unity thesis, all the experiences had by actual human conscious subjects at a time are phenomenally unified in that sense. As we will see, Bayne argues that various special or pathological cases that might seem to challenge the unity thesis can be explained in a way that is consistent with the thesis.

The same applies in the *practical* domain to the self as conscious agent or subject of action. We typically experience all our many actions as being those of a single, ongoing agent or self—a single self that not only acts but also desires, chooses, intends, and controls the many things we do in the *world*, in our *bodies*, and in our *minds* at every conscious moment. Again, the relevant unities are of many types. As in the experiential domain, some practical unities involve a representational dimension—for example, the unified representation of our multiple, simultaneous, active intentions— but others appear to involve a dimension of causal unity that goes beyond the mere unity of contents or representations. Our sense of conscious agency is typically that of unified self as single effective *agent* and *cause*. The unified self appears as a single, complex, causal structure, the common ground and source of all our actions. Like other conscious unities, practical conscious unities can be compromised or absent in nonstandard cases: both cases of normal subjects under special laboratory conditions, and, more often, cases of psychopathology, including dissociative identity disorder, schizophrenia, and dementia. Considering how and why unity is disrupted in such cases may provide important insights into the nature and basis of the unity of consciousness.

Before turning to consider some specific pathological cases in which unity is compromised, it will be useful to review some of the current theories or models of consciousness in which unity plays a major role. All of them are controversial, and they remain at present working hypotheses, but they can provide a theoretical context for better understanding the possible implications of cases in which conscious unity is pathologically absent or diminished.

Perhaps the best known of such theories is the global neuronal workspace model initially proposed by Bernard Baars (1988, 1997) and developed in greater detail by a number of researchers, especially by Stanislas Dehaene and this collaborators in Paris (Dehaene and Nacacche 2001, Dehaene 2014). According to the global workspace (GWS) model, information or other mental contents become conscious when they enter a functionally defined "workspace" that makes them globally available to diverse systems and modules throughout the brain or mind. Conscious contents are thus widely available and highly integrated; all the contents present in the global workspace at a time are simultaneously available to many "consumers" throughout the mind, as well as being highly integrated with each other. The model thus critically involves at least two important forms of unity: (1) a type of access unity—all the relevant contents are available to the same multiplicity of modules—and (2) a type of representational unity—all the relevant contents are themselves integrated with each other. Particular hypotheses have also been proposed as to the neural mechanisms that may underlie the global workspace (Dehaene 2014), but it is the role of the functionally defined workspace that makes unity and integration key features of conscious on the global workspace model.

Unity plays an even more central role in the Integrated Information Theory (IIT) of the neuroscientist Giulio Tononi (2008, 2012). According to Tononi's IIT, consciousness is defined in terms of a measure that he terms "Φ" that combines the quantity of information in a system with the degree of connection or interdependence between the system's informational elements. What makes a system S conscious is that S has a high Φ value because S contains a high level of information that is highly integrated, and the Φ value of S is maximal in that S does not contain any proper subsystem S' with a higher Φ value, nor is S itself a proper part of some S* with a higher Φ value. Given the way in which Φ is defined in terms of information theory, the integration involved in IIT can be regarded as a form of representational unity or integration. All the many informational elements of a system with a high Φ value are unified or integrated in terms of their contents. Tononi's IIT is nonetheless intended as a theory of consciousness in the fullest sense, not just of cognitive consciousness but also of phenomenal consciousness in the experiential "what-it-is-like" sense. To be a system with a high Φ value, according to Tononi and IIT, is to have a subjective point in the conscious experiential sense.

Unity plays a less central but still important role in a detailed neurofunctional theory of consciousness recently proposed by the philosopher Jesse Prinz (2005, 2012). Prinz terms his theory the attended intermediate representation theory of consciousness or AIR theory. According to Prinz's AIR theory, the only perceptual and bodily contents that become conscious are those that are intermediate, both in the processing pathway and in the level of specificity of what is represented. For example, in conscious visual experience we are aware only of the macro spatial features of objects viewed from a particular perspective—their size, shape, color, and orientation from a given viewing angle. We are not conscious of more proximal or micro features of the visual stimulus nor of categorical properties of the object, such as its objective canonical shape specified in a viewer-independent way. It is that limitation that accounts for the IR, intermediate representation aspect, of AIR theory. However, not all intermediate-level representations are conscious. In order to become conscious according to AIR theory, those representations must be attended and thus available to working memory, though not necessarily in working memory. The attentional process has both a neural and functional aspect in AIR theory. The neural aspect involves the amplification and synchronized oscillation of the neural structures underlying the relevant representations. The functional aspect is a matter of the availability of those contents to working memory and thus to many other systems and modules within the mind and brain. It is this aspect that involves unity and integration. All the contents that are conscious are jointly available to working memory and unified in terms of simultaneous access. The relevant unity on the AIR model is thus a form of representational unity, one that involves the joint access and integration of the contents associated with the relevant, conscious, intermediate-level representations.

The philosopher Tim Bayne has argued for a type of conscious unity that he calls "phenomenal unity" (Bayne 2010). According to Bayne, phenomenal unity is both a universal feature of human consciousness and something more than representational unity. Bayne argues for what he calls "the unity thesis": all the experiences had by a conscious human at a given moment are phenomenally unified. According to Bayne, synchronic phenomenal unity is a universal feature of conscious human minds. All the conscious experiences that any of us have at a given moment are all phenomenally unified with each other.

Moreover, Bayne argues that the relevant sort of phenomenal unity is something more than mere representational unity. Although Bayne agrees that conscious experiences can be unified in various representational ways, he claims there is a further type of unity that is distinctly phenomenal and not merely representational (*pace* Tye 2003 and Van Gulick 2014a). As Bayne sees it, when two experiences are simultaneously conscious in our mind, their coconsciousness itself has a phenomenal aspect. There is something that-it-is-like to have experiences *E1 and E2 together* at time *t* that is more than the mere conjunction of the what-it-is-like to have E1 at *t* and the what-it-is-like to have E2 at *t*. It is that further phenomenal aspect of being coconscious that the notion of phenomenal unity aims to capture. Bayne argues that this sort of phenomenal unity can hold between pairs of simultaneous experiences E1 and E2 even when E1 and E2 are not representationally unified and the contents of E1 and E2 are not well integrated. Two experiences can be phenomenally coconscious for us even when we fail to make all sorts of appropriate representational connections between them or their contents.

Pathological cases, especially those involving dissociations and selective deficits of unity, may be of special interest in deciding whether Bayne is right in regarding phenomenal unity as a universal feature of consciousness distinct from representational unity. Such cases can provide evidence relevant to the unity thesis as well as to Bayne's claim about the distinct nonrepresentational nature of phenomenal unity.

As a final theoretical context, let me offer a view that I have argued for elsewhere. It combines the higher-order global state (HOGS) model of consciousness (Van Gulick 2004, 2006) with a virtual self realism (VSR) view of the self (Van Gulick 2014a, 2014b). On the HOGS model, what makes a mental state conscious is that it has been recruited into the integrated global state (GS) that constitutes and underlies one's momentary consciousness. For example, a nonconscious visual perception (VP) becomes a conscious visual perception just if VP gets recruited into one's integrated GS. The primary representation of the visual information will continue to involve activity in the same local regions of the visual cortex, but in the conscious case that activity and its content gets integrated into the larger overall structure and activity of the GS, with likely amplification and feedback onto the local activity. In this regard, the GS part of the HOGS model is similar to the global workspace theory and, perhaps, to AIR theory. The highly integrated nature of the global states provides a form of unity, both of content and of dynamics.

However, the HOGS model differs from other GS models in its claim that the relevant global state also involves a heightened degree of higher-order or reflexive content, the HO aspect of the HOGS models. When information, such as that in VP, gets incorporated into the global state GS, the content is transformed in a way that makes that visual content part of the experience of a conscious self. It is not just that a blue mug is off to the right, but that a blue mug off to the right is present as part of my experienced world. That latter aspect, its presence as an object *in my experienced world*, is also part of the transformed intentionality of VP once it has been recruited into my GS. Unlike the higher-order aspect of more standard HO theories (Rosenthal 1997, Lycan 1996) the HO aspect of the HOGS model is not embodied in a separate higher-order state distinct from the lower-order mental state that it makes conscious. Rather, the higher-order aspect is embodied in the transformed intentionality of the conscious state itself, for example, VP after it has been recruited into the GS. Moreover, as argued elsewhere (Van Gulick 2006), the relevant conscious intentionality involves two additional interdependent forms of conscious unity: the unity of the *experienced world* and the unity of the conscious *subject or self that experiences* that unified world.

Questions thus arise about the nature of the self that is unified in experience, leading to the second part of the overall view, which might be termed, somewhat paradoxically, virtual self realism (VSR) (Van Gulick 2014a, 2014b). On VSR, the self is not a distinct entity, nor is it a special subsystem of the mind or brain. Rather, VSR builds on Daniel Dennett's notion of the virtual self (VS) as the so-called "center of narrative gravity" (Dennett 1992), also recently supported by Tim Bayne (2010). However, it treats that virtual self in a more realistic way in relation to the GS of the HOGS model. Like other virtual-self views, VSR treats the VS as a structure defined by the combined contents of experience. The contents of those many experiences together define the point of view of a unified subject that has those experiences. It is the experiences that define the unified subject rather an independently existing subject that unifies the experiences. However, unlike other, less realist versions of VS theory, such as those found in Dennett and Bayne, VSR regards the resulting self as more than a mere intentional entity. The self of VSR is a real causal entity or structure. When a set of experiences cohere in such a way that they define a virtual self, as they do in the GS of the HOGS model, they together constitute a self. The self is identified with the total ensemble of experiences, but only because they are bound together in a way that defines the point of view of that self (Van Gulick 2014b). Given these five theories as background context— GWS, IIT, AIR, Bayne's unity thesis, and the combination of HOGS and VSR—we can now turn to consider some specific pathologies of conscious unity and what implications they may have. I will focus primarily on three phenomena—unilateral neglect and extinction, dissociative identity disorder, and split brains.

In cases of visual neglect, patients fail to describe or respond in any directed, intentional way to objects that appear in some partial region of their visual field, most typically to those on one side or half of their visual field, as in so-called hemineglect (Milner et al. 2002). If asked to describe what they see, such patients will refer to nothing in the neglected region of their visual field, nor will they engage in any directed behavior toward those objects. In a paradigm example, such patients will fail to eat any of the food on one half of their plates, even while complaining that they are hungry and did not get enough food. The patients' lack of verbal or intentional response to the neglected region of the visual field occurs despite the fact that they appear to process the entire visual field up to a relatively high level of analysis.

Visually based information about the entire scene is processed by the brain, but the patients do not make use of that information in any directed, intentional way. Evidence of several types supports the view that high-level visual information about the neglected regions is being processed (Driver and Mattingley 1998). Patients may show indirect behavioral responses to items or features in the neglected regions. In a much-cited case, a neglect patient was shown line drawings of two houses that were the same except one had large flames coming from the left side of the house. When asked to describe each house, the patient described only features on the right side of each house and did not mention the flames on the one house that had them to its left. The houses were the same on their right sides, and the patient described them as the same overall. Yet when asked which house she preferred, the patient consistently chose the one without the flames (Marshall and Halligan 1988). Though the flames appeared only in the neglected region of the house, and the patient did not describe them or respond to them in any directed, intentional manner, her visual system seemed to be clearly processing them to a degree capable of covertly influencing her choice, perhaps via a subcortical affective pathway.

Hemineglect thus differs from hemianopia, in which half of the visual field is not visually processed because of damage to processing areas. In hemianopia, the information about half of the visual scene is simply not computed or represented in the cortex. By contrast, in hemineglect that information is represented, but it is not available for report or for the guidance of intentional action. One might describe the information as being present but not conscious. However, as we will see next, the conscious/unconscious border is not so clear in these cases.

A special subset of neglect cases involves what is called *extinction*. In these cases, the patient's neglect is contingent on the presence or absence of competing stimuli in the nonneglected field (Rafal and Vuillemumier 2000). If stimuli are presented only to the impaired field, the patient observes them and responds to them verbally and nonverbally. But if competing stimuli are presented at the same time to the nonimpaired field, the patient fails to respond to objects in the impaired field. The perception of competing stimuli from the dominant field thus appears to extinguish the conscious perception of objects in the neglected field.

What should we say about consciousness in such cases of neglect and extinction? Are they cases in which consciousness in absent? Does the patient lack conscious experience of the neglected objects? The behavioral evidence would seem to show that they have no conscious experience of them. Information about objects in the neglected field may be processed and represented in the relevant cortical areas and may even have some indirect, perhaps emotional, effects, but it appears to remain unconscious. The absence of verbal report and intentional action seems to show the patient is not aware of the neglected field. Thus, it may seem plausible to conclude that she lacks conscious experience of it.

However, if, following Ned Block, one distinguishes *access consciousness* from *phenomenal consciousness* (Block 1995, 2007), then the implications for neglect cases are more ambiguous. Clearly, neglect patients are not access-conscious of the objects in their neglected field. Access consciousness is defined in terms of having access to those contents for report, inference, and direction of intentional action, and those are the very things neglect patients lack. However, if one follows Block in taking phenomenal consciousness in the what-it-is-like sense to be distinct from access consciousness, then it remains an open question whether neglect patients are phenomenally conscious of their neglected field. Even if they lack access, they may still have phenomenal experiences of the objects in their neglected field. Is there something in the phenomenal what-it-is-like sense for the neglect patient with respect to the neglected field? Or is it a phenomenal void—a total conscious absence, as lacking in phenomenal consciousness as in access?

A further question arises. If neglect patients do have phenomenal consciousness of objects in their impaired field, to what conscious self are they present? It would seem that a phenomenal experience can occur only if it is an experience *for* some subject or self. There must be some such self or subject *to whom it is present*. If there is a what-it-is-likeness associated with the neglected field, *for whom* is it like something? Phenomenal consciousness of the neglected field thus seems to imply the existence of a phenomenal self distinct from the conscious self associated with the patient's reports and intentional actions. If so, it would involve a major disunity of consciousness; indeed, it would seem to involve the existence of two distinct and disunified conscious selves within the patient. Avoiding that consequence might be a reason to deny the existence of phenomenal consciousness in neglect cases, but that surely does not suffice to settle the matter.

How do the five theoretical models discussed earlier apply to neglect cases, and what implications do they have for conscious unity in such cases? Each of the five analyzes consciousness partly in terms of unity or integration, and, thus unsurprisingly, they imply that neglect involves a lack of unity, though not necessarily a disunity, within consciousness.

For each of the first three models (GWS, IIT, and AIR), the analysis implies a lack of conscious perception resulting from a lack of integration and functional unity. On the GWS model, contents become conscious only when they enter the global workspace and are widely available for consuming systems throughout the mind/brain. Given the neglect patient's lack of response to visual information from the impaired field, the natural GWS explanation would be that it has not been integrated into the global workspace and thus remains unconscious. From the perspective of IIT, the most plausible hypothesis is that information from the neglected field is not integrated into the subsystem of the patient's mind/brain with the highest Φ value, and thus is not conscious in any sense. On AIR theory, the neglected information fails to be conscious because it is not attended—the A of AIR is absent. According to the neurophysiological aspect of AIR theory, that would mean that the neural substrates of the neglected intermediate representations have not been incorporated in a pattern of resonant and mutually amplifying synchronized oscillations in the gamma band (Prinz 2012, 253). With respect to extinction, each of the three theories would argue that the existence of the competing activity drives the neglected contents from the relevant integrated structure that underlies consciousness. Such contents lose out in competition for access to the global workspace; they are driven from the subsystem with the highest Φ value, or they fail to attract sufficient attention in the face of stronger competitors. For Bayne, neglect patients pose a potential counterexample to his unity thesis. If such patients had conscious experience of their neglected field, they might count as cases in which not all the conscious experiences within a given human at a time were phenomenally unified. If there were some phenomenal what-is-like-ness associated with the patient's neglected field, it would seem not to be phenomenally unified with the rest of the patient's conscious experience. Thus unsurprisingly, Bayne (2010) argues that neglect patients do not have conscious experience of their neglected fields and that any residual nonintentional responses that they show to such stimuli—as in the burning house case—can be fully explained by appeal to nonconscious processes.

Finally, the HOGS model analyzes neglect cases in a way that is similar to the first three theories, though it may have additional resources to answer Block's challenge, and the implications of VSR may differ in some important respects. According to HOGS, if the information from the neglected field is not incorporated into the global state GS, it remains unconscious. In that respect HOGS is similar to GWS and IIT and, perhaps, also to AIR. However, the question remains whether the evidence in neglect cases shows only the absence of access consciousness, leaving the presence of phenomenal consciousness a real possibility. The HOGS model, when combined with VSR, has a bit more to say in reply. The GS of the HOGS model involves more than the mere integration of information. It specifically involves an enhanced higher-order aspect that incorporates that information into the unified perspective of a self-aware subject, one of the sort described by VSR. When the patient's neglected contents are not integrated into the GS, they are thus excluded from the ensemble of experiences that constitute the real VS. If the existence of phenomenal experience requires a self or subject to whom those experiences are present, and the VS of VSR provides the only such self that exists, then exclusion from the GS and the associated VS entails that there are no phenomenal experiences of the neglected field, since there is no relevant self for whom or to whom those experiences could be present. Thus, the combination of HOGS and VSR may have more resources to reply to Block's challenge in neglect cases than do the other three integration-based theories.

A second and dramatic form of conscious disunity involves the well-known and somewhat controversial phenomenon of dissociative identity disorder (DID), formerly termed multiple personality disorder. In such cases, a single individual, that is, a single human being, appears to embody a number of distinct persons, or alters, who typically manifest themselves one at a time, though temporally overlapping personalities can also occur in some cases. The alters are distinct in that they typically have quite different characters, including disparate sets of motives, desires, and intentions as well divergent sets of perceptions, beliefs, and memories (Putnam 1989). Moreover, each set of mental states and personal characteristics coheres as a unit or self in much the way that those of a normal single individual do. We all have a diversity of sometimes conflicting psychological states, but we nonetheless experience them as states of a single, continuing individual or self. However, in DID the conflicting features appear to cohere into separate self-like organizational structures that alternate in controlling the patient's speech and behavior, and these may seem to constitute distinct persons.

There is great disagreement about the nature of DID (Hacking 1995, 2006), and even its reality has been disputed, including by some who regard it as largely a therapeutic artifact (Piper and Merskey 2004). However, let us assume that some DID cases involve a genuine multiplicity of at least self-like structures or organizations within a given individual. Initially, we need make no ontological commitment about how to count the number of selves or persons involved in such cases. Leaving ontology to one side, the psychological facts in themselves raise interesting questions about conscious unity, with implications for the five theories we have been considering.

The primary disunity in DID is diachronic. As the patient's various alters come and go, the links of memory and character that normally bind our consciousness into that of a single, temporally extended subject appear to vanish. Sometimes one alter will have memories of the experiences of another, but often such memory links are completely absent. One alter may have no memory access to the past experiences of another. DID can also involve synchronic disunity in which more than one personality or alter appears to be active in a given individual at the same time. One alter may comment on the thoughts or actions of another, or they may struggle for control, which requires them both to be present and active at the same time.

What implications does DID have for the unity of consciousness and for the five integration-based theories we have been considering? In large part, that depends on the actual nature and reality of DID. Are apparent cases of DID really examples of multiple conscious selves embodied simultaneously in a single brain, or might some more modest description suffice to explain the behavioral evidence? The most direct challenge posed by DID is to Bayne's unity thesis. The simultaneous version of DID, in which two or more alters are active at the same time, would refute the unity thesis if those alters were conscious subjects with distinct streams of consciousness. The experiences in those two streams would not be phenomenally unified, contrary to Bayne's thesis. Thus, unsurprisingly, he rejects that interpretation of DID in favor of a less radical view. According to Bayne (2010), the switching between alters involves merely a change in self schemas, organized conceptual structures that we use to represent ourselves. To some degree, we all switch self schemas in our normal, everyday lives. It is just that the differences between the schemas in DID are so much greater, and the patients as a result suffer from the delusion that they are more than one person when, in fact, they are not. Bayne writes, "It is more plausible to suppose that agentive disunity seen in multiplicity is best accounted for in terms of a single stream of consciousness that is successively informed by a variety of psychological schemas, rather than by appeal to parallel streams of experience. The switching between schemas may produce the appearance of phenomenal disunity, but I suggest that this appearance masks an underlying phenomenal unity" (Bayne 2010, 172).

However, the distinction between alternating selves and mere alternating self schemas may not be as clear-cut as Bayne assumes, at least not if one is sympathetic to virtual self (VS) views of the self as I am and as is Bayne himself in the final chapter of his book (Bayne 2010, 289–293). On VS views, the existence of the self depends on of the unified set of experiences that cohere from a single, subjective point of view. The self does not have an existence independent of that coherent set of experiences and the point-of-view they implicitly define. Thus, if the experiences of the DID patients switch between alternative coherent ensembles of experience, each defining a distinct subjective point of view, then that, in itself, may constitute an alternation of selves in the most realist sense actually available. Whether two such ensembles with differing points of view can exist simultaneously within a single human is less clear. It is an empirical matter whether human brains permit such a possibility, but it would not seem to be ruled out by any general theoretical considerations on the VS view of selves.

Moreover, such multiplicity seems compatible with at least some of the other integration-based theories of consciousness we have considered. From the perspective of IIT, whether multiple centers of consciousness could exist within a single brain would depend entirely on whether the structure and organization of that brain was segregated into two nonoverlapping high-information systems, each of which is highly integrated internally but not integrated with the other. If the Φ values of two such systems are higher than any of their subsystems, as well as higher than any larger system of which they are parts, then each would be a conscious subject or self according to IIT. Given that the high Φ regions that IIT identifies with consciousness appear to rely on dynamic integrations with the thalamo-cortical core, the physical architecture of the brain may not permit such a dual organization. But if so, that would be a contingent fact about the specifics of the human brain rather than a general theoretical constraint on consciousness. The IIT model in itself does not rule out a genuine multiplicity of conscious selves within a single individual, organism, or brain.

The compatibility of DID with the global workspace model is less clear, at least with respect to the possibility of distinct, simultaneously conscious alters. GWS models tend to treat the global workspace as a unitary functional structure, though it can allow for degrees to which contents are broadcast and made generally available. Access to the global workspace is competitive, and various constellations of contentful states often work in mutually reinforcing combinations to gain access. The overall organization of contents active in the workspace at a given moment also structures and affects the subsequent state of the workspace and partly determines which new contents are included. Those larger structuring ensembles may include self schemas of the sort that Bayne appeals to in his deflationary model of DID. GWS models might plausibly interpret DID along the less radical lines suggested by Bayne. Different self schemas might alternate in dominating and structuring the contents active in the global workspace, giving the appearance of a multiplicity of distinct conscious subjects or agents. However, like Bayne, proponents of the GWS may be less willing to accept the possibility of simultaneous but distinct conscious agents. In so far as the global workspace is a single functional unit, it may not be able to incorporate two fully coherent self schemas at the same time. Integration of content in the workspace admits of degrees, and so perhaps it might allow for a confused state involving a combination of less-than-coherently unified self schemas. But that would not seem sufficient to produce genuine multiplicity, that is, two distinct, simultaneous, conscious subjects.

With respect to AIR theory, Prinz argues that attention, specifically what he calls "co-attention," plays a primary role in unifying perceptions and other intermediate representations into a single experience at a moment. How many distinct strands of consciousness exist within one brain at a moment will depend on the extent to which various attended intermediate-level representations are coattended at that time. What is required for synchronic phenomenal unity, and thus for unification in a single self, is a physical linkage of resonance between the relevant representations, where Prinz defines resonance as follows: "I will use the term *resonance* to refer to phase coherence or any other pattern of causal dependence between neural populations. The way one population of neurons fires can be said to be resonant with another if and only if the pattern of activity in one depends on the pattern of activity in the other" (Prinz 2012, 254). Attention, specifically coattention, can act to produce such resonance between simultaneous, or nearly simultaneous, groups of neurons that constitute the substrate of diverse experiences, thus phenomenally unifying them in the momentary experience of a single, conscious self. However, not all the attended intermediate representations in a brain at a given moment will be linked by such resonance or coattention. Thus, contrary to Bayne's unity thesis, Prinz's AIR theory allows for the possibility of simultaneous experiences that are not phenomenally unified, not merely in special DID cases, but even in the everyday experience of normal subjects. He admits that when we specifically introspect as to whether two experiences are phenomenally unified, they may always seem to be so. But he argues that may be the result of our looking for unity rather than a reflection of the ordinary state of our experience. Whenever we ask about the unity of two experiences, we coattend them and, thus, produce the resonant link between them that underlies phenomenal unity. But that does not show that there are such links among our experiences when we are not asking ourselves about their phenomenal unity. The act of looking for unity may itself suffice to produce that unity through coattention and resonance whenever we look (Prinz 2012, 271).

Finally, how do DID and the possibility of multiplicity look from the perspective of HOGS and VSR? In some ways, the implications are similar to those for other theories, but in other ways HOGS and VSR offer a somewhat different slant on the issue. Like GWS theory, the HOGS model explains the transition from unconscious to conscious state in terms of incorporation into a larger integrated state of activation. Just as the possibility for multiplicity on the GWS model turns, in part, on whether the global workspace is a unique and single structure, so too, on the HOGS model, it rests in part on the uniqueness of the relevant GS state. Can a brain maintain more than one such integrated GS state at a time? HOGS theory by itself does not rule out such an option. Thus, it may be possible for one individual human to realize two distinct simultaneous GS states, and, if so, that might suffice for genuine multiplicity at a moment. In that respect, HOGS also resembles IIT, which theoretically permits the possibility of two distinct maximum Φ integrated systems within a single brain. Facts about the actual structure and organization of the human brain may prevent the simultaneous occurrence of two GS states or of two separate high Φ states, but theoretically both seem possible.

However, even if it should turn out that human brains cannot maintain two distinct, simultaneous GS states, could a single integrated GS state nonetheless be able to support a multiplicity of selves? There are good, though less than conclusive, reasons to doubt that it could. Like GWS states and IIT states, the GS states of the HOGS model are highly integrated, but they are integrated in specific ways that relate to the HO aspect of HOGS. In particular, they cohere in ways that underlie two key unities within the structure of phenomenal experience: the unity of the *experienced world* and the unity of the *experiencing subject or agent.* Contrary to most other higher-order theories of consciousness, the higher-order intentionality of the HOGS model is not explicitly represented by a distinct metastate, but is implicitly embodied in the reflexive structure of phenomenal experience. And a good part of that implicit, reflexive content relates to the two central and interdependent unities of phenomenal experience: the unity of world-in-relation-to-self and that of self-in-relation-to-world. Thus, insofar as the GS states of the HOGS model cohere in ways that naturally define a single unified self or subject, it may be impossible for a single GS state to support a genuine multiplicity of selves. The question requires more investigation.

Combining HOGS with VSR reinforces the point. According to VSR, an ensemble of experiences constitutes a self only when it coheres in such a way that it defines a unified point of view—that of the conscious subject or self to whom these experiences are present. As noted above, VSR is committed to a greater realism about selves than most other virtual-self views. The self of VSR is real; hence the R of VSR. The relevant self is constituted by the ensemble of relevant experiences and their substrates, but only when they cohere to define a relevant VS—that is, only when they cohere to define a unified, subjective point of view, as well as, perhaps, a focus of agency. Thus, from the perspective of HOGS and VSR, multiplicity appears theoretically possible, but only if the human brain can support two or more simultaneous GS states, each defining a distinct, unified point of view and associated virtual self. However, HOGS and VSR would seem to exclude genuine multiplicity in the context of a single GS state.

Let us turn then to a final form of pathological disunity, that associated with the much-discussed phenomenon of so-called split-brain patients (Sperry 1968). In these happily rare but now very familiar cases, the corpus callossum connecting the two cortical hemispheres is surgically severed for medical reasons, primarily to limit the spread of uncontrolled seizures. The procedure leaves the patients with what seems in everyday situations to be normal behavior and normal consciousness. However, if carefully controlled laboratory presentations are used to provide differing stimuli to their left and right visual fields, such patients show striking dissociations of consciousness and behavior. Their left hands literally do not know what their right hands are doing. Shown one stimulus on the left and a different one on the right, each hand will respond appropriately to its respective stimulus but not to the other. Moreover, such patients typically show verbal knowledge only of the stimuli shown to their right field and not to those in their left field, even though their left hand is able to respond appropriately to the left-field stimuli. Given the typical lateralization of primary language function to the left hemisphere, the right hemisphere, which contralaterally receives it visual input from the left visual field, remains unable to verbally describe what it sees. Thus the question arises: In such cases, is consciousness itself split in two, and how many conscious selves do such patients embody?

Split-brain cases have aroused philosophical controversy for as long as they have been known. The first philosophical discussions (Nagel 1972, Puccetti 1973) appeared soon after the pioneering scientific research was done by Roger Sperry, James Bogen, and Michael Gazzaniga in the 1960s (Gazzaniga et al. 1965, Gazzaniga 1967, Sperry 1968). The literature on them is extensive, and this is not the place to review it. My present aim is merely to consider split brains as another form of pathological disunity from the perspective of our five integration-based theories of consciousness.

Split-brain cases again pose a challenge to Bayne's unity thesis. If split-brain patients embody two conscious selves, they would seem to involve distinct streams of experience that are not phenomenally unified with each other. That would refute the unity thesis. The deflationary strategy Bayne employed against DID does not seem an option with split-brain cases. With respect to DID, Bayne denied the existence of both synchronic and diachronic multiples. He argued that DID does not involve any genuine multiplicity of conscious subjects, but merely a shifting set of self schemas conjoined with a delusion of multiplicity. The differing behavioral abilities and experiential and agentive unities associated with the two hemispheres of split-brain patients seem too robust to be dismissed as mere schema-shifting or delusion.

Thus, Bayne takes a different tact on split-brain cases. He concedes that there are diachronic multiples selves in such cases, but denies they ever occur simultaneously. He opts instead for a rapid-switching model, in which the two selves alternate in existence. Only one exists at a given time, though which one of them exists may switch rapidly and repeatedly over short intervals of time (Bayne 2010). The rapid-switching hypothesis has the value of preserving the unity thesis, which limits its claim of universal phenomenal unity to synchronic unity—all the experiences had by a given human *at a moment* would remain phenomenally unified. Thus recognizing the existence of diachronic multiples poses no threat to the unity thesis. However, the rapid-switching hypothesis seems implausible and a bit ad hoc. For example, split-brain patients seem able to reach for hidden objects with their left and right hands at the same time, each being guided by the stimuli shown to only a single visual field. Perhaps Bayne could appeal to finer details of those experiments to argue that the hands are not really working simultaneously, but the prospects do not look promising. Thus, as others and I have argued elsewhere, the split-brain patients do seem to refute the unity thesis (Prinz 2012, Van Gulick 2014a).

As to the other theoretical perspectives, the implications of split-brain patients seem similar to those for DID. With respect to IIT, Tononi argues that, after the split, the two hemispheres reorganize themselves into separate high Φ systems that are internally integrated, but not integrated with each other (Tononi 2012). Each is thus conscious and constitutes a separate, conscious self. In this respect, Tononi's view echoes that of Sperry's original views about what happens in split-brain patients (see also Marks 1981). Sperry (1976) used the metaphor of cutting a bar magnet in half. If one does so, one does not get a north pole and a separate south pole. Instead, the two halves of the magnet reorganize themselves as two new, complete magnets, each with its own north and south pole. Sperry argued that the analogous thing happens in split-brain patients; each hemisphere reorganizes itself as a complete, unified, conscious mind or self. Similar hypotheses seem plausible from the perspective of AIR theory and on the HOGS and VSR model. Assuming attentional processes remain functional in each hemisphere—which is not certain—then AIR theory would predict that distinct resonant ensembles of active representations would form in each hemisphere and, thus, two streams of consciousness. From the perspective of HOGS and VSR, after the split, each hemisphere coheres to form an integrated GS state that defines a VS point of view and constitutes a separate self.

The implications are perhaps least clear for GWS. If the global workspace is unique and singular, as it is often supposed to be, then proponents of GWS may be inclined to deny that the right hemisphere has access to the global workspace, as shown, for example, by its lack of access to verbal report. And if the right hemisphere has no workspace access, then any contents represented in the right hemisphere would remain unconscious. If so, then there would be no conscious self associated with the right hemisphere. There would be only one conscious self in split-brain patients, and it would be solely associated with the left hemisphere, which would have access to the workspace. Such a negative conclusion about multiplicity would be hard to support given the behavioral evidence in split-brain patients and the range of responses that can be made by their right hemispheres. Alternatively, GWS supporters could argue that, after the split, the brains reorganize to produce two workspaces, each of which is relatively global even though the one associated with the right hemisphere provides more limited access. Each hemisphere might thus embody a distinct, conscious self, just as on IIT, AIR, and HOGS. The global workspace of GWS is defined functionally rather than structurally, and thus there may be no unique, single structure in the brain that it requires. It might be globally distributed across many cortical regions that would make the organization of separate hemisphere-based workspaces possible after commissurotomy.

There are many other pathologies of disunity that may also be relevant in evaluating competing integration-based theories of consciousness, but hopefully the few considered here suffice to demonstrate the value of doing so.

References

Baars, B. 1988. *A Cognitive Theory of Consciousness*. New York: Cambridge University Press.

Baars, B. 1997. *In the Theater of Consciousness: The Workspace of the Mind*. New York: Oxford University Press.

Bayne, T. 2010. *The Unity of Consciousness*. Oxford: Oxford University Press.

Block, N. 1995. On a confusion about the function of consciousness. *Behavioral and Brain Sciences* 18:227–247.

Block, N. 2007. Consciousness, accessibility, and the mesh between psychology and neuroscience. *Behavioral and Brain Sciences* 30:481–548.

Dehaene, S. 2014. *Consciousness and the Brain: Deciphering How the Brain Codes Our Thoughts*. New York: Viking.

Dehaene, S., and L. Nacacche. 2001. Towards a cognitive neuroscience of consciousness: Basic evidence and a workspace framework. *Cognition* 79:1–37.

Dennett, D. 1992. The self as the center of narrative gravity. In *Self and Consciousness: Multiple Perspectives*, ed. F. Kessel, P. Cole, and D. Johnson. Hillsdale, NJ: Erlbaum.

Descartes, R. (1642) 1935. *Meditations on First Philosophy: The Philosophical Works of Descartes Rendered into English, Part I*. Trans. E. Haldane and G. Ross. Cambridge: Cambridge University Press.

Driver, J., and J. Mattingley. 1998. Parietal neglect and visual awareness. *Nature Neuroscience* 1:17–22.

Gazzaniga, M. 1967. The split brain in man. *Scientific American* 217:24–29.

Gazzaniga, M., J. Bogen, and R. Sperry. 1965. Observations on visual perception after disconnexion of the cerebral hemispheres in man. *Brain* 88:221–236.

Hacking, I. 1995. *Rewriting the Soul: Multiple Personality and the Sciences of Memory*. Princeton: Princeton University Press.

Hacking, I. 2006. Making up people. *London Review of Books* 28:23–26.

Kinsbourne, M., and E. Warrington. 1962. A disorder of simultaneous form perception. *Brain* 85:461–486.

Lycan, W. 1996. *Consciousness and Experience*. Cambridge, MA: MIT Press.

Marks, C. 1981. *Commissurotomy, Consciousness, and Unity of Mind*. Cambridge, MA: MIT Press.

Marshall, J., and P. Halligan. 1988. Blindsight and insight in visuo-spatial neglect. *Nature* 336:766–767.

Milner, A., H. Karnath, and G. Vallar. 2002. *The Cognitive and Neural Bases of Spatial Neglect*. Oxford: Oxford University Press.

Nagel, T. 1972. Brain bisection and unity of consciousness. *Synthese* 22:396–413.

Piper, A., and H. Merskey. 2004. The persistence of folly: Critical examination of dissociative identity disorder. *Canadian Journal of Psychiatry* 49:678–683.

Prinz, J. 2005. A neurofunctional theory of consciousness. In *Cognition and the Brain,* ed. A. Brook and K. Akins. Cambridge: Cambridge University Press.

Prinz, J. 2012. *The Conscious Brain.* New York: Oxford University Press.

Prinz, J. 2013. Attention, atomism, and disunity of consciousness. *Philosophy and Phenomenological Research* 86:215–222.

Puccetti, R. 1973. Brain bisection and personal identity. *British Journal for the Philosophy of Science* 24:339–355.

Putnam, F. 1989. *Diagnosis and Treatment of Multiple Personality Disorder.* New York: Guilford Press.

Rafal, R., and P. Vuillemumier. 2000. A systematic study of visual extinction: Between and within-field deficits of attention in hemispatial neglect. *Brain* 24: 1263–1279.

Rosenthal, D. 1997. A theory of consciousness. In *The Nature of Consciousness,* ed. N. Block, O. Flanagan, and G. Güzeldere. Cambridge, MA: MIT Press.

Sperry, R. 1968. Hemisphere deconnection and unity in conscious awareness. *American Psychologist* 23:723–733.

Sperry, R. 1976. Mental phenomena as causal determinants in brain function. In *Consciousness and the Brain,* ed. G. Globus, G. Maxwell, and I. Savodnik. New York: Plenum Press.

Tononi, G. 2008. Consciousness as integrated information: A provisional manifesto. *Biological Bulletin* 215:216–242.

Tononi, G. 2012. *A Voyage from the Brain to the Soul.* New York: Pantheon.

Tye, M. 2003. *Consciousness and Persons.* Cambridge, MA: MIT Press.

Van Gulick, R. 2004. HOGS (higher-order global states)—an alternative higher-order model of consciousness. In *Higher-Order Theories of Consciousness,* ed. R. Gennaro. Amsterdam: John Benjamins.

Van Gulick, R. 2006. Mirror-mirror, is that all? In *Self-Representational Approaches to Consciousness,* ed. U. Kriegel and K. Williford. Cambridge, MA: MIT Press.

Van Gulick, R. 2014a. Getting it all together—phenomenal unity and the self. *Analysis* 74:491–498.

Van Gulick, R. 2014b. E pluribus unum: Rethinking the unity of consciousness. In *Sensory Integration and the Unity of Consciousness,* ed. C. Hill and D. Bennett. Cambridge, MA: MIT Press.

10 Consciousness despite Network Underconnectivity in Autism: Another Case of Consciousness without Prefrontal Activity?

William Hirstein

1 Introduction

Recent evidence points to widespread underconnectivity in autistic brains owing to deviant white matter, the fibers that make long connections between areas of the cortex. Subjects with autism show measurably fewer long-range connections between the parietal and prefrontal cortices. These findings may help shed light on the current debate in the consciousness literature about whether conscious states require both prefrontal and parietal/temporal components. If it can be shown that people with autism have conscious states despite such underconnectivity, this would constitute an argument for the claim that conscious states can exist in posterior cortex without associated prefrontal activity. This in turn lends support to a class of theories according to which *microconsciousness* is possible—consciousness in small areas of cortex without active connections to the prefrontal cortex, as opposed to the higher-order thought (HOT) theory of consciousness, according to which conscious states can only occur when posterior cortical areas (in the parietal or temporal lobes) have active connections to the prefrontal cortex. In this chapter, after listing several candidate examples of consciousness without accompanying prefrontal connections, I will argue that autism provides yet another such example. I will also examine a recent version of the higher-order theory that acknowledges these cases of consciousness without prefrontal activity and, instead depicts consciousness as sometimes requiring higher-order thoughts located in posterior cortex. In the final section, I will examine the consequences of these views for our understanding of the metaphysical nature of consciousness itself—the classic mind-body problem.

Over the last two decades, a surprising number of philosophers have given up on the prospect of developing a materialist theory of consciousness as a brain process. Rather than learning about the brain, they have created new variants of behaviorism called the *embodied mind* or the *extended mind*. Quitting on the original problem, the mind-body problem, has had its rewards. It is flattering to think that there is some special part of us that transcends the material realm, and audiences never tire of having this cherished belief affirmed. Perhaps this special part or property of us even allows us to have free will, in which the nonmaterial part of us is capable of breaking out of the determined materialistic realm. While these philosophers have been ignoring neuroscience, rapid progress is being made. We have our first neuroscientific theories of consciousness, which are in the process of being tested along many fronts. Using imaging techniques, lesion studies, and advanced anatomical and physiological investigation techniques, as well as traditional psychology experiments in which human subjects are shown stimuli and their responses recorded, measured, and analyzed, neuroscientists have begun to narrow down the cortical areas and networks responsible for conscious states. But there are still major obstacles to be overcome, caused partly by a fundamental inability of experimenters to actually be certain that a certain active brain area or network is itself a conscious state.

Among those philosophers and scientists resolved to continue the quest for a materialist theory of consciousness, an interesting debate has emerged between two groups. According to the higher-order thought theory of consciousness, conscious states require at least two components (Rosenthal 1997, 2005, Carruthers 2000, 2005, Kriegel 2009, Kriegel and Williford 2006, Lau and Rosenthal 2011). First, there must be a state in the brain's posterior cortex that constitutes the contents of the conscious state. For instance, in the case of vision, the content of my current state is that which I am visually aware of. But this posterior state must also have active connections to a state in the front of the brain. This frontal state must be directed at the posterior state, or, in different versions, it must be aware of the posterior state, or it must perceive it. More specifically, according to this theory, a state becomes conscious when it either is, or is disposed to be, the object of a higher-order representation of some sort (Carruthers 2007). The event of a state becoming the object of a higher-order thought or representation is the same event as the subject becoming aware of that state. In other words, states become conscious when we become aware of them. This theory has both philosophical and scientific versions (e.g., Baars et al. 2003, Dehaene and Changeux 2011), and this coalescence between the two approaches has made it one of the most clearly delineated and popular theories of consciousness.

According to the alternative approach to a materialistic theory of consciousness, which has become known as the theory of microconsciousness, only one brain state is required in order for consciousness to be present: the state located in the brain's posterior cortex (Zeki and Bartels 1999, Zeki 2007, Lamme 2003, Pins and ffytche 2003, Hirstein 2012). As its name indicates, this theory allows for conscious states to exist in relatively small, restricted areas of brain tissue, without the need for accompanying frontal activity or for any accompanying cortical activity. Those areas that are capable of producing conscious states, taken along with their connected thalamic nuclei, may be spatially contiguous. One candidate for the process that produces microconsciousness is a type of neural binding process in which the activity of a certain subset of neurons making up an area of the cortex (along with portions of the relevant thalamic nuclei) takes on a certain highly synchronized functional pattern (Steriade and Llinas 1988).

2   Candidate Examples of Consciousness without Associated Prefrontal Activity

Contrary to the higher-order thought view of consciousness, there appear to be cases in which conscious states exist in brains without associated prefrontal activity. In this section, I will review several candidate cases (thanks to Gennaro [2012b] for supplying several of these).

Animals and Infants

Consciousness without prefrontal activity may exist in animals and human infants, in that they might have, for instance, "conscious pains without higher-order thoughts about them" (Block 2007, 288). Several different techniques have now verified the claim that the frontal lobes mature, or *myelinate*, slowly throughout childhood, adolescence, and early adulthood (e.g., Klingberg et al. 1999). This process parallels the development of more sophisticated behaviors in children, such as the ability to inhibit actions and the ability to make higher-level decisions. As with most of the candidate examples we will examine, this one is only able to suggest the possibility of consciousness without accompanying prefrontal activity. With no ability to experience the minds of animals and infants directly, along with no canonical neuroscientific criterion for detecting consciousness from the outside using imaging or other measurement techniques (i.e., the very issue under dispute here), we can only put forward good candidates, not proven examples.

Akinetic Mutism

Neurological patients with akinetic mutism syndrome appear to be awake and conscious but are completely unresponsive to stimuli (Mega and Cohenour 1997). They will apparently stare right at you, but show no sign of actually seeing you, and will not respond to any requests or commands. Patients who have recovered from this state (sometimes via the restoration of blood flow to the damaged area) report that they had conscious states, but simply lacked any desire or impetus to respond. What we may have here is a case of consciousness without the prefrontal activity that must act on it before any behavioral intentions can be formed and executed. The conscious states exist, but they just sit there because they lack important causal connections allowing them to interact with the prefrontal lobes.

Meditation

Deep meditative states are characterized by an absence of activity in the prefrontal cortex. According to Lou et al. (2005), subjects deep in meditation show increased blood flow in posterior areas having to do with imagery, along with decreased blood flow to prefrontal executive areas (which make possible tasks such as inhibition, planning, and decision making). Practitioners of meditation speak of "the self" quieting down or "going away" during these states. Indeed, the ensemble of prefrontal executive processes makes a good candidate for what has historically been referred to as the self in philosophy. The list of mental acts that the self or ego performs is actually a list of executive processes (Hirstein 2011). The ego, says Descartes, is, "a thing which doubts, understands, [conceives], affirms, denies, wills, refuses, which also imagines and feels" (Descartes 1967, Second Meditation). This is, I contend, a list of executive processes.

Perceptual Absorption

Perceptual absorption occurs when people are engaged in a perceptual task or while they are absorbed in a movie they are watching, for example. This produces a state similar to the meditative state, characterized by activity in the brain's posterior perceptual regions, but very little prefrontal activity (Grill-Spector and Malach 2004, Goldberg, Harel, and Malach 2006). A related phenomenon occurs when we engage in activities that are conscious but automatic and unthinking, such as our daily drive home from work. We have driven the route so many times that we don't need to think about what we are doing or be aware of our conscious states. We might arrive at home and be rather surprised that we wound up there without any discernable mental effort on our part. Certainly there were conscious visual states in our brains, though: we consciously saw the other cars and the traffic lights. Yet it may be true to say that we were not aware of these states and were not attending to them. Or so I will argue below.

Frontal Damage

There are cases in which patients show severe frontal damage while continuing to experience and report normal conscious states. There are also cases of profound frontal disconnection caused by damage, intentional (e.g., frontal lobotomy) or accidental, in which subjects continue to have relatively normal conscious mental lives (Pollen 2008, Tononi and Koch 2008). Frontal patients may have trouble using those conscious states to form coherent plans or inhibiting them from causing inappropriate or dangerous behavior, but they seem to nevertheless have conscious states.

Schizophrenia

According to the disconnection hypothesis of schizophrenia, the vivid hallucinations that some schizophrenics experience are caused by disruptions of the processing connections between posterior sensory areas and the prefrontal cortex. There is evidence that the fiber bundles that carry the posterior-prefrontal connections are damaged in schizophrenics (Friston 1998). This may indicate that they experience a type of disordered conscious state that is vivid enough to be distracting and annoying but which is chaotic and/or irrational and may cause dangerous behavior, precisely because the frontal lobes are unable to interact with it in the normal manner.

Coma

Rather than accepting the traditional view that coma patients possess no consciousness whatsoever, Owen and his colleagues performed brain imaging on coma patients while they were asked to imagine doing different things (Owen et al. 2007). Quite surprisingly, even though the patients cannot move a muscle or signal the experimenters in any way, their brains showed activity consistent with the different imagery tasks. In this respect, they may be similar to the patients with akinetic mutism in that their brains contain conscious states that reside in posterior cortical regions but which are causally isolated from the prefrontal cortex. Similarly, patients in a minimally conscious state (who are able to show intermittent behavioral responses) exhibited activity in the temporal cortex in response to hearing personal narratives, but were unable to respond to them behaviorally (Schiff et al. 2005).

3 Consciousness in Autism

Autism has two features: (1) network underconnectivity between the posterior and frontal cortices, and (2) executive deficits, both of which support adding it to the list of possible cases of consciousness without associated prefrontal activity. There is now a large body of evidence showing abnormal and inadequate white matter connections (which link up distant areas of cortex) in the autistic brain between posterior perceptual areas and the prefrontal cortex. Assaf et al. (2010) had subjects with autism simply lie still in the scanner as they monitored the functional connectivity among different cortical regions. They found reduced connectivity between the precuneus, a posterior cortical area thought to be an important node for consciousness, and the medial prefrontal cortex. Cherkassky et al. (2006) similarly found anterior-posterior connectivity to be reduced in autism. Monk et al. (2009) found reduced functional connectivity between the posterior cingulate cortex and the medial prefrontal cortex in autism and noted that this lack of connectivity was associated with worse social function in their subjects. Just et al. (2004), as well as Kana, Libero, and Moore (2011), suggest that this functional underconnectivity might underlie the core symptoms of autism. This lack of frontal connectivity appears to be compensated for by increased local connectivity in the posterior cortex. Monk et al. (2009) found increased connectivity between the posterior cingulate cortex and temporal regions in subjects with autism. In addition, they found that increased repetitive behaviors, a core diagnostic symptom of autism, were associated with increased connectivity between the posterior cingulate cortex and the parahippocampal gyrus.

But what is consciousness like in autism? People with autism certainly report having conscious states. Indeed, several reports on autistic savants appear to show that their visual conscious states are quite large, containing much more information that those of normal people. It appears that such subjects do not, in Crick and Koch's (1995) phrase, get an "executive summary" of their visual contents which accentuates the important features, but are in touch with a large amount of raw conscious data. Similarly, subjects with autism show attention to the periphery of the visual field that is actually superior to that of normal people (Joseph et al. 2009). The periphery of the visual field is a good place to tease apart the higher-order thought and the microconsciousness theories, since consciousness in the unattended visual periphery may be another candidate for conscious states without accompanying prefrontal activity (see Lamme 2003, Hirstein 2012). What the people with autism may show that is of interest here is perhaps that a greater amount or percentage of their conscious states can continue to exist in a robust form while not being attended to, that is, not having active causal connections with prefrontal, top-down, attentional processes, which are a type of executive process. Those of us without this gift nevertheless experience a full visual field, although we are bad at reporting what is out there (e.g., Rensink et al. 2003). This brings us to the issue of reportability.

4   Reportability

There is a long tradition in psychology of using reportability as a criterion for the presence of consciousness: subjects can report the presence of a stimulus if and only if they are conscious of it. This criterion may well be an outmoded vestige of behaviorism, however. Behaviorists insisted that any mental state that could not be cashed out in behavioral terms was suspect or not a proper object of science. The criterion also creates a problem in that some theorists are confusing neural processes associated with giving the report with the conscious state the report is about. That is, these theorists regard reportability as essential to consciousness, and they also believe that prefrontal activity is essential to consciousness (e.g., Dehaene and Changeux 2011). The prefrontal activity they are seeing may be due to the processes required to report the state. Thus, according to this line of thought, their belief that prefrontal activity is essential for consciousness is, in some cases, an artifact of their insistence on reportability.

One type of argument against the necessity of reportability to consciousness points out that we are always conscious of more than we are able to report. One simple experiment that shows this exposes a subject briefly to a five-by-five grid of random letters. The subject is shown the grid for a limited period of time and then must report what she saw. Normal people are unable to hold the entire grid in visual short term memory, and hence cannot report all of the letters. But this does not show that there is not a large conscious state containing the entire grid during the exposure period (Block 2007, but see Kouider et al. 2010). Hulme, Friston, and Zeki (2009) argue that they were able to tease apart the neural structures required for consciousness and those associated with reportability by using signal detection theory during the reporting task, a finding which supports the idea that consciousness can be present without reportability.

Some linguistic distinctions may be useful here. There are three grammatically different types of claims we make about consciousness and conscious states. In the subject type, we refer to a person who is the subject of consciousness or of the conscious state, as in "Joe is conscious." This type admits of a grammatically intransitive sense, as in the previous example, as well as a transitive sense, as in, "Joe is conscious of a blue jay," and "Joe is conscious that a blue jay is in the tree." In addition to these two, we use a third type of report that focuses on the mental state, not the subject. This third type allows us to focus on the states themselves, as when we speak of conscious states in general or a conscious state in the subject's brain.

It may be correct to claim that when a person is conscious of x, that person can report awareness of x. But, I suggest, this is because this grammatical form actually describes a fact about the brain in which the prefrontal processes are in contact with the posterior state. But it does not follow from that claim that every conscious state in a person's brain is reportable by her. We need to examine what facts in the brain make reports about conscious states true. To say that "Jan is conscious of x" is to describe a fact in which there is a conscious state in the posterior of Jan's brain that has the right sort of active connections to Jan's ensemble of executive processes, I submit. However, to say that "There is a conscious state in Jan's brain" is to commit only to the posterior brain state, not to the prefrontal connections. Thus, to say "Jan is conscious of x, but she cannot report that x" is, in most ordinary contexts, a contradiction. But to say "There is a conscious state in Jan's brain, but she cannot report its presence or correctly describe it" is not a contradiction. A claim like this might be true, for instance, of the unattended visual periphery. I have argued that the fact that sentences of the form, "Jan is conscious of x," have additional truth conditions (compared to the "there is a conscious state" construction) indicates that the noun phrase of the sentence (in this case, "Jan") is actually making a sort of reference to these extra facts (Hirstein 2012). The extra facts include certain prefrontal executive processes as well as their active reciprocal white matter connections to the conscious state itself, according to my hypothesis. Following Perry and Crimmens, who argue for a much more restricted form of it (Crimmens and Perry 1989, Crimmens 1992), I call this type of reference *tacit reference*.

5   Gennaro's View

Rocco Gennaro places himself in the higher-order thought camp, but he is unique in accepting that prefrontal activity is not required for consciousness (Gennaro 2012a, chapter 9, 2012b). Gennaro makes objections similar to those listed above to experiments that appear to show that prefrontal activity is necessary, that is, that the reportability criterion is a confound. In addition to explicitly noting several of the apparent cases of non-prefrontal consciousness in my list above, he argues that the experiments of Lau and Passingham (2006) and Dehaene et al. (2006) "tend to demand explicit verbal or meta-confidence reporting, introspection, top-down attentional processes, and/or executive functions which are not necessary for first-order conscious states" (2012b). Gennaro similarly criticizes Dehaene and Changeux (2011) by noting that their experiments leave it "undetermined whether [prefrontal] activation *constitutes* [a neural correlate of consciousness] or is a *consequence* of a conscious perception" (2012b). Gennaro notes that, while Lau and Rosenthal (2011) believe that higher-order thoughts are in the prefrontal cortex, he prefers to move away from the idea that higher-order thoughts are to be identified with executive processes in the prefrontal cortex, arguing instead that executive functions such as attention are better understood as introspective abilities than as higher-order thoughts (2012b). "The PFC activity," concludes Gennaro, "likely has more to do with processes that *follow* or *trigger* conscious perceptions rather than being *constitutive* of the [neural correlates of consciousness] themselves" (2012b, see also Gennaro 2012a, especially chapter 9).

If prefrontal activity is not required, then where are the necessary higher-order thoughts? Gennaro cites Tong (2003) approvingly, who argues that, in the case of visual consciousness, activity in primary visual area V1, together with activity in nearby posterior visual cortices, is sufficient for consciousness. Gennaro suggests that this nearby activity is in fact the necessary higher-order thought. Thus he believes that higher-order thoughts can exist at relatively low levels in the processing hierarchy and in the posterior cortex. Notice that this activity is modality specific—the higher-order thought is still in *visual* cortex. This would suggest that the analogous higher-order thoughts in the case of hearing would be in the auditory cortex.

The initial intuition behind the higher-order theory is that a thought becomes conscious when the person becomes aware of it. This implies, I would argue, that the higher-order thought must in some sense stand in for the person herself. We need to be able to say "*I* am aware of that thought." Gennaro would thus need to show that the nearby activity mentioned by Tong can generate such a claim, that is, the nearby activity must be a referent of "I" in some way, or it must be a sort of *self*. If Gennaro's willingness to allow higher-order thoughts to exist alongside their targets in the posterior cortex works, it may save the higher-order theory, but at a cost of abandoning its initial intuitive support. Without that support, where is the independent motive for requiring a higher-order thought? A related objection to Gennaro's attempt to save the higher-order theory is that the different higher-order thoughts need to issue from a single, unified source, otherwise, again, much of the intuitive support for the higher-order theory is lost. In everyday parlance, the self must be unified. I take this to mean that, if we want to be materialists, we need to map the self onto a single, unified brain system. Our mental states must have a kind of connectedness in order for us to think coherently about ourselves. The one who is aware of the bear must be the same one who decides not to run from it. It is crucial, for instance in legal contexts, that the same "I" who made the decision to kill also formed the intention to kill and, in the end, performed the action of killing (Hirstein and Sifferd 2011). Gennaro would thus need to extend Tong's findings to show something like this. There cannot be unrelated higher-order thoughts all over the posterior cortex.

Gennaro has a response to my claim that the lower-level HOTs cannot function as a type of self, however: he first accepts that higher-order thoughts, together with their target conscious states, can be understood as a form of self-consciousness. He then suggests that the higher-order thoughts located in posterior consciousness might be understood as a sort of "pre-reflective self-consciousness" (2012b). In support of this, Gennaro cites Newen and Vogeley (2003), who distinguish five different levels of self-consciousness, ranging from a fairly low-level "phenomenal self-acquaintance" and "conceptual self-consciousness" up to "iterative meta-representational self-consciousness." However, Newen and Vogeley are writing about different types of self-*representations*. They are employing the assumption, reasonable I think, that when a person is conscious of a self-representation, for instance a representation of his body, this counts as a type of self-consciousness. But what Gennaro needs is a type of self, not a self-representation, to serve as something directed at the conscious state that allows us to say "I am aware of that state." Self-representations represent some aspect of the person. Since Gennaro needs something that will represent the conscious state (and, in so doing, make it a conscious state), such states would have to represent two things: some aspect of the self as well as the conscious state. There would need to be an independent argument that the self-representation also represents the conscious state. Gennaro needs a lower-level self, not a lower-level self-representation.

6 Metaphysical Issues

The relation between the higher-order thought and its target is epistemic, since the higher-order thought is supposed to be aware of, or perceive, its target by representing it. But if you include an epistemic component in your definition of consciousness, you have created an epistemic-metaphysical simple and, thereby, made the mind-body problem unsolvable. If you similarly include representation in your definition, you create one thing that must be two things, representer and represented—again, a two-part simple. The "simple" part prevents the analysis from progressing any further. You have combined the conscious state and the subject of that conscious state into a unit that cannot be broken if you still want there to be a conscious state. You are done. And yet there still seems to be great complexity there, with much more to be explained.

Bonding the higher-order thought to its target may create another metaphysical problem: only one person can ever experience that conscious state. Since the higher-order thought is a type of self, or "I" that is aware of its target, that self may be the only one capable of experiencing the target state. That makes conscious states unlike every other physical state in the universe, all of which can be experienced by multiple parties. This is exactly the sort of thing that made the theorists mentioned at the beginning of this article give up on the prospect of developing a satisfying materialistic theory of conscious states, one that depicts them as just like every other physical state. And it encourages dualists, who believe that conscious states are not physical. The most straightforward way to respond to this situation is to show that, in fact, conscious states can be directly experienced by multiple parties, by way of brain-to-brain connections (Hirstein 2012). But, this can only be done if we adopt the microconsciousness theory of conscious states (which allow us to separate the conscious state from the "self"). At the very least, this objection forces the higher-order theorists to refine their theory: Is the target state only conscious when it allies with a certain, particular higher-order thought, or can it become conscious when it allies with any sort of higher-order thought, possibly in the brain of another person?

If there can be posterior consciousness, or microconsciousness, without an accompanying higher-order thought, this may indicate that the problem of consciousness has already been solved. An analysis of the properties of posterior conscious states alone can yield a theory of what consciousness is. The current version of this analysis is that the measurable physical property that best corresponds to those cases in which consciousness is present is binding (Singer 1997). Binding occurs when the entire state is unified by coherent, synchronized oscillations. Even if the problem of consciousness has been solved, however, the other half of the mind-body problem remains. The mind-body problem has two parts: (1) the problem of consciousness, and (2) the problem of the self. The problem of the self is caused by the apparent fact that only I, only this self, can ever experience my conscious states. Thus, according to this conception, my consciousness is deeply private, in that no one else can ever experience it directly. I have suggested that the second problem can be solved by showing (1) the self is the ensemble of prefrontal executive processes (Hirstein 2011), and (2) we can connect one person's self to another person's conscious state (Hirstein 2008, 2012) and, in so doing, breach the wall of mental privacy. Note that if we can achieve this sort of *mindmelding*, we could use it to provide evidence that consciousness exists in the cases mentioned above. We would need to ascertain that the connection itself isn't causing the patient's mental states to become conscious, but there are experimental tests for this. For instance, does anything about the mental state in question change after the connection is made?

Further research on this question will surely illuminate the issues surrounding consciousness, our sense of self, and our minds in general. These issues are difficult, but ultimately resolvable. Breakthroughs in our understanding of consciousness will have immediate medical benefits on exactly the sorts of disorders mentioned in the examples above. If we understand consciousness better, we can better understand its disorders.

Acknowledgments

Many thanks to Xavier Arko, Ty Fagan, Rocco Gennaro, Daniel Hayes, Katrina Sifferd, and Margaret Sumney for their valuable comments.

References

Assaf, M., K. Jagannathan, V. Calhoun, L. Miller, M. Stevens, R. Sahl, J. O'Boyle, R. Schultz, and G. Pearlson. 2010. Abnormal functional connectivity of default mode sub-networks in autism spectrum disorder patients. *NeuroImage* 53:247–256.

Baars, B., T. Ramsey, and S. Laureys. 2003. Brain, conscious experience, and the observing self. *Trends in Neurosciences* 26:671–675.

Block, N. 2007. Consciousness, accessibility, and the mesh between psychology and neuroscience. *Behavioral and Brain Sciences* 30:481–499.

Carruthers, P. 2000. *Phenomenal Consciousness.* Cambridge: Cambridge University Press.

Carruthers, P. 2005. *Consciousness: Essays from a Higher-Order Perspective.* New York: Oxford University Press.

Carruthers, P. 2007. Higher-order theories of consciousness. In *The Stanford Encyclopedia of Philosophy* (Fall 2007 Ed.), ed. Edward N. Zalta. http://plato.stanford.edu/archives/fall2007/entries/consciousness-higher/.

Cherkassky, V., R. Kana, T. Keller, and M. Just. 2006. Functional connectivity in a baseline resting-state network in autism. *Neuroreport* 17:1687–1690.

Crick, F., and C. Koch. 1995. Are we aware of activity in the primary visual cortex? *Nature* 375:121–123.

Crimmens, M. 1992. *Talk about Beliefs*. Cambridge, MA: MIT Press.

Crimmens, M., and J. Perry. 1989. The prince and the phone booth: Reporting puzzling beliefs. *Journal of Philosophy* 86:685–711.

Dehaene, S., and J. Changeux. 2011. Experimental and theoretical approaches to conscious processing. *Neuron* 70:200–227.

Dehaene, S., J. Changeux, L. Naccache, J. Sackur, and C. Sergent. 2006. Conscious, preconscious, and subliminal processing: A testable taxonomy. *Trends in Cognitive Sciences* 10:204–211.

Descartes, R. 1967. *Meditations on First Philosophy*. Trans. E. Haldane and D. Ross. Cambridge: Cambridge University Press.

Friston, K. 1998. The disconnection hypothesis. *Schizophrenia Research* 30:115–125.

Gennaro, R. 2012a. *The Consciousness Paradox: Consciousness, Concepts, and Higher-Order Thoughts*. Cambridge, MA: MIT Press.

Gennaro, R. 2012b. HOT theory and the prefrontal cortex. Paper presented at the "Toward a Science of Consciousness" Conference in Tucson, Arizona, April 10.

Goldberg, I., M. Harel, and R. Malach. 2006. When the brain loses its self: Prefrontal inactivation during sensorimotor processing. *Neuron* 50:329–339.

Grill-Spector, K., and R. Malach. 2004. The human visual cortex. *Annual Review of Neuroscience* 7:649–677.

Hirstein, W. 2008. Mindmelding: Connected brains and the problem of consciousness. *Mens Sana Monographs* 6:110–130.

Hirstein, W. 2011. The contribution of prefrontal executive processes to producing a sense of self. *Mens Sana Monographs* 9:150–158.

Hirstein, W. 2012. *Mindmelding: Consciousness, Neuroscience, and the Mind's Privacy*. Oxford: Oxford University Press.

Hirstein, W., and K. Sifferd. 2011. The legal self: Executive processes and legal theory. *Consciousness and Cognition* 20:156–171.

Hulme, O., K. Friston, and S. Zeki. 2009. Neural correlates of stimulus reportability. *Journal of Cognitive Neuroscience* 21:1602–1610.

Joseph, R., B. Keehn, C. Conolly, J. Wolfe, and T. Horowitz. 2009. Why is visual search superior in autism spectrum disorder? *Developmental Science* 12:1083–1096.

Just, M., V. Cherkassky, T. Keller, and N. Minshew. 2004. Cortical activation and synchronization during sentence comprehension in high-functioning autism: Evidence of underconnectivity. *Brain* 127:1811–1821.

Kana, R., L. Libero, and M. Moore. 2011. Disrupted cortical connectivity theory as an explanatory model for autism spectrum disorders. *Physics of Life Reviews* 8: 410–437.

Klingberg, T., C. Vaidya, J. Gabrieli, M. Moseley, and M. Hedehus. 1999. Myelination and organization of the frontal white matter in children: A diffusion tensor MRI study. *Neuroreport* 10:2817–2821.

Kouider, S., V. de Gardelle, J. Sacker, and E. Dupoux. 2010. How rich is consciousness? The partial awareness hypothesis. *Trends in Cognitive Sciences* 14:301–307.

Kriegel, U. 2009. *Subjective Consciousness*. New York: Oxford University Press.

Kriegel, U., and K. Williford. 2006. *Self-Representational Approaches to Consciousness*. Cambridge, MA: MIT Press.

Lamme, V. 2003. Why visual attention and awareness are different. *Trends in Cognitive Sciences* 7:12–18.

Lau, H., and R. Passingham. 2006. Relative blindsight in normal observers and the neural correlate of visual consciousness. *Proceedings of the National Academy of Sciences of the United States of America* 103:18763–18768.

Lau, H., and D. Rosenthal. 2011. Empirical support for higher-order theories of conscious awareness. *Trends in Cognitive Sciences* 15:365–373.

Lou, H., M. Nowak, and T. Kjaer. 2005. The mental self. In *The Boundaries of Consciousness: Neurobiology and Neuropathology*, ed. S. Laureys. Amsterdam: Elsevier.

Mega, M., and R. Cohenour. 1997. Akinetic mutism: Disconnection of frontal-subcortical circuits. *Neuropsychiatry, Neuropsychology, and Behavioral Neurology* 10: 254–259.

Monk, C., S. Peltier, J. Wiggins, S. Weng, M. Carrasco, S. Risi, and C. Lord. 2009. Abnormalities of intrinsic functional connectivity in autism spectrum disorders. *NeuroImage* 47:764–772.

Newen, A., and K. Vogeley. 2003. Self-representation: Searching for a neural signature of self-consciousness. *Consciousness and Cognition* 12:529–543.

Owen, A., M. Coleman, M. Boly, M. Davis, S. Laureys, and J. Pickard. 2007. Using functional magnetic resonance imaging to detect awareness in the vegetative state. *Archives of Neurology* 64:1098–1102.

Pins, D., and ffytche, D. 2003. The neural correlates of conscious vision. *Cerebral Cortex* 13:461–474.

Pollen, D. 2008. Fundamental requirements for primary visual perception. *Cerebral Cortex* 18:1991–1998.

Rensink, R., K. O'Regan, and J. Clark. 2003. To see or not to see: The need for visual attention to perceive changes in scene. In *Essential Sources in the Scientific Study of Consciousness*, ed. B. Baars, W. Banks, and J. Newman. Cambridge, MA: MIT Press.

Rosenthal, D. 1997. A theory of consciousness. In *The Nature of Consciousness*, ed. N. Block, O. Flanagan, and G. Güzeldere. Cambridge, MA: MIT Press.

Rosenthal, D. 2005. *Consciousness and Mind.* New York: Oxford University Press.

Schiff, N., D. Rodriguez-Moreno, A. Kamal, K. Kim, J. Giacino, F. Plum, and J. Hirsch. 2005. fMRI reveals large-scale network activation in minimally conscious patients. *Neurology* 64:514–523.

Singer, W. 1997. Consciousness from a neurobiological perspective. In *From Brains to Consciousness? Essays on the New Sciences of the Mind*, ed. S. Rose. Princeton, NJ: Princeton University Press.

Steriade, M., and R. Llinas. 1988. The functional status of the thalamus and the associated neuronal interplay. *Physiological Reviews* 68:649–742.

Tong, F. 2003. Primary visual cortex and visual awareness. *Nature Reviews: Neuroscience* 4:219–229.

Tononi, G., and C. Koch. 2008. The neural correlates of consciousness. *Annals of the New York Academy of Sciences* 1124:239–261.

Zeki, S. 2007. A theory of micro-consciousness. In *The Blackwell Companion to Consciousness*, ed. M. Velmans and S. Schneider. Malden: Blackwell.

Zeki, S., and A. Bartels. 1999. Toward a theory of visual consciousness. *Consciousness and Cognition* 8:225–259.

11 A Schizophrenic Defense of a Vehicle Theory of Consciousness

Gerard O'Brien and Jon Opie

1 Introduction: The Road Less Traveled

There is a striking similarity between representation and consciousness. Both possess the remarkable and exceedingly rare property of *aboutness*. Leonardo da Vinci's *Mona Lisa* isn't just a material object with a variety of physical properties; it is *about* a woman with a famously enigmatic smile. Likewise, your current visual experience, whatever its physical basis, is *about* these words. This similarity motivates the following explanatory strategy regarding phenomenal consciousness. Perhaps the brain's capacity to generate conscious states is connected in some profound way with its representational capacities? This explanatory strategy is promising for two reasons. First, it offers the prospect of reducing the elusive and puzzling problem of consciousness to the slightly less elusive and puzzling problem of representation. And second, aligning consciousness with the brain's representational capacities is consistent with our most promising strategy for explaining the evolution of intelligent organisms—the computational theory of cognition.

It is thus not surprising that almost everyone working on consciousness in philosophy and cognitive science pursues this strategy in one form or another. The most straightforward relationship that might obtain between consciousness and the brain's representational capacities is one that *identifies* conscious experiences with the brain's representing vehicles, such that the tokening of a neural vehicle of representation is necessary and sufficient for its content to be conscious. Such an identity would provide an elegant account of the function of consciousness, since it implies that consciousness is none other than the brain's means of representing the world. We call any theory that takes seriously this kind of identity thesis a *vehicle* theory of consciousness (O'Brien and Opie 1999a).

Despite their attractions, vehicle theories are exceedingly rare in the literature. It has been orthodoxy in cognitive science for many years that the brain engages in a great deal of unconscious information processing (Fodor 1983, Kahneman and Tversky 1974, Kihlstrom 1987, Pylyshyn 1984).[1] Consequently, philosophers and scientists alike almost universally assume that neural representation is *insufficient* for consciousness (see, e.g., Carruthers 2011). The relationship between consciousness and the brain's capacity for representation must be more complicated; something else is required for neural representing vehicles to contribute their contents to consciousness (Maia and Cleeremans 2005, 398). What else? Prinz provides the obvious answer: "Most theories assume that mental states become conscious by virtue of a change that takes place within the organism: a difference in how mental representations are processed" (2012, 20). The emphasis here is on what neural representing vehicles *do*, rather than what they *are*. The mere existence of a vehicle of representation is not enough for consciousness; what matters is that it be implicated in some kind of consciousness-making process. We call any theory that adopts this stance a *process* theory of consciousness (O'Brien and Opie 1999a).

Process theories dominate both the philosophical and scientific literature on consciousness, and, consequently, there is a dizzying range of speculations on offer (see, e.g., Baars 1988, Carruthers 2005, Dehaene and Naccache 2001, Dennett 1991, Gennaro 2012, Llinas 2003, Lycan 1996, Prinz 2012, Rosenthal 2005, and Tononi 2004, to cite just a few). But despite their superficial differences, most of these process theories represent variations on the same theme. They assume that consciousness-making is a process in which cognitive subjects *access* the contents of (a subset of) their own representing vehicles.

The idea of conceptualizing consciousness in terms of an access relation between subjects—"selves"—and their own mental states has a long and venerable history in philosophy. The general motivation behind this idea is the widely held assumption that conscious experiences don't just occur *tout court*, but always occur *to someone*:

Conscious experiences do not float around unattached to selves. A conscious experience is always the experience of some self S. An event with representational content or raw feel (if there is such a thing) can exist within S without being one of S's conscious experiences, for example, a representation of stomach acidity used in digestive functioning or a representation of edges used in visual processing. For S to experience E consciously, S (and not just some subsystem of S) must consciously access the relevant feel or content. So ... [a] substantive theory of consciousness necessarily involves a theory of what constitutes a self and of what constitutes access to that self. (Harman 1995, 257)

When philosophers think about the process by which subjects might access their own mental states, they are drawn to the idea of *metarepresentation*: subjects become aware of the representational contents of their own internal states by representing them. This idea yields the various *higher-order representation* theories of consciousness that are currently popular in philosophy (see, e.g., Carruthers 2005, Gennaro 2012, Lycan 1996, Rosenthal 2005). Cognitive scientists, by contrast, tend to unpack the cognitive subject in terms of executive functions such as attention, working memory, and cognitive control. When they come to put flesh on the idea of consciousness-making as a process by which subjects access their own representing vehicles, they typically focus on the role of these executive mechanisms in making information globally available to direct ongoing cognition and behavior. This leads to various *global workspace* and *information integration* theories of consciousness (see, e.g., Baars 1988, Dehaene and Naccache 2001, Llinas 2003, Tononi 2004).

Dennett is well-known for complaining that what he calls *Cartesian materialism*—the idea that consciousness is the transduction of information into a special neural medium—is "the most tenacious bad idea bedevilling our attempts to think about consciousness" (1991, 108). We disagree.[2] To put our cards on the table at the outset, we think this honor should go to the treatment of consciousness as an access relation between cognitive subjects and their own mental states. This is a bad idea because it models all consciousness on one rarefied form of cognition—*self*-consciousness—and thus flies in the face of good evidence for rudimentary forms of phenomenal consciousness in organisms that lack the requisite executive mechanisms or metacognitive abilities (Griffin 2001, Griffin and Speck 2004).[3] And it is a tenacious bad idea with such a tight grip on the imagination of philosophers and scientists that it has stymied the exploration of alternative ways of thinking about consciousness.

In previous work, we have taken the road less traveled and defended a vehicle theory of consciousness. (O'Brien and Opie 1998, 1999a, 2001, 2009). Because this theory identifies conscious experiences with the brain's representing vehicles, it takes consciousness to be an *intrinsic* feature of the neural states that constitute these vehicles. In doing so, it eschews the idea that consciousness is to be understood in terms of an access relation between cognitive subjects and their own internal states and offers a way of thinking about consciousness which doesn't rule out the possibility that it is a far more widespread biological phenomenon than countenanced by the currently fashionable process theories.

Our primary purpose in this chapter is to extend our defense of this vehicle theory. It is split into two parts. In the first (section 2), we provide an overview of a computational approach to cognition that, remarkably, makes it feasible to identify conscious experience with a special neural medium of representation, yet without denying that the brain engages in a great deal of unconscious information processing. This computational framework provides the foundation for the specific vehicle theory at the core of our project, and we will spend much of section 2 exploring its somewhat counterintuitive implications. In the second (section 3), we turn our attention to schizophrenia, perhaps the most debilitating psychopathology of the human mind. We will argue that the delusions associated with this disease, when understood in light of their neurological origins, provide strong evidence for a vehicle theory. Schizophrenia is rightly regarded as a disorder of the self. But, as such, it is a disorder whose phenomenology is inconsistent with any approach that treats consciousness-making as an access relation between selves and their mental states.

2 The Connectionist Vehicle Theory of Consciousness

Two main factors have given rise to the view that neural representation is insufficient for consciousness and, hence, that a vehicle theory of consciousness is a nonstarter. The first is a large body of research which purports to show that conscious experience is *dissociable* from the construction and processing of representations in the brain, in the sense that the latter can and often does occur in the absence of the former. We have in mind here experimental paradigms such as dichotic listening, visual masking, unconscious thought, and priming in decision making, as well as the investigation of neurological disorders such as blindsight. Such *dissociation studies* appear to rule out a vehicle theory. The second is the influence exerted by the *classical* computational theory of mind—the theory that regards cognition as a species of symbol manipulation in the brain. Quite apart from the dissociation studies, it has been a working assumption of classical cognitive science that the brain is home to a vast number of unconscious symbols. The dissociation studies and classicism thus form a perfect alliance. As we saw in the introductory section, they have so conditioned the theoretical climate it is almost universally agreed that the brain's representing vehicles must be processed in some way for consciousness to emerge.

But recent developments in cognitive science suggest that a reassessment of this situation is in order. On the one hand, a significant number of theorists have been highly critical of the experimental methods employed in the dissociation studies. So critical, in fact, it is reasonable to believe that the dissociability of conscious experience and representation has not yet been adequately demonstrated (see, e.g., Acker 2008, Baumeister et al. 2011, Doyen et al. 2012, Dulany 1996, Holender 1986, Huizenga et al. 2012, Maia and McClelland 2004, O'Brien and Opie 1999a, Overgaard 2011, Pratte and Rouder 2009, Shanks and St. John 1994). For example, in a recent wide-ranging review of the experimental paradigms purported to supply evidence of unconscious information processing in human cognition, Newell and Shanks draw the following conclusion:

Our critical analysis points to a surprising conclusion, that there is little convincing evidence of unconscious influences on decision making in the areas we review, and that, as a consequence, such influences should not be assigned a prominent role in theories of decision making and related behaviours. This conclusion is consistent with the view that conscious thoughts are by far the primary driver of behaviour ... and that unconscious influences—if they exist at all—have limited and narrow effects. (Newell and Shanks 2014, 2)

On the other hand, classicism, as a theory of human cognition, is no longer as dominant in cognitive science as it once was. As everyone knows, it has an important competitor in the form of connectionism (Churchland 1995, O'Reilly and Munakata 2000, O'Reilly et al. 2012, Rumelhart and McClelland 1986, Smolensky 1988). But it is still not widely appreciated that, when we look at these issues from the connectionist perspective, we find the terrain considerably altered. Specifically, connectionism, unlike classicism, can allow for unconscious information processing in the brain without jeopardizing the possibility of identifying conscious experience with some species of neural representing vehicle.

In this section we will provide a brief overview of a connectionist vehicle theory of consciousness and tease out its implications for our understanding of the way the brain makes consciousness. We begin with some reflections on the differences between classicism and connectionism as computational accounts of cognition and their relative prospects for supporting a vehicle theory.

2.1 Classicism versus Connectionism: Vive la différence

What the classical computational theory of mind claims about cognition is a familiar story. Classicism takes the generic computational theory of

mind—the idea that the human brain is a biological information proces-
sor—and adds a more specific account of the representing vehicles and
computational processes it deploys (Chomsky 1980, Fodor 1975, 1987,
Newell 1980, and Pylyshyn 1984). According to classicism, the brain is
a *physical symbol system* (Newell and Simon 1976, 116–117), a structure
with the ability to produce complex symbolic expressions and transform
those expressions in ways that respect their meaning. The transformations
involved are governed by so-called *syntactic rules,* that is, that they are sensitive to the formal (syntactic) structure of the symbols on which they act,
just like the program in a digital computer. Such rules come in two possible forms: they are either primitive operations that are "hardwired" into
the brain as a result of normal development, or they are operations that
are explicitly represented in symbols. The distinction here is akin to the
distinction between the rules written on the tape of a Turing machine and
those that are implicit in the behavior of its read/write head. Human cognition is thus conceived by classicists as the rule-governed manipulation of
neurally realized symbols, with the caveat that at least some of those rules
are themselves encoded in symbolic form.

The tenets and implications of the connectionist computational theory
of mind are not yet as widely appreciated as they deserve to be. Connectionism has been variously portrayed as an antirepresentational approach
to cognition, as a formalization of psychological associationism, as a neural
implementation of symbolic computing, and as a none-too-realistic math-
ematical model of the brain. It is none of these. Unlike classicists, who treat
cognition in formal, medium-independent terms, connectionists adopt a
"bottom-up" approach to investigating the mind. This requires an empirical investigation of neural networks with a view to discovering the kind
of information processing that occurs in biological systems of this kind.
According to connectionism, the brain engages in a highly distributed style
of processing reminiscent of computation in analog computers (O'Brien
and Opie 2011). Human cognition consists in the operation of a large collection of parallel distributed processing (PDP) networks in the brain.[4]

To see how connectionism might inform a vehicle theory of consciousness, let's consider how PDP networks represent and process information.
In the abstract, a PDP network is a group of interconnected processing
units, each of which has an *activation level* that is communicated to the rest
of the network via modifiable, weighted connection lines. These units sum
the weighted activity they receive from other units and generate a new activation level that is some threshold function of both current activation and
current input. PDP networks process information by "relaxing" into a stable

pattern of activation in response to the total input they receive. This process is mediated by the connection weights, which determine how activity is passed from unit to unit.

Representation in a PDP network depends on the plasticity of its connection weights.[5] Any change in these weights alters the way the network reacts to input. Consequently, a PDP network can learn to generate an array of output patterns in response to an array of distinct inputs. These stable patterns of activation constitute a transient form of information coding known as *activation pattern representation*. They are the moment-by-moment response of a network to the flux of inputs that impinge on it. But since each network has a relatively stable capacity to generate distinct activation patterns in response to cueing inputs, a PDP network can also be said to *store* a great deal of information. This form of representation, known as *connection weight representation*, is the basis of long-term memory in connectionist systems. Such long-term storage is *superpositional* in nature, because each connection weight contributes to the generation of many different activation patterns. Consequently, the information stored in a network is not encoded in a physically discrete manner. The one appropriately configured network encodes a large *set* of contents corresponding to the set of activation patterns it is capable of generating.

Connectionism thus presents us with two quite distinct styles of representation: activation pattern representation and connection weight representation. Since stable activation patterns are relatively short-term, causally potent responses to current input, whereas connection weights are the basis of long-term memory, we might seek to identify conscious experiences with stable patterns of activation in neurally realized PDP networks. This is the basis of the connectionist vehicle theory of phenomenal consciousness.

The connectionist vehicle theory of consciousness is the claim that conscious experiences are none other than stable patterns of activation in the PDP networks of the brain. Notice that this identity claim does justice to the common sense distinction between information that is unconsciously stored in the brain (in the synaptic connections between neurons) and information that is part of our moment-by-moment experience. The latter consists in the structures that arise when neural activity temporarily stabilizes as a result of feedback both within and between networks. But what of information that operates unconsciously to shape our thought processes and behavior? We have seen that a network's connection weights are responsible for the manner in which it responds to input (by generating activation pattern representations) and, hence, the manner in which it processes information. This means that the mechanism driving the computational operations of a connectionist network is identical to the mechanism responsible for its long-term storage of information. So there is a strong sense in which it is the information unconsciously stored in a network—the network's long-term memory—that actually governs its computational operations.

Classicists are not in a position to defend a vehicle theory of consciousness. Although classicism has a great deal to say about mental representation, its focus on the purely formal properties of cognition is deliberately noncommittal as to how mental representing vehicles are realized in the brain. This is an advertised strength of classicism, because it is apparently required to guarantee the multiple realizability of cognitive processes (but see Opie and O'Brien forthcoming). However, it is fatal for any vehicle theory that, like ours, adopts a bottom-up, biologically naturalistic approach to consciousness. Putting this issue to one side, let's consider what theoretical resources classicism can provide for framing a vehicle theory of consciousness. A classical vehicle theory of consciousness must embrace the distinction between information represented symbolically and information that is implicit in the primitive operations of the cognitive system. But, as we have explained elsewhere (O'Brien and Opie 1999a), it is implausible for a classicist to delegate the cognitive work of the unconscious exclusively to primitive cognitive operations. Standard explanations of reasoning, for example, posit large networks of manifestly *unconscious* beliefs. On the vehicle theory we are considering, such beliefs must be realized as hardwired transformations among the (conscious) symbolic states. The difficulty with this suggestion is that the only model of how beliefs causally influence cognition available to a classicist involves symbolic representation (see Fodor 1987, 25). So, either there is unconscious, symbolically encoded information, or there are no classical explanations of higher cognition. There seems to be no escape from this dilemma for the classicist.

The upshot of all this is that classicism doesn't have the computational resources to offer a plausible vehicle theory of phenomenal consciousness. Any classicist who seeks a computational theory of consciousness is forced to embrace a process theory. The situation is quite different for a connectionist, who can plausibly regard conscious experiences as islands of stable neural activation in a sea of unconscious activity. The latter takes the form of network relaxation processes that are mediated by the superpositionally encoded information stored therein. Unconscious processes thus generate activation pattern representations, which the connectionist is free to identify with phenomenal experiences, since none is required to account for the unconscious activity itself.

2.2   The Multiplicity of Consciousness

Theorists sometimes construe connectionism as the claim that the brain is a single, integrated network and are therefore tempted to attribute network-level properties to the mind as a whole. But this is surely a mistake. Many lines of evidence suggest that the brain has a highly modular architecture. Connectionism treats it as a *collection* of interconnected, specialized PDP networks, each with its own internal structure and patterns of activity. This implies that from moment to moment, as the brain simultaneously processes parallel streams of input and ongoing internal activity, a large number of stable patterns of activation are generated across the brain.

This feature of connectionism has important implications for the vehicle theory of consciousness. According to that theory, stable patterns of activation are identical to elements of conscious experience. Since many such activation patterns are typically being generated at each instant, the vehicle theory implies that global consciousness is a *multiplicity*: a complex aggregate composed of a large number of relatively independent, coconscious elements. Moreover, it implies that the neurological basis of consciousness is *manifold*, that is, that there are a multitude of consciousness-making sites distributed across the brain.

Quite apart from the supposed evidence for the dissociation of consciousness and representation in the brain, many scientists regard this kind of theory as highly implausible. Kanwisher says this:

[To] appreciate the idea that the mere existence of a representation is not likely to be sufficient for awareness, consider the following thought experiment. Suppose cortical area MT [i.e., V5] was surgically removed from a human brain. Suppose further that its interconnections remained intact, and it was kept functional in a dish for some period of time despite the lack of input and output connections to the rest of the brain. Now suppose that a region within MT was microstimulated [in a fashion] that apparently produces a conscious percept when carried out in an intact animal or person. Surely awareness of motion would not occur for an isolated MT in a dish. (Who would see the motion?!) Thus, common sense suggests that perceptual awareness probably requires not only a strong neural representation in a particular cortical area, but access to that representation by at least some other parts of the system. (Kanwisher 2001, 104–105)

What motivates Kanwisher's objection is the idea that consciousness is a matter of a subject's access to their own mental states. On this conception, conscious experiences don't occur in isolation; they always occur *to someone*. The point, of course, is that the vehicle theory embraces the very idea Kanwisher rejects—that conscious experiences are generated by distinct neural circuits in the brain and, hence, *would* be generated by an isolated

MT in a dish (provided that this isolated circuit is capable of the same patterns of activity it generates when part of a normally functioning brain).[6]

According to Cohen and Dennett, this kind of thought experiment does more than show that the vehicle theory of consciousness is counterintuitive; it demonstrates that any theory of this kind is "inherently unfalsifiable and beyond the scope of science" (2011, 358). Here's their reasoning:

> What does it mean to study consciousness without function. Inevitably, theories motivated by this view will define consciousness in their own way … and say whenever that criterion is met, consciousness must occur. But how do we set this criterion? For example, what reason is there is think that local [activation] is conscious experience? … It cannot be based on subjective reports because these reports are the direct result of cognitive functions. … In the face of such clear grounds for doubting such conscious experiences, [vehicle] theories need to provide a reason for claiming that these isolated types of activation involve any kind of consciousness. It is clear, then, that proper scientific theories of consciousness are those that specify which functions are necessary for consciousness to arise. (Cohen and Dennett 2011, 362)

Cohen and Dennett seem to be making the classic mistake of conflating the behavioral criteria for some phenomenon with the phenomenon itself. The issue that divides vehicle and process theories is precisely whether conscious experiences are *intrinsic* or *relational* properties of the brain's representing vehicles. These vehicles undoubtedly have cognitive effects, including the production of subjective reports, that are a vital source of information about conscious experiences. But unless we deny the very existence of intrinsic properties, we cannot fail to distinguish between the local properties of representing vehicles and their distal effects. A vehicle theory identifies conscious experiences with the intrinsic activity of neural PDP networks, activity that is responsible for certain cognitive effects. In this respect, it poses no more of a methodological problem for science than any other theory that countenances hidden properties and mechanisms.[7]

Nonetheless, Kanwisher's thought experiment does highlight a counterintuitive implication of the connectionist vehicle theory: consciousness is a multiplicity. We would argue that this implication is quite consistent with the available evidence. Consider first the evidence of experience. Even a casual inspection of moment-by-moment consciousness reveals its complexity. As you concentrate on the page before you, your consciousness is simultaneously multimodal and multichanneled: visual experiences (the shape of the text), linguistic experiences (what it means), auditory experiences (background noises), tactile experiences (the chair pressing against your body), and so on, combine in your instantaneous phenomenal field. And when you visually experience these words, the other aspects of your phenomenal field don't drop out: you don't stop having auditory experiences or feeling the chair pressing against your legs. By the same token, the various modes of experience are relatively independent of one another. Total deficits in sight and audition are quite common and are brought on by localized damage that can leave the other modalities more or less intact. Experiences are like so many strands in a woven cloth—each strand adds to the cloth, but, since they run side by side, the loss of any one strand doesn't substantially deform or diminish the others—it merely reduces the total area of fabric.

The full significance of this first-person evidence only emerges when considered in the light of the neuroscience. On the basis of deficit studies, we know that the processes underlying conscious experience occur in many different parts of the cortex. Visual processing, for example, is highly modularized. The visual cortex appears to contain discrete subsystems for processing information about color, shape, depth, and motion. When any one of these subsystems is subject to localized damage, the associated aspect of visual experience drops out, more or less independently of the others. Given that such deficits are so tightly correlated with lesions in particular parts of the visual cortex, the most parsimonious hypothesis is that consciousness is generated locally at these very sites.

Other tantalizing evidence comes from work on timing in vision. When subjects are asked to pair rapidly alternating states of two visual attributes—for example, a bar with two possible orientations and two possible colors—there is a systematic misbinding of attributes relative to their actual time of occurrence (Zeki and Bartels 1998, 1583). It appears that color is perceived before orientation, which in turn is perceived before motion, with a delay in motion perception of 60–80 milliseconds (Bartels and Zeki 1998, 2329). Bartels and Zeki take these findings to demonstrate that "consciousness is not a unitary faculty, but ... consists of many micro-consciousnesses" (2327).

It might be objected that information in one sensory modality sometimes *influences* experiences in another. A nice example is the McGurk effect, in which a subject's auditory experience is partly determined by what they see (McGurk and MacDonald 1976). This looks problematic for a vehicle theory, because vision and audition don't appear to be genuinely independent. But the vehicle theory is only committed to the claim that the components of experience are generated locally at the very sites where their contents are fixed. This doesn't imply that distinct content-fixations must be completely unaffected by one another. We know that there are typically a multitude of signals crisscrossing the brain, such that conscious contents not only co-occur, but mutually shape each other. Such influences are perfectly consistent with the vehicle theory, so long as the consciousness-making mechanisms themselves are manifold and localized.

The neuroscientific evidence confirms that consciousness is a complex of relatively independent parts, and it suggests a natural way of interpreting the distributed nature of neural information processing: as a sign that the mind incorporates multiple consciousness-making mechanisms. The connectionist vehicle theory of consciousness makes sense of this. Conscious experience has a highly differentiated synchronic structure precisely because it consists of a multitude of distinct activation pattern representations generated across the brain.

2.3 Multiplicity and Unity

Despite the support for the connectionist vehicle theory we've just rehearsed, this account will still strike many as preposterous, given that, prima facie, it is at odds with the conventional wisdom concerning the *unity of consciousness*. Intuitions about the unity of consciousness have been central to the development of global workspace theories of consciousness. Since a global workspace is normally conceived as a functional bottleneck through which information must pass in order to become conscious, the unity of consciousness can be explained by the existence of this *single* consciousness-making system in the brain (Baars 1988, Dehaene and Naccache 2001). The connectionist vehicle theory, in contrast, holds that the neural basis of consciousness is both manifold and distributed. It treats consciousness as a system of phenomenal elements, each of which is generated at a different site in the cortex. On this account, global consciousness is not *one* thing at each instant, but *many* things (O'Brien and Opie 1998).

It is pertinent at this point, however, to note an ambiguity in the notion of unity employed in both philosophy and cognitive science. To say that consciousness is unified is sometimes to claim that it is literally a single entity, or the product of a single consciousness-making mechanism. But the unity of consciousness is also construed in terms of the *representational coherence* of its contents. For example, Bernard Baars, one of the foremost proponents of global workspace theory, is at pains to highlight what he thinks is the tight focus of instantaneous consciousness in just one dense stream of input. But he also claims that contents fixed in the brain's specialized circuits only gain access to the global workspace when they form *internally consistent* coalitions that out-compete alternative interpretations of the stimuli impinging on our sensory surfaces (Baars 1997).

This second kind of unity is manifest in the consonance of representational contents *between* modalities and in the binding of phenomenal elements *within* modalities. Quotidian experience sometimes provides only one source of information regarding external objects: we hear the bird, but we don't see it, we see the ball (on the roof), but we don't feel it. In these cases, we don't expect our various modes of experience to be in complete accord; their objects, being distinct, have no obligation to be in temporal or spatial register. However, we often have access to a single object via two or more senses. When it comes to our own bodies, in particular, we are information rich. As one types on a keyboard, the sound of one's fingers striking the keys is in synchrony with both the visual and tactile experiences of these events; the location of these same key-strikes, as revealed in visual experience, is compatible with their position in auditory space, and one's proprioceptive and visual experiences of hand position are in accord. Intermodal coherence is pervasive when our senses report on common events or objects. Within modalities, we also discover a great deal of harmony. Vision, for example, provides us with information about color, shape, depth, and motion. But this information is not free-floating; it comes bound together in coherent phenomenal objects whose visual properties covary in a consistent fashion.

The connectionist vehicle theory is not at odds with this kind of unity. For a start, it is not implausible to suppose that when phenomenal contents coincide *temporally*, either within or across modalities, this is entirely due to the simultaneity of their vehicles (see, e.g., Edelman 1989). So when a felt key-strike is temporally aligned with its seen counterpart, this might be explained in terms of a brain architecture that generates simultaneous vehicles in those two modalities. It's reasonable to believe that evolutionary pressures have conspired to wire the brain in this way, given the tight temporal constraints that attend useful interaction with our local environment. Clearly, however, simultaneity of vehicles is not going to have much bearing on *spatial* coherence. When we seek to explain this form of coherence we must contend with what Akins calls the "Spatial Binding Problem," namely, "given that the visual system processes different properties of the stimulus at spatially distinct sites, how is it possible that we perceive the world in the spatially coherent manner that we do?" (1996, 30). However, so long as the contributing sensory systems represent their common object as located in the one place, then the experience of object location ought to be both intermodally and intramodally coherent. In particular, the only intramodal binding we can reasonably expect is a binding at the level of contents. For the various properties of, say, a visual object to be experienced as unified, the visual system need only represent them as occurring in a common region of space. To deal with multiple, co-occurring objects, we need only posit a number of such "content-bindings" realized by multiple, simultaneous representing vehicles.

So it is possible to regard instantaneous consciousness as a multiplicity, as entailed by the connectionist vehicle theory, yet still hold that it is unified. The sense in which consciousness is unified is a not a matter of "oneness," but of representational coherence. It is important to note, however, that representational coherence is not an invariable feature of global consciousness—it is a hard-won computational achievement, as demonstrated by those cases in which the brain fails to construct an integrated model of the world. It is precisely this kind of representational incoherence that is most dramatically on display in schizophrenia. This is the appropriate moment, therefore, to turn to the second part of our defense of the connectionist vehicle of consciousness.

3   The Fragmentation of the Self in Schizophrenia

Schizophrenia is a complex and heterogeneous disease, incorporating at least three distinct subsyndromes: *psycho-motor poverty* (poverty of speech, lack of spontaneous movement, blunting of affect), *disorganization* (inappropriate affect, disturbances of the form of thought), and *reality distortion* (Liddle 1987, Johnstone 1991). The reality distortion syndrome encompasses the so-called positive or psychotic symptoms of schizophrenia, which include (principally auditory) hallucinations and delusions. The leading hypothesis about the cause of the disease is that it results from a communication breakdown between a number of brain regions, especially frontal and cingulate cortices, that implement the executive functions of information integration, attention, working memory, and cognitive control (Andreasen 1997, Barch 2005, Bob and Mashour 2011). Given its symptoms and conjectured neural basis, it is not surprising that the working assumption of most current research in this area is that schizophrenia constitutes a *fragmentation of the self.*

Schizophrenia thus offers a unique window on the operation of the brain. It affords an opportunity to explore the complex relationship between the neural basis of consciousness and the executive functions of the brain and, so, to pitch process theories of consciousness against their connectionist rival. Our contention, in what follows, is that the vehicle theory is the clear winner in this contest. Process theories, precisely because they conceptualize consciousness in terms of an access relation between cognitive subjects and their mental states, render the aberrant phenomenology of schizophrenia inconsistent with the neurological causes of this disease. It simply isn't possible for the self to fragment and yet remain the source of consciousness-making in the brain. Consequently, just as the vehicle theory suggests, the neural basis of consciousness must be independent of the brain's executive systems and, more generally, of the cognitive subject.

3.1 Troubles for Process Theories of Schizophrenic Consciousness

On the face of it, process theories of consciousness have recourse to an attractive way of explaining the strange phenomenology of schizophrenia. Since normal consciousness-making is a process whereby perceptual and cognitive contents are brought together by executive mechanisms to form a unified representation of the world, it would seem that the disordered experiences commonly found in schizophrenia are the result of informational *disintegration*:

[Schizophrenia] may result in part from a disturbance of conscious integration and of its underlying neural substrates. By conscious integration we mean the generation of a coherent neural process that underlies the unity of perception and cognition. Several lines of evidence suggest that, in the normal human brain, a single, coherent neural process is generated through ongoing re-entrant interactions among widely distributed brain areas. ... On these bases, it is worth considering the possibility that several symptoms of schizophrenia may derive not so much from a malfunctioning of a particular brain area, but from a malfunctioning of the re-entrant interactions that are responsible for the functional integration of the activities of the distributed brain areas that give rise to conscious experience. (Tononi and Edelman 2000, 392)

But this is a case where first appearances are highly misleading. The allure of this explanation comes at the price of conflating two distinct conjectures: (i) that the aberrant phenomenology of schizophrenia stems from a malfunction in the mechanisms responsible for integrating information in the brain, and (ii) that consciousness is the product of such mechanisms.

The first of these conjectures is indeed plausible. Consider, for example, the bizarre delusion of *thought insertion*, in which people come to believe that some of the thoughts they experience are not their own:

I look out the window and I think that the garden looks nice and the grass looks cool, but the thoughts of Eammon Andrews come into my mind. ... He treats my mind like a screen and flashes his thoughts onto it like you flash a picture. (Mellors 1970, 17)

This person accepts that the "thoughts of Eammon Andrews" occur in their *own* mind, even if imposed from outside. Although the precise explanation of this delusion is the subject of an intense debate (cf., for example, Frith 1992 with Martin and Pacherie 2013), the consensus is that it is caused by inconsistencies among representational contents as they are fixed in the schizophrenic brain. This failure of integration leads the sufferer to judge some contents as alien intrusions and disown them. Furthermore, it appears to be the result of a desynchronization of neural oscillations among frontal brain regions that implement the various executive functions (Ford et al. 2008, Lee et al. 2003, Park and Thakkar 2010, Uhlhaas et al. 2008).

However, the evidence in favor of this first conjecture need not support the claim that the mechanisms that integrate information in the brain are also in the consciousness-making business. If anything, it points in the opposite direction. For if consciousness-making is dependent on mechanisms that act to integrate information, one would expect their malfunction to cause a general *diminution* in consciousness, rather than the *aberrant* forms of experience that occur in schizophrenia. The fact that their breakdown produces disordered forms of consciousness suggests that such mechanisms are actually responsible for rendering consciousness *representationally coherent* rather than for consciousness-making per se. Information integration is not the material basis of consciousness. It is merely a process by which conscious contents are kept in line with one another.

This suggestion is bolstered by a number of additional findings from the science of schizophrenia. First, there is the well-documented fact that the phenomenology of psychosis, far from manifesting diminution, is marked by *amplification* and *proliferation*. Schizophrenics are burdened with hallucinations, delusions, and other forms of reality distortion (Liddle 1987, Johnstone 1991), which they find frightening and overwhelming. There is too much happening rather than too little. In this sense, schizophrenia is better understood as a *surfeit* of consciousness, rather than its opposite.

Second, the neuroimaging studies of schizophrenics consistently reveal *hypoactivation* of the frontal brain regions implicated in attention, working memory, and cognitive control (Diederen et al. 2010, Park and Thakkar 2010, Satterthwaite et al. 2010). This reduced activity may well be a consequence of the communication breakdowns in the brain that are thought to cause schizophrenia (Uhlhaas et al. 2008, Womelsdorf and Fries 2007). This finding is difficult to reconcile with the claim that executive functions are responsible for consciousness-making. On that hypothesis, one would expect hypoactivation of the frontal cortex to produce a significant reduction in phenomenology, not a proliferation and amplification.

Third, there is the long-standing conjecture that the executive systems in the frontal cortex regulate content-fixation elsewhere in the brain via a process of *inhibition* (Courtney 2004, Miller and Cohen 2001). When coupled with the evidence for frontal hypoactivation and the disordered and intense phenomenology of schizophrenia, a picture of psychosis emerges as consciousness-making that has spun out of control. Crucially, this is *not* because the executive systems are the fundamental source of conscious experience. Rather, it is because such systems play a key role in regulating the *contents* of consciousness. When they fail, consciousness-making around the brain becomes uncoordinated, resulting in florid and exaggerated experiences whose contents are disconnected from one another.

Finally, many theorists have pointed to the significant overlap between the phenomenology of psychosis, on the one hand, and the bizarre experiences induced by psychedelic drugs and dream states, on the other (Hobson, 1999). What is significant, for our purposes, is that the latter appear to issue from the same neurological mechanism responsible for schizophrenic psychosis: hypoactivation of the brain regions associated with the executive functions of cognition (Carhart-Harris et al. 2014, Limosani et al. 2011, Maquet et al. 1996). We are all familiar with the chaotic, sometimes baroque phenomenology of dreaming. What isn't so well known is that people undergoing psychedelic experiences commonly describe them in terms of a general *amplification* of their phenomenology:

It seemed to me that what I had experienced was essentially, and with few exceptions, the usual content of experience but that, of everything, there was *more*. … Looking at a thing one sees *more* of its color, *more* of its detail, *more* of its form. Touching a thing, one touches *more*. Hearing a sound, one hears *more*. Tasting, one tastes *more*. Moving, one is *more* aware of movement. Smelling, one smells *more*. The mind is able to contain, at any given moment, *more*. … Awareness has *more* levels, is many-dimensioned. Awareness is of *more* shades of meaning contained in words and ideas. (Masters and Houston 1966, 11, quoting a subject's account of a mescaline-induced trip)

Accounts of this kind, coupled with the evidence for hypoactivation of the prefrontal cortex in psychedelic states, lead Carhart-Harris and colleagues to speculate that this region of the brain may act to maintain global consciousness in a subcritical state. This state of "secondary consciousness," as they call it, allows for various forms of self-directed cognition and metacognition, and it permits more flexible cognitive control over behavior. But when, under the influence of psychedelic agents, the action of the prefrontal executive systems is curbed, the brain enters a high entropy state of "primary consciousness" characterized by a proliferation of very intense conscious experiences (Carhart-Harris et al. 2014).[8]

The findings we've considered raise a serious problem for process theories that explain consciousness in terms of information integration and cognitive access. On that account, hypoactivation of the prefrontal cortex, together with the coordination failures that inexorably follow, ought to produce a significant attenuation of moment-by-moment consciousness. But all the evidence points in the opposite direction. Unconstrained by the inhibiting and controlling influences of the executive systems, consciousness proliferates, intensifies, and becomes increasingly disjointed.

Hughlings Jackson famously speculated about the role of the frontal cortex and the consequences of damage to this vital brain region:

> The higher nervous arrangements evolved out of the lower to keep down those lower, just as a government evolved out of a nation controls, as well as directs, that nation. If this be the process of evolution, then the reverse process of dissolution is not only "a taking off" of the higher, but is at the very same time a "letting go" of the lower. If the governing body of this country were destroyed suddenly, we should have two causes for lamentation: (1) the loss of services of eminent men, and (2) the anarchy of the now uncontrolled people. (Jackson 1958, 11)

Process theories explain consciousness in terms of the services of eminent men. The aberrant phenomenology of schizophrenia demonstrates that consciousness is actually the preserve of the people.

3.2   The Vehicle Theory and the Disunity of the Schizophrenic Subject

Schizophrenia is a puzzle for process theories of consciousness, but it is grist to the mill of the connectionist vehicle theory. According to that theory, consciousness is generated in a multitude of distinct neural circuits located in many parts of the brain. These circuits are coupled to the frontal cortex, which supports executive systems such as attention, working memory, and cognitive control. Given the role of the executive systems in regulating and coordinating activity elsewhere in the brain, and the likelihood that schizophrenia is caused by hypoactivation of those systems, one would therefore expect precisely the kind of disordered and exaggerated phenomenology seen in psychosis.

Viewed from the perspective of the connectionist vehicle theory, schizophrenia is not a disease of consciousness-making. At its core, it is a disorder of the neural systems responsible for maintaining the coherence of moment-by-moment consciousness. But this suggests something quite radical. If conscious experiences can be produced even when the cognitive subject has begun to disintegrate, then selves and their experiences don't come as a package deal. The conscious self is a hard-won, somewhat fragile computational achievement. It is a cloth woven from many threads, each fiber distinct, yet conformable to the others in the manufacture of something new. What schizophrenia reveals is that the self is an emergent system composed of many subpersonal phenomenal elements; not the pre-condition for consciousness-making, but one of its possible products.

In section 2.3, we discussed a couple of senses in which consciousness might be unified. It might be the product of a single consciousness-making mechanism, as conjectured in global workspace theories. This kind of unity is mandatory, in that disunity is equivalent to unconsciousness. Alternatively, consciousness might manifest a unity in its contents, such that the various modes and elements of experience sensibly hang together. When the brain is functioning normally, that is undoubtedly how things go. We find ourselves in a world of coherent objects, arrayed in space and time in a consistent and principled manner. But of course *we* are objects too: we have minds and bodies, and just as we conceptualize and experience the external world, so also we experience and seek to understand our internal milieu. That part of the phenomenal field we regard as *us* divides quite naturally into experiences of our bodies, and experiences of thoughts, emotions, and other mental phenomena. But beyond all that, seemingly at the core of experience, we have a sense of ourselves as *unified subjects of experience*. This form of unity subtends the *perceiver* rather than the *perceived*. What is the source of this feeling of subject unity?

Consider sensory experience. One of the salient features of the senses is their *perspectival* character: each modality encompasses a space with a privileged locus, a point with respect to which its contents are "projected." According to the connectionist vehicle theory, this locus arises independently in each modality. But so long as the various sensory systems represent their contents as located with respect to the same projective locus—a form of representational coherence—the confluence of these points of view will have the effect of producing a single perceptual subject located at a particular point in space.

Among the senses, the proprioceptive, somesthetic, and vestibular systems play a special role in producing a feeling of embodiment. Most of us are not particularly aware of this feeling, but life without it is extremely difficult. Oliver Sacks describes the tragic case of a woman who suffered acute polyneuritis of the spinal and cranial nerves and subsequently lost all proprioceptive sensations. "Something awful's happened," she tells Sacks, "I can't feel my body. I feel weird—disembodied" (1985, 44). In the complete absence of proprioceptive feedback, this woman recognizes, perhaps for the first time, the feeling of embodiment she once had, but has now lost. Experiences of embodiment are another source of subject unity. But again, our sense of being a single, embodied subject is primarily down to the coherence of the contents fixed by the somatosensory systems. Disruptions of this coherence produce disorders of embodiment with well-documented impacts on the sense of self (see, e.g., Giummarra et al. 2008).

Quite apart from these sensory forms of subject unity, most of us have the capacity to distinguish self-initiated thoughts and actions from mental and behavioral events not of our making. This capacity is associated with experiences of *agency* and our sense of being a unified entity causally responsible for thoughts, imaginings, and behavior. That this sense of agency is distinct from the other forms of subject unity described so far is demonstrated by the fact that it can be selectively impaired (see, e.g., Graham and Stephens 1994). This is exactly what seems to be occurring in the delusion of thought insertion. As we saw, sufferers have no doubt that the rogue thoughts they experience occur in their own minds, and to this extent their basic sense of subject unity is intact. But the representational discontinuity of these thoughts from the contents of other representing vehicles leads them to be regarded as intruders. A unified, agentive self is one of the significant casualties of schizophrenia.

Finally, consider our ongoing personal narrative, the story we tell about ourselves, and to ourselves, practically every waking moment. This stream of self-directed thought gives rise to a uniquely human kind of subject unity—one that Dennett has famously dubbed "the self as a center of narrative gravity" (1991, 1992). Whether we regard the narrative self as real or merely a useful abstraction, its unity depends on the representational coherence of a multitude of linguiform representing vehicles. This kind of unity is also a casualty of schizophrenia. A compelling explanation for the auditory hallucinations experienced by some schizophrenics is impairment to the sense of agency associated with their self-narrative, such that the latter is experienced as emanating from outside the mind (Diederen et al. 2010, Frith 1992, 2012).

4 Conclusion

Let us finish by pulling together the various threads of *our* narrative. Our task in this chapter has been to take the road less traveled and defend a *vehicle* theory of consciousness. The attraction of such theories is their simplicity: since they identify conscious experiences with the brain's representing vehicles, they hold that consciousness just is the brain's representational medium. Despite this virtue, vehicle theories are unfashionable in contemporary philosophy and cognitive science because of the widespread assumption that neural representation is insufficient for consciousness—something has to happen to the brain's representing vehicles, according to most theorists, in order for their contents to be rendered conscious. And it is this assumption that leads to the *process* theories of consciousness that dominate the literature.

Our defense of a vehicle theory has been divided in two parts. In the first, we argued that the widely held assumption that neural representation is insufficient for consciousness is largely the result of classical conditioning—of the influence, that is, of the classical computational theory of mind on how theorists think about the format of representation in the brain. It is certainly true that classicism doesn't have the representational resources to support a vehicle theory of consciousness. But connectionism, we argued at some length, does. At this juncture, therefore, our vehicle theory took on a distinctively connectionist hue: conscious experiences, we proposed, are identical with stable patters of activation in neural-realized PDP networks. We then spent a little time investigating some of the initially counterintuitive, but ultimately empirically defensible, implications of this proposal—most strikingly, that our global consciousness at each instant, far from being a unity, is a *multiplicity* (a complex aggregate composed of a large number of relatively independent, coconscious elements) and that the neurological basis of consciousness is *manifold* (there are a multitude of consciousness-making sites distributed across the brain).

In the second part of our defense, we used schizophrenia as a battleground on which to pitch process theories of consciousness against our connectionist rival. Process theorists portray consciousness as posterior to, and indissolubly bound up with, the cognitive subject. Phenomenal properties and states can only exist when a coordinating, organizing, remembering, self-reporting subject is at hand. From this perspective, the fragmentation of the brain's executive functions inevitably fragments and dissolves consciousness. But schizophrenia, we argued, teaches us to think differently about the relationship between consciousness and the self. Conscious experience doesn't dissolve in the face of damage to the cognitive subject; it becomes more complex and more intense. That is, schizophrenia is a disease of *self*-making, not *consciousness*-making. This is just what one would expect on our connectionist vehicle theory. Consciousness is the product of multiple, interdependent mechanisms, a system of subpersonal phenomenal elements, whose unity, such as it is, represents a significant computational achievement, rather than the touchstone of experience. Those elements, in turn, are none other than a set of transient representing vehicles that encapsulate the brain's current take on its environment and itself.

Notes

1. If a slew of recent popular books can be trusted, the cognitive unconscious is a powerful, intelligent, and adaptive information-processing system that automatically and reflexively enables us to respond rapidly to current task demands and, in so doing, is responsible for our successful survival in the world (Gigerenzer 2007, Gladwell 2005, Kahneman 2011, Lehrer 2009, Wilson 2002). The focus on unconscious information processing has become so great in certain quarters that Eagleman, in another recent popular book, crows about the "dethronement" of consciousness:

> The conscious you—the *I* that flickers to life when you wake in the morning—is the smallest bit of what's transpiring in your brain. … Your consciousness is like a tiny stowaway on a transatlantic steamship. … Over the past century, neuroscience has shown that the conscious mind is not the one driving the boat. A mere four hundred years after our fall from the center of the universe, we have experienced the fall from the center of ourselves. (Eagleman 2011, 4, 193)

2. Indeed, not only is Cartesian materialism not the most tenacious bad idea bedeviling our attempts to think about consciousness, it is not even a bad idea (see O'Brien and Opie 1999b).

3. To be fair, many of the proponents of this way of treating consciousness are aware of the difficulties it creates for explaining animal consciousness and have attempted various kinds of responses. For a representative example, see Gennaro 2012, chapter 8.

4. In this context, we regard PDP networks as idealized models of real neural networks, which aim to capture their most computationally salient properties (see, e.g., Churchland and Sejnowski 1992, chapter 3, O'Brien 1998, and Opie 1998).

5. For good general introductions to the representational properties of connectionist systems, see Bechtel and Abrahamsen 2002, chapter 2, Churchland 1995, Churchland and Sejnowski 1992, chapter 4, and Rumelhart and McClelland 1986, chapters 1–3.

6. It seems clear, for example, that cortical regions such as MT require more than sensory inputs to function normally. A number of theorists point to the role of the reticular formation in switching on these cortical regions, so that their activity is consistent with their information-processing functions. The evidence for this is that most anesthetics disable the connections between the reticular formation and the cortex that implement this switch (Alkire and Miller 2005, Zeki 2001). This is important because, from the perspective of the connectionist vehicle theory, mere activity in specialized cortical circuits is insufficient for conscious experience. Such circuits must be capable of settling into stable patterns of activity. We conjecture that anesthetics work by disabling the conditions under which such stable patterns can form.

7. We have in mind theories of the very small, such as atomic physics, and the very large, such as cosmology.

8. We are indebted to Chris Letheby for drawing our attention to the relevance of the neuroscientific literature on psychedelic experience to the current project.

References

Acker, F. 2008. New findings on unconscious versus conscious thought in decision making: Additional empirical data and meta-analysis. *Judgment and Decision Making* 3:292–303.

Akins, K. 1996. Lost the plot? Reconstructing Dennett's multiple drafts theory of consciousness. *Mind and Language* 11:1–43.

Alkire, M., and J. Miller. 2005. General anesthesia and the neural correlates of consciousness. *Progress in Brain Research* 150:229–244.

Andreasen, N. 1997. Linking mind and brain in the study of mental illnesses: A project for a scientific psychopathology. *Science* 275:1586–1593.

Baars, B. 1988. *A Cognitive Theory of Consciousness*. Cambridge: Cambridge University Press.

Baars, B. 1997. In the theatre of consciousness: Global workspace theory, a rigorous scientific theory of consciousness. *Journal of Consciousness Studies* 4:292–309.

Barch, D. 2005. The cognitive neuroscience of schizophrenia. *Annual Review of Clinical Psychology* 1:321–353.

Bartels, A., and S. Zeki. 1998. The theory of multi-stage integration in the visual brain. *Proceedings of the Royal Society of London, Series B: Biological Sciences* 265: 2327–2332.

Baumeister, R., E. Masicampo, and K. Vohs. 2011. Do conscious thoughts cause behavior? *Annual Review of Psychology* 62:331–361.

Bechtel, W., and A. Abrahamsen. 2002. *Connectionism and the Mind: Parallel Processing, Dynamics, and Evolution in Networks*. Malden, MA: Wiley-Blackwell.

Bob, P., and G. Mashour. 2011. Schizophrenia, dissociation, and consciousness. *Consciousness and Cognition* 20:1042–1049.

Carhart-Harris, R., R. Leech, P. Hellyer, M. Shanahan, A. Feilding, E. Tagliazucchi, D. Chialvo, and D. Nutt. 2014. The entropic brain: A theory of conscious states informed by neuroimaging research with psychedelic drugs. *Frontiers in Human Neuroscience*. doi:10.3389/fnhum.2014.00020.

Carruthers, P. 2005. *Consciousness: Essays from a Higher-Order Perspective*. Oxford: Oxford University Press.

Carruthers, P. 2011. Higher-order theories of consciousness. In *The Stanford Encyclopedia of Philosophy*, ed. E. Zalta. http://plato.stanford.edu/archives/fall2011/entries/consciousness-higher/.

Chomsky, N. 1980. Rules and representations. *Behavioral and Brain Sciences* 3:1–62.

Churchland, P. M. 1995. *The Engine of Reason, the Seat of the Soul: A Philosophical Journey into the Brain.* Cambridge, MA: MIT Press.

Churchland, P. S., and T. Sejnowski. 1992. *The Computational Brain.* Cambridge, MA: MIT Press.

Cohen, A., and D. Dennett. 2011. Consciousness cannot be separated from function. *Trends in Cognitive Sciences* 15:358–364.

Courtney, S. 2004. Attention and cognitive control as emergent properties of information representation in working memory. *Cognitive, Affective, and Behavioral Neuroscience* 4:501–516.

Dehaene, S., and L. Naccache. 2001. Towards a cognitive neuroscience of consciousness: Basic evidence and a workspace framework. *Cognition* 79:1–37.

Dennett, D. 1984. Cognitive wheels: The frame problem of AI. In *Minds, Machines, and Evolution,* ed. C. Hookway. Cambridge: Cambridge University Press.

Dennett, D. 1991. *Consciousness Explained.* Boston: Little, Brown.

Dennett, D. 1992. The self as a center of narrative gravity. In *Self and Consciousness: Multiple Perspectives,* ed. F. Kessel, P. Cole, and D. Johnson. Hillsdale, NJ: Erlbaum.

Diederen, K., S. Neggers, K. Daalman, J. Blom, R. Goekoop, R. Kahn, et al. 2010. Deactivation of the parahippocampal gyrus preceding auditory hallucinations in schizophrenia. *American Journal of Psychiatry* 16:427–435.

Doyen, S., O. Klein, C.-L. Pichon, and A. Cleeremans. 2012. Behavioral priming: It's all in the mind, but whose mind? *PLoS ONE* 7:e29081.

Dulany, D. 1996. Consciousness in the explicit (deliberative) and implicit (evocative). In *Scientific Approaches to Consciousness,* ed. J. Cohen and J. Schooler. Hillsdale, NJ: Erlbaum.

Eagleman, D. 2011. *Incognito: The Secret Lives of the Brain.* New York: Pantheon.

Edelman, G. 1989. *The Remembered Present: A Biological Theory of Consciousness.* New York: Basic Books.

Fodor, J. 1975. *The Language of Thought.* Cambridge, MA: MIT Press.

Fodor, J. 1983. *The Modularity of Mind.* Cambridge, MA: MIT Press.

Fodor, J. 1987. *Psychosemantics.* Cambridge, MA: MIT Press.

Ford, J., B. Roach, W. Faustman, and D. Mathalon. 2008. Out-of-synch and out-of-sorts: Dysfunction of motor-sensory communication in schizophrenia. *Biological Psychiatry* 63:736–743.

Frith, C. 1992. *The Cognitive Neuropsychology of Schizophrenia*. Hillsdale, NJ: Erlbaum.

Frith, C. 2012. Explaining delusions of control: The comparator model 20 years on. *Consciousness and Cognition* 21:52–54.

Gennaro, R. 2012. *The Consciousness Paradox: Consciousness, Concepts, and Higher-Order Thoughts*. Cambridge, MA: MIT Press.

Gigerenzer, G. 2007. *Gut Feelings: The Intelligence of the Unconscious*. New York: Viking Press.

Giummarra, M., S. Gibson, N. Georgiou-Karistianisa, and J. Bradshaw. 2008. Mechanisms underlying embodiment, disembodiment, and loss of embodiment. *Neuroscience and Biobehavioral Reviews* 32:143–160.

Gladwell, M. 2005. *Blink: The Power of Thinking without Thinking*. New York: Penguin.

Graham, G., and G. L. Stephens. 1994. Mind and mine. In *Philosophical Psychopathology*, ed. G. Graham and G. L. Stephens. Cambridge, MA: MIT Press.

Griffin, D. 2001. *Animal Minds: Beyond Cognition to Consciousness*. Chicago: University of Chicago Press.

Griffin, D., and G. Speck. 2004. New evidence of animal consciousness. *Animal Cognition* 7:5–18.

Harman, G. 1995. Phenomenal fallacies and conflations. *Behavioral and Brain Sciences* 18:256–257.

Hobson, A. 1999. *Dreaming as Delirium: How the Brain Goes Out of Its Mind*. Cambridge, MA: MIT Press.

Holender, D. 1986. Semantic activation without conscious awareness in dichotic listening, parafoveal vision, and visual masking: A survey and appraisal. *Behavioral and Brain Sciences* 9:1–66.

Huizenga, H., R. Wetzels, D. Van Ravenzwaaij, and E. Wagenmakers. 2012. Four empirical tests of unconscious thought theory. *Organizational Behavior and Human Decision Processes* 117:332–340.

Jackson, H. 1958. *Selected Writings of Hughlings Jackson*. New York: Basic Books.

Johnstone, E. 1991. Defining characteristics of schizophrenia. *British Journal of Psychiatry. Supplement* 13:5–6.

Kahneman, D. 2011. *Thinking: Fast and Slow*. London: Allen Lane.

Kahneman, D., and A. Tversky. 1974. Judgements under uncertainty: Heuristics and biases. *Science* 185:1124–1131.

Kanwisher, N. 2001. Neural events and perceptual awareness. *Cognition* 79:89–113.

Kihlstrom, J. 1987. The cognitive unconscious. *Science* 237:1445–1452.

Lee, K., L. Williams, M. Breakspear, and E. Gordon. 2003. Synchronous gamma activity: A review and contribution to an integrative neuroscience model of schizophrenia. *Brain Research Reviews* 41:57–78.

Lehrer, J. 2009. *The Decisive Moment: How the Brain Makes Up Its Mind.* London: Canongate Books.

Liddle, P. 1987. The symptoms of chronic schizophrenia: A re-examination of the positive-negative dichotomy. *British Journal of Psychiatry* 151:145–151.

Limosani, I., A. D'Agostino, M. Manzone, and S. Scarone. 2011. The dreaming brain/mind, consciousness, and psychosis. *Consciousness and Cognition* 20:987–992.

Llinas, R. 2003. Consciousness and the thalamocortical loop. *International Congress Series* 1250:409–416.

Lycan, W. 1996. *Consciousness and Experience.* Cambridge, MA: MIT Press.

Maia, T., and A. Cleeremans. 2005. Consciousness: Converging insights from connectionist modelling and neuroscience. *Trends in Cognitive Sciences* 9:397–404.

Maia, T., and J. McClelland. 2004. A re-examination of the evidence for the somatic marker hypothesis: What participants really know in the Iowa Gambling Task. *Proceedings of the National Academy of Sciences of the United States of America* 102: 16075–16080.

Maquet, P., J.-M. Peters, J. Aerts, G. Delfiore, C. Degueldre, A. Luxen, et al. 1996. Functional neuroanatomy of human rapid-eye-movement sleep and dreaming. *Nature* 383:163–166.

Martin, J.-R., and E. Pacherie. 2013. Out of nowhere: Thought insertion, ownership, and context-integration. *Consciousness and Cognition* 22:111–122.

Masters, R., and J. Houston. 1966. *The Varieties of Psychedelic Experience.* New York: Holt, Rinehart & Winston.

McGurk, H., and J. MacDonald. 1976. Hearing lips and seeing voices. *Nature* 264: 746–748.

Mellors, C. 1970. First-rank symptoms of schizophrenia. *British Journal of Psychiatry* 117:15–23.

Miller, E., and J. Cohen. 2001. An integrative theory prefrontal cortex function. *Annual Review of Neuroscience* 24:167–202.

Newell, A. 1980. Physical symbol systems. *Cognitive Science* 4:135–183.

Newell, A., and H. Simon. 1976. Computer science as empirical inquiry: Symbols and search. *Communications of the ACM* 19:113–126.

Newell, B., and D. Shanks. 2014. Unconscious influences on decision making: A critical review. *Behavioral and Brain Sciences* 37:1–61.

O'Brien, G. 1998. The role of implementation in connectionist explanation. *Psycoloquy* 9 (6), http://www.cogsci.ecs.soton.ac.uk/cgi/psyc/newpsy?connectionist-explanation.3.

O'Brien, G., and J. Opie. 1998. The disunity of consciousness. *Australasian Journal of Philosophy* 76:378–395.

O'Brien, G., and J. Opie. 1999a. A connectionist theory of phenomenal experience. *Behavioral and Brain Sciences* 22:127–148.

O'Brien, G., and J. Opie. 1999b. A defence of Cartesian materialism. *Philosophy and Phenomenological Research* 59:939–963.

O'Brien, G., and J. Opie. 2001. Connectionist vehicles, structural resemblance, and the phenomenal mind. *Communication and Cognition* 34:13–38.

O'Brien, G., and J. Opie. 2009. Vehicles of consciousness. In *The Oxford Companion to Consciousness*, ed. T. Bayne, A. Cleeremans, and P. Wilken. Oxford: Oxford University Press.

O'Brien, G., and J. Opie. 2011. Representation in analog computation. In *Knowledge and Representation*, ed. A. Newen, A. Bartels, and E. Jung. Stanford, CA: CSLI Publications.

Opie, J. 1998. Connectionist modelling strategies. *Psycoloquy* 9 (30), http://www.cogsci.ecs.soton.ac.uk/cgi/psyc/newpsy?9.30.

Opie, J., and G. O'Brien. forthcoming. The structure of phenomenal consciousness. In *The Constitution of Phenomenal Consciousness: Toward a Science and Theory*, ed. S. Miller. Amsterdam: John Benjamins.

O'Reilly, R., and Y. Munakata. 2000. *Explorations in Computational Neuroscience*. Cambridge, MA: MIT Press.

O'Reilly, R., Y. Munakata, M. Frank, T. Hazy, et al. 2012. *Computational Cognitive Neuroscience*. Wiki Book. http://ccnbook.colorado.edu.

Overgaard, M. 2011. Visual experience and blindsight: A methodological review. *Experimental Brain Research* 209:473–479.

Park, S., and K. Thakkar. 2010. "Splitting of the mind" revisited: Recent neuroimaging evidence for functional disconnection in schizophrenia and its relation to symptoms. *American Journal of Psychiatry* 16:366–368.

Pratte, M., and J. Rouder. 2009. A task-difficulty artefact in subliminal priming. *Attention, Perception and Psychophysics* 71:1276–1283.

Prinz, J. 2012. *The Conscious Brain: How Attention Engenders Experience*. Oxford: Oxford University Press.

Pylyshyn, Z. 1984. *Computational and Cognition*. Cambridge, MA: MIT Press.

Rosenthal, D. 2005. *Consciousness and Mind*. Oxford: Oxford University Press.

Rumelhart, D., and J. McClelland, eds. 1986. *Parallel Distributed Processing: Explorations in the Microstructure of Cognition*, vol. 1: *Foundations*. Cambridge, MA: MIT Press.

Satterthwaite, T., D. Wolf, J. Loughead, K. Ruparel, J. Valdez, S. Siegel, et al. 2010. Association of enhanced limbic response to threat with decreased cortical facial recognition memory response in schizophrenia. *American Journal of Psychiatry* 167: 418–426.

Shanks, D., and M. St. John. 1994. Characteristics of dissociable human learning systems. *Behavioral and Brain Sciences* 17:367–447.

Smolensky, P. 1988. On the proper treatment of connectionism. *Behavioral and Brain Sciences* 11:1–23.

Tononi, G. 2004. An information integration theory of consciousness. *BMC Neuroscience* 5:42.

Tononi, G., and G. Edelman. 2000. Schizophrenia and the mechanisms of conscious integration. *Brain Research Reviews* 31:391–400.

Uhlhaas, P., C. Haenschel, D. Nikolic, and W. Singer. 2008. The role of oscillation and synchrony in cortical networks and their putative relevance for the pathophysiology of schizophrenia. *Schizophrenia Bulletin* 34:927–943.

Wilson, T. 2002. *Strangers to Ourselves: Discovering the Adaptive Unconscious*. Cambridge, MA: Belknap Press of Harvard University Press.

Womelsdorf, T., and P. Fries. 2007. The role of neuronal synchronization in selective attention. *Current Opinion in Neurobiology* 17:154–160.

Zeki, S. 2001. Localization and globalization in conscious vision. *Annual Review of Neuroscience* 24:57–86.

Zeki, S., and A. Bartels. 1998. The asynchrony of consciousness. *Proceedings of the Royal Society of London, Series B: Biological Sciences* 265:1583–1585.

12 Prediction Error Minimization, Mental and Developmental Disorder, and Statistical Theories of Consciousness

Jakob Hohwy

1 Introduction

It is possible to distinguish top-down and bottom-up approaches to the task of constructing a theory of consciousness. *Top-down* approaches are by far the most common: begin with a list of characteristics of consciousness, then hypothesize a functional or neural mechanism that could explain these characteristics, and, finally, seek to procure evidence for this hypothesis.

The top-down approach is guaranteed to be about consciousness, but it is not guaranteed to relate particularly well to actual neural mechanisms or to overall brain function. The top-down approach is also hostage to the list of characteristics, which can often be selective; different conceptions of the key characteristics of consciousness can make theories difficult to compare.

The top-down approach is also sometimes conducted in a more empirically informed way: begin with a list of characteristics of consciousness, procure evidence for their neural correlates, use that correlate to develop a hypothesis about the neural mechanism, and, finally, test this hypothesis further. The neural correlates version of the top-down approach has a better chance at connecting with neural mechanisms. Oddly, it has proven difficult to form solid theories of consciousness on the basis of findings from the neural correlates of consciousness. Findings are heterogeneous and not easy to harness and unify.

A *bottom-up* approach, in contrast, does not begin with a list of characteristics of consciousness; instead, it begins with a general theory about brain function—about what kind of organ the brain is and what it does—and then it uses that general theory to locate characteristics of consciousness.

The bottom-up approach is rarer, in part because there are not many global theories of brain function with an explanatory reach that could potentially encompass characteristics of consciousness. It is, however, a desirable approach because it adds explanatory strength when a phenomenon (here consciousness) is *discovered* to be explainable within an independently supported theoretical framework. It also seems unlikely that consciousness ultimately would be explainable in a way divorced from a general theory of brain function: consciousness does not seem to be a dissociable module, but is integrated with overall brain function, and its heterogeneity must be accounted for within a unified framework. Here, I explore whether characteristics of consciousness can be discovered and explained under the purview of a specific, new, and increasingly influential general theory of brain function, namely that given by the prediction error minimization framework (also known as the free energy principle; for a programmatic statement, see Friston 2010).

A number of psychopathologies, neurological and developmental disorders, and perceptual illusions impact on the characteristics of consciousness. For example, delusions and hallucinations modulate our conscious experience of the world and challenge our sense of self; depersonalization disorder changes our sense of presence; autism impacts the coherence of our experience of the world and undermines aspects of social cognition; full body illusions reveal the plasticity of our bodily self-awareness. Therefore, psychopathology, developmental disorders, and unusual perceptual phenomena are important test cases for any given theory of consciousness. Theories of consciousness will be supported if they can help explain how malfunction to the proposed neural mechanism could lead to psychopathology and disorders of conscious experience.

The relevance of psychopathology and disorders of conscious experience can also be seen in a different way, related to the bottom-up approach to theories of consciousness. There is an enormous amount of psychiatric, neuroscientific, and psychological research on mental and developmental disorder and other perceptual perturbations; often this research is associated with significant theories of psychopathology and their neural underpinnings. This means that empirical findings and theories about psychopathology should be seen as a constraint on theories of consciousness: it would be odd if the basic mechanism for consciousness is entirely independent of the neural mechanisms impacted in psychopathology and neurodevelopment. This again suggests that there will be explanatory benefits in considering a more bottom-up approach to theories of consciousness. Thus, we would explore the mechanisms suggested in research on psychopathology in the hope of discovering how they may relate to characteristics of consciousness. Here, I go one step further and consider how prediction error minimization (the free energy principle) offers a unified explanation of types of mental and developmental disorder that are all relevant to consciousness.

I have suggested that it may be useful to adopt a more bottom-up approach to the construction of a theory of consciousness: explore a general theory of brain function with a view to discovering how characteristics of consciousness may arise. I have also suggested that findings on psychopathology and disorders of conscious experience should constrain theories of consciousness. With this in mind, I review the free energy principle as it relates to certain disturbances of perception, action, and attention. This suggests that various key characteristics of consciousness find a natural home in this general theory of brain function. I then consider how the free energy principle may fit with a contemporary theory of consciousness, namely a Bayesian metacognitive theory recently proposed by Hakwan Lau. This theory is, in turn, shown to be closely related to the global neuronal workspace theory, suggested by Dehaene and others, and I argue that it is unrelated to the higher-order thought theory suggested by Rosenthal and others. This serves to combine the bottom-up approach with some top-down approaches and suggests that certain aspects of quite different theories will survive within the broader account of brain function.

The chapter is thus an invitation to reconsider theories of consciousness as constrained by findings on psychopathology, under a general theory of brain function. This suggests that a naturalistic approach to consciousness integrates well with a broader view of what the brain is and what it does, namely the notion of prediction error minimization. Further, aspects of contemporary theories of consciousness may be refound within this broader perspective; specifically, the proposal is that the ignition of representational content into the global neuronal workspace is determined by action-related representation of the precisions of internal, probabilistic representations.

2 Prediction Error Minimization

Consider the following broad, simple, but also far-reaching claim: the brain's main job is to maintain the organism within a limited set of possible states. This is a fairly trivial claim, since it just reflects that there is a high probability of finding a given organism in some and not other states, combined with the obvious point that the organism's brain in good working order helps explain this fact. It is the brain's job to prevent the organism from straying into states where the organism is not expected to be found in the long run. This can be turned around such that, for any given organism, there is a set of states where it is expected to be found and many states in which it would be surprising to find it. Indeed, we might define the organism's phenotype in terms of the states we expect it to be found in, on average and over time. This way of putting it then defines the brain's job: it must keep the organism within those expected states. That is, the brain must keep the organism out of states that are surprising for it, given the organism it is—or, in general, the brain must minimize surprise.

Here surprise should not be understood in commonsense terms in which a surprise party, say, is surprising. Surprise is technically surprisal or self-information, which is a concept from information theory. It is defined as the negative log probability of a given state, such that the surprise of a state increases the more improbable it is to find the creature in that certain state (in this sense, a fish out of water experiences a lot of surprise). Surprise is then always relative to a model, a set of expectations (being out of water is not surprising given a human being's expectations). States in which an organism is found are described in terms of the causal impact from the environment on the organism (for example, the differences to the fish from being in water vs. being out of water). This, in turn, can be conceptualized as its sensory input, in a broad sense, including not just the visual and auditory input but also important aspects of sensation such as thermoreception, proprioception, and interoception. Surprising states are then to be understood as surprising sensory input, and the brain's job is to minimize the surprise in its sensory input—to keep the organism within states in which it will receive the kind of sensory input it expects.

The question then is how the brain accomplishes the minimization of surprise. It cannot assess surprise directly from the sensory input because that would require knowing the relevant probability distribution as such. To do this, it would need to, impossibly, average over an infinite number of copies of itself in all sorts of possible states in order to figure how much of a surprise a given sensory input might be, relative to what it should expect. This means that to do its job, the brain needs to do something else: it must harbor and finesse a model of itself in the environment, against which it can assess current sensory input.

Assume then that the brain has a model—an informed guess—about what its expected states are, and that it uses that model to generate hypotheses that predict what the next sensory input should be. Now the brain has access to two quantities, which it can compare: on the one hand, the predicted sensory input and, on the other, the actual sensory input. If they match, then the model generating the hypothesis is a good one. Any difference between them can be conceived as prediction error because it means that the predictions were erroneous in some way. For example, if a certain frequency in the auditory input is predicted, then any difference from what the actual auditory input turns out to be is the prediction's error.

The occurrence of prediction error means the model is not a perfect fit to the sensory samples after all, and so, to improve the fit, the overall prediction error should be minimized. In the course of minimizing prediction error, the brain averages out uncertainty about its model and, hence, implicitly approximates the surprise. It is guaranteed to do this by minimizing the divergence between the probability of the selected hypothesis and the posterior probability of the hypothesis given the evidence and the model; this is a Kullback–Leibler divergence, which is always zero (when there is no divergence) or positive, and which therefore creates an upper bound on the surprise—minimizing this bound will therefore approximate surprise.

The key notions here are that the brain acts to maintain itself within its expected states, which are estimated in prediction error minimization. This is known as the free energy principle, where free energy can be understood as the sum of prediction error (for this and the following, see key papers by Friston and Stephan 2007, Friston 2010, as well as introductions in Clark 2013 and Hohwy 2013b).

Prediction error minimization itself instantiates probabilistic, Bayesian inference, because, as mentioned, it means the selected hypothesis becomes the true posterior. Consider that Bayesian inference is a process wherein a given hypothesis, h, is revised in light of new evidence, e. The key question is how much to change h for every sample e. Intuitively speaking, h should change a lot if e is far from h, and little if there is a good fit between e and h. These terms relate to prediction error because they capture how well h predicts e. This, in turn, can be cashed out in terms of likelihood, that is, the probability of e given h. Speaking in simple formal terms, the prediction error is then captured by the likelihood. The update rule for h given e should reflect the aim of having low prediction error. It should also incorporate weighting by the prior probability of h, such that if one is already quite certain of h, then the size of the prediction error should count for less. We have here the basic elements of Bayesian inference, since the posterior probability is proportional to the product of prior and likelihood. One way to engage in inference is to directly calculate the posterior, but this requires inversion of the likelihood to obtain the posterior, which can be formally intractable. Instead, if on average and over time the prediction error is kept low, then the chosen hypotheses that accomplish this must have been good ones, and Bayesian inference (the true posterior) would then be approximated.

Applied to the brain, this idea then focuses on how the brain infers the causes of its own sensory input by minimizing the error in its predictions of the sensory input. If it can minimize prediction error, then the models of the causes of the sensory input it has used to generate the predictions must be good ones, revealing the true environmental causes. Overall, on this view, the brain becomes a better and better model of the world (including itself), and this model can be considered the agent since it acts (as we shall explain in more detail below) to maintain itself in certain states in the world.

Prediction error minimization can occur in a number of ways, all familiar from debates on inference to the best explanation and many heuristic descriptions of scientific inference. The central principle is that, on average and over the long run, the chances of encountering surprise should be minimized. First, the model parameters can be revised in the light of prediction error, which will gradually reduce the error and improve the model fit (as described above). This is *perception*, and it corresponds to how a scientist seeks to explain away surprising evidence by revising a hypothesis. Here, perception is conceived most fundamentally as a kind of (unconscious) causal inference: using Bayes to infer the causes of sensory input. Second, the model parameters can be kept fixed and used to generate predictions, in particular, proprioceptive predictions, which are delivered to the classic reflex arcs and fulfilled there until the expected sensory input is obtained. This is *action*, and it corresponds to how a scientist may retain a hypothesis and control the environment for confounds until the expected evidence obtains. Since action is prediction error minimization with a different direction of fit, it is labeled *active inference*. Third, the model parameters can be precisified such that prediction error minimization occurs on the basis of trustworthy, *precise* prediction error; this amounts to gain control and functionally becomes *attention*. This corresponds to assessment of variance in statistical inference and to how a scientist is guided more by precise measurements than imprecise ones. Fourth, the model parameters can be *simplified* (*cf.* complexity reduction) such that the model is not underfitted or overfitted, both of which will generate prediction error in the long run. This corresponds to Bayesian model selection, where complexity is penalized, and to how a scientist will prefer simpler models in the long run even though a more complex model may fit the current evidence very well.

From the simple starting point of an organism maintaining itself within certain states, we then get the idea that the brain is a model of its environment, and is considered an agent, which through statistical inference minimizes its own prediction error.

3   Disturbances of Prediction Error Minimization: The Role of Expected Precisions

With the conception of overall brain function as long term, average prediction error minimization, captured in terms of statistical inference (optimal model fitting), we can now consider how inference might be disturbed.

The prediction error minimization idea says that all the brain ever does is minimize the error of predictions about its sensory input, formed on the basis of an internal model of the world and the body. The better these predictions are, the less error there is.

To be meaningful, such inference must be guided by reliable signals. Therefore, a key part of inference is to estimate the precisions (or variance) of the prediction error (or sensory input). As mentioned above, this implies that the brain must keep track of the varying levels of noise and uncertainty in the environment and adjust accordingly how much it relies on the sensory input according to such expected precisions. Mechanistically, this is tied to adjusting the gain on sensory input; functionally, it is attention (Feldman and Friston 2010, Hohwy 2012). Simply put, the brain's predictions of sensory precision control the "gates of perception": we attend to signals that are expected to be precise, and those signals tend to dominate perception.

Optimizing expected precisions is, however, difficult statistically because it is itself a type of inference, in need of further, higher-order assessment of precision. Clearly, to avoid regress, at some point levels of such inference about inference must become uninformative. This induces a certain fragility to a prediction error minimizing system, which suggests that some psychopathologies and some neurodevelopmental problems may be tied to inference on expected precisions. The basic idea would be that inferences on precisions are difficult to get right because they are less stringently supervised by the error signal from the world than first-order inference itself. This would thus be an area of inference that is more prone to individual differences and that is more volatile and difficult to adjust in the face of injury and developmental and genetic disturbance (see Hohwy 2013b). This speaks to elements of misperception, psychopathology, and developmental disorder in a number of ways, as I will now discuss.

Often, mental and developmental disorder spare immediate, basic perception of the world and manifest instead in more subtle, circumscribed, accumulative symptoms. This is consistent with the construction of models that may minimize prediction error reasonably well in the short run, but which, on average and over the long run, are less optimal at prediction error minimization. This could occur as a result of suboptimal learning of the changing, context-dependent levels of precision in the sensory input. The impact of such problems with expected precisions would be relatively domain-general, because expected precisions do not concern the concrete origin of the signal itself but, instead, the quality of the signal (we can assess the precision of a signal without knowing what it signals, like a statistician crunching numbers; this fact will be important in section 6, when I turn to theories of consciousness). Being domain-general means that problems with expected precisions will tend to percolate to many levels and local domains in an agent's overall perceptual and cognitive state. This is a good fit to the often-heterogeneous presentation of mental and developmental disorder, as well as to the diverse areas in which perceptual illusions can be present.

Prediction error minimization occurs in a hierarchical manner, with prediction errors and predictions being shunted up and down between distinct levels of the cortex (the cortical hierarchy) while being assessed for precision at all levels and gain-controlled accordingly. This hierarchy builds up representations in a rich, context-dependent fashion, beginning with fast-changing sensory attributes (e.g., transient change of contrast) at low levels and progressing to slower and slower regularities (e.g., movement of objects, changing of seasons) as the prediction error moves up. Conversely, regularities at slower time scales work as control parameters on regularities at faster time scales, meaning that current perception becomes context-dependent and modulated by learned expectations (e.g., how input from a partially occluded object will change over time depending on the expected causal interaction with the occluder).

In this way, perceptual content is harnessed in a rich, context-dependent, causally informed, hierarchical model (for further description, see Hohwy 2013b, chapter 1, 3). This implies that disturbances to prediction error minimization can occur in a number of different ways, according to where in the hierarchy the malfunction is centered and what the upstream and downstream ramifications are. Similarly, malfunction of optimization of expected precision would be able to occur in some and not other parts of the hierarchy, with more or less subtle results. For example, differences in the expected precisions of low-level prediction error will have flow-on effects in the revision of higher-level hypotheses about the world. This happens under the rational principle that if the evidence cannot be trusted in a particular uncertain or ambiguous situation, and a decision must nevertheless be made, then one's prior conceptions about the situation should be given more weight. This might relate to aspects of psychosis, such as delusions and hallucinations. Conversely, if prior expectations of precision at higher levels are deemed uninformative, then there will be less context-dependent, longer-term or global, modulation of processing of low-level sensory attributes. This might relate to sensory differences and lack of global coherence in autism.

Optimization of expected precision is crucial to *action* as well as perception. That is to say, just as attentional gain determines how perception occurs, it determines how action occurs. This claim builds on a simple idea, which, however, challenges commonsense notions of action.

As a basic starting point, assume just that the brain represents various states and orders them according to how probable it is that the system is in these states (where representations are hypotheses or probability density functions). Some of these represented states will be close to actuality and some will be further removed, that is, some will carry more information than others about the current causes of sensory input. If a representation is false, then one possibility is that perceptual inference will be engaged and the representation adjusted to fit with the world. But this direction of fit requires that the prediction error is expected to be precise. If, for some reason, current prediction error is expected to be imprecise, then perceptual inference should be halted and, instead, active inference will be engaged: the selected representation will be held fixed even though it currently generates prediction error, and the body plant will fulfill its predictions instead. This is then a probabilistic mechanism, which propels action.

The current sensory input (or prediction error) can be expected to be imprecise for a variety of reasons. As a simple example, consider entering a darkened room and (actively) turning on the light because the current visual stimuli are expected to be imprecise under circumstances of darkness. In sensorimotor terms, current proprioceptive input (or prediction error) may suggest that the agent is stationary but this input may be expected to be increasingly imprecise as time passes, as it is unlikely that agents remain stationary for very long periods of time. As a consequence, current proprioception is quickly trusted less, and is increasingly sought explained away in favor of new representations, which are in fact false, on which the agent predicts precise prediction error. In the manner of a self-fulfilling prophesy this ensures action occurs, albeit on the basis of extracting regularities about precisions from nature (Brown, Adams et al. 2013, Van Doorn, Hohwy et al. 2014).

Many questions can be asked about this notion of active inference, such as where the in-fact false representations come from and how movement trajectories are processed. These are addressed in the literature (Friston 2012, Friston, Schwartenbeck et al. 2013, Shipp, Adams et al. 2013), but for present purposes what matters is that under the prediction error minimization scheme, action is tied to expected precisions. This means that if psychopathology and some developmental disorders are tied to disordered precision optimization, then their associated motor and, in a broader perspective, decision-making differences can also be addressed.

The relation between expected precisions and action in psychopathology is relevant to, for example, catatonia and waxy flexibility in schizophrenia, which may be related to low expected precision for in-fact false representations, or, conversely, overly high confidence in the current hypothesis that the patient is not moving (Brown, Adams et al. 2013). Autism is characterized by many movement-related differences, including clumsiness and gait differences, which might be related to problems with updating expected levels of proprioceptive precision (Paton, Hohwy et al. 2011, Palmer, Paton et al. 2013, Hohwy and Palmer 2014).

Overall, these considerations suggest that disturbances to the expected precision of prediction error may be a good candidate for explaining aspects of psychopathology and developmental disorders in a unified manner.

4   Precision Processing in Illusions, Psychopathologies, and Developmental Disorder

I now review a variety of illusions, psychopathologies, and developmental disorders, which in different ways tap into central characteristics of conscious experience. These conditions have been linked to disturbances in precision optimization, and I thus make a case that prediction error minimization provides the unifying, underlying mechanism for these characteristics of conscious experience. Hence, by beginning with a general theory of brain function, we can discover how aspects of conscious experience arise, namely when considering how disturbances to the basic mechanism relate to psychopathology and disorder.

4.1   Illusion and Bodily Self-Awareness

Perceptual illusions are not psychopathologies as such, though they do share elements with psychotic states such as delusions (Hohwy 2013a). Some illusions are relevant to our understanding of perceptual binding, which is often considered a key characteristic of human conscious experience in the sense that the science of consciousness would be furthered if the mechanisms underlying binding could be revealed.

Consider, for example, the ventriloquist effect, where typically an auditory input is bound to (or captured by) a visual input, such that they appear, falsely, to co-occur spatiotemporally. This happens in Bayes optimal integration, where the precisions (i.e., inverse of variance about the mean) of each input is estimated and weighted relative to each other (Alais and Burr 2004). In this way, an imprecise auditory input is weighted less than a more precise visual input (and vice versa), and their colocation is determined accordingly. Obviously, such weighting only makes sense against a prior expectation about the precisions of these inputs in the given kind of context.

In the larger perspective, the ventriloquist effect induces a situation with high prediction error, namely where the expected common cause of the sensory input is not evidenced unequivocally through the individual sensory estimates. A perceptual inference therefore places the common cause in the environment according to Bayes' rule.

This probabilistic perspective suggests that multisensory binding illusions relate directly to the central mechanisms for prediction error minimization: precision optimization in perceptual inference. In other words, by considering the behavior of a prediction error minimization system under conflicting sensory input and prior expectations about their common causes, together with expected precisions, we can discover how binding occurs (Hohwy 2013b, chapter 5).

Other illusions concern binding but also more subtle issues concerning the sense of bodily self-awareness, which is a key characteristic of conscious experience. Examples are the rubber hand illusion and the full body illusion (Botvinick and Cohen 1998, Ehrsson 2007, Lenggenhager, Tadi et al. 2007). Both of these illusions throw light on bodily self-awareness because they show how easy it is to change the otherwise robustly appearing sense that we belong in our own bodies and have our experience and first-person perspective centered where the body is located.

The rubber hand illusion occurs when the experimenter taps synchronously on the participant's real hand, hidden from view, and on a visible rubber hand. After a while, most people feel as if the felt touch is located on (or close to) the rubber hand, that it is caused by the experimenter's hand tapping on the rubber hand, and that it is as if the rubber hand belongs to them. Threatening the rubber hand then leads to a fear response, as measured with skin conductance (and can be assessed in a number of additional ways). Similarly, participants will often make the inaccurate proprioceptive estimate that their real hand has drifted toward the rubber hand. Here, a simple visuotactile-proprioceptive sensory conflict leads to perceptual inference, which challenges life-long priors about the boundaries of the body. This illusion likely also involves precision-weighted integration under expected precisions, for example, in virtue of the expectation that proprioceptive precision decreases relatively fast when the limb is stationary.

The rubber hand illusion suggests that bodily self-awareness is more a transient conclusion to a perceptual inference, based on all the sensory evidence available in the moment, than a robust anchor for our sense of self. This is then captured nicely by the inferential nature of prediction error minimization, including precision optimization.

The full body illusion enhances this verdict about bodily self-awareness. Illusions of this type are basically full-body versions of the rubber hand illusion. For example, a participant wears head-mounted goggles attached to a camera recording herself from the back, such that she sees herself from the back. She is tapped on the back and sees her own virtual body in front of herself, being tapped. A proportion of participants will, after a while, feel that the tapping occurs in front of them and will move around in space as if they are placed in that forward location. There are many variations of this theme, each displaying how easy it is to change bodily self-awareness for the whole body. For example, adult participants can be given the illusion that they shake hands with themselves, or that they have been shrunk into a Barbie doll-sized body (Petkova and Ehrsson 2008, van der Hoort, Guterstam et al. 2011).

Full body and rubber hand illusions can deeply challenge the worldview of participants. For example, in a variation of a virtual reality version of the rubber hand illusion, what the participant sees is not that the rubber hand is being touched by the experimenter's finger, but that the experimenter's finger moves up and down above the rubber hand. Surprisingly, this does not break the illusion; instead, it produces an even stronger illusion, with supernatural, bizarre content, that there is an "invisible extension" of the experimenter's finger extending down to the rubber hand, or that the experimenter's finger is a "spectral gun," or that "opposing magnets" have been implanted into the skin (Hohwy and Paton 2010). In full-body versions of this kind of experiment, it is possible to make people experience that their torso is being threaded by a giant needle (unpublished data). This speaks to elements of psychotic experiences, such as delusions, where people adopt bizarre beliefs supposedly in response to unusual experiences. From a prediction error perspective, the sensory input produces greater-than-expected uncertainty, and top-down hypotheses are engaged to deal with this new error, even if those hypotheses have very low prior probability to begin with. I return to delusion formation below.

4.2 Presence, Depersonalization, and Self

On a strictly prediction error minimization framework, the brain infers the causes of its sensory input, even if those causes originate within the body itself. This means there can be interoceptive prediction error. Emotions and bodily sensations may then arise as the brain explains away interoceptive prediction error, again under expectations for how precise (or salient) these internally generated signals will be.

This inferential take on interoception adds to the idea that bodily self-awareness arises in prediction error minimization because not only the visible boundaries of the body but also its internal states, which we appear to be intimately familiar with, depend on inferring hidden causes behind a sensory veil. Evidence for this inferential approach to interoception has been found in a study of the rubber hand illusion, where illusion strength increased when the tapping was done in synchrony with the heartbeat, suggesting that interoceptive states are treated as hidden, to-be-inferred external causes of sensory input, which codetermine the sense of bodily presence (Suzuki, Garfinkel et al. 2013).

The inferential approach to interoception also can explain a further, deep characteristic of conscious experience, namely the sense of presence, that is, the "subjective sense of reality of the world and of the self within the world" (Seth, Suzuki et al. 2012). The key idea is that the sense of presence is secured when interoceptive signals are successfully explained away by top-down predictions, and, conversely, that the sense of presence is compromised when interoceptive signals cannot be explained away as precisely as expected. This may happen when top-down predictions become imprecise. Intuitively, this creates a kind of distance to—a lack of "familiarity" with—the bodily causes of sensory input. This may be what characterizes depersonalization disorder, where the sense of reality of the self is compromised.

Philosophically speaking, depersonalization would manifest as a disturbance to the minimal, nonreflective sense of self, namely the sense that each occurrent experience is in a nonreflective manner experienced as "mine." Self-awareness in a broader, temporally extended sense can also be placed within a prediction error minimization framework. This follows from the simple observation that the states of the agent itself interact with the states of the wider environment to cause changes in the flow of sensory input to the agent. What you sense depends, in part, on your own mental states and the states of your body as it moves around (Hohwy 2007). This entails that the self must be itself be modeled internally, such that these changes to sensory input can be predicted and explained away efficiently and precisely. This means self-awareness could be tied to a representation of a cause of one's sensory input, which happens to be oneself. This is a special cause, different from other modeled causes, because it must factor in heavily in active inference, where the agent's internal and bodily states are brought into new interactions with the environment: it is a cause that is object to more direct control than other causes of sensory input, and this could help explain why it attains a special role in our conscious experience.

The internal model of oneself as a cause of sensory input must carry hallmarks of the self to be able to minimize prediction error on average and over time. It must have parameters carrying information about long-term but detail-poor regularities, such as character traits, and it must represent shorter-term but more detail-rich regularities, such as memories of particular interactions. Insofar as the self is an inferred, internal model of external causes, it too should be subject to disturbances to estimation of the precision of prediction error. For example, one can imagine that underestimation of the precision of sensory input produced during action means that the input signal is trusted less, and that the model of the self is then given disproportionate weight and is, in turn, revised less well and in a more fragmented manner. This could potentially lead to inflated models of self (cf. delusions of grandeur, where self is imputed with powers it hasn't got) or deflated models of self (cf. delusions of alien control, where own action is misattributed to other). In this manner, something as simple as picking out the signal from the noise during action, and deconvolving interacting causes accordingly, could relate directly to self-awareness. (For further discussion of self and prediction error minimization, see Apps and Tsakiris 2014, Hohwy 2007, Limanowski and Blankenburg 2013.)

4.3 Delusions

I have explored the prediction error framework and found that simple disturbances to statistical inference on sensory input can be associated with quite profound characteristics of conscious experience. On a couple of occasions, I noted potential links to psychotic phenomena, in particular delusions, and I now discuss these links in more detail.

Precision plays various roles in (hierarchical) Bayesian inference. We have focused on the expected precision of the sensory input (or prediction error), which in Bayesian terms concerns the likelihood of the evidence given the hypothesis (imprecise evidence means the likelihood will be low). In this way, precise sensory input will weight the posterior probability in favor of the likelihood. But the precision or confidence of the prior belief also matters, in the sense that very precise priors will weight the posterior in its favor. In this way, the posterior belief is hostage to the precisions of the prior and prediction error.

In a hierarchical setting, as mentioned above, the precisions (as well as means or expectations) of probability distributions are themselves treated as unknown parameters and are then subject to inference by higher levels. In other words, inference is always approached under top-down expectations about precisions. The weightings of priors and likelihoods in inference are, therefore, subject to the ability to build up expectations of precisions. For the reasons mentioned in the previous paragraph, it is easy to see how these expectations can be difficult to estimate confidently. Given the hierarchy, it is also easy to see how simple deficits in expected precisions can give rise to cascading, detrimental effects.

For example, if sensory input is expected to be very imprecise (if the signal from the world has proven hard to extract from the noise), then inference will be biased in favor of internal models of the world—the posterior will reflect the prior and be poorly guided by the input. This can explain how delusions become entrenched and appear unrevisable. Further, if, over time, an internal model of the world remains poorly guided by the world, then error minimization will take other routes (integration with other poorly supervised models and skewed complexity reduction). It is likely that such evidentially insulated revision could lead to the warped belief systems seen in psychosis.

Here emerges an interesting point about the emergence of conscious experience, under the assumption that conscious experience is determined by the posterior (i.e., by the hierarchically distributed conclusion to unconscious perceptual inference). The internal model of the world is probably never static but is constantly open to revision. This is captured in the idea that a hyperprior maintained in the brain (i.e., a prior about precisions harbored high in the hierarchy and modulating many lower-level inferences) is that the world changes. In other words, the precision of the sensory input in a given situation will decline at a rate appropriate for that level (for an application of this principle to basic perception, see Hohwy, Roepstorff et al. 2008).

In terms of conscious experience, this predicts that there will always be some dynamic, experiential fluctuation, even in the absence of sensory input (for example, dreaming; see Hobson and Friston 2012) or under dampened-down levels of sensory input, such as the case for psychosis just considered. The prediction error landscape is expected to change, making the current state expensive in prediction error terms and forcing the brain to change its model. In the absence of robust guidance for the world, this will then likely contribute to imagery, hallucinations, and delusions.

So far, we have considered the possibility that in schizophrenia there is disturbed optimization of precisions of prediction error minimization, in particular that there may be excessive expectations of imprecision in the sensory input. Similarly, it is possible that there is increased imprecision, lack of confidence, in the top-down predictions of sensory input, leading to poor attenuation of prediction error and, therefore, spurious prediction error, which can misguide the revision of internal models (Adams, Stephan et al. 2013, Hohwy 2013b).

4.4 Autism Spectrum Disorder

The opposite of the case just considered is when there are excessive expectations of precision in the sensory input, or where some top-down predictions are too confident. In that kind of case, the individual will be caught up in the sensory input and will fail to integrate individual sensory attributes under higher, more global, long-term expectations. That is, if prediction error is expected to be very precise, then sensory input will tend to drive perceptual inference. If perceivers assume they are in a context where sensory input can be trusted (i.e., it is precise), then they should sample more vociferously, update their internal hypotheses vigorously in the light of the prediction error, and rely less on prior conceptions to impose disambiguation on the input.

Overly confident prediction can arise when context fails to modulate predictions. Context-independence is a type of localized processing, where the possibility of causally interfering factors on a particular signal tend to be ignored. This will lead to unexpected prediction error. For example, an auditory cause (a pedestrian-crossing signal) produces a sound at 1Hz frequency but is modulated by other factors (malfunction to its mechanism), so instead produces a sound at about 0.3 Hz. If the possibility of malfunction is not factored in, then the 0.3Hz frequency is a highly salient prediction error, which is difficult to explain away. Somewhat paradoxically, then, when higher levels of the hierarchy become relatively uninformative, lower-level predictions can become overly confident.

This maps reasonably well onto elements of sensory differences in autism spectrum disorder (ASD). Expecting too much precision in the prediction error is a kind of attention grabbing: the gain on low-level error units is set too high, and there is a preoccupation with sensory input, as is often seen in ASD. Specifically, this preoccupation happens in a less context-dependent, less globally integrated way, capturing the lack of "central coherence" characteristic of autism (Happe and Frith 2006, Simmons, Robertson et al. 2009, Hohwy and Palmer 2014). Having overly confident, context-independent predictions is a kind of endogenous attention allocation that also increases local focus and speaks to the hypersensitivity to surprise often reported in individuals with ASD. These different elements can also be applied to sensorimotor processing (Paton, Hohwy et al. 2011, Palmer, Paton et al. 2013), which would relate to some of the motor elements of ASD (e.g., clumsiness).

Accordingly, there is now a growing move to understand ASD in terms of prediction error minimization (Pellicano and Burr 2012, Friston, Lawson et al. 2013, Hohwy 2013b, Van Boxtel and Lu 2013, Van de Cruys, Evers et al. 2014). We believe a key element of this approach to ASD has to do with the way state-dependent levels of noise and uncertainty are learned (Palmer, Paton et al. 2013). As noted above, levels of uncertainty change depending on context. This means that the gain on prediction error should change depending on context, and this gain has to be learned. This is a kind of second-order learning about the reliability of prediction error minimization, which can be difficult to correct. It also seems that it can give rise to a highly heterogeneous manifestation of sensory differences, because prediction error minimization will depend heavily on not only second-order uncertainty learning but also on which contexts the individual finds him or herself in or manages to construct for him or herself.

For the prediction error minimization approach to ASD to be successful, it will also have to explain the social aspects of ASD, which are central to its clinical manifestation. There are various attempts to do this. Our approach is to treat mentalizing as just more causal inference, namely on hidden mental states of other people. This social causal inference would be subject to all the requirements of causal inference in general and will be implemented with prediction error minimization. In other work, we have considered how this may impact specifically social processes such as solving coordination problems and creating common (rather than mere mutual) knowledge (Hohwy and Palmer 2014).

ASD is not often discussed in the literature on consciousness science. This is perhaps because it is primarily viewed as a social cognitive disorder. But autism is characterized by many perceptual differences too, and the prediction error minimization scheme is a promising tool to begin a novel, unified explanation of autism; in addition, it may be misguided to think that social aspects have no role to play in a theory of consciousness (Frith 1995, Hohwy 2013b, chapter 12).

5   Precision Processing and Characteristics of Consciousness

The approach so far has been to begin with a recent, general account of overall brain function, based on the notion of prediction error (or free energy) minimization. This account makes perceptual inference central and should, thus, be able to provide a starting point for an exploration of perception that has some of the characteristics of consciousness. We focused in particular on the optimization of precisions of prediction errors, noted how such precision processing may be disturbed and, in the preceding sections, linked that to a range of illusions and mental and developmental disorders. Looking across this sample of disordered prediction error minimization, a list of characteristics, which are particularly important for consciousness science, has transpired.

Some of these characteristics include the binding of individual sensory attributes in coherent percepts, in particular across sensory modalities. This relates to the key notion of the binding problem: explaining how conscious perception seems bound rather than disparate in spite of the functional segregation of processing of individual stimuli in the brain (Roskies 1999).

The shaping of conscious perception in the meeting of bottom-up sensory input and top-down expectations is captured in prediction error minimization too, and it is modulated by expected precisions. Simply put, changes in the precisions of priors and of likelihoods in Bayesian prediction error minimization will readily change posterior estimates, that is, the conscious upshot of perceptual inference. This is apparent in the gating of sensory input and the degrees of reliance on priors, exemplified in delusions and sensory differences in autism.

The unity and context-dependence of conscious experience may be related to the relative weighting, under expected precisions, of predictions and prediction error. Subtle differences in the confidence of predictions or the expected precisions of input may give dramatic differences in the overall central coherence of experience and the salience of environmental events.

We also saw that precision processing in prediction error minimization relates to more subtle characteristics of conscious experience such as bodily self-awareness, interoceptive sensations, and the sense of presence. This is important because conscious perception is not merely a matter of representing contents but of imbuing those contents with a richer kind of integrated, embodied, experienced significance.

A part of this story also relates to the representation of self and other. For the case of ASD, we made the point that other people's mental states must be inferred. This means that the individual must maintain a model of other people's mental states. This is based on a general point: other people's mental states are causes in the world that may interact with other environmental causes and thus produce nonlinearity in the sensory input, making it more difficult to predict confidently (for example, you may expect to find the treasure where you left it but you must temper this prediction with the contextual knowledge that other people desire treasures too). Importantly, this point holds for representations of oneself too. Your own interactions with the environment also create nonlinearities in the sensory input (for example, a cat partially occluded behind a fence will be experienced differently depending on how you move relative to the fence). Consequently, in order to predict your sensory input, you need to model yourself as an interacting cause in the environment. This means that you need long-term and short-term expectations about yourself, including optimized expectations for the precisions of your own impact on your sensory input. This may relate to our self-consciousness and to disturbances of selfhood seen in psychosis and, perhaps, ASD.

The first-person perspective characteristic of conscious experience refers to the idea that experience always seems to be centered on a particular locus, namely the subject's own locus, and to be dependent on changes in this locus. This can be understood in terms of internal modeling of the trajectory of the self set in a hierarchy of prediction error minimization. Conscious percepts would be determined concurrently through various, linked levels of the cortical hierarchy. At low levels, sensory attributes that change at fast time scales are processed, whereas, at higher levels, attributes that change over slower time scales are processed. Levels reciprocally constrain each other, and this gives an integrated, overall percept, which must reflect the unique perspective of the agent, because processing at all levels must take the interacting, causal factors into account. In the light of this, it is likely that the first-person perspective will be impacted by problems with the optimization of prediction error minimization, somewhat as is seen in schizophrenia and ASD.

At a general level of description, the prediction error minimization framework furnishes a role for attention within an account of conscious perception. This is because, as I have intimated a couple of times, the optimization of precisions of prediction error fits the functional role of attention very well—indeed, it may *be* attention (Feldman and Friston 2010). Since expected precisions are essential for prediction error minimization in a world with state-dependent levels of noise, it follows that attention is necessary (but not sufficient) for an account of conscious perception. This provides a principled way to begin reconciling attention with consciousness, something that has been discussed extensively in the literature on consciousness (Van Boxtel, Tsuchiya et al. 2010, Hohwy 2012).

In the application of the prediction error minimization framework to mental and developmental disorder, a further element transpires, which is rarely noticed in the science of consciousness, namely *individual differences*. The framework provides a principled way to understand why the same stimuli can generate different experiences among different people: perceptual content depends on priors, on the computation of likelihoods, and on the difficult business of maintaining a proper balance between them through optimization of precisions and the other tools of statistical inference. There is, therefore, some promise that this framework can make contact with recent findings on such individual differences in consciousness science (Kleinschmidt, Sterzer et al. 2012).

More aspects of conscious experience can be accommodated with prediction error minimization. We have largely left out two key aspects with great relevance for consciousness. First, complexity reduction, which is the brain's method for reducing prediction error minimization in the long run, when neither perceptual nor active inference is engaged. This may help explain key aspects of dreaming (Hobson and Friston 2012), which is often seen as an important test case for a theory of consciousness (Windt and Metzinger 2007, Windt and Noreika 2011). Second, action, which is conceived as active inference under this framework, namely the organism's recruitment of the motor plant to change its own sensory input to fit its predictions (and thus maintain itself in its expected states). This clearly has an enormous impact on sensory processing. We hinted at this when we noted the imperative to model oneself to enable prediction of the sensory consequences of one's own actions. But the impact of active inference is wider than this (for discussion and further references, see Hohwy 2013b). Active inference will play a central role in the discussions of contemporary theories of consciousness below.

To sum up, the prediction error minimization framework is a general account of brain function. This suggests that it should apply to conscious experience. This application is founded in the fact that prediction error minimization furnishes perceptual inference. But a focus on inference and the formation of representational content is not enough, in itself, to motivate that prediction error minimization can help explain consciousness. To motivate this, the account needs to speak specifically to some of the key characteristics of conscious experience. Consideration of how prediction error minimization may be disturbed in illusions and in mental and developmental disorder displays ways in which this rather austere framework in fact captures quite deep and subtle key characteristics of perception, which are all clearly within the dominion of consciousness science. It therefore seems reasonable to harness consciousness science within this broader theory of overall brain function.

In terms of philosophical methodology, we here treat *conscious experience* as a *cluster concept*: the property of having a certain conscious experience is the property of having a certain perceptual content characterized by members of the cluster of related core properties: binding, multisensory integration, bottom-up/top-down weighting, sense of presence, first-person perspective, action-dependence, self and other representation, and so on. We then develop theoretical frameworks that could describe the complex, interconnected functional roles associated with these properties and search for neurobiological mechanisms that could realize the functional roles associated with such a cluster of properties. It turns out that the prediction error minimization framework is a promising candidate for unifying this philosophical project: inference gives contents, and action and precision optimization in a hierarchical setting captures the cluster of characteristics.

Introspection and our commonsense grasp of the concept of conscious experience determine what goes into the initial defining cluster of core properties. There is bound to be some degree of variance in different individuals' intuitions about which properties are indispensable for classifying some experience as conscious. I believe the list presented here is not an unreasonable starting point.

It is, of course, possible to object that a key ingredient is missing from the cluster of core properties, namely that the experiences are *phenomenally* or *qualitatively* conscious—that there is "something it is like" to enjoy them. This property relates to the hard problem of mind-body metaphysics. And it seems this theoretical, probabilistically based approach, as most others, is silent on phenomenality. The state of play in much contemporary theorizing about consciousness, to the extent the hard problem is properly acknowledged, is that this rather glaring omission is not detrimental to the scientific project of finding a theory of consciousness. Indeed, the theories of consciousness to be considered in the next section are such that it can be argued that their basic neuronal mechanism can be in place without phenomenality being necessitated. Simply put, though the issue is certainly much debated (Gennaro 2012), it seems to me none of the theories on the market has near enough resources to withstand the argument against physicalist or materialist metaphysics of consciousness (Chalmers 1996). The best one can do is, instead, to hope for something less than necessitation of phenomenality from the story about neural activity. This could be in the form of an inference to the best explanation to the conclusion that, say, a version of (perhaps restricted type-type) mind-brain identity is true (Hohwy 2010). The best explanation would be the one that best explains most of the properties of the cluster defining conscious experience. The inference pattern would be this: since theory T explains the cluster better than relevant alternative theories, properties of T's posited neural mechanism are identical to properties of consciousness. Uniquely, the prediction error minimization explanation has a crucial "best-maker" here, since it *integrates* so well with an overall view of brain function and with general theoretical developments in other areas such as machine learning and AI.

6   Prediction Error Minimization and Theories of Consciousness

The prediction error minimization framework is both a global theory of brain function and well placed to explain core characteristics of consciousness. Existing, top-down theories of consciousness seek to explain core characteristics of conscious experience and are intended to be biologically plausible. It would be odd, then, if there was no overlap in the mechanisms suggested by theories of consciousness and the prediction error framework. In this section, I consider a specific theory and reconceptualize some of its features in prediction error minimization terms.

In thinking about mental and developmental disorder, I have focused primarily on the role of precision optimization in hierarchical prediction error minimization. A recent theory of perceptual consciousness, which is also partly motivated by thinking of cases of perceptual disturbance, seems particularly likely to fit this focus. This is a theory based on signal detection theory proposed by Hakwan Lau, according to which "perceptual consciousness depends on our Bayesians decisions, i.e. criterion setting, based on … higher order representations [of the variance of probability density functions]" (Lau 2008). In the following, I will explain aspects of this theory, and I will disconnect it from the higher-order thought theory with which it is initially presented and, instead, via the notion of active inference, connect it to global neuronal workspace theory. (I also note that Lau is currently developing his views in new directions.)

If the objective is to minimize the error in a discrimination task (to have as many hits and correct rejections as possible), then it is crucial to set the decision criterion optimally. This requires estimating the probability of the target being present given a certain internal signal, and this is a task that requires higher-order representation of the variance of the involved probability distributions. The system needs to learn what the probability distributions look like in order to meaningfully decide how to respond to a given signal (e.g., firing rate). Lau explains that,

given that the optimal criteria are determined by the probability distributions for the stimuli, one's knowledge of these distributions is important. However, the distributions describe the probabilistic behavior of the internal signal, which has to be learned over time. The learning of one's own internal signal produces representations concerning the internal signal, which itself is a representation of the external stimuli. (Lau 2008, 39)

A crucial part of the argument for this approach to consciousness concerns misrepresentations, namely cases where it can be argued that criterion setting is involved in false negatives or false positives, which are reflected in changes in conscious perception. Lau considers blindsight, hallucinations, and dreams in this regard. In a similar vein, one could consider some of the other mental and developmental disorders we have discussed above in terms of criterion setting in signal detection. In this sense, Lau's theory is well placed to make illusion, psychopathology, and developmental disorder central for an understanding of consciousness.

These misrepresentations are important because they can demonstrate dissociation between mere signal detection and criterion setting. In blindsight, for example, there is detection of the signal, as revealed under forced-choice conditions, but it seems the criterion remains set conservatively, such that the newly weakened signal is deemed below the criterion, and therefore the subject reports no conscious experience. In dreams and hallucinations, the criterion may be set too low, such that an essentially noisy signal is deemed above the criterion. Lau also cites evidence of signal detection and criterion setting in a clever experiment in healthy participants where everything but the criterion is kept constant across conditions (Lau and Passingham 2006); the idea concerning blindsight has also been modeled computationally (Ko and Lau 2012). Together, this provides reason to think that conscious perception occurs when a signal is deemed above the criterion (modulo confidence intervals) rather than merely when the signal is discriminable.

As presented so far, Lau's theory does not in itself suggest *why* there should be any link between conscious perception and criterion setting. It is evidence for some degree of covariation between conscious experience and criterion setting, but the account does not begin with an independent theoretical reason for why they should covary. This is not a problem for the theory as such, since the evidence for covariation is compelling in its own right. It would, however, be desirable to explore why such covariation might exist.

Lau notes that his theory is metacognitive, because it is an internal operation on a representation (assessing the variance of an internal probability density). This fact about the theory is then used by Lau to link it with a well-known theory of consciousness, namely higher-order thought theories of consciousness (Rosenthal 1997). According to classic versions of such theories, conscious perception requires a higher-order thought about a lower-order mental state, such that the subject having the thoughts becomes aware of the lower order's content. Crucially, it is this idea of *becoming aware* that links the austere, functionalist idea of higher-order representation with consciousness.

I think, however, it is a mistake to connect Lau's elegant theory with higher-order thought theories—for pretty much the same reasons Lau himself presents:

In the present model, the higher order representation represents a scale by which the first-order representation (the internal signal) could be interpreted. The internal signal carries no fixed meaning unless one is to have some access to the higher order representations; a firing rate of 5Hz in the early visual cortex could mean that a signal is very likely to be present, or very unlikely to be so, depending on the higher order representations. Similarly, the higher order representations do not make sense outside of the context of the internal signal. This way, a mismatch between the levels in the above sense is simply not possible: their content cannot directly contradict, because they are never meant to duplicate each other. (Lau 2008, 46–47)

That is, the metacognitive representation does not carry information about what the lower level represents. It is a second-order statistical representation of its variance. This implies that higher-order thought theory cannot get any purchase here: there is no way that a representation of the variance of a probability distribution could cash out the idea of *becoming aware of* what that distribution carries information about. Though Lau's theory is certainly metacognitive in some sense, it is not metacognitive in a sense that can relate to the main impetus for the higher-order thought theory of consciousness. (There is much variation within the higher-order thought class of theories, in particular relating to how such theories handle misrepresentation, which is a critical issue [Gennaro 2012]. The preceding remarks do not pertain to higher-order thought theories per se; they only seek to decouple Bayesian metacognitive theories from such theories. For all I say here, it thus remains highly likely that higher-order thought theories in their own right will contribute significantly to the science of consciousness.)

Lau's theory is thus still in want of some theoretical framing. What I will attempt to do now is to situate it within the broader prediction error minimization framework, to explore whether this will allow some kind of principled connection to consciousness.

At the beginning of this section, I mentioned that Lau's theory seems to fit the focus on precision processing in prediction error minimization.

This should be clear from the notion that the representation of precision is just the representation of variance (precision being the inverse of variance). If the brain is indeed a prediction error minimizer (and if the world has state-dependent levels of uncertainty), then the brain must be engaged in second-order statistical inference, that is, in representing the properties of its own probability distributions. This is something that can be described using either signal detection theory, or Bayes' rule, or the minimization of free energy. So Lau's proposed computational mechanism would find a natural home in a prediction error minimizing brain.

However, this move does not, in itself, connect it to consciousness. The reason is that precision processing is ubiquitous in hierarchical inference. There is no meaningful perceptual inference, whether conscious or not, without second-order statistics. Even at very low levels of the hierarchy (e.g., early visual cortex), which on many accounts are candidates for unconscious mental states, there must be this kind of metacognition. This makes it difficult to explain a key element of Lau's theory, namely that it seems the prefrontal cortex is especially involved in criterion setting. In other words, there seems to be something special (prefrontal) about the kind of precision processing that covaries with consciousness, which is not captured straightforwardly by the role of precision processing in prediction error minimization.

One move here is to provide circumstantial evidence that precision processing, at some level in the hierarchy, is likely related to conscious perception. This is based on the considerations given in the previous sections, suggesting that precision processing is especially relevant for a series of key characteristics of conscious perception. It would therefore not be surprising if conscious perception were in a more general sense related to precision processing, via the approach suggested by Lau.

However, though I believe such circumstantial evidence is of some importance, I would like to briefly speculate about a deeper, more principled reason why the kind of precision processing central to conscious perception should be of a special (prefrontal) kind. This speculation will involve the use of active inference to link precision with consciousness.

I noted earlier that precisions are central to action. Action is engaged for precise hypotheses, and high precision prediction error is sought out in active inference. The process may somewhat simplistically be described like this: there is a landscape of various hypotheses seeking to minimize prediction error, with different degrees of success. Each of these hypotheses is precision weighted, so depend on some metacognitive process. In order to engage active inference, the system must, in a more global sense, assess this prediction error landscape and select a hypothesis, preferably one with good precision. This selection process seems to require a fairly global perspective, consistent with processing at high, prefrontal levels of the hierarchy. The proposal is therefore that representation of the variance of lower-level distributions acquires the profile identified by Lau when, specifically, action is about to be engaged. The system, as it were, asks itself which hypothesis is a worthy candidate for the costly process of testing in action; it doesn't care what the hypotheses are about, only whether they are precise enough to be likely to make a healthy prediction error minimization return through action. This mechanism might be seen in action under states of uncertainty, where several hypotheses offer themselves up as reasonable explanations of the sensory input. For example, under binocular rivalry conditions, different stimuli (e.g., a face and a house) are presented to each eye, and conscious perception alternates between them rather than presenting a fused percept to consciousness. Under such conditions, there is uncertainty about which hypothesis the system should adopt as the best explanation of the sensory input. In response to such uncertainty, the system then seems to recruit higher levels of activity, including prefrontal areas, in an effort to rank them according to their precision and then engage action (such as eye movement) to increase the confidence in the chosen hypothesis. There is some evidence that precision optimization and active inference are involved in rivalry in this manner. Attention is a key modulator of binocular rivalry, consistent with attention's role as increasing the precision-weighted gain on prediction error and, thereby, the precision ranking of the attended stimulus. In addition, when the imperative to act is removed (e.g., by not requiring introspective reports from participants), activity in general moves away from prefrontal areas and rivalry concurrently begins to slow down or cease (Frässle, Sommer et al. 2014).

In this sense, the prefrontal areas as it were sculpt the response space by selecting the (precise) hypotheses the organism should consider for action. This is, in fact, a function that has been proposed for the dorsolateral prefrontal cortex, which shows up in many different studies and which is highlighted especially by Lau (Elliott, Dolan et al. 2000). Here, action can take many different forms, including introspective report, behavioral indication of discriminated targets, exploration, goal directed, planned movement, as well as simple actions like eye and head movement.

The next question to ask is why such overall precision representation should be related to conscious perception, or, in other words, why selection of a (precise) hypothesis for action should be related to conscious perception? I can only offer brief speculations here, but it seems likely that hypotheses that are selected for action are made available to multiple cognitive consumer systems, namely to let these systems figure out how best to use the hypothesis to minimize prediction error in some kind of action or other. This would let the metacognition involved in selection of a hypothesis coincide with what some theorists claim is central to consciousness, namely so-called "ignition" of a content into the global neuronal workspace (Dehaene and Changeux 2011). The specific take on this theory, in prediction error terms, is that the global workspace is used to generate predictions of sensory input on the presumption that the selected hypothesis is true. These predictions, when deemed precise enough, are then sent to motor systems for fulfillment, in accordance with the notion of active inference. Notice that in this interpretation of global workspace theory, processing in the workspace has been given a unified function, in terms of active inference. It may be best to consider this a subsumption of elements of workspace theory under prediction error minimization, rather than a version of the workspace theory in its own right. (Notice also that a straightforward marriage of a Bayesian metacognitive theory with global workspace theory may not be feasible; for discussion, see Lau and Rosenthal 2011.)

This section began by asking how the prediction error minimization scheme fits with theories of consciousness. We picked Lau's signal detection theory as the most attractive candidate. We noted how this theory in fact has little to do with the higher-order thought theory of consciousness and, therefore, is in want of a theoretical link to consciousness. By interpreting the theory in the broader prediction error minimization setting, in particular, the way action is incorporated, such a link may appear, namely in the shape of a different theory—the global neuronal workspace theory. One may therefore speculate that the mechanism that triggers "ignition" into the workspace of a content is not mere evidence accumulation, as suggested by Dehaene (2011), but precision optimization in a global, prediction error minimization setting. In this way, there is scope for a meaningful marriage of aspects of Lau's theory and the global neuronal workspace theory, under the auspices of prediction error minimization. (The link between global neuronal workspace theory and active inference is explored further in Hohwy 2013b, chapter 10, with a focus on the unity of perceptual experience.)

For the case of blindsight, the implication would be that the signal is so imprecise that it is not picked for selection for active inference, so not made available to the global workspace, and, therefore, it does not become conscious. Only under highly unusual forced-choice conditions is the information made available. Importantly, the blindsighter is keenly aware that he or she is guessing, which suggests that there is extremely high uncertainty about what the sensory input would be like were the chosen hypothesis true. This indicates that active inference is not engaged in a normal way, with full ignition into the cognitive consumer systems.

This proposed marriage of the metacognitive account with the global neuronal workspace sits reasonably well with some of the mental and developmental disorders we have looked at so far, at least as far as they are also disorders of consciousness. It seems reasonable to suspect that, in many of these disorders, it is not just precision optimization that has gone awry but also, consequent upon this, the selection of hypotheses for active inference (the sculpting of the response space). This should impact on which hypotheses are ignited into the global workspace and how certain patients might fare in their processing of them. This, in turn, should be reflected in action and behavior in these patient groups, such that the actions selected are poorly suited for prediction error minimization in the long run. In fact, people with schizophrenia have incredibly disrupted behavior, as do people with autism. These groups also have a range of more subtle motor differences, which in some cases are consistent with the idea that precision optimization is suboptimal in the long run (see, e.g., Palmer, Paton et al. 2013).

I want to add one last consideration. I have suggested that the prediction error minimization framework may combine well with both the metacognitive theory and with the global neuronal workspace theory. Sometimes, these types of theories are thought to imply that there is only conscious experience when content is accessed or re-represented. For example, that it makes no sense for a content to be conscious if it is not made available to, for example, introspective report (for discussion, see Block 2008). I don't think this follows from the way these theories have been incorporated into the prediction error framework. It seems entirely possible that there can be conscious experience on the basis of hypotheses that are not yet selected for ignition into the workspace. Such conscious experience may be fairly imprecise and ambiguous, because the hypotheses in question have not received a boost in certainty through active inference. But this lack of precision does not, on its own, entail that there is no conscious experience at all.

7   Concluding Remarks

This has been a wide-ranging attempt to connect theories of consciousness with overall theories of brain function, using as a leverage accounts of illusions as well as mental and developmental disorder. I focused, in particular, on the prediction error minimization framework, which is a promising general account of brain function. When applied to perceptual illusions and mental and developmental disorder, this framework was demonstrated to be highly relevant for a set of core properties of consciousness. This approach was in turn related to a contemporary, metacognitive Bayesian theory of consciousness and, through that, to global neuronal workspace theory.

The upshot is that this bottom-up approach to consciousness science is promising: we can discover aspects of consciousness in a general account of brain function. This contrasts with more traditional top-down approaches, designed to capture consciousness but potentially disconnected from the brain's overall job. Psychopathology, developmental disorder, and perceptual illusions are crucial for bringing out the full explanatory prowess of this approach. When considering contemporary theories of consciousness under this approach and, in particular, under the prediction error minimization framework, the selection of mental representations into consciousness transpires as related to precision optimization in action, which is a new strand in theorizing about consciousness.

Acknowledgments

I wish to thank Felix Blankenburg, Anil Seth, Giulio Tononi, and Sid Kouider for many helpful discussions about prediction error and consciousness. I am also grateful to Hakwan Lau for comments on an earlier draft.

References

Adams, R., K. Stephan, H. Brown, C. Frith, and K. Friston. 2013. The computational anatomy of psychosis. *Frontiers in Psychiatry* 4:47. doi:10.3389/fpsyt.2013.00047.

Alais, D., and D. Burr. 2004. The ventriloquist effect results from near-optimal bimodal integration. *Current Biology* 14:257.

Apps, M., and M. Tsakiris. 2014. The free-energy self: A predictive coding account of self-recognition. *Neuroscience and Biobehavioral Reviews* 41:85–97.

Block, N. 2008. Consciousness, accessibility, and the mesh between psychology and neuroscience. *Behavioral and Brain Sciences* 30:481–499.

Botvinick, M., and J. Cohen. 1998. Rubber hands "feel" touch that eyes see. *Nature* 391:756.

Brown, H., R. Adams, I. Parees, M. Edwards, and K. Friston. 2013. Active inference, sensory attenuation, and illusions. *Cognitive Processing* 14:411–427.

Chalmers, D. 1996. *The Conscious Mind*. Oxford: Oxford University Press.

Clark, A. 2013. Whatever next? Predictive brains, situated agents, and the future of cognitive science. *Behavioral and Brain Sciences* 36:181–204.

Dehaene, S. 2011. Conscious and nonconscious processes: Distinct forms of evidence accumulation? *Biological Physics* 60:141–168.

Dehaene, S., and J.-P. Changeux. 2011. Experimental and theoretical approaches to conscious processing. *Neuron* 70:200–227.

Ehrsson, H. 2007. The experimental induction of out-of-body experiences. *Science* 317:1048.

Elliott, R., R. Dolan, and C. Frith. 2000. Dissociable functions in the medial and lateral orbitofrontal cortex: Evidence from human neuroimaging studies. *Cerebral Cortex* 10:308–317.

Feldman, H., and K. Friston. 2010. Attention, uncertainty, and free-energy. *Frontiers in Human Neuroscience* 4:215. doi:10.3389/fnhum.2010.00215.

Frässle, S., J. Sommer, A. Jansen, M. Naber, and W. Einhäuser. 2014. Binocular rivalry: Frontal activity relates to introspection and action but not to perception. *Journal of Neuroscience* 34:1738–1747.

Friston, K. 2010. The free-energy principle: A unified brain theory? *Nature Reviews. Neuroscience* 11:127–138.

Friston, K. 2012. Policies and priors. *Computational Neuroscience of Drug Addiction: Springer Series in Computational Neuroscience* 10:237–283.

Friston, K., R. Lawson, and C. Frith. 2013. On hyperpriors and hypopriors: Comment on Pellicano and Burr. *Trends in Cognitive Sciences* 17:1.

Friston, K., P. Schwartenbeck, T. Fitzgerald, M. Moutoussis, T. Behrens, and R. Dolan. 2013. The anatomy of choice: Active inference and agency. *Frontiers in Human Neuroscience* 7:598. doi:10.3389/fnhum.2013.00598.

Friston, K., and K. Stephan. 2007. Free energy and the brain. *Synthese* 159:417–458.

Frith, C. 1995. Consciousness is for other people. *Behavioral and Brain Sciences* 18:682–683.

Gennaro, R. 2012. *The Consciousness Paradox: Consciousness, Concepts, and Higher-Order Thoughts*. Cambridge, MA: MIT Press.

Happe, F., and U. Frith. 2006. The weak coherence account: Detail-focused cognitive style in autism spectrum disorders. *Journal of Autism and Developmental Disorders* 36:5–25.

Hobson, J., and K. Friston. 2012. Waking and dreaming consciousness: Neurobiological and functional considerations. *Progress in Neurobiology* 98:82–98.

Hohwy, J. 2007. The sense of self in the phenomenology of agency and perception. *Psyche* 13:1–13.

Hohwy, J. 2010. Mind–brain identity and evidential insulation. *Philosophical Studies* 153:377–395.

Hohwy, J. 2012. Attention and conscious perception in the hypothesis testing brain. *Frontiers in Psychology* 3:96. doi:10.3389/fpsyg.2012.00096.

Hohwy, J. 2013a. Delusions, illusions, and inference under uncertainty. *Mind & Language* 28:57–71.

Hohwy, J. 2013b. *The Predictive Mind*. Oxford: Oxford University Press.

Hohwy, J., and C. Palmer. 2014. Social cognition as causal inference: implications for common knowledge and autism. In *Social Ontology and Social Cognition*, ed. M. Gallotti and J. Michael. Dordrecht: Springer.

Hohwy, J., and B. Paton. 2010. Explaining away the body: Experiences of supernaturally caused touch and touch on non-hand objects within the rubber hand illusion. *PLoS ONE* 5 (2): e9416.

Hohwy, J., A. Roepstorff, and K. Friston. 2008. Predictive coding explains binocular rivalry: An epistemological review. *Cognition* 108:687–701.

van der Hoort, B., A. Guterstam, and H. Ehrsson. 2011. Being Barbie: The size of one's own body determines the perceived size of the world. *PLoS ONE* 6 (5): e20195.

Kleinschmidt, A., P. Sterzer, and G. Rees. 2012. Variability of perceptual multistability: From brain state to individual trait. *Philosophical Transactions of the Royal Society of London, Series B: Biological Sciences* 367:988–1000.

Ko, Y., and H. Lau. 2012. A detection theoretic explanation of blindsight suggests a link between conscious perception and metacognition. *Philosophical Transactions of the Royal Society of London, Series B: Biological Sciences* 367:1401–1411.

Lau, H. 2008. A higher order Bayesian decision theory of consciousness. *Progress in Brain Research* 168:35–48.

Lau, H., and R. Passingham. 2006. Relative blindsight in normal observers and the neural correlate of visual consciousness. *Proceedings of the National Academy of Sciences of the United States of America* 103:18763–18768.

Lenggenhager, B., T. Tadi, T. Metzinger, and O. Blanke. 2007. Video ergo sum: Manipulating bodily self-consciousness. *Science* 317:1096–1099.

Limanowski, J., and F. Blankenburg. 2013. Minimal self-models and the free energy principle. *Frontiers in Human Neuroscience* 7:547. doi:10.3389/fnhum.2013.00547.

Palmer, C., B. Paton, J. Hohwy, and P. Enticott. 2013. Movement under uncertainty: The effects of the rubber-hand illusion vary along the nonclinical autism spectrum. *Neuropsychologia* 51:1942–1951.

Paton, B., J. Hohwy, and P. Enticott. 2011. The rubber hand illusion reveals proprioceptive and sensorimotor differences in autism spectrum disorders. *Journal of Autism and Developmental Disorders* 42 (9): 1870–1883.

Pellicano, E., and D. Burr. 2012. When the world becomes too real: A Bayesian explanation of autistic perception. *Trends in Cognitive Sciences* 16:504–510.

Petkova, V., and H. Ehrsson. 2008. If I were you: Perceptual illusion of body swapping. *PLoS ONE* 3 (12): e3832.

Rosenthal, D. 1997. A theory of consciousness. In *The Nature of Consciousness: Philosophical Debates*, ed. N. Block, O. Flanagan, and G. Güzeldere. Cambridge, MA: MIT Press.

Roskies, A. 1999. The binding problem. *Neuron* 24:7–9.

Seth, A., K. Suzuki, and H. Critchley. 2012. An interoceptive predictive coding model of conscious presence. *Frontiers in Psychology* 2:395. doi:10.3389/fpsyg.2011.00395.

Shipp, S., R. Adams, and K. Friston. 2013. Reflections on a granular architecture: Predictive coding in the motor cortex. *Trends in Neurosciences* 36:706–716.

Simmons, D., A. Robertson, L. McKay, E. Toal, P. McAleer, and F. Pollick. 2009. Vision in autism spectrum disorders. *Vision Research* 49:2705–2739.

Suzuki, K., S. N. Garfinkel, H. D. Critchley, and A. K. Seth. 2013. Multisensory integration across exteroceptive and interoceptive domains modulates self-experience in the rubber-hand illusion. *Neuropsychologia* 51 (13): 2909–2917.

Van Boxtel, J., and H. Lu. 2013. A predictive coding perspective on autism spectrum disorders: A general comment on Pellicano and Burr 2012. *Frontiers in Psychology* 4:19. doi:10.3389/fpsyg.2013.00019.

Van Boxtel, J., N. Tsuchiya, and C. Koch. 2010. Consciousness and attention: On sufficiency and necessity. *Frontiers in Psychology* 1:217. doi:10.3389/fpsyg.2013.00019.

Van de Cruys, S., Evers, K., Van der Hallen, R., Van Eylen, L., Boets, B., Lee de-Wit, L., and Wagemans, J. 2014. Precise minds in uncertain worlds: Predictive coding in autism. *Psychological Review* 121 (4): 649–675.

Van Doorn, G., J. Hohwy, and M. Symmons. 2014. Can you tickle yourself if you swap bodies with someone else? *Consciousness and Cognition* 23:1–11.

Windt, J., and T. Metzinger. 2007. The philosophy of dreaming and self-consciousness: What happens to the experiential subject during the dream state? In *The New Science of Dreaming*, vol. 3: *Cultural and Theoretical Perspectives*, ed. D. Barrett and P. McNamara. Santa Barbara, CA: Praeger Publishers/Greenwood Publishing.

Windt, J., and V. Noreika. 2011. How to integrate dreaming into a general theory of consciousness—a critical review of existing positions and suggestions for future research. *Consciousness and Cognition* 20:1091–1107.

13 Passivity Experience in Schizophrenia

Philip Gerrans

1 Introduction

In this chapter, I provide an explanation of a specific form of conscious experience that has a well-defined neural correlate. The experience in question is the passivity experience characteristic of some schizophrenic delusions, and the neural correlate is hyperactivity in the right inferior parietal lobe (rIPL) (Eidelberg and Galaburda 1984, MacDonald and Paus 2003, Sirigu et al. 2003, Danckert et al. 2004, Ganesan et al. 2005, Rizzolatti et al. 2006, Rushworth and Taylor 2006). Patients with schizophrenia sometimes find themselves performing actions without experience of the "sense of agency" that normally accompanies action. They rationalize this "passivity" experience in delusions of alien control. They say things such as, "I felt myself touched in such a way as if I were hypnotized, electrified, or generally controlled by some sort of medium or some other will," or "The force moved my lips. I began to speak. The words were made for me" (Frith and Done 1989, Spence et al. 1997, Spence 2001, Blakemore et al. 2002, Blakemore et al. 2003)

The crucial feature of the account I provide is that the sense of agency and its pathological counterpart, passivity experience, originate at the borderline between relatively reflexive, bottom-up, and reflective, top-down control of action. The sense of agency is generated in the process of taking deliberate, attentive control of an action. Think of defusing a bomb or carefully threading a needle. In cases such as these, we engage a suite of cognitive processes that enable high-level, visually-guided control of movement. Such cases contrast with more automatic forms of bodily control in which control is delegated to lower-level systems that manage the sensorimotor interface in a relatively reflexive way. Think, for example, of walking down a long staircase with evenly spaced steps or playing a reflex volley at tennis. The sense of agency arises in the shift from one form of reflexive control to more reflective, deliberate control. Precisely because the two forms of control operate as part of the same hierarchical system whose functioning is context-dependent (walking is reflexive until you start picking your way through a minefield or stumble on an uneven surface), the sense of agency is an evanescent phenomenon.

This explanation contains the germ of a theory of consciousness in the idea that we become conscious in the transition to high-level control. The boldest way to state the idea would be to say that if the representations we use to control our behavior were perfectly accurate, leading to instantaneously successful action, we would not be conscious. Consciousness enables reflective, deliberate control of action.

This is reflected in the architecture of motor control. When movements are initiated, a "prediction" of the sensory consequences is generated and compared to sensory feedback produced by the movement. When a movement is perfectly accurate, it produces predicted feedback and, consequently, there is no error to be corrected and no need to engage higher levels of conscious control. We need to become conscious to detect and correct errors that cannot be dealt with automatically by systems that evolved to manage the sensorimotor interface with the world (Blakemore et al. 2002). This idea suggests that consciousness of agency fluctuates according to the degree of successful engagement with the world. As Elisabeth Pacherie puts it:

> Our ordinary experience of agency may be simply a rather diffuse sense of a coherent ongoing flow of anticipations and sensory feedback. It may be that it is only when we are voluntarily attending to what we are doing, or in the case of a serious mismatch between predicted and actual outcome that we become explicitly aware of what we are attempting to do as opposed to what we are actually doing. (Pacherie 2001, 174)

Pacherie suggests that the more successful our activity, the less conscious we are of ourselves as actors, precisely because the mind is a predictive coding system. As I noted earlier, the idea can be developed as a theory of consciousness in general—as Clark (2013) and Hohwy (2013), for example, have suggested—but here I focus on the specific case of passivity experience. The reason is that forward model versions of the predictive coding theory have been used to interpret the neural and clinical evidence for some decades, so there exists a solid body of evidence comparing the way schizophrenic and other pathological and nonpathological populations experience the intentional control of action (Frith et al. 2000, Wolpert and Ghahramani 2000, Blakemore et al. 2002). Another reason for focusing on this case is that it exemplifies something important to explanation: mechanisms matter. The abstract structure of the forward model theory is attractive, but it obviously applies equally well to robots or any motor-control system. What matters, from our point of view, is the way the human brain implements that architecture in such a way that a description of the implementation architecture can serve as a basis for inference to the best explanation of the relationship between neural and conscious states.

In the final section, I connect the predictive coding explanation of passivity experience with some other theories of consciousness with which it shares some features: the attentional, higher order, and global broadcast theories of consciousness. In my framework, concepts such as attention, higher order control, and global workspace play a fairly natural role as descriptors of essential aspects of a predictive coding system. It is hard to see how such a system could work without the ability to focus processing resources on salient information carried by error signals (attention) and allow that information to dominate cognitive processing (global workspace), including the metarepresentational and executive processes that constitute higher-order cognition. The predictive coding explanation suggests that error signals both attract, and are amplified by, attentional processes, and it offers an account of the nature of attention as a mechanism for increasing signal-to-noise ratio in the error signal. Attention does not make states conscious, but without attention sustaining, amplifying, and sharpening the relevant signal, it is likely that an error signal would not dominate the global workspace sufficiently to be the focus of higher-order executive processes.

One advantage of the predictive coding framework is that problematic postulates of other theories can be abandoned in favor of a description of the flow of information in a hierarchical architecture according to principles of error correction. Experience, including the sense of agency, is not generated by an attentional "searchlight," by a quasi-perceptual inner sense, or by a specific metarepresentational capacity directed at a lower-order representation. In abandoning these postulated mechanisms, however, we can preserve the essential insights of the theories that generate them.

In the remainder of the chapter, I apply this framework to the explanation of the sense of agency.

2 Predictive Coding

Helmholtz (1866) noted that if the eyeball moves to the left while we look at an object, the retinal image of the object moves to the right. The identical retinal displacement is produced by movement of an object if the eyeball does not move. Thus retinal displacement is intrinsically ambiguous between movement of objects in the world and movement of the eyeball. However, endogenously caused displacements are not sensed as movement of the seen object because the displacement is *predicted* by the visual system to be a consequence of the movement of the eyeball. *Only unpredicted displacement is sensed as movement.* This insight has modest and radical theoretical consequences. The modest one is that the visuomotor system dynamically computes the discrepancy between predicted and actual states: this leads to the predictive coding model of neural computation and the project of discovering how it is implemented in the visuomotor system. The radical consequence is that the representational content of visual experience, *our image of the world*, is constituted by the difference between predicted and actual sensory states. An even more radical extension of this conclusion would be that this explanation of visual experience applies to consciousness in general. I don't think that the radical conclusion could be made (or refuted) a priori. If it were to be substantiated, we would have to see how the predictive coding theory fared as an inference to the best explanation of a wide variety of types of experience. Here I pursue the idea for the case of passivity experience. First, however, we need to state the essential features of the predictive coding theory, since the details of architecture and implementation are essential to the explanation of passivity experience.

Predictive coding theories treat the mind as a hierarchically organized cognitive system that uses representations of the world and its own states to control behavior. All levels of the cognitive hierarchy exploit the same principle: error correction (Friston et al. 2006, Hohwy et al. 2008, Seth et al. 2011, Hohwy 2013). Each cognitive system uses models of its domain to predict its future informational states, given actions performed by the organism or its subsystems. When those predictions are satisfied, the model is reinforced; when they are not, the model is revised or updated, and new predictions are generated to govern the process of error correction. Discrepancy between actual and predicted information state is called *surprisal* and represented in the form of an error signal. Error signals are referred to higher-level supervisory systems. These systems have access to a larger database of potential solutions and generate an instruction whose execution will cancel the error and minimize surprisal (Friston 2003, Hohwy et al. 2008). The process iterates until error signals are canceled by suitable action.

Applied to the case of action, predictive coding theory yields versions of the forward model theory of motor control captured in the diagram in figure 13.1. The basic idea is that a system moves from state to state by estimating its current state (for example, hand in open grasp 5 cm above an object) and comparing that to a goal state (grasping the object). The difference between current and desired state generates the inverse model that tells the system what it needs to do to reach a goal state—in this case, lower the hand 5 cm and close the fingers around the object. This allows the system to generate motor commands to take it from the current state to the goal state. These commands operate in a descending interactive hierarchy, since even the simplest action has complex components.

The crucial part of the theory is that, as Helmholtz noted, the system is controlled by comparing the predicted sensory consequences of the action (grasping the object) to the actual sensory consequences of movement. In this case, my motor system predicts proprioceptive changes as my arm and hand follow the grasping trajectory and sensory consequences such as the feeling of pressure and weight as I grab the object. I could also predict visual feedback: the sight of the object nestled in my grasp. Actual sensory reafferences are compared to predicted ones. If they match, no further action is needed. If they do not match, an error signal is generated, and the process iterates to produce corrective action canceling the error signal.

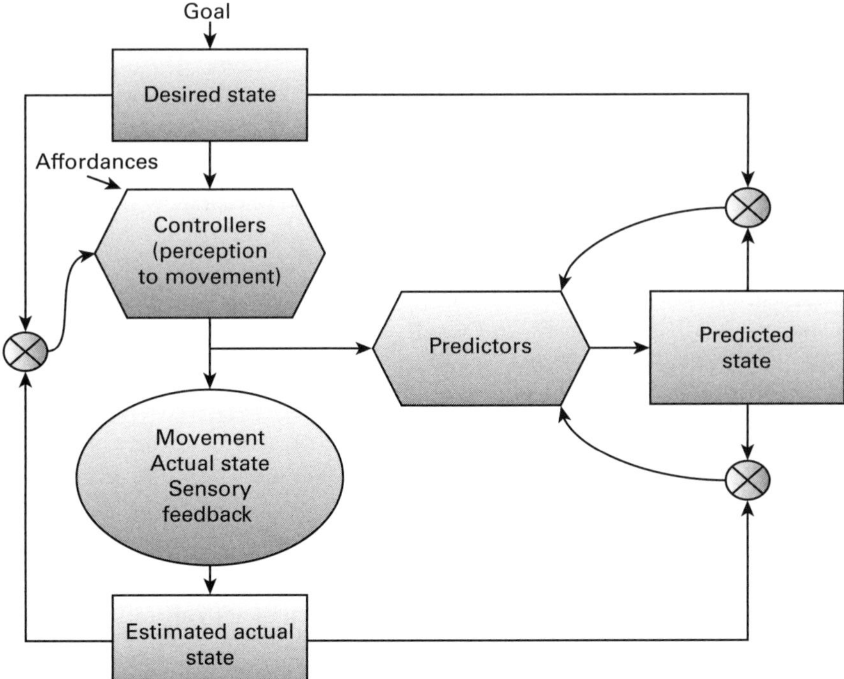

Figure 13.1

In fact there is no single forward model for any action but, instead, a complex hierarchy, since even the simplest movement involves a complex array of interacting systems. Think of reversing a car into a parking space. Visual information gained, not only by eye movement but also by adjusting posture and head alignment, has to be combined with the sense of motion of the car felt through the body and translated down the motor hierarchy into subtle adjustments of pressure on the brake and accelerator and rotational movements of the steering wheel. If I hit the car in the next bay, I may decide to start all over again. This would involve reprogramming the whole hierarchy from the top down with a new goal state and intention.

Most of the processing in the hierarchy is automatic and reflexive and exploits coding formats and time scales that are opaque to introspection. However, the fact that we can decide to carefully repark the car, learn the piano by carefully reading the score, or decide to change our tennis service motion tells us that high-level representations of goals and intentions can be translated into the neurocomputational vocabulary of lower-level sensorimotor systems that implement them.

Andy Clark has provided an interpretation of this process of translation that suggests that the apparatus of prediction and error correction operates seamlessly between levels and modalities of the mind.

All this makes the lines between perception and cognition fuzzy, perhaps even vanishing. In place of any real distinction between perception and belief we now get variable differences in the mixture of top-down and bottom-up influence, and differences of temporal and spatial scale in the internal models that are making the predictions. Top level (more "cognitive") models intuitively correspond to increasingly abstract conceptions of the world and these tend to capture or depend upon regularities at larger temporal and spatial scales. Lower level (more "perceptual") ones capture or depend upon the kinds of scale and detail most strongly associated with specific kinds of perceptual contact. But it is the precision-modulated constant content-rich interactions between these levels, often mediated by ongoing motor action of one kind or another, that now emerges as the heart of intelligent, adaptive response. (Clark 2013, 10)

Clark suggests that, in principle at least, executive control can cancel surprisal all the way down. Our beliefs should be able to modify lower-level predictions and comparisons. That conclusion, however, seems an artifact of the formalization of predictive coding theories as Bayesian inference. Or perhaps as a result of the fact that, viewed at the very bottom level of computational processing, all cognition is neural activation that can be described in the same vocabulary of ion channels and action potentials. Thus, at the highest levels of abstraction and the lowest levels of neural engineering, the mind is seamless. However, at the intermediate levels of computation, differences are significant. For example, perceptual illusions can be explained in terms of predictive coding and so can processes of belief revision. However, one continues to see illusions of motion even when one believes that the shapes are stationary. Beliefs do not change perceptual processes directly.

This point is important for our concerns here because the type of experiences we are interested in in this chapter typically arise at the borderline between lower-level, semi-reflexive and higher-level, deliberative control. The sense of agency is generated precisely because the interaction between levels is not seamless. There is an intermediate level of representation at which we experience the world in formats that enable us to act on it deliberately. The sense of agency arises at that level when we attempt to modulate error signals generated when lower-level action control systems fail.

So far I have only sketched a theory and provided no empirical evidence in support. Much of that evidence comes from pathologies in which the sense of agency is lost or inappropriately generated. Before looking at some of that evidence, it is worth noting that the theory sketched so far makes some specific predictions.

We should expect that pathologies of the sense of agency arise in cases of the transition from reflexive to reflective control. Furthermore, the loss of the sense of agency should not compromise activities that can be entirely carried out by lower-level systems. Thus we might expect, for example, that someone who has lost the sense of agency might claim that she is not driving the car while still successfully reflexively changing lanes to avoid the car ahead.

Another prediction is that the neural correlate of loss of sense of agency (hyperactivity in the rIPL) is, in effect, an error signal that cannot be modulated from the top down, so to speak.

3   Pathologies of Control and the Sense of Agency

The sense of agency is difficult to isolate phenomenologically—so much so that one might doubt whether it even exists. Why would one think that one experiences oneself *qua* agent of an action in addition to the experience of performing the action itself? If you introspect, it is hard to find a feeling that is the feeling of *you* reading or washing the dishes rather than the feeling of reading or washing the dishes. However, some people report that they are not washing the dishes—that their bodies are performing the actions, but they are not the author of those actions. And these people are having some kind of experience different from yours and mine as we stand despondently at the sink.

There are two main reasons why it is so hard to identify the experience of agency.

The first is that sense of agency is not something to which we would normally attend. In that respect it resembles the phenomenology of "familiarity." When we recognize a person, we are not usually aware of any phenomenology. Only in pathological cases such as the Capgras delusion, in which recognition is not accompanied by familiar affective response, is the normal presence of a sense of familiarity salient (Breen et al. 2001, Ellis and Lewis 2001, Brighetti et al. 2007). The second is that the performance of actions produces a variety of sensory consequences: proprioceptive, muscular contraction, and sensory reafference (Jeannerod 2006). Somewhere in among this phenomenological flux is the sense of agency, competing where necessary for attentional and executive resources.

To isolate the sense of agency, we need "pure" cases where experience can be attributed entirely to the control of action rather than the experience of action itself. Deafferented patients provide examples. If one asks a deafferented patient to move a limb, the normal process of initiation of a movement is unimpaired. The intention to move generates a motor instruction and a prediction of the reafferent sensory consequences (contraction of muscles, proprioceptive changes in sense of position, and perception of movement). However, because the limb is deafferented, no such feedback is produced. Nonetheless, the patient experiences a sense of effort.

In such cases, "sense of effort" is a way of becoming aware, not of bodily feedback (because the patient is deafferented), but of being the agent of the action—that is, being the intentional author and trying to control the action according to that intention (Jeannerod 2006).

Deafferented patients can accurately sense the differences in effort involved in trying to make different actions, such as lifting light or heavy objects, and the same phenomena can be produced in healthy patients who are temporarily deafferented. Lafargue and collaborators have conducted an elegant set of experiments with hemiparetic patients asking them to compare or estimate the efforts involved in making and attempting actions with paralyzed and nonparalyzed limbs. In the absence of feedback from the deafferented limbs, patients seem to rely on the sense of effort. Similarly, a patient with no proprioceptive feedback has the capacity to become aware of her efforts to produce actions (Lafargue et al. 2003, Lafargue and Sirigu 2006, Lafargue et al. 2008, Lafargue and Franck 2009).

Another way to produce this phenomenon is via cases of imaginary action. Imaginary actions involve intentions, motor instructions, and the consequent predictions of feedback, but, because motor output is inhibited, there is no sensory reafference. Nonetheless, patients experience a phenomenology of agency and can use that phenomenology to control the imaginary action. It is an interesting feature of imaginary actions that they obey Fitts's law, which says that duration of an action is a function of difficulty (Danckert et al. 2002, Danckert et al. 2004).

What these cases suggest is that the phenomenology of agency is something that is generated in the control of action and recedes when action is successfully guided by sensory feedback. The feeling of controlling an action arises when neural activity that normally decays quickly is maintained when there is no reafference to cancel it. This activation then becomes, in effect, an error signal that attracts prefrontal resources (Saoud et al. 2000, Danckert et al. 2002, Danckert et al. 2004). This is why Jeannerod says:

If motor preparation, which normally lasts for a very brief period of time, could be prolonged, the intention to act would become progressively a motor image of the same action. If this were the case, then the non conscious to conscious transition would be only determined by the time allowed for the preparation process to access awareness and to become conscious. *Actions which fail or which are cancelled at the last moment may be situations where a non-conscious program is transformed into a conscious image.* (Jeannerod 1994, 190; my italics)

The actual mechanism involved is circuitry linking areas involved in motor preparation and execution to the rIPL. rIPL is a sensory integration area that, in this case, functions as a comparator comparing anticipated to actual feedback. "A corollary of the motor signal involved in intended effort, in the supplementary motor area (SMA), could be sent to attenuate parietal activity" (Lafargue and Franck 2009, 284). This is called the *corollary discharge* or *efferent copy* in forward models. It "tells" the parietal cortex that a motor instruction to produce a certain movement has been issued and that consequent sensory feedback generated by the movement is reafferent rather than afferent. It does so by *attenuating* activity in the parietal cortex so that when predicted (reafferent) feedback arrives it does not produce the same level of activation as afferent signals.

Thus, when a movement is initiated, activity in the IPL is initially attenuated (the prediction). If the movement is unsuccessful, preattenuated activity rises, driving further attempts to reduce it by adjusting the movement. When that signal of discrepancy is sustained in the project of top-down control of action, a sense of agency arises. In other words, when we are trying to integrate different sources of information to cancel those signals of discrepancy as part of attentively guided actions, and we are not instantaneously successful, we feel a sense of agency. The sense of agency is produced by the attempt to control movement, which, in effect, is the attempt to reduce the prediction error signaled by activity in the IPL (Eidelberg and Galaburda 1984, Blakemore and Sirigu 2003, Rizzolatti et al. 2006). This is what is meant by cancellation of predictions. When inputs to parietal circuitry are predicted, activation, already down-regulated, rises less than when inputs are unpredicted.

4   Schizophrenia

These considerations suggest that if activity in the IPL cannot be modulated, a person will be in the position of observing or experiencing bodily movements initiated by her but will be unable to use prediction error to fine-tune the movements. Consider threading a needle. In such a case, we typically move slowly and carefully, integrating proprioceptive and visual information to control fine movements. As we make the right adjustments, activity in the right IPL is reduced and subsides to baseline levels.

Imagine, however, that baseline levels of activation in the IPL are initially too high and cannot be attenuated. In such a case predictions, which consist of attenuation of rIPL activation, cannot be made. Nor can error be signaled, since error consists of unpredicted rise in level of activity in the IPL. Nor can action be properly controlled from the top down, since that requires modulation of activity in the IPL as predictions are matched to feedback.

This seems to be the situation in which schizophrenics find themselves. They are unable to modulate activity in the IPL using sensory information—especially visual—while performing controlled actions. Activation in inferior parietal areas, which would otherwise be attenuated by properly functioning prediction circuitry, is not attenuated in schizophrenia (Spence 2002, Danckert et al. 2004, Maruff et al. 2003). Unlike the Jeannerod cases, they observe movements they have initiated, but neither the initiation of those movements nor the reafferent feedback modulates IPL activity. Thus, schizophrenic patients cannot recruit fluctuations in rIPL activation, consequent on execution of their intentions, to help them control the task, and they report the result as a feeling of passivity. For example, while painstakingly icing a cake, the schizophrenic patient sees the words "happy birthday" emerging but does not experience the proportionate waxing and waning of activity in the IPL as she controls the nozzle. She is writing but does not feel as if she is.

This account predicts that schizophrenic passivity experience should not be characterized by problems with automatic control, and passivity experience should be associated with unusual activation in parietal networks involved in controlled processing.

In an important experiment (Jeannerod et al. 2003), subjects traced a path from their body midline to a target directly in front of them. The subject's view of their moving hand was occluded until the final 30 percent of the movement. For the first 70 percent, patients saw a computer-generated trace of the movement path. In some trials, the experimenters introduced a deviation of 15 percent into the movement path so that, if uncorrected, the trace would veer off to the right. Subjects were able to compensate for the perturbation during the occluded section of the movement, with the result that when the hand came into view, the hand was to the left of the midline. This accords with the idea that automatic control does not depend on explicit visual feedback but must use the automatic motor loop, measuring body feedback against a prediction.

This idea has been substantiated in many experiments that suggest that, in the case of automatic movements, patients compare actual to anticipated *proprioceptive* feedback. This fast, automatic process involves the modulation of rIPL activity by the cerebellum. This is why patients were able to sense the perturbation and correct for it, even though they were not explicitly aware of it.

In Jeannerod and collaborators' experiment, schizophrenics' automatic performance was no different from that of neurotypical subjects (Jeannerod et al. 2003). They were able to correct for the perturbation in the absence of visual feedback. This finding is consistent with now-numerous experimental and lesion studies suggesting that automatic motor control does not require the explicit representation of visual information. Reviewing this literature, Danckert, Saoud, and Maruff express the consensus stating that "on-line monitoring and adjustment of action [automatic processing] is unaffected in patients with schizophrenia" (2004, 253).

The experience of passivity, then, is more likely to arise in deliberate, visually guided control of action. The experiment described above provides a way to test this idea, because the last 30 percent of the movement is not occluded and, when the hand appears, it is fifteen degrees to the left of a straight line to the target. Schizophrenics with positive symptoms made attribution errors in this case, leading to the conclusion that "online control can coexist with a tendency to misattribute the source of error" (253).

A series of further experiments pursues the idea that passivity experience arises when predictive circuitry misfires during deliberate control of action.

For example, Mlakar et al. asked schizophrenics to deliberately manipulate a joystick. They were able to do so correctly but reported vivid passivity experiences (Mlakar et al. 1994). This suggests that the automatic components of the action hierarchy were unaffected, and that the sense of agency is generated when the action becomes the object of higher-level processing. Spence et al. pursued this paradigm in the course of a PET study, with the same result (Spence et al. 1997).

These cases substantiate the idea that schizophrenic passivity experience arises, as Pacherie predicts, when action is being controlled from the top down using explicit visual information. Passivity experience results from the failure to attenuate activity in the parietal cortex, especially the inferior parietal cortex, essential to the integration of visual and bodily information in controlled processing. In such a case, the subject has no signals that actions are under her control.

In an elegant study, Blakemore, Oakley, and Frith (2003) hypnotized subjects whose arms were attached to a pulley apparatus and told them that, in one condition, they would be asked to raise their arms and, in a second, that the pulley would raise their arms. The pulley did not actually exert any force. Highly hypnotizable subjects moved their arms in both conditions, but in the second case they reported no feeling of agency, attributing the movement to the pulley. In effect, hypnosis induced the passivity experience for controlled action characteristic of delusions of alien control. PET imaging showed increased activation in the parietal cortex and cerebellum in cases where the subject attributed the source of the movement to the pulley (Blakemore et al. 2003).

Blakemore treats this as evidence that predictions available to consciousness are represented in the parietal cortex and automatic predictions unavailable to consciousness in the cerebellum. This is consistent with findings that patients with cerebellar but not parietal lesions have difficulty with automatic control of action but not with generating a sense of effort when they attend to those actions (Sirigu et al. 2003).Thus Blakemore and Sirigu summarize the consensus view in these cases that awareness of self-initiation of action depends on attenuation of activity in the right inferior parietal cortex by the SMA: "The prediction made by the parietal cortex is concerned *more with high level prediction such as strategic planning actions"* (2003, 243; my italics). Furthermore they suggest that "perhaps the predictions made by the parietal cortex can be made available to consciousness" (2003, 243).

To summarize, schizophrenic subjects seem to have difficulty generating the sense of agency that normally arises when a person switches to controlled monitoring of action. Controlled monitoring normally involves strategic attenuation of activation in parietal areas as a consequence of motor instructions, and schizophrenics have abnormally high baseline activation levels in these parietal networks. Not only that, but controlled monitoring involves the ability to modulate activity in the rIPL consequent on successful performance. Once again, the hyperactivity in the rIPL makes this difficult for schizophrenic patients. The precise cause of this hyperactivity is not known.

Interestingly, activity in the left and right IPL appears to be anticorrelated. That is to say that an increase of activity in one area is correlated with a decrease in the other. Because of the anticorrelation between left and right parietal areas, some authors speculate that the sense of agency has its substrate in activity in the left parietal cortex. For example, Grézes and Decety write as if this is the case, treating the left and right parietal cortex as specialized for representations of "self" and "other" (Grézes and Decety 2001). However, from the point of view of the motor control system, the left and right parietal cortex are correlated with self- and other-initiated movements, not because they intrinsically represent self and other, but because their response to sensory representations of movement trajectories is different according to whether those trajectories are predicted consequences of upstream motor signals.

5 Implications

I have argued that the sense of agency and its pathological counterpart, passivity experience, have a neural basis in the way activity in the rIPL is modulated in the context of high-level control of action. This might suggest endorsement of a higher-order theory of consciousness. However, the account is not suggesting that we become conscious of information represented by high levels of activity in the rIPL because that information is metarepresented by higher-order states such as beliefs, some kind of metaperception, or inner sense. There are well-known difficulties with these versions of higher-order thought (HOT) theories. In any case, the predictive coding architecture involves a continuous hierarchy of cognitive systems, with higher levels supervising lower level ones. The metalevel relationship between belief and perception, or sensation, although it is hierarchical, captures only two levels of the hierarchy that have familiar folk psychological counterparts. In fact, the predictive coding account suggests that, provided the architecture exists for referral of errors, there is, in principle, no reason why any information cannot become conscious. It does not follow that information represented in conscious experience directly informs the subject of the nature of the error that produced it. Emotional and bodily experiences are paradigm cases of information that is encoded and transmitted in formats that make that information opaque to introspection. Often, high-level cognition has to work hard to interpret and explain experiences referred from lower-level systems. Indeed, this seems the obvious explanation for the fact that passivity experience is rarely reported as such but more often reported in the form of a delusion of alien control. The anomalous experience is interpreted and reported in conceptual vocabulary that enables rationalization and communication of experiences that do not wear their content on their face.

The account is close in spirit to versions of HOT theories on which first-order mental states (the signal of prediction error in this case) are conscious in virtue of possessing a property that makes them available to be the target of higher-order states. On this view, the signal of prediction error is just such a property: it is designed to make the relevant information available to higher levels of cognitive processing. How high the error signal rises in the hierarchy and the form it takes depends on whether and how it is canceled at any level in the hierarchy.

This point is relevant to a common objection to some versions of HOT theories that seem to require higher-order processing of a type familiar to humans (explicit propositional attitudes) in order for an organism to be conscious. Thus, one might wonder if animals that lack our executive and conceptual capacities can be conscious. However, three-year-olds, chimpanzees, and other animals can surely meet the requirements of sustaining and modulating a signal of prediction error in sensorimotor processing in the context of refining and revising an action. They can maneuver their bodies slowly and carefully to realize a goal even though they cannot represent the process in familiar conceptual vocabulary. Daniel Povinelli and John Cant (1995) once suggested that a key input to the development of self-awareness in primates was the need to carefully move from branch to wavering branch. This required slow and careful reaching and grasping and testing of weight-bearing properties of the fragile target. My suggestion is that a marmoset or spider monkey precariously negotiating fronds in the forest canopy might experience herself as an agent in exactly the same way we do when balancing precariously (walking the plank in a Japanese game show, for example). What really matters to HOT theories should not be anthropomorphic restrictions on the nature of relevant higher-order and lower-order processes (why should octopodae not be conscious) but the presence of a predictive coding hierarchy enabling top-down control. The suggestion here is consistent with versions of HOT theories that arguably do not rule out animal or infant consciousness (e.g., Gennaro 2012). Such theories require forms of executive control and/or metarepresentation that take a different form than the symbolic metarepresenting vehicles that form part of standard theories. My suggestion is that, ontogenetically and phylogenetically, some forms of predictive coding can provide a candidate for higher-level processes involved in conscious control.

Of course, if metaphysics is the study of what there is *necessarily,* this account will not satisfy metaphysicians of consciousness. After all, a robot spider monkey or bomb defuser may have predictive coding architectures. However, here my sympathies are with Peter Carruthers (2011) in his lucid discussion of the issue. Perhaps "explained properties [feelings of agency and passivity] are *constituted by* the explaining ones [signaling of prediction error], in such a way that nothing *else* needed to be added to the world once the explaining properties were present, in order for the world to contain the target phenomenon" (22).

Similar points can be made about the relationship between attention and consciousness. The predictive coding account suggests that some experiences are made to command attention: those signal problems that cannot be dealt with quickly and automatically at lower levels. The account of attention most amenable to the predictive coding account treats attention not as a searchlight or a higher-order faculty that can be trained on experiences. Rather, it is a mechanism, or suite of mechanisms, that determines which of the innumerable competing patterns of neural activity dominate a (metaphorical) global workspace. In other words, attention is a way of optimizing cognitive resource allocation. More precisely, in the predictive coding framework, as Hohwy puts it: *"conscious* perception can be seen as the upshot of prediction error minimization and *attention* as the optimization of precision expectations during such perceptual inference" (2012, 1, my italics).

On this view, attention is a way of maximizing the signal-to-noise ratio in an error signal. For example, is an object heavier than my motor system predicted, or are my arm muscles just tired from participating in motor control experiments? The proprioceptive feedback that reaches the rIPL is ambiguous between these two interpretations. It only carries information that reafference is unpredicted. In such a situation, I need to inspect the target and my arm and switch to top-down visual guidance, increasing and precisifying my effort. If this error signal is the most salient in context, for example, if I am trying to push the "Off" lever in a nuclear power station meltdown scenario, then attention will ensure that other experiences lose the battle to dominate the global workspace, and I am primarily conscious of a sense of effort. William James said "Attention, belief, affirmation, and motor volition, are … four names for an identical process, incidental to the conflict of ideas alone, *the survival of one in spite of the opposition of the others*" (1880, 31, my italics).

James was alluding to the fact that what is present to the mind (belief, commitment, decision) is the result of a selective process. Global workspace theories of consciousness depend on the same insight. Only information that is suitably formatted to be the object of executive processes and is most salient in cognitive context dominates the global workspace. So-called executive processes are just those that manage these metacognitive operations. Attention and working memory are really two aspects of the same necessary condition for any metacognitive operation. Attention is a matter of selective biasing of information processing, so that some representations take precedence in working memory. Biasing mechanisms exist at all levels in the hierarchy, but, in the case of consciousness, these mechanisms bias executive processes to the processing of surprisal, which propagates to the top of the hierarchy.

Most attentional theories of consciousness founder on problem cases that challenge the necessity and/or sufficiency of attention to make an informational state conscious (Mole 2011, Wu 2014). I would claim that *for the cases I discuss*, attention to the information represented by top-down modulated activation in the rIPL is necessary and sufficient for the sense of agency and its pathological counterparts. Unless we attend to the signal, we won't be conscious of it, and once we do attend we are guaranteed to be conscious of it *provided no other information becomes more salient and captures attention.* Thus sufficiency is a context-dependent matter.

The account is similar in spirit to the global workspace theory of Stanislas Dehaene (Dehaene and Naccache 2001) and the attentional account of Jesse Prinz (2012). Prinz argues that we are conscious of represented information that integrates stimulus properties in a way that makes them available to working memory. The necessary level of integration is "intermediate" in the sense that it is the output of sensory or perceptual processing rather than higher-level processing. We attend to intermediate-level representations because lower-level ones are too piecemeal and fragmented to be of use to planning and deliberation. We need to respond to representations of objects and their properties such as color, not preliminary computations of spatial and spectral properties, because we need to decide how to deal with objects, for example. Attention gives us the perspective on the world we need to decide how to act in it. As Prinz puts it:

Consciousness makes information available for decisions about what to do, and it exists for that purpose. … If consciousness were for theoretical reasoning, we might be conscious of more abstract representations. (Prinz 2012, 203)

Prinz then goes on to provide a theoretically inflected description of the relevant mechanism: "Consciousness arises when and only when vectorwaves that realize intermediate-level representations fire in the gamma range, and thereby become available to [the particular neurofunctional kind of process that is] working memory … these neurons play psychological roles that are essential for consciousness" (293, 289).

I sympathize entirely with Prinz's project of trying to explain consciousness by combining implementation-level description of mechanistic functioning with functional considerations (the role of consciousness in executive control). I also agree that the level at which an empirically based account gains traction is the intermediate level at which representations are referred to higher-order functioning. Like him, I set aside metaphysical objections to the account in favor of providing a description of the relevant mechanisms in sufficient detail to substantiate an inference to the best explanation.

In some ways my account (following that of Hohwy) is slightly more fundamental than Prinz's. Prinz concentrates on the neural mechanisms that make intermediate-level representations available to working memory and which thereby constitute attention. I concentrate on the computational and functional properties that such representations would need to have in order to be the kind of representation which meets Prinz's requirements—namely, they have to be those signals of prediction error, which, in context, are the most salient for the organism.

It would be interesting to see whether an intermediate-level neural circuit firing in gamma vector wave range that was *not* a signal of prediction error would necessarily be attended to. Prinz would have to say yes to such a question. Even if he is right, however, it might well be the case that the property of entering working memory possessed by activation patterns in the gamma range evolved to enable us to attend to prediction error in order to clarify the information represented in experience as a prelude to executive response. After all, on both his and my account, what is of primary importance is the ability to detect and respond to signals from the world at odds with the subject's model of it.

The account given here is not a metaphysical account of consciousness per se but an empirically-informed account of one puzzling form of consciousness: passivity experience. I have tried to show that implementation details of neural mechanisms matter and need to be complemented by an account of the mind's functional and computational architecture. The predictive coding model of the mind can be made consistent with other accounts—HOT, attentional, dispositionalist—precisely because those accounts must be situated against something like the framework suggested here. If there is a single message, it is that consciousness is a borderline phenomenon arising in the allocation of cognitive resources to signal of prediction error. As such, we should expect to detect and explain it as a dynamic, even evanescent phenomenon that occurs within an ongoing process of cognitive control.

References

Blakemore, S., D. Oakley, and C. Frith. 2003. Delusions of alien control in the normal brain. *Neuropsychologia* 41:1058–1067.

Blakemore, S., and A. Sirigu. 2003. Action prediction in the cerebellum and in the parietal lobe. *Experimental Brain Research* 153:239–245.

Blakemore, S., D. Wolpert, and C. Frith. 2002. Abnormalities in the awareness of action. *Trends in Cognitive Sciences* 6:237–242.

Breen, N., N. Coltheart, and D. Caine. 2001. A two-way window on face recognition. *Trends in Cognitive Sciences* 5:234–235.

Brighetti, G., P. Bonifacci, R. Borlimi, and C. Ottaviani. 2007. "Far from the heart far from the eye": Evidence from the Capgras delusion. *Cognitive Neuropsychiatry* 12: 189–197.

Carruthers, Peter. 2011. Higher-order theories of consciousness. In *The Stanford Encyclopedia of Philosophy* (Fall 2011 Ed.), ed. Edward N. Zalta. http://plato.stanford.edu/archives/fall2011/entries/consciousness-higher/.

Clark, A. 2013. Whatever next? Predictive brains, situated agents, and the future of cognitive science. *Behavioral and Brain Sciences* 36:181–204.

Danckert, J., Y. Rossetti, T. D'Amato, J. Dalery, and M. Saoud. 2002. Exploring imagined movements in patients with schizophrenia. *Neuroreport* 13:605.

Danckert, J., M. Saoud, and P. Maruff. 2004. Attention, motor control, and motor imagery in schizophrenia: Implications for the role of the parietal cortex. *Schizophrenia Research* 70:241–261.

Dehaene, S., and L. Naccache. 2001. Towards a cognitive neuroscience of consciousness: Basic evidence and a workspace framework. *Cognition* 79:1–37.

Eidelberg, D., and A. Galaburda. 1984. Inferior parietal lobule: Divergent architectonic asymmetries in the human brain. *Archives of Neurology* 41:843–852.

Ellis, H., and M. Lewis. 2001. Capgras delusions: A window on face recognition. *Trends in Cognitive Sciences* 5:149–156.

Friston, K. 2003. Learning and inference in the brain. *Neural Networks* 16: 1325–1352.

Friston, K., A. Gjedde, R. Näätänen, and A. Hansen. 2006. Predictive coding and the mind: Prospects and perspectives. http://www.pet.au.dk/~andreas/ccc/predictive/PredCodWorkshop.doc.

Frith, C., S. Blakemore, and D. Wolpert. 2000. Explaining the symptoms of schizophrenia: Abnormalities in the awareness of action. *Brain Research Reviews* 31: 357–363.

Frith, C., and D. Done. 1989. Experiences of alien control in schizophrenia reflect a disorder of central monitoring in action. *Psychological Medicine* 19:353–363.

Ganesan, V., M. Hunter, and S. Spence. 2005. Schneiderian first-rank symptoms and right parietal hyperactivation: A replication using FMRI. *American Journal of Psychiatry* 162:1545.

Gennaro, R. 2012. *The Consciousness Paradox: Consciousness, Concepts, and Higher-Order Thoughts*. Cambridge, MA: MIT Press.

Grézes, J., and J. Decety. 2001. Functional anatomy of execution, mental simulation, observation, and verb generation of actions: A meta-analysis. *Human Brain Mapping* 12:1–19.

Helmholtz, H. v. 1866. *Handbuch der Physiologischen Optik*. Leipzig: Voss.

Hohwy, J. 2012. Attention and conscious perception in the hypothesis testing brain. *Frontiers in Psychology* 3:96.

Hohwy, J. 2013. *The Predictive Mind*. New York: Oxford University Press.

Hohwy, J., A. Roepstorff, and K. Friston. 2008. Predictive coding explains binocular rivalry: An epistemological review. *Cognition* 108:687–701.

James, W. 1880. The feeling of effort. *Mind* 5:582.

Jeannerod, M. 1994. The representing brain: Neural correlates of motor intention and imagery. *Behavioral and Brain Sciences* 17:187–201.

Jeannerod, M. 2006. *Motor Cognition: What Actions Tell the Self*. New York: Oxford University Press.

Jeannerod, M., Farrer, C., Franck, N., Fourneret, P., Posada, A., Daprati, E., and Georgieff, N. 2003. Action recognition in normal and schizophrenic subjects. In *The Self in Neuroscience and Psychiatry*, ed. T. Kircher and A. David, 380–406. Cambridge: Cambridge University Press.

Lafargue, G., A. D'Amico, S. Thobois, E. Broussolle, and A. Sirigu. 2008. The ability to assess muscular force in asymmetrical Parkinson's disease. *Cortex* 44:82.

Lafargue, G., and N. Franck. 2009. Effort awareness and sense of volition in schizophrenia. *Consciousness and Cognition* 18:277–289.

Lafargue, G., J. Paillard, Y. Lamarre, and A. Sirigu. 2003. Production and perception of grip force without proprioception: is there a sense of effort in deafferented subjects? *European Journal of Neuroscience* 17:2741–2749.

Lafargue, G., and A. Sirigu. 2006. The nature of the sense of effort and its neural substratum. *Revue Neurologique* 162:703–712.

MacDonald, P., and T. Paus. 2003. The role of parietal cortex in awareness of self-generated movements: A transcranial magnetic stimulation study. *Cerebral Cortex* 13:962.

Maruff, P., P. Wilson, and J. Currie. 2003. Abnormalities of motor imagery associated with somatic passivity phenomena in schizophrenia. *Schizophrenia Research* 60:229–238.

Mlakar, J., K. Jensterle, and C. Frith. 1994. Central monitoring deficiency and schizophrenic symptoms. *Psychological Medicine* 24:557–564.

Mole, C. 2011. *Attention Is Cognitive Unison: An Essay in Philosophical Psychology.* New York: Oxford University Press.

Pacherie, E. 2001. Agency lost and found: A commentary on Spence. *Philosophy, Psychiatry & Psychology* 8:173–176.

Povinelli, D., and J. Cant. 1995. Arboreal clambering and the evolution of self-conception. *Quarterly Review of Biology* 70:393–421.

Prinz, J. 2012. *The Conscious Brain: How Attention Engenders Experience.* New York: Oxford University Press.

Rizzolatti, G., Ferrari, P., Rozzi, S., and Fogassi, L. 2006. The inferior parietal lobule: Where action becomes perception. *Novartis Found Symposium* 270:129–140; discussion 140–125, 164–129.

Rushworth, M., and P. Taylor. 2006. TMS in the parietal cortex: Updating representations for attention and action. *Neuropsychologia* 44:2700–2716.

Saoud, M., Y. Coello, P. Dumas, N. Franck, T. d'Amato, J. Dalery, and Y. Rossetti. 2000. Visual pointing and speed/accuracy trade-off in schizophrenia. *Cognitive Neuropsychiatry* 5:123–134.

Seth, A., K. Suzuki, and H. Critchley. 2011. An interoceptive predictive coding model of conscious presence. *Frontiers in Psychology* 2:395.

Sirigu, A., E. Daprati, S. Ciancia, P. Giraux, N. Nighoghossian, A. Posada, and P. Haggard. 2003. Altered awareness of voluntary action after damage to the parietal cortex. *Nature Neuroscience* 7:80–84.

Spence, S. 2001. Alien control: From phenomenology to cognitive neurobiology. *Philosophy, Psychiatry & Psychology* 8:163–172.

Spence, S. A. 2002. Alien motor phenomena: A window on to agency. *Cognitive Neuropsychiatry* 7:211–220.

Spence, S., D. Brooks, S. Hirsch, P. Liddle, J. Meehan, and P. Grasby. 1997. A PET study of voluntary movement in schizophrenic patients experiencing passivity phenomena (delusions of alien control). *Brain* 120:1997–2011.

Wolpert, D., and Z. Ghahramani. 2000. Computational principles of movement. *Nature Neuroscience* suppl. 3:1212–1217.

Wu, W. 2014. *Attention*. New York: Routledge.

14 From a Sensorimotor Account of Perception to an Interactive Approach to Psychopathology

Erik Myin, J. Kevin O'Regan, and Inez Myin-Germeys

1 Introduction

According to the sensorimotor approach to perception and perceptual awareness, perceptual experience should be seen fundamentally as a way of interacting with the environment (O'Regan and Noë 2001, O'Regan 2011). What distinguishes perceptual experiences is the different ways in which a perceiver perceptually engages with the environment. What sets apart hearing from seeing, for example, are the differences between the patterns of auditory versus visual engaging with the world. Similarly, within a single (sub) modality such as color vision, what sets apart an experience of red from an experience of green are also the differences in the modes of interaction with the environment that are involved. It has been argued by sensorimotor theorists that this relocation of emphasis from the brain to the interaction with the environment, or "going wide" (the phrase is from Hutto and Myin 2013, chapter 8), offers a fruitful perspective on stubborn problems regarding understanding the nature of phenomenal consciousness.

After having reviewed the sensorimotor approach to perceptual experience and what underlies its claims on allowing understanding of perceptual consciousness, we will investigate a similar shift of emphasis away from an internal (or brainbound) approach to an interactive approach in the study of psychopathology. Indeed, such a shift is implemented in approaches to psychopathology that focus on the role of person-environment interactions in the study of the positive and negative phenomena of psychosis, by means of ambulatory monitoring (see Myin-Germeys et al. 2009). Underlying such approaches is a view of psychopathology as involving altered ways of interacting with one's local context. In this paper, we will focus on the similarities between the sensorimotor view of perception and the interactive view to psychopathology. We will explore potential synergies and discuss the gains that could be obtained by turning one's view outward.

2 "Going Wide" for Perceptual Awareness: the Sensorimotor Approach

2.1 The Narrow Take on Consciousness

"What is consciousness?" remains, to many, a baffling question, especially if one considers the qualitative or phenomenal aspects of consciousness. The experience of seeing a purple rose, the sensations of holding an ice cube or tasting vanilla seem, in all their subjective, phenomenal glory, not easy to reconcile with a world made up of photons, quarks, waves, and energy.

It is natural to frame questions about the scientific understanding of consciousness in terms of the potential of neuroscience to elucidate awareness, including its qualitative complexities and depths. The burden regarding consciousness then lies on neuroscience: it is the study of the brain that should bring the required scientific understanding of consciousness. It *should*, which means it also could fail. Theorists who focus on neuroscience as the place where the battle for consciousness should be decided are divided between optimists and pessimists. Optimists reckon that more closely studying the brain will unlock the secrets of consciousness. For example, in his book *The Quest for Consciousness: A Neurobiological Approach*, Christof Koch admits to being guided by "a hunch that the NCC [Neural Correlates for Consciousness] involve specific biological mechanisms" (Koch 2004, 101). He looks for "particular mechanisms that confer onto coalitions of neurons properties that correspond to attributes of conscious percepts" (Koch 2004, 103). Koch thinks the very nature of the branch of biology he pursues motivates his approach to consciousness:

The specificity that is a hallmark of molecular and cellular biology suggests that the correlates of consciousness are based on equally particular biological mechanisms and gadgets, involving identifiable types of neurons, interconnected in some special way and firing in some pertinent manner. (Koch 2004, 105)

Pessimists about the prospects of neuroscience, on the other hand, see the existence of consciousness as an indication of the limits of neuroscience and, by implication, of science in general. This position has been defended, famously, by Colin McGinn, who despairs of the possibility of intelligibly elucidating how "the water of biological tissue" turns "into the wine of consciousness" (McGinn 1989, 348).

Despite coming to radically differing conclusions, the common platform for both optimists and pessimists is the initial assumption that one should turn to neuroscientific or brain-based properties if one wants to understand how consciousness in a physical world is possible. What splits them apart is a different assessment of whether this expectation will be met.

Enter the sensorimotor approach to perception and perceptual awareness. Crucially, it disagrees with both optimists and pessimists regarding their commonly held tenet that the secret to understanding consciousness lies in the brain. Sensorimotor theorists do agree with pessimists in holding that one does not have to expect that the links that will be found between brain processes and experiences will be enlightening or illuminating when it comes to understanding the phenomenal feel of experience. Unlike the pessimists, however, sensorimotor theorists do not see this lack of intelligible relation between brain processes and phenomenal consciousness as showing that neuroscience, or science in general, fails to reach a goal it could be reasonably expected to attain. The problem lies not with (neuro)science, but with the expectation that the "laws" of phenomenal consciousness should be found in the brain.

For what would it mean that the "laws of phenomenal consciousness" (O'Regan and Block 2012) would be found in the brain? It would mean that some intracranial process could be intelligibly related to phenomenal feel. It would mean that, through such neural-phenomenal laws, it could be shown how qualitative consciousness was generated by the physical processes in the brain. On the left-hand side of such laws, one would find a neural process; on the right-hand side, a phenomenal feel, and the laws themselves would make their correspondence intelligible. The example that has become iconic for the identity theory of the fifties and sixties, the philosophy that proposed that mental states are brain states, can still serve: C-fibers on the neural side and pain on the other side (Smart 1958). This example was scientifically simplistic both regarding the complexity and variety of neural processes underlying pain, as well as concerning the complexity of pain awareness (see Grahek 2007 for a philosophical discussion of some of these issues). However, what has been philosophically revealing about the example holds regardless of any complications of the left-hand or right-hand side of such a law. For it seems that, whatever brain process one substitutes on the left-hand side and whatever feel on the right-hand side, the relation between them remains brute and, in itself, unexplained or unintelligible. Observation of this bruteness can drive theorists who set out from strong expectations regarding the brain in the two different directions corresponding to our optimist/pessimist division. Some might hope that, despite first appearances, there might be deeper neural laws to be uncovered so that the left-hand side will one day be filled in with a worthy candidate able to be revealingly related to feel and, thus, to its right-hand counterpart. Yet it is hard to see how anything on the neural side might fulfill such a role. Whatever will be found, it will be some objective process, itself apparently lacking any of the subjective, qualitative feels present on the right-hand side—the feel of, for example, red, sweetness, or pain. It is precisely the fact that there is a general issue about relating objective brain processes to phenomenal feels that drives pessimists to declare consciousness to lie beyond the limits of neuroscience—and when coupled with the expectation that neuroscience is the relevant science for elucidating consciousness, this conclusion transforms into a pessimistic assessment of the potential of science itself regarding consciousness.

2.2   Why and How the Sensorimotor Approach Goes Wide

From the sensorimotor approach comes a different proposal: instead of aiming to find intelligible physico-phenomenal laws inside the confines of the cranium, one looks elsewhere. In particular, if one wants to find an intelligible relation between the phenomenal and the physical, one must look at the interactions between an organism and its environment. In other words, the sensorimotor approach proposes to "go wide" when looking for the laws of qualitative consciousness instead of narrowly peeking inside the brain.

Tactile examples have served the sensorimotor approach well in illustrating the strategy of going wide. Consider the qualitative experience one has when pressing something hard, such as a piece of marble. A narrow strategy would expect to find the secret of the particular quality of hardness by considering the brain processes involved in the experience. As pessimists will be keen to point out, it looks as if no properties likely to be encountered in the brain—be they neural firings, neural connections, electricity, chemistry, or quantum mechanics—will ever connect intelligibly with hardness. But prospects change, so the sensorimotor approach insists, when one turns to the pattern of interaction that a perceiving agent will enact when it experiences something as hard. Typically, the agent will push or press and encounter resistance. Even under more forceful pushing, the hard object will not yield. In general, so the sensorimotor account proposes, perceptual experiences are constituted by interactions characterized by precise patterns of ways in which worldly stimulation changes with specific actions on the part of the perceiver—so-called patterns of sensorimotor contingency (O'Regan and Noë 2001, O'Regan 2011). Having a certain perceptual experience with a certain phenomenal quality corresponds to embodying or enacting an interaction characterized by a specific pattern of sensorimotor contingencies. According to the sensorimotor approach, this account for perceptual feel works across the board. It doesn't apply accidently only to touch but, rather, to all of the sensory modalities. Seeing and having the phenomenal experience of a color too consists, according to the sensorimotor approach, in embodying a pattern of interaction typical for a certain color. This color pattern consists of such facts as that moving in such and such a way with respect to a surface will change the light reaching the eye in such and such a way. Though the example of color undoubtedly has less intuitive appeal than a tactile example, pursuing this sensorimotor approach in the context of color has led to striking empirical results. For example, it has been shown to be possible to account for the special role that the focal colors red, yellow, green, and blue play in perception in terms of the finding that surfaces of these colors have the particularity that they alter incoming light in a simpler way than other surfaces (Philipona and O'Regan 2006, 336) —thus affording a set of different interactions with the world— rather than, as is usually done, in terms of the structuring of experience by the peculiarities of neurophysiological processes, in particular the opponent channels (Degenaar and Myin 2014a, 395).

The sensorimotor approach not only casts light on the specific feel of experiences within a modality, such as the phenomenal experience of hard or red, but also on the phenomenal quality of the different sensory modalities. Having a visual experience, as opposed to having, for example, an auditory experience, should, according to the sensorimotor approach, also be understood by "wide laws" of interaction. In a visual experience, moving or closing the eyes will have certain effects on how one's visual system is stimulated, whereas it will have no such systematic effects on input from the ears. A sensorimotor account has also been offered of the specific perceptual quality of experience. Perceptual experiences are different from thoughts because only the perceptual organism-environment interactions have features like "bodiliness" and "grabbiness" (O'Regan, Myin and Noë 2005, O'Regan 2011). "Bodiliness" concerns the fact, characteristic of perceptual interactions, that movements of the perceiver will have systematic changes on the incoming stimulation. "Grabbiness" refers to complementary typical aspect of a situation of perceptual interaction: certain changes in the perceptual environment—such as a sudden flash of light or a loud sound— will tend to attract perceptual attention and/or cause bodily reorientation. It is because of bodiliness and grabbiness that a perceiver is "immersed" in a perceptual situation. Conscious thinking about something has neither bodiliness nor grabbiness. Even if what you are thinking about would suddenly cease to exist, in most cases, this would have no immediate effects on your thoughts about it. These differences in the laws governing interaction with the environment, so the sensorimotor theory defends, hold the key to the phenomenal difference between thinking and perceiving.

The sensorimotor approach has often been taken to reserve a primordial role for action in perception. No doubt, such understanding has been promoted by the rhetoric that helped the approach to secure a prominent place in recent discussion, as in the phrase that "visual consciousness … is something we do" (O'Regan and Noë 2001, 970), rather than "something that happens to us, or in us" (Noë 2004, 1). It needs to be kept in mind, however, that the primary aim of the sensorimotor approach is to tie perception and perceptual awareness to an organism's interaction with its environment. Interaction with an environment involves both affecting the environment and being affected by it—as is clear from the discussion of the concepts of bodiliness and grabbiness in the previous paragraph. So, even if some formulations might suggest otherwise, the sensorimotor account does have room to accommodate those aspects of experience that have primarily to do with how an organism is acted on or affected by the environment (Hutto 2005).

Why is going wide a better strategy for attempting to understand consciousness than looking for narrow neural-phenomenal laws? A first consideration is that going wide connects with how we already understand awareness in our everyday speaking and writing, in literature, but also in science. Take the famous way of speaking about phenomenal consciousness as the "what it is like" aspect of experience (Nagel 1974). If we ask what it is like to enter an airplane, to feel something hard, or see a bright red, the answers refers to the situations in which we have those or similar experiences. We might say that what it is like to enter an airplane is like entering a tunnel, that feeling something hard is like pushing something that resists, or that seeing bright red is like seeing an overilluminated surface of glossy red plastic. Even experiences that don't involve much actual interaction, such as dreams or near-death experiences, are described in terms of doing things in, and being affected by, an environment.

In other words, when we talk about our experiences in nontheoretical or nonphilosophical contexts, we do so by invoking the kinds of interactions the experiences normally arise in. Going wide and referring to interactions is the natural way to talk and, therefore, think about experience. The narrow approach, on the other hand, at least allows—and arguably even *dictates*—that the wide laws are only contingently related to the phenomenal feels. That is, on the narrow view, there is no fundamental connection to the interactions a certain feel is associated with and the "what it is like" of the feel. From the point of view of our pretheoretic understanding of phenomenology, this narrow focus, or disregard of the wide interactions, is puzzling. It directs us away from the circumstances under which experiences normally happen and toward "pure" experiences unrelated to the worldly engagements such experiences normally form a part of.

Of course, congruence with pretheoretical understanding shouldn't carry too much weight in arguing for a theoretical stance toward anything, including experience. A second basis for support for the sensorimotor approach lies in scientific advantages. In particular, sensorimotor theorists claim their approach provides new insights and initiates new experimental paradigms in fields such as vision with distorting goggles, sensory substitution, neural plasticity, and change blindness (O'Regan and Noë 2001, Hurley and Noë 2003, O'Regan 2011). The pattern that sensorimotor theorists discern in this research is that what one perceptually experiences is determined by how one interacts with the world, rather than by how sensory input is oriented, where it is received on the body, and which are the brain areas most involved in enabling the experience.

A third set of considerations for going wide is philosophical. They can be introduced by stating a standard countermove to the thesis that the laws of phenomenology are wide (O'Regan and Block 2012). A common reaction met by the sensorimotor approach is that it cannot be a correct approach to consciousness because the laws of phenomenology *must be* narrowly brainbound because of the (alleged) fact that one can have perceptual awareness without involvement of the wide laws. In dreams, paralysis, or stimulation of the brain under experimental or medical conditions, experience can supervene on the brain and on the brain *only*, irrespective or independent of any interactive situations or surroundings. In a further step, one can then reason that, if the phenomenology can supervene on nothing more than the brain in noninteractive situations, then one can conclude that, also in interactive situations, it supervenes on the brain only. Finally, one can conclude from such "narrow supervenience" that the laws of phenomenology are narrow too (see Ned Block's parts in O'Regan and Block, 2012 for a clear formulation of this way of reasoning).

From an interactive perspective, this standard line of reasoning is not as solid as it might prima facie look. In the first place, one can question the assumptions made about supervenience of experience on the brain only. Philosophers often assume that a mere mention of the existence of dreams, hallucinations—or even the possibility thereof—or thought experiments about brains-in-vats establish brainbound supervenience for experience in general. Philosophers of a different persuasion have recently raised serious challenges about these standard moves regarding supervenience. Cosmelli and Thompson (2010) have argued in great detail that everything we know about biology implies that the brain needs a body and some form of interaction with the environment in order for it to maintain a stable and continuous form of experience. Ken Pepper (2014) has raised the issue of whether one can validly draw inferences about what experience "really is" by setting out from experience under abnormal conditions (as in dreams), rather than from experiences under standard conditions.

Even if one leaves aside such worries about the starting assumptions of the standard reasoning, additional problems can be raised about the inference from narrow supervenience to narrow laws of phenomenology or narrow physico-phenomenal laws. These problems concern the very idea of a narrow law of phenomenology. In order to be genuinely narrow, such a law would have to make reference only to narrow, and thus noninteractive, properties. On the *physico*, or brain side of the law, one can easily envisage how this could be done. It could be done, among other possibilities, by referring to the kinds of neural properties mentioned in the quotes by Christof Koch in section 2.1. In order to keep the *phenomeno*-side properly narrow, it would have to contain a description of experience in which experience is characterized in a way that does not contain any reference to interactive situations in which the experiences often, or even only occasionally, figure. The description serving in the experiential part of the law would require that a pure and self-contained "atom" of sensation could be distilled and described (Cooke and Myin 2011).

Such genuinely narrow experiences would by their very (narrow) nature only be contingently or nonessentially connected to, or associated with, behaviors, actions, and interactions. If the bonds between experiences and interactions became tighter, the experiences would stop being genuinely narrow. That is, narrow experiences might have typical causal links to (inter)actions, but those links would not affect the phenomenal character of the experience. In principle, a particular narrow experience might have causal links to (inter)actions entirely different from those it is normally causally linked to, without any change in phenomenal feel. For example, one would have to hold that it was at least conceptually coherent, and possibly empirically possible, to swap phenomenal feels inter- and intramodally. Where person A would have normal color experiences when being visually confronted with a colored world, person B would, under the same circumstances, have no color but olfactory experiences. Some philosophers embrace these consequences and think that only a concept of phenomenal feel that leads to these consequences will be satisfactory. Opposed to this, theorists of sensorimotor persuasion will point out that these consequences are unpalatable and in fact show the untenability of the concept of phenomenal experience that lies at their basis (see Dennett 1988, Cooke and Myin 2011, and Myin, Cooke, and Zahidi 2014, for arguments to this effect, supported by thought experiments).

A fourth and final consideration in favor of wide laws is practical: whatever the philosophical niceties, in fact, even if it were granted that some narrow conception of phenomenality might be tenable, it remains the case that, in any practical context, we go wide or operate on a wide conception of phenomenality. That is, when we want to intervene on phenomenal feels, in the large majority of cases, we intervene on interactions. If we want someone to experience the taste of a delicate dish, we feed him or her that dish instead of directly intervening on the brain. In other words, if there was a case to be made for metaphysically narrow laws, it would still not matter for any other purpose than metaphysics (on a certain—not unchallengeable—conception of metaphysics). We would still continue in any practical context to deal with consciousness in our usual wide ways.

3 "Going Wide" to Understand Psychopathology

3.1 The Primacy of Interaction, Once More

In the previous sections, we have given reasons for skepticism about the prospects of a strictly narrow account of the feel of perceptual experience. The core consideration we relied on concerned the nature of experience. Experience, so we defended, fundamentally concerns interactions: how a subject (or organism) interactively affects its environment and is affected by its environment. As a consequence, an understanding of experience always involves relating experience to the interactional context that it normally arises in—even when one considers experiences that occur outside of their standard interactive context. None of this leads us to deny the role brain factors play in experience, but it does imply that brain factors will not provide a deeper understanding of experience—a kind of understanding that is more profound than the one that is offered by considering experiences in their normal, interactive contexts. The outlook is that we will make sense of the contribution of brain factors to experience by seeing the way the brain enables interactions rather than by understanding interactions in terms of brain factors. To return to the phenomenal redness of red: this will not be more deeply comprehended by seeing how it derives directly from a brain mechanism. Rather, brain mechanisms involved in the experience of red are understood as such because of their direct, or derived, role in the kinds of interactions typical for "red."

Does it make sense to adopt a wide approach in the study of psychopathology too? Much of the research in the last twenty years aiming at a better understanding of psychopathology has had a narrow orientation. Just as the brain has seemed the obvious place to turn to when one wants to answer questions about the phenomenal feel of consciousness, so the brain has seemed to many the obvious place to turn to when one wants to make sense of psychopathology. Thus, most research of psychopathology in the last two decades has been devoted to a closer investigation of the brain. But is this narrow focus more appropriate when it comes to studying psychopathology than when it comes to understanding the phenomenal feel of consciousness?

A way in which this narrow orientation often finds expression is in the characterization of psychopathology as a brain disorder or brain disease. Thomas Insel states, in a TEDx presentation at the California Institute of Technology, that the problem is that we call these "brain disorders" mental or behavioral disorders (Insel 2013). The idea of psychopathology as a disease or the "disease model" (Borsboom and Cramer 2013) is predicated on a difference between a disease-specific set of symptoms and an underlying cause from which those symptoms flow forth. This underlying cause is necessarily independent of the symptoms and ideally, but not necessarily, unitary: it then is a robust phenomenon that can be characterized and manipulated on its own, irrespective of the symptoms, which can show variety. The disease model seems to be appropriate in some cases of somatic pathology, when a single underlying factor, such as the presence of a virus, can lie at the basis of a multitude of specific and related symptoms. One can treat the disease by going after the virus: once that has been removed, the symptoms will subside, whereas interfering with (some of the) symptoms will not necessarily affect the virus (Borsboom and Cramer 2013).

But it remains an open question whether the disease model applies to psychopathology. In order to tackle this question, it pays off to start by having a closer look at the actual phenomena of interest. Most research on psychopathology has been devoted to understanding the neural underpinnings of psychiatric conditions such as major depression, bipolar disorder, or schizophrenia. However, the validity of these diagnostic categories has been questioned (van Os 2009, 2010), given that there is no symptomatic specificity (e.g., depression is common in major depressive disorder, bipolar disorder and schizophrenia), no etiological specificity (e.g., there is genetic overlap between schizophrenia and bipolar disorder), no prognostic specificity, and no treatment specificity that can distinguish one diagnosis from another. As a consequence, it seems that the most basic requirement coming from the disease model, namely, that there exist identifiable and distinct diseases to begin with, is not met.

Furthermore, it has consistently been demonstrated that psychiatric symptoms are dimensional rather than categorical in nature. Symptoms of depression, anxiety, bipolar disorder, autism, and psychosis are all present at a subclinical level in the general population and form a continuum with normal variation and clinical symptoms at the extreme ends (van Os, Linscott, Myin-Germeys, Delespaul, and Krabbendam 2009). Disregarding this continuous nature of symptoms and conceiving of psychopathological phenomena as distant from everyday mentality might have been another motivation for the search for narrow factors (neural, genetic, or otherwise) outside of experience as the way of making sense of psychopathology.

One can also raise issues about the very idea of underlying causes. In order to be genuinely *underlying*, the phenomena that act as causes should be able to exist independently from the symptoms—just as a virus can exist independently of its pathological effects in a body (a similar point is made in Fuchs 2012). In the previous section, we saw that sensorimotor theorists defend that the way brain states or properties are characterized in perceptual terms—that is, as visual, auditory, tactile—depends on what kinds of perceptual person-environment interactions these brain states and properties are, or have been, involved in. In other words, the criterion for deciding whether or not a brain area should be characterized in perceptual terms is stated in terms of interactions (or wide, as we have said) and not in terms of noninteractively (or narrow) characterized brain properties. Exactly the same applies in the domain of psychopathology. For whether a narrowly specified property or feature is a valid candidate for being an underlying cause depends on wide—symptom-related—criteria. Whether some brain property can form (part of) the underlying cause for a certain form of psychopathology is determined by investigating how the property or feature correlates with symptoms. If the property or feature does not correlate with symptoms in some required way (however that is defined), it is discarded as a candidate underlying cause. Importantly, the reverse does not happen: symptoms are not discarded as genuine symptoms when a correlation between symptoms and a narrow property turns out not to meet some requirement. That is, if a candidate for underlying property (narrowly described) is not correlated in the required way with symptoms, one retracts the assumption that the narrow property forms the underlying cause, rather than retracting the idea that the symptoms are genuinely symptomatic.

3.2   The Interactive Approach in Action

The foregoing provides reasons to study psychopathology by studying symptoms in an interactive framework. In an interactive, wide approach, symptoms constitute specific ways a subject interacts with his or her environment. Interaction in psychopathology is different from nonpsychopathological ways of interaction, but it is at the same time deeply related.

It is by having a closer look at symptoms that one can discern how going wide, in contrast to taking a narrow stance, is both theoretically mandatory and practically beneficial. Let us start at the theoretical end first and ask what sort of results and what kind of understanding a wide approach in the study of psychopathology leads to. Psychopathological symptoms are natural experiences emerging in the realm of normal daily life. Taking a wide approach thus involves the study of how these psychopathological symptoms arise and change in a person's interaction with her context. In order to grasp these interactions, one needs instruments to track them and chart their dynamics. Momentary assessment approaches using structured diary techniques, such as the experience sampling method (ESM) (Myin-Germeys et al. 2009) or ecological momentary assessment (EMA) (Shiffman, Stone, and Hufford 2008), allow one to systematically study experiences, including psychopathological symptoms, in the realm of daily life. They make possible real-time monitoring of variation in experiences as well as the context in which they occur. Subjects fill out questionnaires regarding their current thoughts, feelings, and psychopathological symptoms, as well as regarding the context (where the person is, what the person is doing, the company the person is with) and appraisals of this context. Participants fill out the questionnaire at semirandom time points, typically between four and ten times a day, for a number of consecutive days. Earlier studies used paper-and-pencil approaches combined with a preprogrammed watch to provide the signal; currently, personal digital assistants and apps are available (Kimhy, Myin-Germeys, Palmier-Claus, and Swendsen 2012). This provides a number of consecutive data-points for each subject, allowing one to study within-moment interactions as well as interactions over moments in time.

Is it possible to identify specific patterns of interactions associated with psychiatric symptoms following this approach? Let's focus on one example here, that of psychotic disorder. Psychotic disorders are characterized by positive symptoms, such as hallucinations (mainly hearing voices) and delusional ideas (such as paranoia or ideas of reference), and negative symptoms, such as lack of motivation, anhedonia, and lack of social interaction. Several studies using experience sampling methodology have been conducted in subjects with psychotic symptoms (e.g., Oorschot, Kwapil, Delespaul, and Myin-Germeys 2009 for an overview).

A first finding coming out of these studies is that symptoms such as paranoid ideation or hallucinations show huge variation over time (Oorschot et al. 2012, Thewissen, Bentall, Lecomte, van Os, and Myin-Germeys 2008), meaning that the intensity of these symptoms fluctuates highly from one moment to the next. The relevant question would then be whether we can identify interactional changes associated with these fluctuations over time. Both affective/subjective and situational factors have been associated with increases in psychotic symptoms. For example, an increase in anxiety and a decrease in self-esteem have been shown to precede an increase of paranoia (Oorschot et al. 2012, Thewissen et al. 2008, Thewissen et al. 2011). The experience of subjective stress has also been associated with increased levels of psychotic symptoms (Myin-Germeys, Delespaul, and van Os 2005, Myin-Germeys and van Os 2007). Both of these findings are found across the whole psychosis continuity, in clinical patients but also in persons with lower-level psychotic experiences (Lataster, Myin-Germeys, Derom, Thiery, and van Os 2009). Situational factors have been associated with psychosis as well. Sleep disturbances are associated with increased levels of paranoia (Freeman, Pugh, Vorontsova, and Southgate 2009), whereas cannabis use results in more intense hallucinations (Henquet et al. 2010). The social context has also been found to be of relevance. More paranoia has been reported when people are accompanied by strangers compared with times when they are with friends or family (Collip et al. 2011). However, at the upper end of the continuum—where the threshold of the symptomatic lies—this interaction changes. Patients with clinical levels of paranoia report high levels of paranoia irrespective of the company they are in.

Apart from allowing us to track how psychotic symptoms vary in response to the context, ESM studies have established that people with psychotic experiences are, in general, more responsive to the environment. When persons with psychosis encounter stress—even minor daily hassles—they not only become more psychotic, but they also show increased negative affect, thus overreacting to this negative environment (Myin-Germeys and van Os 2007, Myin-Germeys, van Os, Schwartz, Stone, and Delespaul 2001). Interestingly, they also are more reactive to a positive environment. When they encounter positive events, they will gain more in the sense that their positive affect will increase more compared to control subjects (Oorschot et al. 2013). Similarly, they experience more positive affect from being in social company (Oorschot et al. 2013). Overall, there seems to be a higher responsivity to the environment compared to persons without these disorders. This has led to the proposal of renaming schizophrenia as "salience dysregulation syndrome" (van Os 2009), which would reflect a more accurate description of the changes in person-environment interaction defining its psychotic symptoms.

Let's take a closer look at negative symptoms. Negative symptoms are among the most disabling psychopathological symptoms—they are poorly understood and hard to treat. What understanding of these negative symptoms does a wide approach provide? An interesting example is anhedonia, defined as reduced hedonic capacity, or the loss of the ability to enjoy things that were previously enjoyable, and considered a core feature of schizophrenia. Although patients with schizophrenia score higher on anhedonia, both with self-assessment scales (Blanchard, Mueser, and Bellack 1998, Cohen et al. 2005) and when questioned by trained interviewers (Earnst and Kring 1997), experimental studies with emotion-inducing stimuli found no difference in positive affect between patients and healthy controls (Cohen and Minor 2010). Experience sampling studies in real life, on the other hand, have found overall lower levels of positive affect in patients compared to controls (Myin-Germeys, Delespaul, and deVries 2000, Oorschot et al. 2013). What could explain these paradoxical findings? One explanation is related to the difference between anticipatory pleasure (related to future activities) and consummatory (in the moment) pleasure (Gard et al. 2007). One ESM study found that patients indeed had more difficulty with anticipatory pleasure, although their consummatory pleasure was intact (Gard et al. 2007). Second, it was investigated whether reduced positive affect in patients as measured in the ESM studies reflected diminished hedonic capacity or merely resulted from less pleasurable life circumstances (Oorschot et al. 2013). Indeed, patients reported fewer pleasant events, but when a pleasant event happened, they reported equal or even more positive affect compared to healthy controls. So, combining both findings, patients are capable of experiencing pleasure in the moment. However, they may be less likely to seek out opportunities to engage in activities when their ability to anticipate which potential experiences will be rewarding is impaired (Oorschot et al. 2013).

The picture that emerges from the foregoing wide approach to psychopathology is that of psychopathology as a specific pattern of interaction related to, but differing from, nonpathological patterns of interaction. Crucially, the relevant patterns of interaction are thoroughly context-sensitive. The example of anhedonia just described illustrates this: anhedonia does not form a stable context-invariant building block of psychopathology, but it needs itself to be specified in terms of context-sensitive ways of affecting, and being affected by, a particular environment. This repeats, for symptoms, what we argued is the case for brain properties: how precisely they relate to psychopathology has to be established by inquiring about which contextualized interactions they are involved in.

3.3 Practical Implications of Going Wide: Interactive Therapy

The most important reason to improve understanding of psychopathology is the high burden associated with psychiatric illness and the need for better treatment to relieve this burden. A recent study in Europe estimated that well over one third of the population in any given twelve-month period suffers from a mental disorder, most of which are not treated (Wittchen et al. 2011). Furthermore, treatment prospects are minimal to modest. Despite enormous developments in pharmacological interventions, which are still the primary therapeutic approach for most psychiatric disorders, the morbidity and mortality rate associated with psychiatric disorders has not changed (Insel 2012).

The most widely used psychosocial intervention is cognitive-behavioral therapy (CBT). Cognitive-behavioral therapy is aimed at changing the thinking that is assumed to underlie action and behavior. However, the results of CBT are mixed, with effects often in the small range (Cuijpers et al. 2014, Szentagotai and David 2010, Turner, van der Gaag, Karyotaki, and Cuijpers 2014). Furthermore, it remains unclear what the active component is in the therapy, and "how much of it is due to what was added to traditional behavior therapy" (Hayes, Villatte, Levin, and Hildebrandt 2011). CBT runs the risk of falling prey to an intellectualist and cognitivist view of mentality. According to this view, thoughts, understood as attitudes to mental representations, play a key role in most aspects of human mentality. Emotions, for example, are understood as having self-related beliefs, taken to be propositional attitudes or attitudes-toward-a-propositional-content as core components. Therapy is then aimed at changing the mental representations or thoughts that are taken to drive dysfunctional mental life. Varga (2014) has argued in great detail how what he calls a CT (for cognitive therapy) view of mentality is problematic. He points out that many cases of thinking and emotion do not seem to be driven by explicit thoughts or representations at all. He gives the example of moods, which have been analyzed as embodied attitudes directly toward the world, rather than toward a representation of it (Ratcliffe 2008). "Feeling low," for example, "is both characterized by the way in which the world appears, namely as lacking attractive 'affordances,' and the way the body feels: slow and heavy" (Varga 2014, 182). This take on moods in particular and on thinking and mental phenomena in general obviously fits within the wide approach advocated here, as the focus fully comes to lie on contextualized patterns of affecting and being affected by one's environment. Many of such patterns might not be mediated by thoughts—irrespective of whether they are taken to be explicit or implicit—or indeed by any representational contents (Hutto and Myin 2013). If such is true, any therapy that always aims for such explicit thoughts or contentful episodes as the place to intervene will be inadequate.

Two caveats need to be made here. Of course, action and behavior (of humans *and* animals) is complex and rich—for example, by being infused with expectations or suspicions. What should be resisted is the temptation to model these expectations as explicit or content-carrying thoughts. There is no logical need for this, as an expectation can exist as a sensitivity or adaptation to a particular context. An animal can be on alert when nearing a particular place because, based on its own history, it expects the presence of another animal at that place. But nothing logically requires that such sensitivity should only be explicable by a content-carrying inner episode, let alone one involving a proposition (Degenaar and Myin 2014b). Second, nothing stands in the way of admitting that at least some human actions are mediated by episodes specifiable only in terms of content (which can only be spelled out in terms of natural language). A youngster could start to smoke by having inferred that, by doing so, she would look cool to another youngster. Even in such cases, there remains the question of to what extent one can change the course of action resulting from the thought by intervening in the realm of thoughts. If our protagonist, at an older age, later comes to think she should not smoke, this change alone might have little behavioral effect. Of course, on the other hand, it should by no means be precluded that one can provoke important changes in a wide range of mental attitudes, and the interactions related to them, by changing content-involving attitudes, as the effects of propaganda testify. Most importantly, however, whatever the extent and role of explicit thought in human action and behavior, it can't be assumed that contentful, thought-mediated action must be the model for all intelligent interactions, regardless of whether they involve humans or animals.

The so-called third generation of contextualized cognitive-behavioral approaches may come closer to directly targeting the relevant patterns of interactions. Contextualized cognitive-behavioral approaches are said to be "particularly sensitive to the context and functions of psychological phenomena, not just their form, and thus tend to emphasize contextual and experiential change strategies" (Hayes et al. 2011). Hayes, the founding father of acceptance and commitment therapy (ACT), distilled three common components in these contextualized therapies (Hayes et al. 2011). A first component relates to issues of acceptance, detachment, and emotion regulation. Rather than focusing on the content of thoughts or feelings, these therapies are aimed at the relation of the subject to his or her thoughts or feelings. Although this has been framed as a content-versus-context distinction, these therapies thus still seem to emphasize thoughts and feelings as central.

A second component Hayes identified is flexible attention or attention to the now. Most of these third-generation therapies include elements of mindfulness or awareness toward the present moment, which may "increase one's sensitivity to important features of the environment and one's own reactions" (Hayes et al. 2011). We would claim that it is actually the changes in the person-environment interaction that form the crucial component of these therapies, whereas researchers so far have claimed their success lies in targeting and reducing maladaptive depressogenic cognitive processes such as rumination or thought suppression. Of course, this is not to deny that interactions might change as a result of changes in these cognitive processes, but only to emphasize that one should not assume that interactive changes can only occur as a consequence of such changes.

A final component in contextualized therapies includes meaningful action, such as motivation to change and behavior activation (Hayes et al. 2011). This component may come closest to explicitly targeting person-environment interaction. For example, behavioral activation therapy uses activity scheduling and mood monitoring to alter the "environing contingencies influencing the client's depressed mood and behavior" (Hayes et al. 2011). Using experience sampling methodology, this approach could be taken one step further to directly target the way the person is interacting with her environment, as it occurs in real life. One study aimed to improve momentary positive affect by providing ESM-derived feedback on the association between positive affect and the context (Kramer et al. 2014). The therapy consisted of six consecutive weeks of ESM using a palmtop (three days/week) and additional weekly standardized feedback on personalized patterns of positive affect. In this feedback, participants received information on their level of positive affect over the three-day period, on the amount of time spent in certain contexts, and, most importantly, on the association between the two. For example, someone would get feedback that the highest level of positive affect was reached while being involved in active relaxation. However, the actual amount of time spent in active relaxation may be very limited. Similarly, someone may experience higher levels of positive affect when in the company of friends, whereas this person may spend most of his time on his own. The standardized feedback did not include any directive on what the person should change; it only provided information regarding the contextualized patterns of positive affect. This randomized clinical trial in 102 depressed patients receiving antipsychotic medication showed that the supplementary ESM-derived feedback resulted in a significant and clinically relevant stronger decrease in depressive symptoms as measured by a clinician (–5.5 points on the Hamilton Depression Rating Scale) as well as by self-report (inventory of depressive symptoms) compared to the control condition of treatment as usual. This improvement was found up to six months after the end of the therapy (Kramer et al. 2014). The positive findings were not only owing to the continual self-monitoring, since a semiexperimental group doing experience sampling without the weekly feedback did not show a similar improvement. This study is just one example. However, it shows that interventions directly focusing on person-environment interactions are feasible and indeed provide an added clinical value.

4 Conclusion

We have suggested that just as a sensorimotor perspective on perception and awareness successfully goes wide, that is, incorporates person-environment interactions as fundamental to perceptual consciousness, so also should a successful approach to psychopathology. Indeed, we showed that an interactive approach fundamentally adds to our understanding of psychopathology. Furthermore, developments in current psychological therapies are now manifesting a shift toward impacting on person-environment interactions. Therapy components such as mindfulness, behavioral activation, and even acceptance and detachment may all impact on the specific person-environment interactions that constitute the symptoms. Still, this is mainly an implicit consequence rather than an active target of the intervention. We claim that explicitly targeting person-environment interactions, as has been done in the ESM behavioral activation study, presents a way forward toward improving psychological interventions. Following a wide approach might, thus, not only prove theoretically fruitful but might also have considerable applicable clinical benefits.

Acknowledgments

The authors wish to thank, besides the editor of this volume, in particular Sanneke de Haan and Lucia Foglia for excellent comments on a previous draft.

Erik Myin's research is supported by the Research Foundation Flanders (Research projects GOB5312N and GO48714N). J. K. O'Regan acknowledges the support of European Research Council (ERC) Advanced grant 323674 "FEEL." The research of Inez Myin-Germeys is supported by ERC Consolidator grant "INTERACT" (ERC-2012-StG—309767).

References

Blanchard, J., K. Mueser, and A. Bellack. 1998. Anhedonia, positive and negative affect, and social functioning in schizophrenia. *Schizophrenia Bulletin* 24:413–424.

Borsboom, D., and A. Cramer. 2013. Network analysis: An integrative approach to the structure of psychopathology. *Annual Review of Clinical Psychology* 9:91–121.

Cohen, A., T. Dinzeo, T. Nienow, D. Smith, B. Singer, and N. Docherty. 2005. Diminished emotionality and social functioning in schizophrenia. *Journal of Nervous and Mental Disease* 193:796–802.

Cohen, A., and K. Minor. 2010. Emotional experience in patients with schizophrenia revisited: Meta-analysis of laboratory studies. *Schizophrenia Bulletin* 36:143–150.

Collip, D., M. Oorschot, V. Thewissen, J. Van Os, R. Bentall, and I. Myin-Germeys. 2011. Social world interactions: How company connects to paranoia. *Psychological Medicine* 41:911–921.

Cooke, E., and E. Myin. 2011. Is trilled smell possible? How the structure of olfaction determines the phenomenology of smell. *Journal of Consciousness Studies* 18 (11–12): 59–95.

Cosmelli, D., and E. Thompson. 2010. Embodiment or envatment? Reflections on the bodily basis of consciousness. In *Enaction: Toward a New Paradigm for Cognitive Science*, ed. J. Stewart, O. Gapenne, and E. Di Paolo. Cambridge, MA: MIT Press.

Cuijpers, P., M. Sijbrandij, S. Koole, M. Huibers, M. Berking, and G. Andersson. 2014. Psychological treatment of generalized anxiety disorder: A meta-analysis. *Clinical Psychology Review* 34:130–140.

Degenaar, J., and D. Myin. 2014a. The structure of color experience and the existence of surface colors. *Philosophical Psychology* 27:384–400.

Degenaar, J. and E. Myin. 2014b. Representation-hunger reconsidered. *Synthese* 191:3639–3648.

Dennett, D. 1988. Quining qualia. In *Consciousness in Modern Science*, ed. A. Marcel and E. Bisiach. Oxford: Oxford University Press.

Earnst, K., and A. Kring. 1997. Construct validity of negative symptoms: An empirical and conceptual review. *Clinical Psychology Review* 17:167–189.

Freeman, D., K. Pugh, N. Vorontsova, and L. Southgate. 2009. Insomnia and paranoia. *Schizophrenia Research* 108:280–284.

Fuchs, T. 2012. Are mental illnesses diseases of the brain? In *Critical Neuroscience: A Handbook of the Social and Cultural Contexts of Neuroscience*, ed. S. Choudhury and J. Slaby. New York: Wiley-Blackwell.

Gard, D., A. Kring, M. Gard, W. Horan, and M. Green. 2007. Anhedonia in schizophrenia: Distinctions between anticipatory and consummatory pleasure. *Schizophrenia Research* 93:253–260.

Grahek, N. 2007. *Feeling Pain and Being in Pain*. Cambridge, MA: MIT Press.

Hayes, S., M. Villatte, M. Levin, and M. Hildebrandt. 2011. Open, aware, and active: Contextual approaches as an emerging trend in the behavioral and cognitive therapies. *Annual Review of Clinical Psychology* 7:141–168.

Henquet, C., J. van Os, R. Kuepper, P. Delespaul, M. Smits, J. Campo, and I. Myin-Germeys. 2010. Psychosis reactivity to cannabis use in daily life: An experience sampling study. *British Journal of Psychiatry* 196:447–453.

Hurley, S., and A. Noë. 2003. Neural plasticity and consciousness. *Biology and Philosophy* 18:131–168.

Hutto, D. 2005. Knowing what? Radical versus conservative enactivism. *Phenomenology and the Cognitive Sciences* 4:389–405.

Hutto, D., and E. Myin. 2013. *Radicalizing Enactivism: Basic Minds without Content*. Cambridge, MA: MIT Press.

Insel, T. 2012. Next-generation treatments for mental disorders. *Science Translational Medicine* 4 (155): 155–119.

Insel, T. 2013. Thomas Insel: Towards a new understanding of mental illness. http:// www.ted.com/talks/thomas_insel_toward_a_new_understanding_of_mental_illness.

Kimhy, D., I. Myin-Germeys, J. Palmier-Claus, and J. Swendsen. 2012. Mobile assessment guide for research in schizophrenia and severe mental disorders. *Schizophrenia Bulletin* 38:386–395.

Koch, C. 2004. *The Quest for Consciousness: A Neurobiological Approach*. Englewood, CO: Roberts.

Kramer, I., C. Simons, J. Hartmann, C. Menne-Lothmann, W. Viechtbauer, F. Peeters, and M. Wichers. 2014. A therapeutic application of the experience sampling method in the treatment of depression: A randomized controlled trial. *World Psychiatry: Official Journal of the World Psychiatric Association (WPA)* 13:68–77.

Lataster, T., I. Myin-Germeys, C. Derom, E. Thiery, and J. van Os. 2009. Evidence that self-reported psychotic experiences represent the transitory developmental expression of genetic liability to psychosis in the general population. *American Journal of Medical Genetics, Part B, Neuropsychiatric Genetics* 150B (8): 1078–1084.

McGinn, C. 1989. Can we solve the mind–body problem? *Mind* 98:349–366.

Myin, E., E. Cooke, and K. Zahidi. 2014. Morphing senses. In *Perception and Its Modalities*, ed. D. Stokes, M. Matthen, and S. Biggs. New York: Oxford University Press.

Myin-Germeys, I., P. Delespaul, and J. van Os. 2005. Behavioural sensitization to daily life stress in psychosis. *Psychological Medicine* 35:733–741.

Myin-Germeys, I., P. Delespaul, and M. deVries. 2000. Schizophrenia patients are more emotionally active than is assumed based on their behavior. *Schizophrenia Bulletin* 26:847–854.

Myin-Germeys, I., M. Oorschot, D. Collip, J. Lataster, P. Delespaul, and J. van Os. 2009. Experience sampling research in psychopathology: Opening the black box of daily life. *Psychological Medicine* 39:1533–1547.

Myin-Germeys, I., and J. van Os. 2007. Stress-reactivity in psychosis: Evidence for an affective pathway to psychosis. *Clinical Psychology Review* 27:409–424.

Myin-Germeys, I., J. van Os, J. Schwartz, A. Stone, and P. Delespaul. 2001. Emotional reactivity to daily life stress in psychosis. *Archives of General Psychiatry* 58:1137–1144.

Nagel, T. 1974. What is it like to be a bat? *Philosophical Review* 83:435–450.

Noë, A. 2004. *Action in Perception*. Cambridge, MA: MIT Press.

Oorschot, M., T. Kwapil, P. Delespaul, and I. Myin-Germeys. 2009. Momentary assessment research in psychosis. *Psychological Assessment* 21:498–505.

Oorschot, M., T. Lataster, V. Thewissen, R. Bentall, P. Delespaul, and I. Myin-Germeys. 2012. Temporal dynamics of visual and auditory hallucinations in psychosis. *Schizophrenia Research* 140:77–82.

Oorschot, M., T. Lataster, V. Thewissen, M. Lardinois, M. Wichers, J. van Os, et al. 2013. Emotional experience in negative symptoms of schizophrenia—no evidence for a generalized hedonic deficit. *Schizophrenia Bulletin* 39:217–225.

O'Regan, J. K. 2011. *Why Red Doesn't Sound Like a Bell: Understanding the Feel of Consciousness*. Oxford: Oxford University Press.

O'Regan, J. K., and N. Block. 2012. Discussion of J. Kevin O'Regan's *Why Red Doesn't Sound Like a Bell. Review of Philosophy and Psychology* 3:89–108.

O'Regan, J. K., E. Myin, and A. Noë. 2005. Sensory consciousness explained (better) in terms of "corporality" and "alerting capacity." *Phenomenology and the Cognitive Sciences* 44:369–387.

O'Regan, J. K., and A. Noë. 2001. A sensorimotor account of vision and visual consciousness. *Behavioral and Brain Sciences* 24:939–1031.

Pepper, K. 2014. Do sensorimotor dynamics extend the conscious mind? *Adaptive Behavior* 22:99–108.

Philipona, D., and J. K. O'Regan. 2006. Color naming, unique hues, and hue cancellation predicted from singularities in reflection properties. *Visual Neuroscience* 23:331–339.

Ratcliffe, M. 2008. *Feelings of Being: Phenomenology, Psychiatry, and the Sense of Reality.* Oxford: Oxford University Press.

Shiffman, S., A. Stone, and M. Hufford. 2008. Ecological momentary assessment. *Annual Review of Clinical Psychology* 4:1–32.

Smart, J. J. C. 1958. Sensations and brain processes. *Philosophical Review* 68:141–156.

Szentagotai, A., and D. David. 2010. The efficacy of cognitive-behavioral therapy in bipolar disorder: A quantitative meta-analysis. *Journal of Clinical Psychiatry* 71: 66–72.

Thewissen, V., R. Bentall, T. Lecomte, J. van Os, and I. Myin-Germeys. 2008. Fluctuations in self-esteem and paranoia in the context of daily life. *Journal of Abnormal Psychology* 117:143–153.

Thewissen, V., R. P. Bentall, M. Oorschot, M., J. à Campo, T. van Lierop, J. van Os, and I. Myin-Germeys. 2011. Emotions, self-esteem, and paranoid episodes: An experience sampling study. *British Journal of Clinical Psychology* 50:178–195.

Turner, D. T., M. van der Gaag, E. Karyotaki, and P. Cuijpers. 2014. Psychological interventions for psychosis: A meta-analysis of comparative outcome studies. *American Journal of Psychiatry* 171 (5): 523–38.

van Os, J. 2009. A salience dysregulation syndrome. *British Journal of Psychiatry* 194:101–103.

van Os, J. 2010. Are psychiatric diagnoses of psychosis scientific and useful: The case of schizophrenia. *Journal of Mental Health* 19:305–317.

van Os, J., R. Linscott, I. Myin-Germeys, P. Delespaul, and L. Krabbendam. 2009. A systematic review and meta-analysis of the psychosis continuum: Evidence for a psychosis proneness-persistence-impairment model of psychotic disorder. *Psychological Medicine* 39:179–195.

Varga, S. 2014. Cognition, representations, and embodied emotions: Investigating cognitive theory. *Erkenntnis* 79:165–190.

Wittchen, H., F. Jacobi, J. Rehm, A. Gustavsson, M. Svensson, B. Jonsson, et al. 2011. The size and burden of mental disorders and other disorders of the brain in Europe 2010. *European Neuropsychopharmacology* 21:655–679.

Contributors

Alexandre Billon is Associate Professor in the University of Lille, France. His work focuses on self-consciousness, and he is a member of the "Consciousness and the Self" team at the Institut Jean Nicod. He has recently published several articles on the philosophical significance of depersonalization.

Andrew Brook is Chancellor's Professor of Philosophy and Cognitive Science at Carleton University in Ottawa, Canada, a former president of the Canadian Philosophical Association, and a former Director of the Institute of Cognitive Science (ICS) at Carleton. He is a licensed psychoanalyst and is the current president of the Canadian Psychoanalytical Society. He has a DPhil from the University of Oxford and has published about 120 works.

Paula Droege is a Senior Lecturer in Philosophy at Pennsylvania State University, University Park, Pennsylvania. Her research on philosophical theories of consciousness proposes an essential role for temporal representation in conscious states. She is the author of *Caging the Beast: A Theory of Sensory Consciousness* (John Benjamins, 2003) and several articles on consciousness theory.

Rocco J. Gennaro is Professor of Philosophy and Philosophy Department Chair at the University of Southern Indiana. He specializes in philosophy of mind/cognitive science and consciousness, but also has strong interests in metaphysics, ethics, and early modern history of philosophy. He has published seven books and numerous papers in these areas, and his most recent book is *The Consciousness Paradox: Consciousness, Concepts, and Higher-Order Thoughts* (MIT Press, 2012). He is also the Philosophy of Mind/ Cognitive Science Area Editor for the *Internet Encyclopedia of Philosophy* and is working on a book entitled *Consciousness* for Routledge.

Philip Gerrans is a Professor in the Philosophy Department at the University of Adelaide, Australia. His main research interest is the use of psychological disorder to study the mind. He has written on developmental disorders (autism and Williams syndrome), cognitive neuropsychiatry, and, more recently, on moral psychopathologies (such as psychopathology) and the emotions. A unifying theme is the interaction between self-referential cognitive processes and those processes that represent the external environment or abstract concepts. He is an Associate of the Swiss Centre for Affective Sciences. His current research is a project on the relationship between emotional processing and self-representation in psychiatric disorders.

William Hirstein is a Professor of Philosophy at Elmhurst College, in Elmhurst, Illinois. He received his PhD from the University of California, Davis, in 1994, studying with Richard Wollheim and John Searle, and, as a postdoctoral researcher, with Patricia Churchland and V. S. Ramachandran. He has published articles on phantom limbs, autism, consciousness, sociopathy, and the misidentification syndromes. He is the author of several books, including *On the Churchlands* (Wadsworth, 2004), *Brain Fiction: Self-Deception and the Riddle of Confabulation* (MIT Press, 2005), and *Mindmelding: Consciousness, Neuroscience, and the Mind's Privacy* (Oxford University Press, 2012).

Jakob Hohwy is Associate Professor of Philosophy at Monash University, Melbourne, Australia. He founded the Cognition and Philosophy Lab in the philosophy department at Monash and conducts interdisciplinary experiments in philosophy, psychiatry, and neuroscience. Hohwy's research focuses on contemporary theories in theoretical neurobiology, and he is the author of *The Predictive Mind* (Oxford University Press, 2013).

Uriah Kriegel is a research director at the Jean Nicod Institute in Paris, France. His books include *Subjective Consciousness: A Self-Representational Theory* (Oxford University Press, 2009) and *The Varieties of Consciousness* (Oxford University Press, 2015).

Timothy Lane is Dean of the College of Humanities and Social Sciences at Taipei Medical University, and Director of the Brain and Consciousness Research Center at Taipei Medical University's Shuang Ho Hospital. He is also a research fellow at Academia Sinica's Institute of European and American Studies. His principal research interests include scientific and philosophical investigations of the content and levels of consciousness, especially as these pertain to understanding self. He is the author of articles in such journals as the *Journal of Philosophy*, *Analysis*, *Phenomenology and the Cognitive Sciences*, *Consciousness and Cognition*, the *Southern Journal of Philosophy*, and *Synthese*.

Thomas Metzinger is Professor of Theoretical Philosophy at the Johannes Gutenberg-Universität Mainz and an Adjunct Fellow at the Frankfurt Institute for Advanced Study (FIAS). He is also Director of the Neuroethics Research Unit in Mainz and Director of the MIND Group at the FIAS. Metzinger is past president of the German Cognitive Science Society (2005–2007) and of the Association for the Scientific Study of Consciousness (2009–2011). His focus of research lies in analytical philosophy of mind and cognitive science, as well as in connections between ethics, philosophy of mind, and anthropology. He has received a number of awards and fellowships, including a five-year GRC Fellowship by the Gutenberg Research College (2014–2019). In the English language, he has edited two collections on consciousness (*Conscious Experience*, Imprint Academic, 1995; *Neural Correlates of Consciousness*, MIT Press, 2000) and one major scientific monograph developing a comprehensive, interdisciplinary theory about consciousness, the phenomenal self, and the first-person perspective (*Being No One: The Self-Model Theory of Subjectivity*, MIT Press, 2003). In 2009, he published a popular book, which addresses a wider audience and discusses the ethical, cultural, and social consequences of consciousness research (*The Ego Tunnel—The Science of the Mind and the Myth of the Self*, Basic Books).

Erik Myin is Professor of Philosophy at the University of Antwerp, where he is head of the Centre for Philosophical Psychology. He has published papers on topics relating to mind and perception in philosophical, interdisciplinary, and scientific journals. He is, with Dan Hutto, coauthor of *Radicalizing Enactivism: Basic Minds without Content* (MIT Press, 2013).

Inez Myin-Germeys is Professor of Ecological Psychiatry at Maastricht University, The Netherlands. She also heads the Division of Mental Health within the school of Mental Health and Neuroscience at the same university. Inez Myin-Germeys has published over 200 papers in the field of psychology and psychiatry, and she was awarded an ERC consolidator grant in 2012.

Myrto Mylopoulos is a postdoctoral researcher at the Institut Jean Nicod in Paris, France. She received her PhD in Philosophy from the Graduate Center, City University of New York, in 2013. Starting in 2015, she will be Assistant Professor of Philosophy and Cognitive Science at Carleton University in Ottawa, Canada.

Gerard O'Brien is a Professor in the Department of Philosophy at the University of Adelaide, Australia. His primary research interests are the computational foundations of cognitive science, consciousness, mental representation, and neurocomputational models of cognition. He also dabbles in naturalized approaches to ethics and values.

Jon Opie is Senior Lecturer in the Philosophy Department at the University of Adelaide, Australia. He studied theoretical physics and then philosophy at Flinders University, before taking up a PhD and an ARC postdoctoral fellowship at Adelaide. His primary research interests are in the philosophy of mind, cognitive science, and the philosophy of science. Jon was a member of the McDonnell Project in Philosophy and the Neurosciences.

Kevin O'Regan is former director of the Laboratoire Psychologie de la Perception, CNRS, Université Paris Descartes. After early work on eye movements in reading, he was led to question established notions of the nature of visual perception and to discover, with collaborators, the phenomenon of "change blindness." His current work involves exploring his "sensorimotor" approach to consciousness in relation to sensory substitution, sensory adaptation, pain, color, space perception, and developmental psychology and robotics. He has recently published the book *Why Red Doesn't Sound Like a Bell: Understanding the Feel of Consciousness* (Oxford University Press, 2011).

Iuliia Pliushch is currently a PhD student at Johannes Gutenberg-Universität Mainz working on the topic of self-deception. She received the degree Magistra Artium in philosophy at Johannes Gutenberg-Universität Mainz in 2011.

Robert Van Gulick is Professor of Philosophy and Director of the Cognitive Science Program at Syracuse University. His work addresses topics including consciousness, intentionality, and self-understanding from the perspective of nonreductive physicalism and teleopragmatic functionalism.

Index

Acceptance and commitment therapy (ACT), 362–364

Acquaintance theory, 30–31, 36, 46

Action consciousness, 16, 76–85, 88–96

Agentive awareness, 76, 117

Agentive quality, 81–85, 90, 117, 131n24

Agnosia, 2, 12–14

Akinetic mutism, 252–253

Akinetopsia, 13

Alexithymia, 13

Algedonic sensations, 34

Alienation argument, 36–39, 47

Alienation experience, 17, 32–47, 55, 92, 104, 107, 110–114, 117, 122–127

Amnesia, 11–12, 17, 141, 151, 155, 213

Anarchic hand syndrome (AHS), 12, 16–17, 77–82, 84–88, 90–94, 103, 117–120

Anhedonia, 358, 360

Animals, 22n3, 184–185, 251, 338, 362

Anosognosia, 2, 11–12, 15, 57, 60, 62, 64, 66–67, 179, 185, 194–195, 214

Anton's syndrome, 10, 62, 151

Apraxia, 12, 79

Asomatognosia, 12, 214

Asymbolia, 123, 125

Attended intermediate representation theory (AIR), 19, 231–237, 241, 245

Autism spectrum disorder (ASD), 13, 19, 249, 254–255, 294, 301–302, 308–310, 320, 357

Autobiographical memories as experienced (AME), 217–219, 222

Baars, B., 10, 19, 113, 144, 230, 276

Balint's syndrome, 14, 211

Bayesian theory, 20, 182, 189, 295, 297–298, 306, 310, 314, 316, 319, 330

Bayne, T., 2, 18–19, 57–58, 60–62, 76, 95, 141, 156–157, 194, 210, 212, 216–220, 229, 232–234, 237, 239–244

Bermúdez, J., 65, 84, 188

Billon, A., 45, 60, 104–105, 107–108, 110–118, 129n15

Blakemore, S., 77–78, 83, 154, 336

Blindsight, 2, 111, 113–115, 268, 315, 319

Block, N., 5, 43, 111, 113–114, 116, 236–238, 251, 255, 353

Bodily self-awareness, 66, 294, 302–304, 310

Body swap illusion, 12

Bortolotti, L., 41, 57, 61

Bottini, G., 33, 57, 60–61, 105, 107, 109

Brain bisection, 209–212, 215–221

Brentano, F., 8, 31, 144–145, 184

Capgras syndrome, 13, 61, 125, 154–156, 158, 332

Carruthers, P., 4, 22n3, 76, 147, 250, 266–267, 339

Charles Bonnet syndrome, 14

Clark, A., 20, 182, 326, 330
Cognitive-behavioral therapy (CBT), 361
Cognitive dissonance, 174, 198n8, 198n11
Cold control theory (CCT), 121
Comparator model, 154–155
Confabulation, 14, 17, 58–60, 63, 67, 106, 141–142, 147, 150–159
Connectionism. *See* Parallel distributed processing (PDP)
Consciousness. *See also* Global workspace theory (GWT); Higher-order thought (HOT) theory; Self-model theory of subjectivity (SMT); Subjectivity theories of consciousness; Vehicle theory of consciousness
  access, 5, 11, 113–114, 236–237
  phenomenal, 5, 15, 19, 21, 29–30, 44, 46, 95, 104, 110–116, 122, 231, 236–237, 265, 267, 271–272, 347, 349
  philosophical theories of, 5–11
  transitive, 4, 75
  unity of, 2, 62, 210–212, 230, 236, 239, 276
Cotard syndrome, 12, 38, 48n9

Dalla Barba, G., 151–152
Darwin, C., 143–146, 152–153, 157–159
Deafferentation, 119
Dennett, D., 9–10, 18, 156, 158, 213, 220–222, 234, 267, 274, 284
Dependent personality disorder, 14
Depersonalization, 15–17, 33–38, 42–46, 48n7, 55, 64, 66, 69, 103, 108, 110, 114–117, 123, 294, 304–305
Descartes, R., 143–144, 152, 227, 252
de Vignemont, F., 37, 48n10, 57, 64–69
Dissociative identity disorder (DID), 1, 11–12, 18–19, 209–213, 219–224, 234, 238–244
Dual control model, 85
Dysexecutive syndrome, 14, 210–211

Epistemic agent model (EAM), 186–189

Feinberg, T., 57–59, 107
First-order representationalism (FOR), 5–6, 17
For-me-ness, 29–30, 104, 123
Free energy principle, 294–297
Fregoli delusion, 14
Frith, C., 77–78, 82–83, 88, 154–155, 279, 325–326
Full body illusion, 294, 303–304
Funkhouser, E., 169–172, 175–176

Gallagher, S., 39–40, 49n15, 96n3, 110
Gennaro, R., 7–9, 15–16, 22n3, 104–108, 147, 256–258, 313, 316
Global workspace model (GWS), 144–145, 230–233, 236–237, 240–242, 245. *See also* Global workspace theory (GWT)
Global workspace theory (GWT), 10, 19, 276, 283, 319–320, 327, 339–340. *See also* Global workspace model (GWS)
Graham, G., 39, 49n15, 76, 95

Hamilton Depression Rating Scale, 364
Hayes, S., 361–363
Hemiagnosia, 14
Hemianopia, 235
Hemineglect, 14, 19, 33, 214, 234–238
Heterophenomenology, 10
Higher-order global states (HOGS), 9, 19, 233–234, 237–238, 241–245
Higher-order perception (HOP), 7, 147
Higher-order representation (HOR), 7, 30, 36–37, 46, 119–120, 147, 250, 267, 314, 316
Higher-order thought (HOT) theory, 1, 7–9, 11, 15–16, 22n3, 55–59, 62–65, 68–70, 71n6, 91, 95, 105–110, 117–122, 124, 249, 258, 337–339
Hohwy, J., 19–20, 169, 182, 302–305, 328, 339

Humphrey, N., 18, 213, 220–223
Husserl, E., 31, 144–145, 160n5

I-concepts, 57, 64–66, 70
Immune to error through misidentification (IEM), 16, 55–56, 67–70
Integrated information theory (IIT), 19, 231, 236–237, 240, 242, 244
Interpretationism, 18, 221
Introspection, 8, 18, 55, 62, 124, 144, 168, 181–182, 186, 194–195, 257, 313, 330, 338. *See also* Reflection; Self-consciousness

Jaspers, K., 15, 29, 31–35, 47
Jeannerod, M., 189, 332–335

Kanwisher, N., 273–274
Koch, C., 253–254, 348
Korsakoff syndrome, 151
Kriegel, U., 9, 15–16, 30, 37, 41, 60, 66–67, 104–118, 122–123

Lane, T., 15–17, 36–37, 55–59, 62–64, 68–69, 128n1
Lau, H., 119–120, 257, 295, 314–319
Liang, C., 15–17, 36–37, 55–59, 62–64, 68–69, 128n1
Locke, J., 1, 7, 31

Mele, A., 171–174, 176, 178–179
Memory, 2, 11, 13–14, 38, 62, 123, 142, 152–153, 155, 157, 210, 213, 217, 220, 222–223, 228–229, 232, 238–239, 255, 267, 271–272, 278, 280, 282, 340–341
Metzinger, T., 10, 17–18, 167, 171, 179–187, 193
Millikan, R., 141, 148
Mine-ness, 15, 29, 34, 40
Mirrored-self-misidentification disorder, 11–12, 68
Mirror neurons, 108

Mortality salience (MS), 178
Müller-Lyer illusion, 149
Multiple drafts model (MDM), 9–10
Multiple personality disorder (MPD). *See* Dissociative identity disorder (DID)
Mylopoulos, M., 16, 84, 105, 107, 117–122, 131n24

Nagel, T., 4–5, 212, 352
Narcissistic personality disorder, 14
Nelkin, D., 169–172

Obsessive compulsive disorder (OCD), 15
Ownership, mental state, 11, 13, 15–16, 35, 55–56, 59, 63–65, 69, 97n4, 105, 117, 214

Pacherie, E., 60–61, 76, 80, 84, 326, 336
Parallel distributed processing (PDP), 270–274, 285
Parietal lobe (activity), 19, 55, 79, 113–115, 249, 325, 333–337
Passivity experience, 20, 77–78, 117, 123, 125, 325–341
Phantom limb, 2, 12, 56, 59
Phenomenal model of the intentionality relation (PMIR), 184
Phenomenal self-model (PSM), 18, 167–168, 179–184, 188, 190–196
Prediction error minimization, 19, 294–295, 297–321
Predictive coding, 326–328, 330–331, 337–339
Prefrontal cortical activity, 19, 113, 115, 120, 249, 251–257, 260, 281, 317–318, 333
Prinz, J., 4, 19, 231, 237, 241, 244, 266, 340–341
Proprioception, 64, 66, 68–69, 82, 117, 214, 296, 301
Prosopagnosia, 14

Qualia, 5–6, 10

Reflection, 144, 241, 269
Rosenthal, D., 4, 7–8, 30, 36–37, 55–59, 63–64, 68–70, 77, 91, 94–95, 105–108, 118–120, 147, 257, 266–267, 295, 316
Rubber hand illusion, 12, 65, 303–305

Sacks, O., 2, 152, 283
Schizophrenia, 2–3, 11, 13, 16–17, 19–21, 33, 35, 38, 42, 77, 82, 90, 110–114, 154–155, 179, 192, 210–211, 230, 253, 268, 278–285, 302, 307, 311, 320, 325, 334–337, 356, 360
Self-awareness, 9, 11, 32–33, 62, 64, 305–306. *See also* Bodily self-awareness
Self-consciousness, 2, 17–18, 141–142, 147–148, 150–153, 157, 159, 167–168, 179, 182, 196, 258, 267, 311
Self-deception (SD), 13, 17–18, 58, 67, 141
Self-model theory of subjectivity (SMT), 10, 18, 167, 179–180, 183
Self-reference, 16, 18, 103–104, 122–127, 181–183
Self-representational theory, 8–9, 11, 15, 17, 30–31, 36, 46, 66, 76, 103, 108, 110, 114, 124, 180, 186–187, 258
Sensorimotor control, 83, 85–87, 92, 94, 120
Sensorimotor theory, 10–11, 347–357
Shoemaker, S., 16, 56, 67, 69, 222
Sierra, M., 34–35, 43, 46, 64, 108, 115, 117
Simultagnosia, 211, 228
Somatoparaphrenia, 11, 13, 15–17, 33–37, 42, 55–69, 103–108, 214
Split-brain, 2, 13, 19, 210, 243–245
Subjectivity principle (SP), 30, 35–37, 104

Subjectivity theories of consciousness, 15–16, 18, 29–39, 43–44, 46–47, 103–104
Surprisal, 296, 328, 330, 340
Switch hypothesis (switching model), 18, 215–219, 239–240, 244

Terror management theory (TMT), 168, 178, 196
Thin immunity principle (TIP), 56, 68–69
Thought insertion, 11, 13, 15, 32–33, 37, 40–41, 45, 78, 111, 130, 154–155, 158, 279, 284
Tononi, G., 19, 231, 244
Transcranial magnetic stimulation (TMS), 110, 121
Transitivity principle, 7, 77, 81, 90–91, 94
Transparency, 6–7, 18, 168, 179–182, 193–196
Two factor model of delusion, 17, 70n2, 78, 141, 154–155
Two-neural-network model, 115–116

Underconnectivity, 1, 249, 254
Utilization behavior (UB), 79–82, 85–95

Van Leeuwen, N., 169, 171, 191
van Os, R., 356–360
Varga, S., 361–362
Vegetative state (VS), 126–127
Vehicle theory of consciousness, 19, 265–285
Virtual self realism (VSR), 19, 233–234, 237–238, 241–243, 245
Visual agnosia, 1–2
von Hippel, W., 178, 190, 193, 198n11

Wide intrinsicality view (WIV), 9, 108, 128n3
Wittgenstein, L., 67, 70